Champions of a Free Society

Champions of a Free Society

Ideas of Capitalism's Philosophers and Economists

EDWARD W. YOUNKINS

LEXINGTON BOOKS

A division of
ROWMAN & LITTLEFIELD PUBLISHERS, INC.
Lanham • Boulder • New York • Toronto • Plymouth, UK

LEXINGTON BOOKS

A division of Rowman & Littlefield Publishers, Inc.
A wholly owned subsidiary of The Rowman & Littlefield Publishing Group, Inc.
4501 Forbes Boulevard, Suite 200
Lanham, MD 20706

Estover Road
Plymouth PL6 7PY
United Kingdom

British Library Cataloguing in Publication Information Available

Library of Congress Cataloging-in-Publication Data

Younkins, Edward Wayne, 1948–
  Champions of a free society : ideas of capitalism's philosophers and economists /
Edward W. Younkins.
     p. cm.
  Includes bibliographical references and index.
  ISBN-13: 978-0-7391-2647-9 (cloth : alk. paper)
  ISBN-10: 0-7391-2647-4 (cloth : alk. paper)
  ISBN-13: 978-0-7391-2648-6 (pbk. : alk. paper)
  ISBN-10: 0-7391-2648-2 (pbk. : alk. paper)
  ISBN-13: 978-0-7391-3053-7 (electronic)
  ISBN-10: 0-7391-3053-6 (electronic)
  1. Capitalism—Philosophy. 2. Free enterprise—Philosophy. 3. Economics—
Philosophy. I. Title.
  HB501.Y682 2008
  330.12'20922—dc22   2008020632

Printed in the United States of America

♾™ The paper used in this publication meets the minimum requirements of American
National Standard for Information Sciences—Permanence of Paper for Printed Library
Materials, ANSI/NISO Z39.48–1992.

For my parents, who taught me to love liberty, to accept responsibility, to respect reality, and to trust the judgment of my own mind.

Contents

Part IV: The Contemporary Period

Part V: The Philosophy of Freedom: In Retrospect and Prospect

Preface

The possibility of men living together in peace and to their mutual advantage without having to agree on common concrete aims, and bound only by abstract rules of conduct, was perhaps the greatest discovery mankind ever made.

—Friedrich Hayek

My 2002 book, *Capitalism and Commerce*, explained the concepts and moral values upon which a free or capitalistic society is built. Included among the concepts and values explained and discussed were: natural law, natural rights, individualism, personal responsibility, negative freedom, morality, freedom of association, civil society, the nature of true communities, the free market, private ownership, work, contract, the nature and responsibilities of the corporation, voluntary unionism, progress, entrepreneurship, technology, justice, law, power, authority, constitutionalism, and pluralism. This work introduced people to the idea of a free market as a moral institution with a theoretical framework rather than as simply a pragmatic means of efficient production. It was about freedom and the discovery of the type of society men require to engage in their own happiness-pursuing activities.

Whereas *Capitalism and Commerce* was organized around concepts and moral values, *Champions of a Free Society* is constructed around great thinkers of the past who were influential in developing the political and economic thought of the Western world. Its main purpose is to provide a survey and overview of the ideas of leading individual philosophers and economists of freedom. This current book is designed to make clear the principal theoretical ideas of a wide array of these outstanding thinkers. In *Champions of a Free Society* I have endeavored to provide a guide to political and economic thinking about the desirability and construction of a free society that is intelligible to the educated layperson. Gaining glimpses into the genius of earlier ages is likely to be interesting and fruitful for any culturally literate person. To absorb oneself in the ideas of the masters is a magnificent intellectual experience.

Champions of a Free Society is intended to introduce the thoughtful reader to the most important thinkers who have contributed to developing what we could call the classical liberal or libertarian worldview. Speculation regarding the nature of a free society began over 2,500 years ago and has grown through the centuries. Throughout the ages, many thinkers have observed that intrusiveness in the lives, conduct, or behavior of individuals is a barrier to progress, prosperity, happiness, the spread of knowledge, and so on. They have asserted the moral primacy of the individual human person against the claims of any social collectivity. In order to know how ideas on political and economic freedom unfolded, it is necessary to immerse oneself in intellectual history.

A study covering such a long period of time requires selection from a great variety of thinkers. Such an investigation is necessarily selective and interpretative by virtue of what is omitted, what is included, and by the method of presentation of what is included therein. I have attempted to include those thinkers whose ideas have had substantial influence, are the most relevant, and are the most interesting. In several cases, I have selected neglected thinkers who have written underappreciated intellectual gems or who have anticipated recent political and economic thought. In choosing to study particular thinkers I have made the judgment that others are less relevant and/or less interesting. Of course, my own predispositions have influenced my judgment and choices of what thinkers to include. Some of the thinkers I have included others would leave out and some that I have failed to include others would find to be indispensable to the subject matter.

I am not impartial or neutral. My own attachment is to what could be termed classical liberalism, classical individualism, or perhaps flourishing individualism. This book represents my attempt at a serious but accessible introduction to the great philosophers and economists who sowed the seeds of liberty, the harvest of which we reap the benefits of today. I have worked to provide a substantial guide for the general reader who desires to grasp the fundamental ideas that have advanced human understanding of man's nature and his place in the universe.

My primary concern is with those thinkers who want to construct a social order in which individual freedom can be maximized and who seek to defend liberty on ethical and moral grounds. Many such thinkers believe that a proper political and economic system cannot be separated from the realm of natural law and that there are universally applicable truths that do not depend on the circumstances of time and place. They hold that a completed political and economic philosophy demands an account of man and an appropriate ethical framework. As yet, we have no such definitive finished comprehensive system.

Such a system would have to incorporate and explain how there is an intimate connection between economic science and an objective normative framework for understanding human life. Given that all objective knowledge in our one universe is interrelated in some manner, it follows that the discovery of a truth-based economics and of a moral philosophy based on the nature of man and the world would be consistent with one another. Because truth is consistent, it follows that economics and morality are inextricably related parts of one individual body of knowledge. Such a transdisciplinary approach must be driven by the demands of truth and must include free will if it is to make a well-founded case for a free society. The long-run success of a political and economic system depends on an overarching theoretical perspective that includes a solid ethical foundation that appeals to an independent ontological order. The integrity and comprehensiveness of such a worldview requires metaphysical content. To succeed in our quest, we must have viable, sound, and proper conceptions of man's nature, knowledge, values, and actions.

Champions of a Free Society provides an historical retrospective of the pursuit of political and economic truth. It provides a framework for analyzing and evaluating the speculations of the great philosophers and economists throughout history. Because no study is really separate, our concern is with all those disciplines and thinkers who deal with freedom, human action, and the moral and economic choices people make. We are concerned with those thinkers who want to construct a social order in which individual liberty can be maximized. This involves the consideration of trends and changes in related disciplines and in the underlying intellectual climate. Because of the inextricably related nature of the real world, boundaries are necessarily blurred between man's artificially constructed academic disciplines. Thinkers from one particular academic area seek light from other complementary branches of study.

This survey of major liberal and libertarian ideas will outline and describe each thinker's philosophy of liberty. The goal of this book is to present the development of ideas from before the early Greeks to the current day in language that permits generally educated readers to understand, recognize, and appreciate their significance. The book's chronological approach considers the thinkers, their ideas, and their schools of thought as they have developed over the course of time. This volume's unified approach presents a breadth of coverage and a manageable organization that effectively and efficiently summarizes and integrates the ideas of diverse philosophers and economists of a free society. As author, I assert no pretense with respect to the originality of interpretation and presentation or regarding the profundity of my analysis or synthesis of the ideas presented. The absence of reference notes in this book does not imply that these interpretations of various thinkers' ideas originate with me or are my own. These expository essays on the ideas of these champions of a free society are aimed at the lay reader and are more interpretative than they are critical. Scholars will certainly find my exegetic approach deficient in terms of the footnote-laden approach of conventional academic debate. However, I do believe that this book provides an excellent means for acquainting readers with the essential ideas of the thinkers included therein. These chapters represent a non-specialist's account of these thinkers' works and ideas. My goal is to make their ideas available to a great number of readers through the use of clear, non-technical explanations of their ideas.

A major message of *Champions of a Free Society* is that it is important to study the ideas of the past and to be respectful of the wisdom found in former times. The point is not when great thinkers wrote their works and espoused their ideas, but rather the content of their books and the truth of their ideas. There is much unfulfilled illuminative potential to be found in the ideas, theories, and perspectives of the past. There has been a long and fruitful tradition of political and economic discourse. Over time, an increasing number of thinkers have joined the debate.

In part, this book is an outgrowth of the lectures, covering much the same ground, that I gave during the spring of 2006 in my History of Economic Thought course at Wheeling Jesuit University. Of course, from the transdisciplinary way in which I approached this course it could very well have been called History of Political and Economic Philosophy. *Champions of a Free Society* has not been specifically designed as a textbook, but it is suitable for courses in history of economic thought, political economy, political philosophy, or political and economic philosophy.

After an introduction, the book is divided into the following five sections: (1) Ancient and Medieval Periods; (2) Early Modern and Renaissance Periods; (3) The Late Modern Period; (4) The Contemporary Period; and (5) The Philosophy of Freedom: In Retrospect and Prospect. Whereas *Capitalism and Commerce* supplied a "bank" of fundamental ideas that provide the groundwork for the free enterprise system, *Champions of a Free Society* provides a "bank" of the essential ideas of the great thinkers who developed those ideas. Sections 1 through 4 of this work essentially constitute a handbook of their fundamental ideas. The chapters included in these sections are primarily devoted to a presentation of a particular thinker's basic ideas. Although it may be desirable to do so, the chapters do not have to be read in progression in order to be understood by the reader. Most of the chapters represent self-contained treatments of the thinker at hand. At the end of each chapter I have included a list of recommended readings for those who wish to study a given thinker in greater depth and detail. The final section of the book provides a summary of the preceding chapters and looks to the future and toward the potential integration of the ideas of past and current thinkers into a logical and systematic worldview. In particular, an attempt will be made to integrate various insights into a broad natural law and natural-rights-based analytic and normative science of liberty.

Over the years, many people have contributed importantly to this work by reading and commenting on all of it, various portions of it, or drafts of my essays containing ideas that appear in it. I am extremely grateful to the following individuals for their useful observations and suggestions and for their help in my efforts to clarify my ideas: Charles W. Baird, Doug Bandow, Roger E. Bissell, Walter Block, David Boaz, Peter Boettke, Samuel Bostaph, James M. Buchanan, Bruce J. Caldwell, Robert L. Campbell, Bryan Caplan, Shelly Carenbauer, Scott Carpenter, Rafe Champion, Tyler Cowen, Ricardo Crespo, Paul Cwik, Douglas Den Uyl, Thomas J. DiLorenzo, Richard M. Ebeling, John B. Egger, Kenneth G. Elzinga, Reginald Firehammer, Fred Foldvary, Arthur Foulkes, Thomas Frecka, Milton Friedman, Richard Fuerle, Joseph S. Fulda, Sean Gabb, Roger Garrison, Stephen Grabill, Bettina Bien Greaves, Homayoun Hajiran, Stuart K. Hayashi, Jeffrey M. Herbener, Stephen Hicks, Robert Higgs, Beth Hoffman, Steven Horwitz, John Hospers, Edward L. Hudgins, Matthew Humphries, Candice E. Jackson, Richard C. B. Johnsson, Hubert Jöngen, David Kelley, Stephan Kinsella,

Shawn E. Klein, William E. Kline, George Leef, Yuval Levin, Loren Lomasky, Roderick T. Long, Spencer MacCallum, Tibor Machan, Russell Madden, Uskali Maki, John E. Mansuy, Martin Masse, Nigel Meek, Thomas Michaud, Jan Narveson, Ron Nash, C. James Newlan, Michael Novak, Alysha Pannett, Jason Pappas, Neil Parille, Lindsay Perigo, William H. Peterson, Karen M. Phillips, Ralph Raico, Douglas B. Rasmussen, Lawrence W. Reed, Beth Reiley, Sheldon Richman, Brent Robinson, Llewellyn Rockwell, Joseph Rowlands, Peter Saint-Andre, Ken Schoolland, Larry Schweikart, Chris Matthew Sciabarra, Larry J. Sechrest, Fred Seddon, Frank Shostak, Aeon Skoble, Mark Skousen, Barry Smith, Russell Soble, Gennady Stolyarov, Chris Tame, William Thomas, Jeffrey Tucker, Murray Weidenbaum, Walter E. Williams, Gary Wolfram, Thomas Woods, Stephen Yates, Andre Zantonavitch, and Gloria L. Zúñiga.

Of course, inclusion in the above list does not indicate endorsement of this book or agreement with the ideas expressed within it. It does mean that each person on the list has assisted me in some way with this current project. Most of all, I am indebted to my secretary at Wheeling Jesuit University, Carla Cash, for her most capable and conscientious help in bringing this book to print.

Finally, in the end, it is only I who can be found responsible for any errors found in this book.

Edward W. Younkins
Wheeling Jesuit University

Introduction

The history of thought and ideas is a discourse carried on from generation to generation. The thinking of later ages grows out of the thinking of earlier ages. Without the aid of this stimulation intellectual progress would have been impossible. The continuity of human evolution, sowing for the offspring and harvesting on land cleared and tilled by the ancestors, manifests itself also in the history of science and ideas. We have inherited from our forefathers not only a stock of products of various orders of goods which is the source of our material wealth; we have no less inherited ideas and thoughts, theories and technologies to which our thinking owes its productivity.

—Ludwig von Mises

For more than 2,500 years, great thinkers have devoted their efforts toward the determination of the best social order based on their investigations and understandings of human nature. Many have concluded that free societies are superior because they are in agreement with human nature. Not all thinkers accepted liberty as their primary principle, and those who did were not always consistent in their arguments for a free society. Nonetheless, political and economic philosophy has drawn the attention of the great minds of all ages who have asked questions regarding the morally appropriate or just political and economic system and who have explained the moral premises and postulates that they maintain should underpin such a system. Many thinkers have sought to discover universal principles that underlie political economy under all historical circumstances. It follows that political and economic philosophy is essential and fundamental to an understanding of the nature and role of the state and of man's relationship to it.

Throughout history, creative thinkers have produced normative, descriptive, and explanatory ideas that have deeply influenced the character and course of world history. There has been longevity of political and economic ideas as many notions that had been introduced in a past social order frequently influence later thought and action. By studying the masters, the discerning reader will detect the foreshadowings, parallels, and similarities of many supposedly new doctrines in the writings of long ago. Many of the ideas that have contributed to Western political thought have emerged gradually or became more clearly formulated over long periods of time. It can be enlightening to study the development of political and economic ideas by searching for their origins, variations, continuity, interrelationships, and appearances. It is possible to consider the development of political and economic philosophy as progressive in the sense that each succeeding generation learns something from the thought of preceding eras.

This introductory chapter offers an overall view of the history of political and economic thought with respect to the desirability of free societies as it has found expression in the writings of many major philosophers and economists who have sown the seeds and watered the roots of modern free societies. This chapter also provides a brief overview of my own political and economic perspective as it has resulted from my study of the diverse political and economic philosophies of freedom of the past.

The ideas discussed in this book range from the social speculations of Lao Tzo to the modern efforts of the twentieth century based on philosophical and empirical work. Of course, the purpose of such a survey is to provide an integrated and meaningful portrait of the field. This book is written for individuals who want to learn more about the philosophical foundations of political and economic freedom. It is an introduction and a guide to the principal theoretical ideas on liberty that the most influential and creative thinkers in history have produced. The goal is to provide in one place an introduction for the general reader to the great ideas of the liberal and libertarian tradition.

This work is by no means a comprehensive or complete history of political and economic thought. It is primarily a history of liberal thought in which I have attempted to include the most influential and pertinent thinkers. Such a history of ideas is selective by nature and has been influenced by my own interests and predilections. By choosing to study certain thinkers, I have made the judgment that others are less relevant or less interesting. Of course, the selection and emphasis in a survey covering such a long period of time inevitably results in difficult decisions and regrettable omissions.

The idea of equal freedom has been approached from various standpoints. Liberal moral, political, and economic demands have been grounded in the theories of natural law and natural rights as well as by reference to utilitarian theories and have been both religious and secular in nature. Despite this historical variability, the desirability of a free society has remained a basic and important perspective. The history of the idea of freedom is an account of what is perhaps the most important speculation of the human mind. By studying the great thinkers of the past, a person can discern recurring ideas and problems. Such a reader will notice that many thinkers are inconsistent and how ideas have developed and changed or have remained the same over time.

This book is organized around great thinkers of the past and the chapters are arranged chronologically, tracing the development of political and economic thought from antiquity to the present time. A chronological arrangement of the great thinkers had been followed in order to elucidate the evolutionary process in political and economic thinking as ideas blend into one another. These thinkers have sought to answer questions dealing with the nature of man, the purpose and justification of the political power of the state, and the relationship between government authority and individual freedom. This book thus considers the history of man as the evolved and involved story of the idea of freedom.

Ancient and Medieval Periods

It is necessary to start our study somewhere and it is logical to begin our intellectual history with an account of ancient thought. Oriental ideas inherited from a remote past have come down to us through the great philosophers of ancient Greece. Liberal ideas can be detected in the writings of the Chinese philosopher Lao Tzu (604-531 B.C.), who viewed individual happiness as the basis of a good society. An opponent of taxation and war, Lao Tzu taught that rulers should take no willful action and that government should not interfere with actions of peaceful people. He was explicitly against the use of force and called for the avoidance of violence.

Greek philosophy has exerted a profound impact on Western thought through a continuous line of thinkers beginning with Plato, Aristotle, Zeno, and so on. Through Christianity, Greek ideas have had a continuous but varying effect upon political and economic thought. During the Middle Ages and medieval period Greek thought in economics and natural philosophy was sustained and passed on to modern thinkers. For example, the value of freedom was a component of the Greek city-state tradition as well as of the Roman Empire and its laws, and in time became part of the feudal structure and municipal constitutions of the medieval period. Another important idea that began with the Greeks was the notion of a higher law by which everyone, including rulers, could be judged. The origins of such an idea can be traced back to Aristotle, who envisioned a higher metaphysical and moral goal that is applicable for individuals and the polity.

Aristotle (384-322 B.C.) taught that to make life fully human (i.e., to flourish) an individual must acquire virtues and make use of his reason as fully as he is capable. His realistic theory of knowledge included the need for specific individual interpretation with respect to a person's actions because of the multitude of various human circumstances and capabilities. Rather than insisting on ascetic living, Aristotle states that human beings are to develop their powers and to live well and comfortably—men exist for the sake of the good life. He said that each citizen should aim at a good life—the life of the *polis*. Aristotle was devoted to the *polis* which has the goal of promoting the good and the virtuous.

For Aristotle, civil society (i.e., a good human community) could activate many of a person's natural capacities. He explained man's social nature by pointing out his capacity to learn from others and the potential contribution of such knowledge to each person's flourishing and happiness (i.e., *eudaimonia*). Aristotle's idea of *eudaimonia* is close to twentieth-century thinker, Ayn Rand's, "noncontradictory state of joy."

Aristotle has provided us with many economic concepts. For him, as for other Greek thinkers, the economic element is subordinated to the political and to the ethical—his economics is embedded in his politics and grew out of his political and moral philosophy and was presented in the context of philosophy. Aristotle denied the labor theory of value, hinted at the marginalist concept of value and the law of diminishing utility, distinguished between use value and exchange value, differentiated between natural and unnatural forms of exchange, identified various types of justice, identified the problem of commensurability, stated that the natural acquisition of property enables men to live a good life in the *polis*, and explained that the use of money facilitates the equalization of want satisfaction.

Greek philosophers generally disparaged some forms of acquisition activities and looked down upon money making. Aristotle was no exception and believed that there were limits to the legitimate role of commercial activity. He viewed estate or household management as natural and commerce and usury as unnatural and was disturbed by the prospect of the unlimited accumulation of wealth. Aristotle noted that in the pursuit of wealth as exchange value there are no limits to the end it seeks, whereas limits are set to wealth as use value. Aristotle recognized the function of money but for him interest appears to be contrary to nature and money making also seems to be rather unnatural. He says that wealth should be a means and not an end.

Epicurus (341-270 B.C.) furthered the development of the idea of individualism by asserting the moral primacy of the person against any social collectivity. He speaks of independence through the restriction of wants and said that even the state is unnecessary if one's wants are few and small enough. Epicurus explains that virtue and wisdom are causes of pleasure, that anxiety and pain are obstacles to happiness, and that reason helps people to live pleasurably. As an atomistic materialist, he viewed the mind or soul as bodily and as a group of atoms that disperse upon death. His ethical naturalism explains that virtues are necessary for happiness. People should live without fear and should live fully engaged in one's projects. The goal is to have freedom from pain of body and from trouble of mind (i.e., mental anguish). Viewing pleasure as tranquility, he recommends limiting one's desires and eliminating the fear of gods and of death. Epicurus placed a high value on friendships and voluntary alliances and cautioned people to avoid politics and public life whenever and wherever possible. The Epicurean instrumental idea of justice is that it is an agreement to neither harm nor to be harmed.

The Epicurean basis for individualism was furthered by the Stoics, who also nourished the concept of natural law. Both the teaching of Epicurus and Stoicism emphasized the here and now. Both taught that happiness results from virtue, that it is best to render one's needs and desires to the bare minimum, and that one can be happy independent of comforts and political circumstances. Both envisioned justice as protecting what we would call individual rights today and did not justify political arrangements to the extent that they contribute to virtue. Natural law, as defined by Stoicism, had a great influence on Roman law. The

Stoic maxim was "to live in accordance with nature." The main vehicles for the tradition of natural law were Roman Stoicism for theoretical philosophy and Roman law for the practice of legislation. The emphasis in the Roman model was on personal and civil freedom and on individual political rights. From the Romans, we have received laws pertaining to economic practices and elements of the legal framework of the state.

During the long period known as the Middle Ages, the Church was an important influence in temporal affairs along with political and moral philosophy. Traditions of the divine order and spiritual individualism called for the integrity and independence of each person's soul before God and proclaimed the Church as the main protector of each person's spiritual sovereignty as opposed to political authority. Christianity's idea of common humanity led to the claim of equal rights for all persons. During the Middle Ages constitutional government, which places limitations upon the sphere of public authority, became linked to natural law. During this period, economics called for charity and fair prices of goods and services.

Aristotle's thought is reflected in the works of Thomas Aquinas (1225-1274), who said that reason apprehends the first principles of natural law. Aquinas was a student of Albert the Great and brought together ideas from Aristotle and the Church Fathers such as Augustine. Aquinas recognized that there is a natural diversity in the attributes and desires of human beings that differentiate one from another. His natural-law-based arguments brought together Aristotelian and patristic ideas. Aquinas viewed natural law as the objective standard against which positive laws may be judged. His body of political and economic thought was constructed on a Catholic understanding of the world and included an emphasis on natural law. The framework of his cosmology combined Greek rationalism with Christian supernaturalism.

Aquinas did not believe that humanity has any separate existence apart from particular concrete persons. He saw the person as an individual, created in the image of God, who is able to inquire and choose and who is free, responsible, and unique in his calling. Like Aristotle, Aquinas maintained that human beings are social and political animals by nature. Like Aristotle, and the later Adam Smith, Aquinas said there was a natural inclination of human persons to feel affiliation or friendship with their fellow human beings. He affirmed the necessity of human law for orderly social life and looked at customs as a consideration when creating new laws.

Aquinas's moral and legal reflections had an Aristotelian flavor. Both Aquinas and Aristotle saw ethics and moral and legal reasoning as an inexact science. Aquinas said that natural law is produced by unaided reason which can discern man's natural end. However, he claimed that some truths of revelation cannot be known by natural reason. He saw the individual as ordered to a supernatural goal that transcends the temporal sphere.

For Aquinas, nature is the basis for political philosophy and the state is the agency that supplies the temporal needs of man and helps him in his task of human flourishing. Recognizing the limits of law, he states that human law cannot eliminate every evil and that when it attempts to eradicate all evils, it inevitably destroys many good things as well. Noting that each person has a supernatural end that the state is not qualified to deal with, he proclaims that the state should not erect arbitrary impediments to stifle a person's spiritual life. He says that to a Christian there are needs that cannot be fulfilled in the political order.

Following Aristotle, Aquinas refers to commutative justice as rules regarding the exchange of goods and services among individuals. He focused on the ethical aspects of prices raising issues of justice and equity. Aquinas followed Aristotle in condemning usury and taught that natural wealth serves man as the solution for his natural wants. He viewed money as a form of artificial wealth which has no natural limits to its accumulation and which is not a direct remedy for natural wants. Aquinas maintained that private possessions were necessary for human life.

Spanish scholastic economists of the sixteenth century were concerned primarily with ethics and furthered Thomistic doctrines. These Spanish theologians of the School of Salamanca worked to understand the process of exchange in order to evaluate moral problems they saw accompanying the spread of commerce. These medieval scholastics also looked for reasons to raise the image of the businessman's activities, but they still held the usury doctrine—the prohibition of interest-taking.

Early Modern and Renaissance Periods

With the weakening of religious and feudal bases of rulership, Thomas Hobbes (1588-1679) began a new approach which emphasized the derivation of authority through the use of individual rationality to create formal systems of political and economic thought. His conclusions are therefore based on rational deductions from assumptions regarding human nature.

Hobbes laid some foundations for a self-interested economic approach to human social life. He explained that each person acts to satisfy his desires and that the proper object of each person's will is some subjectively understood good for himself. His notion of rights signifies a power to behave as a person would regularly be inclined to act rather than as a moral justification of being free to act in particular ways. The self, for Hobbes, was atomistic, isolated, antisocial, and amoral. He envisioned each person as driven by passions such as the fear of death and the instinct to survive. He also saw the endless and insatiable character of man's desires. Hobbes said that people are equal in their boundless desires and unlimited claims and that in the state of nature every person is against every other person. This condition drives people to create an unnatural union by agreeing to give up their freedom for the sake of life and peace. For Hobbes, social and political order is an artificial human construction.

Concerned with the idea of the dissolution of authority, Hobbes's goal was to attain peace rather than liberty. He saw civil society as possible only if there is a government to make and enforce laws. Without government, society would return to a state of nature as a state of war. Individuals must give up their own power and transfer it to a sovereign who would become both law giver and law enforcer. His social contract theory says that sovereignty must be absolute if there is to be secure property, enforceable contracts, and the possibility of economic life. Hobbes's economics is a corollary which is embedded in his political philosophy. The Hobbesian solution is to frame and contain interpersonal relationships by delegating authority and mediation to a Leviathan State.

According to Spinoza (1632-1677), the state comes into existence because social order (i.e., peace) is a necessary condition for the exercise of each person's individual power of self-preservation. He argued that politics is not appropriate for the production of virtue and he wanted to protect the state from the diverse judgments of proponents of the various many religions. Spinoza detranscendalizes the state and makes the Bible and other religious documents irrelevant to politics. He did not want to interweave political and religious sentiments. Spinoza said that the purpose of the state is to secure freedom (i.e., the avoidance of physical conflict), harmony, and order. His minimal liberal state is concerned with security and physical well-being. Political life has a very limited function that does not deal with attaining one's perfection or blessedness. Spinoza dismisses any type of moralistic perfectionist politics—he removes politics from moral perfection. He thus expounds a perfectionist individual ethics and nonperfectionist politics.

Spinoza's orientation toward perfection or well-being defines virtue in terms of an individual's power of acting. He says that to be active is to be antipolitical. Freedom, for Spinoza, means unimpeded flourishing. For Spinoza, something is free that exists from the necessity of its nature alone and that is determined to act by itself alone. He says that the foundation of virtue is self-preservation, that the good is whatever makes a person more perfect, and that natural law sets bounds on what can be attained. We find a self-perfectionist meaning of autonomy in Spinoza. He explains that individuals naturally seek autonomy and to develop their rational powers in order to defeat external obstacles. The perfection of reason is the perfection of man. He says that a man is free to the extent that he is guided by reason.

Spinoza maintains that democracy promotes the conditions of reason and individual expression. He says that democracies are the most compatible with natural individual liberty. Spinoza advocates the subordination of all religions (which can be boiled down to justice and charity) to the state and the confinement of religion to private faith in the form of inward worship of God. Concerned with the civil strife caused by religion, he advises toleration of opposing religious beliefs as the best policy for the state. He argued that every person should be free to think and say what he likes and can even discuss the law short of sedition. Spinoza noted that freedom of philosophy is necessary for the protection of piety and public peace.

John Locke (1632-1704) argued that people have natural rights prior to the existence of government. He reasoned that a state of nature stabilized by natural law predated the social contract and that people are not born into political communities. Locke maintained that by nature all individuals are equal and free both before and after the foundation of the state. He saw the state of nature as one of peace, good will, and mutual assistance and preservation—unlike Hobbes, Locke's state of nature is not a state of war.

According to Locke, men may form a civil society even before the existence of the state and, when in that civil society, make their natural rights more secure by agreeing to respect each others' labor and property—within civil society, economic institutions, including money, may develop through mutual consent and in the absence of any political contact. People form a government in order to protect their natural rights. Government is established to secure natural rights when people perceive that they are not powerful enough to thwart those who refuse to acknowledge their moral sovereignty. Consent of the governed is necessary to form a political community and such consent may be tacitly given. Locke rests political obligation on a social contract or agreement to transfer the powers that each person possessed in the state of nature to a democratic sovereign. There exists a rational purpose for government which is the protection of individual rights. If the government exceeds that role then the people can revolt. Locke explains that representative government is the best way to ensure that government stays within legitimate purpose. He also recognizes the danger of leaving absolute power to any one person or group of persons. Consent is the underpinning of government and fixes its limit. He acknowledges the right of people to depose rulers who do not abide by the social contract.

Locke assumed the original divine donation of the world and explained that God wanted happiness on earth for his created beings. He said that the laws of nature expressed God's commandments, that reason could apprehend them, and that men were subject to natural moral law. According to Locke, people require liberty, property, and health because the chief end set by the Creator is survival. Locke explained that the moral and legal possession of property is a precondition of freedom. He saw man's labor as the origin and justification of private property when a man, who has property in his own body, mixes his labor with previously unowned property and removes it from the common state.

David Hume (1711-1776) prepared the way for the French physiocrats and for Adam Smith. His powerful, skeptical, intellectual argument rejects the ordinary view of causality. In addition, he looked to sentiments or emotions as the primary source of morality. Rather than view the passions as evil, Hume applauded the sympathetic mechanisms of morality—he maintained that reason cannot lead to action without the passions and that moral action stems from sympathy. He said that the permanent principles of the moral and intellectual virtues are sympathy and utility and that justice is the community of sentiment that keeps society stable and well-organized. Of course, his skepticism is problematic when he attempts to argue for the existence of permanent truths that can be discovered. Hume was concerned with the state and its relationship to the happiness of its citizens—he envisioned a trade-off between the power of the state and personal freedom and contended that an action was virtuous, rather than corrupt, if it resulted in public benefits. Hume distinguished both happiness from wealth and money from wealth and taught that labor is the source of wealth and that people will supply labor only if they have an incentive to do so. He also noted that luxury and avarice are required for national progress.

The French physiocrats (1755-1775) are regarded as the first organized school of economists. Their approach, like that of Adam Smith, was primarily deductive. These French economists emphasized the worth of agriculture and enriched economics with concepts such as "circular flow" and "equilibrium." Whereas the mercantilists emphasized economic regulation, money-making, and the importance of manufacturing, the physiocrats advocated agriculture and favored economic freedom at home and abroad. The physiocrats saw agriculture as the key to economic growth because of its ability to generate a financial surplus. They contended that, in a well-ordered state, taxation would be levied on the landholding class who are the ultimate producers. In addition, the French economists viewed the natural order of society as the basis of natural rights. A notable accomplishment of the physiocrats was to embody economics in their great system of political and social philosophy.

A. R. J. Turgot (1727-1781), a French public official, engaged in pragmatic reforms based on his systematic writings in economics. Like the physiocrats, he placed a premium on agriculture. Turgot taught that interest rates are determined by supply and demand and explored the nature of value which he saw as unique to each individual. He saw that there was no natural unit that can be used to measure value and developed a primitive theory of subjective value grounded in utility. Turgot also developed an early version of the law of diminishing returns. In addition, he explained that the savings of one period became the investment of the next period—advances come out of savings. Turgot saw economic evolution as a process of endless innovation. Because of the potential of the human mind, he firmly believed in the progressive accumulation of knowledge and steady advance. However, he was concerned with different rates of progress among nations and the influence of culture, genius, and entrepreneurship on these rates in his famous philosophy of history.

Adam Smith (1723-1790) was a moral philosopher whose economic ideas were part of a comprehensive system of social science rooted in moral philosophy. One can see the influence on Smith of Aristotle and of the Stoic tradition reaching back to the Greeks through the medieval and rational natural law thinkers. Smith also drew upon the work of the sixteenth- and seventeenth-century Spanish scholastic theologians. He followed Hume in his *Theory of Moral Sentiments* and the French physiocrats in his *The Wealth of Nations*. Smith retained the French economists' preference for agriculture over manufacturing, and like them, was against the economic policy of mercantilism. In part, he constructed his own system on the foundation of the physiocratic system.

According to Smith, nature presents people with phenomena and it is the purpose of the philosopher to find the principles that connect the phenomena. He employs the natural law tradition and natural theology to appeal to human nature as the foundation for an orderly moral sphere. As a moral philosopher, Smith sought to elucidate the principles of human nature and their connecting principles. He wanted to understand human beings as they are and as they ought to be if they were to realize their own *telos*. It is clear that nature is the key to Smith's project. Smith proposed the existence of a benevolent deity who designed a systematic universe that coordinates the actions of autonomous individuals. This deity is said to also have designed the forces which through unintended consequences makes possible the evolution of mankind.

Smith explained morality as expressing the moral sentiments of human nature—he saw the natural inclination of sympathy toward the interests of others as the foundation for moral human development. He explains that people are encouraged to associate because they find mutual sympathy (i.e., the mutual accord of sentiments) pleasurable. Psychological dispositions and feelings are viewed as related to morality and the propriety of an action is seen as dependent on the appropriations of the motivating sentiment.

The concept of sympathy involves seeing things from someone else's point of view. According to Smith, a man's character cannot develop without other human beings—a man would not have any moral sentiments without other individuals. He observes that direct sympathy or fellow feeling is the origin of the virtues. People form their first perceptions of right and wrong through immediate sense experience and feelings. Viewing sentiments as prior to virtues, Smith sees virtues and moral order as emanating from a process of sympathetic interaction.

Smith developed the idea of an impartial spectator to account for the formation of people's judgments of themselves and of others. This involves removing one's self out of his natural context and attempting to view his own conduct and that of others at a distance from himself. The judgment of moral approval or disapproval is the extent of an agreement or disagreement between a person's reaction and the imagined reaction of the impartial spectator. Smith's spectatorial vision calls each person to desire the virtue of being praiseworthy.

For Smith, both ethics and economics are rooted in the moral sentiments of human nature—moral sentiments have an impact on ethics and economics. He saw that the connecting principle in ethics is sympathy and that it is commercial ambition in economics. This led to his distinction between the higher virtues and the lower virtues.

In *The Wealth of Nations* Smith proposed a system of natural liberty where markets can work like an invisible hand. This system included the division of labor, competition, capital accumulation, and a laissez-faire government that supplies a system of justice. The state exists primarily for the defense of life and property and for the advance of justice. He explains that, in order to preserve society, nature has placed a desire for justice in human beings' personalities. Smith teaches that the invisible hand disposes human actions toward the general good despite the failings of human agents—commercial ambition aimed at private interests secures the public benefit. For Smith, economic phenomena are closely linked to physical and biological nature. He saw that the economy had a natural order that was self-governed in a similar fashion as the physical world was governed.

Smith observes that each person is more deeply interested in what concerns himself and thus will first attend to his own happiness. He also contends that men suffer from the delusion that goods will make them happier, but also that this delusion is actually a good thing because society benefits when people strive to attain wealth. Individuals are deceived by nature into acting in a socially beneficial manner. The universe is a great system built by a deity with the goal of the maximization of human happiness.

Society is needed in order to have the higher self and to develop the higher and nobler virtues. People are driven by both the motivation to better their conditions and the desire for mutual sympathy. Smith explains that self-command is a virtue which evidences the realization of true wisdom. Self-command involves learning to control one's appetites in the interest of a higher devotion to the whole. It follows that, for Smith, moral experience is a combination of emotions, reason, and a constrained form of free will that can choose only from among the sentiments a man experiences.

The Late Modern Period

John-Baptiste Say (1767-1832) generally popularized the views of Adam Smith, although he discarded Smith's labor theory of value. Like Smith, Say sought to discredit mercantilist doctrines. He saw government intervention as an obstacle and said that taxation cannot cause a nation to be more prosperous. Say opposed arbitrary fiat money, consumptionism, and credit creationism.

Say maintained that, in order to be a consumer, a person must first be a producer of a good that will exchange for money (i.e., something that is desirable to others). Production (i.e., supply) generates the income necessary for the demand of other products and services. In other words, products are bought ultimately with other products—the supply of certain goods constitutes demand for other goods. Say understood the metaphysical primacy of production.

He taught that general overproduction or underproduction can be no more than a momentary phenomenon. Economic disruptions occur only if goods are not produced in correct proportions to one another. Say denies that there is any glut or general overproduction in an economic downturn. He says that general underconsumption is impossible although political events can cause prolonged unemployment. Emphasizing the interconnection of markets, Say explains that free markets do clear through the rationing function of the price system.

Say recognized the creative role of the entrepreneur and liked technological change. He said that innovation can destroy jobs in the short run but that it creates jobs in the long run. Say understood that when money is saved it would then be invested. He rejected claims that excessive saving (or an unfavorable trade balance) would reduce demand for a country's products. He also saw no need for government to pass laws to fabricate demand.

Herbert Spencer's (1820-1903) positive, optimistic, and deterministic theory of inevitable progress had a significant impact in the United States. He saw progress as the outcome of the natural process of evolution. Spencer advocates the "law of equal freedom" which holds that everyone is free to do as he wishes as long as he does not impinge upon the freedom of others to do likewise. In his writings, he applies this law to every area of state action. Spencer equated justice with equal liberty and saw law as a restriction of liberty. He observes that when government thwarts competition it causes more suffering in the long run.

According to Spencer, equal freedom favors societies that internalize it. Spencer sees society as an aggregation of individuals—individuals are primary and people are responsible for their own lives. A Lamarckian with respect to the inheritance of acquired characteristics, he maintained that acquired characteristics were passed on to one's offspring. Noting the inevitable law of causation in human affairs, Spencer taught that each individual should experience the natural effects of his own actions. He observed that living beings seek what is conducive to their lives (i.e., values) and that such activity fosters social and moral progress.

Society is subject to evolution from an incoherent homogeneity to a coherent heterogeneity—positive social change involves differentiation. As societies evolve functions become more specialized. Spencer explains that society evolves naturally through the adaptation of its functions to changing conditions until the ideal state is reached. This involves a transition from a militant society to an industrial society. He said that under peaceful conditions the less government and fewer regulations the better.

An agnostic with respect to religion, Spencer endorses a type of gradual progressivism. He thus ironically endorses both a destiny of social perfection and the idea that government interference is an obstacle to its attainment. In his ethics, Spencer argued for a kind of rational egoism. Of course, this is problematic because his determinism keeps him from endorsing a theory of free will.

Abstract economic theory make its greatest advances as a result of the doctrines developed at the University of Vienna by a group of economists known as the Austrian School. Carl Menger (1840-1921), the father of Austrian economics, taught that knowledge begins with induction and that economic subjectivism is compatible with philosophical realism. The desire of Menger, whose approach was close to Aristotelian philosophy, was to uncover the real nature or essence of economic phenomena. As an immanent realist, Menger was interested in essences and laws as manifested in this world. His economics subscribes to economic realism in its conception of the existence and epistemic attainability of what Adam Smith had viewed as the "Invisible Hand." Menger's economic theory was a general and abstract theory which attempted to unify all true fragments of economic knowledge.

Holding that causality underlies economic laws, Menger taught that theoretical science provides the tools for studying phenomena that exhibit regularities. He distinguished between exact types and laws that deal with strictly typical phenomena and empirical-realistic types and laws that deal with truth within a particular spatio-temporal domain. Menger's exact approach involves deductive-universalistic theory and looks for regularities in the coexistence and succession of phenomena that admits no exceptions and that are strictly ordered. His theoretical economics is concerned with exact laws based on the assumptions of self-interest, full knowledge, and freedom. Menger's exact theoretical approach involves both isolation and abstraction from disturbing factors.

Menger, like the much later Ayn Rand, argued that the ultimate standard of value is the life of the valuer and espoused a type of contextually relational objectivity in his value theory. He defined value as the importance of a good in satisfying one's needs. Menger also distinguished between economic and non-economic goods, developed a theory of marginal value, and investigated the implications of time and uncertainty.

Menger was also concerned about the way in which institutions arise and incorporated ontological and methodological individualism and spontaneous order in his genetico-compositive understanding of social phenomena. For example, he said that money is a product of human action and not of human design.

The Contemporary Period

Ludwig von Mises (1881-1973) was dissatisfied with Menger's Aristotelian methodology and value theory and therefore laid out his own view of economics and its fundamentals. Insisting on the a priori character of economic science, Mises relied upon aprioristic reasoning as the foundation of his thinking and work. He wanted to gain knowledge through purely conceptual and deductive reasoning from first principles. Mises wanted to study what is necessary and universal about actual actions performed by real human beings. He saw human action as the ultimate given. Mises explains that a person's introspective knowledge that he is conscious and that he acts is a fact of reality independent of external experience. He said that action is reason applied to purpose and wanted to understand purposeful human action in an open-ended world of uncertainty.

Mises named the study of human action "praxeology." He maintained that the categories of praxeology are universally valid because they reflect the structure of the human mind and the natural world. Mises said that the statements and propositions of economics are a priori, are not derived from experience, and do not proceed from inductive generalizations. He contended that economic theory rests on a body of truths independent of time and place. Included among these truths are the notions of causation, valuation, means and ends, scarcity, choice, opportunity cost, social cooperation, marginal utility, the time-preference theory of interest, the laws of exchange, and so on.

Misesian economics is descriptive, value-free, and apolitical. Mises explains that value judgments are subjective and cannot be argued about. The value of goods is thus in the minds of acting people and the content of human action is determined by the personal judgments of each individual. According to Mises, economics is a value-free science of means, rather than of ends, that describes but does not prescribe. He says that whether people act to attain happiness or some other goal is irrelevant for praxeological economics.

Economics deals with chosen human aims and values. Mises says that human reason and freedom play roles in every action. Values are freely chosen and a person can decide to initiate a chain of causation because he has free will—actions are self-generated and goal-directed. Mises understands that the study of human action can be used to make a value-free case for freedom. Mises observes that voluntary social cooperation springs from human action because higher production and greater prosperity in society arise from the division of labor. Each person is more likely to attain his own goals in a free society. Misesian value-free economics thus shows that only free-market capitalism can create a social order of freedom, peace, and prosperity.

Ayn Rand (1905-1982) constructed an entire integrated and coherent philosophy to underpin her ethics and politics, which stress individual happiness and natural rights. In her normative argument for classical liberal ideas Rand places freedom as a precondition for virtue. She derives an objective ethics based on the nature of man as a goal-seeking entity with the end goal as life as man *qua* man. According to Rand, happiness relates to a person's success as a unique, rational human being possessing free will.

Rand's rational epistemology holds that knowledge is based on the observation of reality and that it is possible to gain objective knowledge of both facts and values. She explains that a concept is a mental integration of factual or perceptual data and that properly formed concepts are objective and contextual. Her epistemology transcends both apriorism and empiricism. Although she refers to essences or concepts as epistemological rather than metaphysical, she actually means relational and contextual.

Rand says that at the root of the concept of value is the conditional characteristic of life and that ethics is an objective metaphysical necessity. Morality is a means to the end of life and ethics deals with concepts which Rand sees as rational and objective. Viewing reason as man's means of survival, she maintains that man's primary choice is to focus his consciousness. Rand saw the virtues as inextricably linked and as the means to obtaining the values which, along with the virtues, enable people to attain their happiness.

Murray Rothbard (1926-1995) developed a type of neo-Aristotelian natural law and natural rights theory. He derives the content of natural law and speaks in terms of natural law and natural rights. Rothbard combined natural law theory using an Aristotelian or Randian approach with the praxeological economics of Austrians such as Mises. He differs from the neo-Kantian Mises in his epistemology and instead returns to the Aristotelian epistemology of Menger to find the action axiom as based in empirical reality. Rothbard believed Mises to be on shaky grounds with his extreme aprioristic approach to epistemology. However, he did embrace nearly all of Misesian economics.

Rothbard saw rights as essential to a libertarian social order. He thus advocated his nonaggression principle and the right to self-defense. Working largely within the Lockean logic of self-ownership, homesteading, and exchange,

Rothbard became an ideologically committed zero-state economist who saw no role for government to play. For him political exchange equals coercion and market exchange equals voluntary agreement. Viewing the state as a vehicle of institutionalized crime, he supported free competition in the provision of defense and judicial services.

Rothbard's market-anarchist program is the instantiation of his libertarian moral theory which does not constitute a prescription for personal morality—it merely constructs a social ethics of libertarianism as a political philosophy. Basically, he holds that individuals can select their own personal values but should not endeavor to enforce their ideas of morality upon other people. He sees the nonaggression principle as consistent with diverse moral stances.

Friedrich A. Hayek's (1899-1992) system is based on his views regarding the scope and limits of human reason. As a critic of central planning, Hayek argued for the impossibility of using Cartesian deliberative reasoning to engineer society. He said that the fatal conceit of political bureaucrats was their undue faith in the power of reason. According to Hayek, the impossibility of social planning comes about from the fact that we are all governed by rules of which we have no knowledge.

For Hayek, social order is not a purposive construction. He claims that the spontaneous order of the market forms itself. There are social rules, the most fundamental of which elude conscious articulation. These rules are products of a process of evolutionary selection. Hayek spoke of spontaneously grown institutions such as language, law, morals, and other conventions. Through trial and error, language, morals, law, and so on involve imitation of successful neural rules combining and spreading throughout the population. He said that the human mind is an evolutionary product and that the order we find in the world is assigned to it by the mind's creative activity.

Hayek's evolutionary theory of morality tells of man's long-evolved moral instincts. According to Hayek, moral standards are the products of evolution, man is socially constituted, and individuals submit themselves to social rules. He sees ethics as emotive, says there is no rational basis for moral rules, and fails to ground his system on explicit moral principles. Hayek explains that people adopt rules of conduct that foster effective collective life in a social environment and that such norms are required because both the individual and society are limited epistemologically.

Hayek contends that the majority of knowledge (particularly social knowledge) is of a tacit practical character. Such tacit knowledge is frequently not known consciously and is unable to be communicated to a central authority. He says that this tacit knowledge is used through a kind of discovery process. Hayek explains that there is a wide dispersal of bits of knowledge which cannot be centralized but which does determine social outcomes.

Milton Friedman (1912-2006) was an adamant and consistent advocate of liberty who taught that the free market is necessary to generate political freedom. He maintained on empirical grounds that only competitive markets can coordinate the components of a complex society. Friedman argued that the methods of economic science can be used to refute the claims of statists and interventionists. He, therefore, conducted countless empirical, historical, and quantitative studies of the failures of government intervention. It is thus apparent that Friedman had a lack of interest in the more philosophical questions regarding freedom.

Friedman employed the economic tools of the Keynesian in his studies. His goal was to use empirical evidence to resolve differences with respect to policy recommendations. Ironically, this proselytizer and spokesman for freedom employed a social engineering approach to help the state to intervene more efficiently to do what it should not be doing in the first place. Friedman was willing to discuss incremental changes that go in the right direction toward his ideal of a minimal state.

Friedman held that a theory is useful if it can be used to predict and to control events. His positive economics was thus aimed at making ever more accurate predictions. For him, theories are explanatory hypotheses that can be tentatively accepted. Friedman said that we can never prove a theory—we can only fail to disprove it. He was a falsificationist and an instrumentalist who argued that the realism or unrealism of the assumptions of an economic theory is no guide to its usefulness. Friedman warned economic theorists who value the realism of assumptions that they must take into account each new event and assimilate it in the theory at hand. For him, abstraction involves a theory in which many characteristics of reality are designated as absent from the theory—he failed to understand that abstraction could be non-precise.

James M. Buchanan (1919-) wants to study government as an integral part of the economy. He applies the methodology and tools of modern economics to the study of political processes and government failure. Buchanan also examines the reasons why government fails to produce the desired results.

Buchanan developed contractual and constitutional bases for his Public Choice theory. Using deductive logic he illustrates how a social contract between free individuals could result in a limited constitutional government. An avowed Hobbesian contractarian procedural liberal thinker, Buchanan contends that individuals agree to a social contract because they want to survive. He says that people choosing behind a veil of ignorance would likely unanimously select the principle of utility embodied in a social contract.

He explains that there are two levels of collective choice—the level of constitutional politics and the level of ordinary politics. Constitutional politics establishes boundaries over what ordinary politics is allowed to do. Buchanan explains that the unanimity principle does not apply to the stage of the post-constitutional operations of the government. He cites the high cost and difficulty (or impossibility) of applying the unanimity principle in practice to make decisions at the post-constitutional level. It follows that a less than unanimity rule relates to this stage. Buchanan notes that ordinary political decisions are usually made by majority voting. He observes that majority voting makes it too easy to fund government activities that benefit ever-changing coalitions and that the constitutional level is where debate about redistribution belongs. Buchanan thus argues for a new social contract that requires much higher than majority agreement for ordinary political decisions. He also wants additional spending, taxing, and term limits at the constitutional level regarding what government officials can do.

Buchanan's social contractarian approach dismisses the possibility of natural law, natural rights, and of an absolute natural moral order. He arrives at contractarian individual rights merely from people having reached an agreement not because there is a natural order of things that determine natural rights.

Robert Nozick (1938-2002) attempted to justify the state and to refute the anarchist position. He uses rational analysis and deduction to argue for the idea of the spontaneous origin of the state as dominant protective agency. Nozick's conclusion was that a single defense agency could arise from anarchy to become an effective minimal state without violating anyone's rights. He says that a free society based on a minimal state will lead to social consequences that correspond to people's moral intuitions.

Nozick contends that a state-like entity would eventually emerge out of anarchy through a series of natural incremental stages. After a period with competing protective agencies, he envisions a dominant protective agency forcing other independent agencies into subjugation to itself. Nozick explains that this dominant protective agency will protect the rights of all as just compensation to those who were not previously its own clients. He says that to become the minimal state the dominant protective agency (or ultraminimal state) is morally obligated to compensate the prohibited would-be subscribers to the services of the independents by providing them with protection services. The minimal state supplies protection services to everyone within its domain and does not permit anyone else to use force or to settle disputes without its expressed permission.

Nozick may be open to the criticism that the state could have been established immorally if force is used against the independents and/or the clients of the independents to gain its monopoly. In addition, Nozick simply assumes the existence of Lockean natural rights and does not try to derive them from the nature of man and the world. He says that the state's coercive apparatus is limited to what he calls the "ethics of respect" for individual rights.

Thomas Sowell (1930-) is a strong and articulate advocate of classical economics and the free market. His constrained vision of man accepts him as self-interested and limited in his knowledge and his capabilities. Each person acts based on his own limited information and is subject to constraints, trade-offs, and incentives. Building on the insights of Hayek, Sowell maintains that knowledge on a societal scale takes the form of social experiences such as traditions and habits. He says that systemic rationality is superior to individual intentional rationality. He speaks of systemic causation in legal traditions, family ties, social customs, and so on. According to Sowell, people have insufficient personal knowledge to rely on reason alone. He explains that dispersed knowledge forms the architecture of our institutions, that society is a collection of overlapping and interconnected decision makers, and that social benefits result from systemic effects of people pursuing their own self-interest within the limits of laws and customs. Sowell emphasizes that prices economize on the knowledge needed for particular decisions.

Michael Novak (1933-), a leading Catholic philosopher and theologian, is a passionate proponent of a free society and has tirelessly advanced his notion of democratic capitalism, consisting of an economy based on markets, a democratic polity based on the rule of law and on checks and balances, and a moral-cultural system that is pluralistic and liberal. Novak advocates the natural system of liberty and articulates a moral theory and theological underpinning for the ideals of democratic capitalism. For him, democratic capitalism embodies a social order in which people may realize their personal dignity, freedom, and personhood. Novak explains that democratic capitalism recognizes the most important common good—the individual freedom of each human being. He says that a free society needs to be populated by those who resist the temptation to violate the natural rights and freedom of others who hold contrary views or who act in disagreeable (but not coercive) ways. Novak's idea of democratic capitalism incorporates positive sum conceptions of man, nature, and wealth, thereby promoting productivity, innovation, and risk-taking.

The Philosophy of Freedom

What can we learn from a survey of political and economic philosophies throughout history? Can we put them together by drawing from many or all of them to construct a powerful emergent libertarian synthesis that is a true reflection of the nature of man and the world properly understood? Is it possible to reframe the argument for a free society into a consistent reality-based whole? Are we able to attain an overarching theoretical perspective and to construct a sound truth-based paradigm with internally consistent components?

Because ultimately the truth is one, there is an essential interconnection between objective ideas. It is thus possible to integrate truths gleaned from thinkers of the various periods of time. We could say that the universe of all true knowledge in all of its diversity has a unity whereby its different parts illuminate each other. It follows that political and economic thought draws upon nearly every phase of human knowledge. Some political and economic ideas have changed and developed over time and many have stayed essentially the same. There has been a rich tradition of political and economic discourse with respect to the nature and fundamental properties of reality and regarding the political arrangements that are indispensable to attain a free society. A wide variety of political and economic philosophies can be found to be related, mutually illuminating, and mutually relevant. Each thinker has basic assumptions and beliefs regarding the nature of man and there is a close connection between one's concept of the nature of man and his political and economic philosophy.

During the long course of Western political thought several basic ideas have played an important role. These include, but are not limited to, the existence of natural moral law and natural rights, the moral and rational character of man, the limited nature of the state, the superiority of democratic rule and constitutional government, and the desirability of subsidiarity. Such ideas emphasize a certain unity in political and economic thought which connects us with ancient times.

A paradigm that appeals to and reflects reality as an independent ontological order will help people to understand the world and to survive and flourish in it. A proper political and economic philosophy must be based on the nature of man and the universe. Once this knowledge is gained, then we can ascertain the role the state should have. Necessary prescriptions are embedded in the nature of things and they are discoverable through observation, logic, and a rational epistemology. What is required is philosophical realism in the natural law tradition. Natural law can provide man with general and universal principles. This will permit the construction of the best political regime based on the framework of the naturality of human society. Our goal is to have a paradigm in which the views of reality, human nature, knowledge, values, action, and society make up an integrated whole.

A proper political and economic philosophy demands an account of man's nature as determined by reason. Man is a rational agent with a free and self-determinative will who is capable of deliberation and choice. A human being has metaphysical liberty and can therefore initiate, by his mental activity, much of what he does in life. Thinking is not automatic, but human beings can use their free will to focus, to think, and to initiate. It follows that human beings can make choices about right and wrong, that they are self-responsible to do the right thing, and that they require a private domain that others must respect. The idea of metaphysical freedom is connected to responsibility and with the related notions of virtues, vices, and human flourishing. It follows that mutual non-interference is primary regarding both freedom and the demands of moral virtues. Mutual non-interference is a required condition for both a free society and for a virtuous society.

Natural rights are metanormative principles that regulate the conditions under which moral conduct and human flourishing can take place. The individual right to liberty secures the possibility of self-direction in a social context. To secure individuals' natural rights, men must seek to establish the structural political conditions that protect that possibility. Each person must be accorded a secure moral space over which he has freedom to act and to pursue his personal flourishing. Individual human flourishing is the standard underpinning the assessment that a goal is rational and should be sought. People are moral agents whose project it is to excel at being the particular human being that one is.

Human flourishing must be achieved through a person's own efforts. Each person has reason and free will and the capacity to initiate conduct that will enhance or inhibit his flourishing. Rationality, the cardinal virtue for human flourishing, can only gain expression which a man has responsibility for his own choices. A person's flourishing depends upon his cognition at a conceptual level. Individuals must be free to discern, select, and pursue their own goals and to form their own groups and associations. Each person must be free to choose to initiate the mental processes of focusing and thinking on becoming the best person he can be as the context of his own existence.

Natural rights are universal, are good for human beings in general, and are based on the common attributes of human beings. As political principles, they are general and uniform and establish proper rules of social interaction. Once they are secured, what is good for the life of each man in his individual instantiation becomes a possibility—the notions of morality and human flourishing apply only to individual human beings whose *telos* it is to develop their virtues and potentialities in accordance with their facticity.

A proper political and legal system is not totally separated from the realm of ethics based on the nature of man and the world. However, ethics are not all of one kind nor at the same level. Some directly prescribe moral conduct and others regulate the conditions under which moral conduct may occur. A political and legal system regulates such conditions and should be concerned only with rights as universal metanormative principles and not with the promotion of personal virtue, morality, or flourishing. Political life is properly concerned solely with peace and security. Such a distinction between politics and morality makes great sense. It follows that the minimal state is only concerned with justice in a metanormative sense—not as a personal virtue.

Ayn Rand has demonstrated that metaphysics and epistemology are inextricably connected. She explains that knowledge is based on the observation of reality and that, to gain objective knowledge, a person must use the methods of induction, deduction, and integration. Induction and deduction are complementary and go hand-in-hand. Because concepts refer to facts, knowledge has a base in reality and it is possible to derive valid concepts using the rules of logic—a person is able to define objective principles to guide his cognitive processes. It follows that conclusions reached through the proper application of reason are objective. Rand maintains that it is possible to gain objective knowledge of both facts and values. People have the capacity to determine what is in their own best interest and to act on such determination. Thinking is self-produced and human beings can will and initiate behavior.

Human beings can think but thinking is not automatic. A person must use his free will to focus and to use his rational consciousness. A man knows he has volition through the act of introspection—he can introspectively observe that he can choose to focus his consciousness or not. A man's distinctiveness from other living species is his ability to initiate an act of consciousness. Free will is critical to human existence and human flourishing.

People value because they have needs as living, conditional entities. The predominant value theory among Austrian thinkers is Ludwig von Mises's subjectivist approach. This approach takes personal values as given and assumes that individuals have different motivations and prefer different things. By contrast, some Austrians follow Carl Menger, the father of Austrian economics, in agreeing with Ayn Rand that the ultimate standard of value is the life of the valuer and that objective values support man's life and originate in a relationship between man and his survival requirements. This approach sees value as a relational and objective quality dependent on the subject, the object, and the context involved. Objective values depend upon both a person's humanity and his individuality. Each person has the potential to use his unique attributes and talents in his efforts to do well at living his own individual life. It is possible for a person to pursue objective values that are consonant with his own rational self-interest.

Production, the means to gaining one's material values, metaphysically precedes their distribution, exchange, and consumption. To survive and flourish, people must produce what is required for their existence. Goods must be produced before they can be consumed. Consumption follows production and production (i.e., supply) is the source of consumption (i.e., demand). Productiveness is a virtue—individuals tend to be productive and to flourish when they practice the related virtues of rationality and self-interest.

Austrian praxeological economics (i.e., the study of human action) has been used to make a value-free case for liberty. This economic science deals with abstract principles and general rules that must be applied if a society is to have optimal production and economic well-being. Misesian praxeology consists of a body of logically deduced, inexorable laws of economics beginning with the axiom that each person acts purposefully. Mises was off base with his neo-Kantian epistemology which views human action as a category of the human mind. Fortunately, Murray Rothbard demonstrated how the action axiom could be derived using induction and a natural law approach.

Although Misesian economists hold that values are subjective and Objectivists argue that values are objective, these claims are not incompatible because they are not really claims about the same things—they exist at different levels or spheres of analysis. The value-subjectivity of the Austrians complements the Randian sense of objectivity. The level of objective values dealing with personal flourishing transcends the level of subjective value preferences.

Austrian Economics is an excellent way of looking at methodological economics with respect to the appraisal of means but not of ends. Misesian praxeology therefore must be augmented. Its value-free economics is not sufficient to establish a total case for liberty. A systematic, reality-based ethical system must be discovered to firmly establish the argument for individual liberty. Natural law provides the groundwork for such a theory and both Objectivism and the Aristotelian idea of human flourishing are based on natural law ideas.

An ethical system must be developed and defended in order to establish the case for a free society. An Aristotelian ethics of naturalism states that moral matters are matters of fact and that morally good conduct is that which enables the individual agent to make the best possible progress toward achieving his self-perfection and happiness. According to Rand, happiness relates to a person's success as a unique, rational human being possessing free will. We have free choice and the capacity to initiate our own conduct that enhances or hinders our flourishing as human beings.

A human being's flourishing requires the rational use of his individual human potentialities, including his talents, abilities, and virtues in the pursuit of his freely and rationally chosen values and goals. An action is considered to be proper if it leads to the flourishing of the person performing the action. A person's flourishing leads to his happiness. Each person is responsible for voluntarily choosing, creating, and entering relationships in civil society that contribute toward his flourishing. Civil society, a spontaneous order, is based on voluntary participation and is made up of natural and voluntary associations such as families, private business, voluntary unions, churches, clubs, charities, and so on. The related notions of subsidiarity and of a pluralistic society spring from the reality of human nature.

Virtues and goods are the means to values and the virtues, goods, and values together enable human beings to attain their flourishing and happiness. Virtues must be applied, although differentially, by each individual in his task of human flourishing. The pursuit of one's flourishing is driven by reason and reason requires the consistent practice of the virtues. Such a "virtue ethics" is agent-centered, agent-based, agent-relative, and contextual. Choosing and making the proper response in particular concrete circumstances is the concern of moral living. A person must identify and abide by rational principles if he is to flourish. The major virtues provide these rational principles.

Both economics and ethics are concerned with human choice and human action. Human action, the subject of both economics and morality, is the common denominator and the link between economic principles and moral principles. Both economic law and moral law are derived from natural law. Because truth is consistent, it follows that economics and morality are inextricably related parts of one indivisible body of knowledge. Because natural law regulates the affairs of men, it is the task of both economists and philosophers to discover the natural order and to adhere to it. There is an intimate connection between economic science and an objective, normative framework for understanding human life.

It follows that all of the disciplines of human action are interrelated and can be integrated into a paradigm of individual liberty based on the nature of man and the world. A study of human action grounded as a true anthropology of the human person provides insights into both economics and moral truths. Economic and moral principles are part of one inseparable body of thought.

It should not be surprising to find that the discoveries of a truth-based economics and of a moral philosophy based on the nature of man and the world are consistent with one another. There is one universe in which everything is interconnected metaphysically through the inescapable laws of cause and effect. True knowledge must also be a total in which every item of knowledge is interconnected. All objective knowledge is interrelated in some way, thus reflecting the totality that is the universe.

Because no field is totally independent of any other field, there are really no discrete branches of knowledge. There is only cognition in which subjects are separated out for purpose of study. That is fine for purposes of specialization, but, in the end, we need to reintegrate by connecting one's specialized knowledge back into the total knowledge of reality. We need to think systemically, look for the relationships and connections between components of knowledge, and aspire to understand the nature of knowledge and its unity. Ultimately, the truth is one. There is an essential interconnection between objective ideas. It follows that academicians should pay more attention to systems building rather than to the extreme specialization within a discipline.

Philosophy provides the conceptual framework necessary to understand man's behavior. To survive a person must perceive the world, comprehend it, and act upon it. To survive and flourish, a man must recognize that nature has its own imperatives. He needs to have viable, sound, and proper conceptions of man's nature, knowledge, values, and action. He must recognize that there is a natural law that derives from the nature of man and the world and that is discoverable through the use of reason.

A sound paradigm requires internal consistency among its components. By properly integrating insights gleaned throughout history we have the potential to reframe the argument for a free society and elucidate a theory of the best political regime on the basis of man, human action, and society. This natural-law-based paradigm would uphold each man's sovereignty, moral space, and natural rights and accords each person a moral space and natural rights. It would hold that men require a social and political structure that recognizes natural rights and accords each person a moral space over which he has freedom to act and pursue his personal flourishing. See the following exhibit for an example diagram of what such a paradigm might look like. Specifically, it would consist of (1) an objective, realistic, natural-law-oriented metaphysics; (2) a natural rights theory based on the nature of man and the world; (3) an objective epistemology which describes essences or concepts as epistemologically contextual and relational rather than as metaphysical; (4) a biocentric theory of value; (5) praxeology as a tool for understanding how people cooperate and compete and for deducing universal principles of economics; and (6) an ethic of human flourishing based on reason, free will, and individuality.

A Paradigm for a Free Society

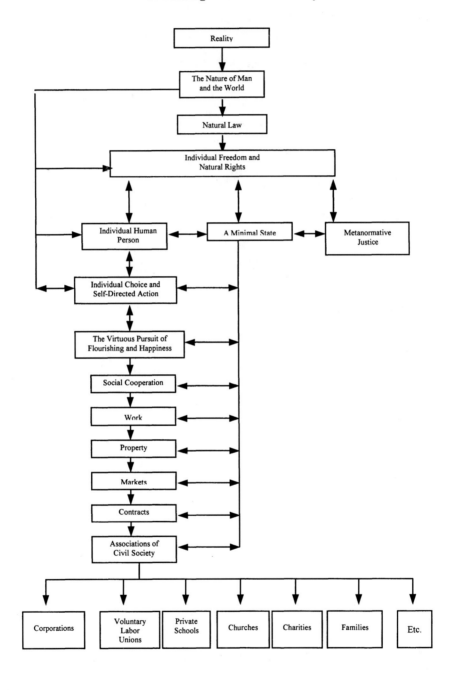

Recommended Reading

Backhouse, R. E. *Economists and the Economy: The Evolution of Economic Ideas* 2nd ed. New Brunswick, NJ: Transaction Press, 1994.

Barry, Norman P. *On Classical Liberalism and Libertarianism*. New York: Palgrave MacMillan, 1987.

Blaug, Mark. *Economic Theory in Retrospect*. Cambridge: Cambridge University Press, (1985) 1992.

Boaz, David. *Libertarianism: A Primer*. New York: Free Press, 1997.

Bonar, James. *Philosophy and Political Economy*. New Brunswick, NJ: Transaction Publishers, 1992.

Brue, Stanley L. *The Evolution of Economic Thought*. Mason, OH: Thomson Learning, 2000.

Buchholz, Todd. *New Ideas from Dead Economists*. New York: A Plume Book, 1990.

Buckle, Stephen. *Natural Law and the Theory of Property*. Oxford: Oxford University Press, 1991.

Canterbury, Ray. *The Literate Economist: A Brief History of Economics*. New York: Harper Collins, 1995.

Conway, David. *Classical Liberalism: The Unvanquished Ideal*. London: MacMillan, 1997.

Copleston, Frederick. *A History of Philosophy*. New York: Doubleday, 1985.

Doherty, Brian. *Radicals for Capitalism*. New York: Public Affairs, 2002.

Ebenstein, William, and Alan O. Ebenstein. *Great Political Thinkers: Plato to the Present*. Austin, TX: Holt Rinehart and Winston, 2000.

Finnis, John. *Natural Law and Natural Rights*. Oxford: Oxford University Press, 1980.

Gierke, Otto von. *Natural Law and the Theory of Society*. Translated by Ernest Barker. Boston, MA: Beacon Press, 1957.

Gordon, Scott. *The History and Philosophy of Social Science*. London: Routledge, 1991.

Höffding, Harold. *History of Modern Philosophy*. New York: Dover Publications, 1924.

Hospers, John. *Libertarianism: A Political Philosophy for Tomorrow*. Los Angeles, CA: Nash Publishing, 1971.

Hursthouse, Rosalind. *On Virtue Ethics*. New York: Oxford University Press, 2002.

Hutchison, T. W. *A Review of Economic Doctrines, 1870-1929*. Oxford: Oxford University Press, 1953.

Jones, W. T. *A History of Western Philosophy*. New York: Harcourt, Brace, & World, 1962.

Kenny, Anthony. *A Brief History of Western Philosophy*. Oxford: Blackwell, 1998.

Langholm, O. *The Legacy of Scholasticism in Economic Thought: Antecedents of Choice and Power*. Cambridge: Cambridge University Press, 1998.

LeFevre, Robert. *The Fundamentals of Liberty*. Santa Ana, CA: Rampart Institute, 1988.

Lepage, Henri. *Tomorrow Capitalism*. LaSalle, IL: Open Court, 1978.

Lomasky, Loren E. *Persons, Rights, and the Moral Community*. Oxford: Oxford University Press, 1987.

Lowry, S. T. *The Archaeology of Economic Ideas: The Classical Greek Tradition*. Durham, NC: Duke University Press, 1987.

Lowry, S. T., and B. Gordon, eds. *Ancient and Medieval Economic Ideas and Concepts of Social Justice*. Leiden, Netherlands: E.J. Brill, 1998.

Machan, Tibor. *Individuals and Their Rights*. LaSalle, IL: Open Court, 1989.

———. *Capitalism and Individualism*. New York: St. Martin's Press, 1990.

Meek, R. L., ed. *Precursors of Adam Smith, 1750-1775*. London: Dent, 1973.

Mises, Ludwig von. *Liberalism in the Classical Tradition.* Irvington, NY: Foundation for Economic Education, (1927) 1985.

Newman, Stephen L. *Liberalism at Wits' End.* Cornell University Press, 1984.

Norton, David. *Personal Destinies.* Princeton, NJ: Princeton University Press, 1976.

Price, B. B., ed. *Ancient Economic Thought.* London: Routledge, 1997.

Rasmussen, Douglas B. "Community versus Liberty." In *Liberty for the Twenty-First Century.* Edited by Tibor R. Machan and Douglas B. Rasmussen. Lanham, MD: Rowman & Littlefield, 1995.

Rasmussen, Douglas B., and Douglas J. Den Uyl. *Norms of Liberty: A Perfectionist Basis for a Non-Perfectionist Politics.* University Park: Pennsylvania State University Press, 2005.

Robbins, L., S. G. Medema, W. J. Samuels, eds. *A History of Economic Thought: The LSE Lectures.* Princeton, NJ: Princeton University Press, 1998.

Roncaglia, Allesandro. *The Wealth of Ideas: A History of Economic Thought.* Cambridge: Cambridge University Press, 2005.

Rowley, Charles Kershaw, ed. *Classical Liberalism and Civil Society.* Cheltenham, UK: Edward Elgar, 1998.

Rutherford, M. *The Economic Mind in America: Essays in the History of American Economics.* London: Routledge, 1998.

Sabine, George H. *A History of Political Theory.* New York: Holt, Rinehart, & Winston, 1961.

Schumpeter, J. A. *History of Economic Analysis.* London: Allen & Unwin; Routledge, (1954) 1986.

Shue, Henry. *Basic Rights.* Princeton, NJ: Princeton University Press, 1980.

Spiegel, Henry William. *The Growth of Economic Thought*, 3rd edition. Durham, NC: Duke University Press, 1971.

Staley, Charles. *A History of Economic Thought: From Aristotle to Arrow.* Boston, MA: Blackwell, (1989) 1992.

Strauss, Leo. *Natural Rights and History.* Chicago, IL: University of Chicago Press, 1953.

Strauss, Leo, and Joseph Cropsey, eds. *History of Political Philosophy.* Chicago, IL: University of Chicago Press, 1987.

Tuck, Richard. *Natural Rights Theories: Their Origin and Development.* Cambridge: Cambridge University Press, 1979.

Veatch, Henry B. *For an Ontology of Morals.* Evanston, IL: Northwestern University Press, 1971.

———. *Human Rights: Fact or Fancy.* Baton Rouge, LA: Louisiana State University Press, 1985.

Windelband, Wilhelm. *History of Philosophy.* New York: Harper and Row, 1958.

Younkins, Edward W. *Capitalism and Commerce: Conceptual Foundations of Free Enterprise.* Lanham, MD: Lexington Books, 2002.

———, ed. *Philosophers of Capitalism: Menger, Mises, Rand, and Beyond.* Lanham, MD: Lexington Books, 2005.

PART I

ANCIENT AND MEDIEVAL PERIODS

Chapter 1

Lao Tzu's Naturalistic Metaphysics, Ethics, and Politics

If I keep from meddling with people, they take care of themselves.
If I keep from commanding people, they behave themselves.
If I keep from preaching at people, they improve themselves.
If I keep from imposing on people, they become themselves.

—Lao Tzu

Lao Tzu (Laozi), an older contemporary of Confucius, lived in the sixth century B.C., and is thought to be the founder of Taoism. The conjectured years of his life are 604-531 B.C. The legendary Taoist philosopher, whose name can be translated as the "Old Master," wrote a manual of self-cultivation and government, as well as a metaphorical account of reality, called *Daodejing* (a.k.a. *Tao te Ching*), translated as "Book of the Way and Its Power" and recognized as a masterpiece in Chinese philosophy.

Tao or *Dao* can be translated as "the Way" or the way nature is. It means a road or alternatively the process of reality itself. It is a pathway or a heading in a particular direction along a road. Referring to the natural flow of things, *Tao* counsels man to follow the course of nature and to seek the path of least resistance much like water does. It is the way of human life when it progresses in harmony with the universe. Actions taken in conformity with nature are more productive and easier to perform than attempting to go against nature. For Lao Tzu, nature encompasses natural phenomena, the spiritual, and the social, including sociopolitical institutions.

Tao is said to be the force that flows throughout all life and the one existing thing that connects the many things. The *Tao* underpins all things and sustains them. It is the source of the One within all as all existence derives its being from *Tao*. *Tao* is the life principle according to Lao Tzu. It is a name for the ground of all being. *Tao*, the origin and goal of things, antecedes the world and all differentiation.

According to Lao Tzu, *Tao* is the source of original, necessary, undifferentiated *qi*-energy that brings forth and nourishes all entities. *Tao* is the beginning of all things. In actualizing itself *Tao* posits objects, thereby producing the world. *Qi*-energy creates the universal *yin* and *yang* forces that then blend to produce the harmonic *qi*-energy that endows human beings. *Tao* is thus a fundamental creative process that is concurrently and paradoxically a negating process conferring life but also reclaiming it. There is an ebb and flow of the forces of reality. For Lao Tzu, opposites, as evaluative dichotomies, are interdependent, and play a prominent role in his pantheistic philosophy. Taoism expresses a materialist form of pantheism and denies the existence of a personal creator God. Gods play no role and exercise no influence in human lives.

Te is the power or virtue that is spontaneously produced from *Tao*. *Te*, a descriptive term, is power or virtue, as in the healing virtue of certain plants. *Te* is the *Tao* at work. Lau Tzu teaches that there is no need for human tampering with the flow of reality and espouses "nonwillful action," "effortless action," or "to act naturally." A person should thus follow the way things spontaneously increase or decrease. "Inaction" permits a person to flourish and to attain happiness. The term *wu wei* means nonaction, or more accurately, nonassertive action. *Wu wei* is the core of Lao Tzu's naturalistic ethics. The act of *wu wei* can be translated as the paradoxical "do nothing" and can be viewed as the most supreme kind of action that gets things done in a seemingly effortless manner. *Tao* can be viewed as general "laws of nature" or natural law that cannot be changed, but which can be used to attain one's goal. It involves men's authentic actions while they perform as though not acting. One can use free will in accordance with the *Tao* or against it. Assertive use of the will is against the nature of *Tao* and its workings in the universe and is to be avoided. Nonassertive use of the will is preferable if it involves the resistance of someone's assertive use of the will or if it is employed to advance *Tao* and its operations in the world. Lao Tzu explains that the operations of *Tao* are intrinsically determined and not brought about by assertive action or desire. It is only the assertive use of the will that interferes with the spontaneous evolution of *Tao*.

Lao Tzu recommended withdrawal from society and retreat into contemplation. He set an ethical goal for the individual only in the retreat into the wisdom and values of the inner self. His ideal society is one in which people live in simplicity, harmony, and contentment, and are not bothered by ambition, desire, or competitive striving. Desires cause harmful relationships between the self and others and lead men to appropriate things for their own satisfaction. Desires are evoked by the attractiveness and variety of things. Lao Tzu counsels people to make their desires negligible, to minimize their personal interests, to limit and diminish the self and the self-other distinction, and to return the self to a state of primitive contentment. He denounces the gratification of one's appetites and senses and the search for wealth and status. A person who lives according to his true being and nature will seek solitude and creative quietude and will act through freedom from desires, selflessness, softness, moderation, and openness to all things. He will follow a peaceful, simple, and frugal way of life not searching for wealth, power, or fame. Such a person will reject intolerance, hatred, and unnecessary violence and will embrace love and harmony. Lao Tzu is thus presenting a way of life by which a person could escape being harmed by the world.

For Lao Tzu, causal evils bring about human suffering in the world. The human sufferings produced by causal evils are consequent evils. He explains that causal evils originate from the use of the human will. Causal evil results when a person asserts something in thought or action against his own nature, other individuals, or the natural world. Lao Tzu's goal is to eliminate causal and consequent evils from the world. Life without such suffering is the ideal state of existence. He is talking about man-made sufferings and not natural ones. A natural death is to be welcomed but early, violent, and untimely deaths are to be prevented.

Lao Tzu maintains that inaction is the proper function of government. He is concerned with realizing peace and sociopolitical order. He wants to allow each individual as much freedom as possible. It follows that a Taoist ruler will not use coercion or permit others to use it against peaceful people. The government must not assert its will against individuals to exploit, dominate, or interfere with them. Although rulers possess weapons, it is preferable that they are not used. It is apparent that Lao Tzu views politics within a larger ethical context.

He says that a good ruler is inconspicuous, humble, and demands nothing. It is not that the supreme emperor does not govern, but that he governs in such a way that is totally in accordance with the wills of his people. Lao Tzu contends that codified rules and laws result in a society that is more difficult to care for. The more ordinances and laws, the more robbers and thieves there will be. When the state takes "no action" the people of themselves will be transformed. When the government engages in no activity the people will prosper. He says that life should be happy in a small state and that, without laws or compulsion, men would live in harmony.

Lao Tzu disapproves of aggressive measures such as war, cruel punishment and heavy taxation which express a ruler's own desire for power and wealth. He cautions the ruler not to be oppressive with military strength. War is evil, brings suffering, and is a most assertive use of the will. Wars involve conflicts of wills usually for wealth, power, or fame. To practice peace is to practice the *Tao*. Lao Tzu asks by what authority the ruler presumes to act upon others. He recommends the restraint of judges and observes that the internal violence of the state is embodied in cruel punishments—especially the death penalty. With respect to taxation, he says that the people starve because the ruler eats too much tax grain. Rulers thus prosper at the expense of the masses. Lao Tzu did not value competition and observed that exploitation or oppression of citizens by a ruler is a type of willful action or competition. He explains that peaceful actions do not require moral justification, but that coercive actions do require moral justification. Lao Tzu lived during a militant period and wanted to avoid constant feudal warfare and other conflicts.

It is obvious that Lao Tzu viewed the state as a likely oppressor of the individual. He thought that any truth in government abides in nonaction and in weakness. The state should not be an organization of functionaries. Lao Tzu thus opposed a multitude of laws and thought that the state should and could control by means of noninterference. He observed that the fulfillment of others and of things results not from the prominence of a ruler's virtues but from the withdrawal of self.

Lao Tzu criticized the civilization of his own time because of its wars, government oppression, taxation, and the lofty values of human culture. He was skeptical with respect to the utility of the artificiality and over-refinement of civilization. He was not totally opposed to technical and social contrivances. Lao Tzu did not completely dismiss technology but he was worried that it may engender a false sense of progression.

He says that the fall from the *Tao* is caused by government and society having lost the truth. The fall from the *Tao* stems from desire, intention, and self-striving. The use of free will can interfere with *Tao*. People, including rulers, should therefore avoid determined action and strong will. A person should be passive and not try to change anything. A sage would move and live naturally and would be empty of pretense and free from desires. He would not attempt to help life along or make a display of himself. A sage would claim moral ignorance, would understand the reversibility of things in the world, and would endeavor to create a peaceful atmosphere.

Lao Tzu's life-oriented philosophy advanced a doctrine of liberation of the individual through withdrawal. He speaks from the standpoint of perfection and eternity. In his radical naturalistic conception of the universe, individual happiness is the basis of a good society. He advocates nonaction both in personal fulfillment and in the sociopolitical order. His perfect ruler takes no willful action. In battle his principle is defense without aggression. He does not believe in revolution. Simplicity and spontaneity are keys to the truth. He says that nature does nothing but leaves nothing undone. Lao Tzu's ethics advocates withdrawal from society, contemplation, and cultivation of internal virtues. As a quietist, he says man cannot solve social problems but he can forsake them.

Recommended Reading

Barrett, T. H. *Taoism under the T'ang*. London: Wellsweep Press, 1996.

Baxter, William H. "Situating the Language of the *Lao-tzu:* The Probable Date of the *Tao-te-ching*." Pp. 231–53 in *Lao-tzu and the Tao-te-ching*, edited by Livia Kohn and Michael LaFargue. Albany: State University of New York Press, 1988.

Bokenkamp, Stephen R. *Early Daoist Scriptures*. Berkeley: University of California Press, 1997.

Boltz, William G. "Textual Criticism and the Ma Wang Tui *Lao-tzu*." *Harvard Journal of Asiatic Studies* 44 (1984): 185–224.

————. "Lao tzu Tao te ching." Pp. 269–92 in *Early Chinese Texts: A Bibliographical Guide*, edited by Michael Loewe. Berkeley: University of California, Institute of East Asian Studies, 1993.

Chan, Wing-tsit. "The Natural Way of Lao Tzu." Chapter 6 in *A Source Book in Chinese Philosophy*. Princeton, NJ: Princeton University Press, 1963.

————. *The Way of Lao Tzu*. Indianapolis, IN: Bobbs-Merrill, 1963.

Chen, Ellen M. "Nothingness and the Mother Principle in Early Chinese Taoism." *International Philosophical Quarterly* 9.3 (1969): 391–405.

————. *The Tao Te Ching: A New Translation with Commentary*. New York: Paragon House, 1989.

Creel, Herlee G. *What is Taoism? And Other Studies in Chinese Cultural History*. Chicago, IL: University of Chicago Press, 1970.

Csikszentmihalyi, Mark, and Philip J. Ivanhoe, eds. *Religious and Philosophical Aspects of the Laozi*. Albany: State University of New York, 1999.

Girardot, Norman J. *Myth and Meaning in Early Taoism*. Berkeley: University of California Press, 1983.

Graham, Angus. *Disputers of the Tao: Philosophical Argument in Ancient China*. LaSalle, IL: Open Court, 1989.

————. "The Origins of the Legend of Lao Tan." Pp. 23–41 in *Lao-tzu and the Tao-te-ching*, edited by Livia Kohn and Michael LaFargue. Albany: State University of New York Press, (1986) 1998.

Hansen, Chad. *A Daoist Theory of Chinese Thought*. New York: Oxford University Press, 1992.

Hardy, Julia. "Influential Western Interpretations of the *Tao-te-ching*." Pp. 165–88 in *Lao-tzu and the Tao-te-ching*, edited by Livia Kohn and Michael LaFargue. Albany: State University of New York Press, 1998.

Henricks, Robert. *Lao-Tzu: Te-Tao Ching*. New York: Ballantine, 1989.

Ivanhoe, Philip J. *The Daodejing of Laozi*. New York: Seven Bridges Press, 2002.

Kaltenmark, Max. *Lao Tzu and Taoism*. Translated by Roger Greaves. Chicago, IL: Stanford University Press, 1969.

Kohn, Livia. "Laozi: Ancient Philosopher, Master of Longevity, and Taoist God." Pp. 52–63 in *Religions of China in Practice*, edited by Donald S. Lopez. Princeton, NJ: Princeton University Press, 1996.

————. "The Lao-Tzu Myth." Pp. 41–63 in *Lao-tzu and the Tao-te-ching*, edited by Livia Kohn and Michael LaFargue. Albany: State University of New York Press, 1998.

Kohn, Livia, and Michael LaFargue. *Lao-tzu and the Tao-te-ching*. Albany: State University of New York Press, 1998.

Kohn, Livia, and Harold Roth. *Daoist Identity: History, Lineage, and Ritual*. Honolulu: University of Hawaii Press, 2002.

LaFargue, Michael. *The Tao of the Tao Te Ching*. Albany: State University of New York Press, 1992.

Lau, D. C. *Lao Tzu Tao te Ching*. Harmondsworth: Penguin Books, 1963.

Lin, Paul J. *A Translation of Lao Tzu's Tao Te Ching and Wang Pi's Commentary*. Ann Arbor: Center for Chinese Studies, University of Michigan, 1977.

Liu, Xiaogan. *Laozi*. Taipei: Dongda, 1997.

Mair, Victor. *Tao Te Ching: The Classic Book of Integrity and the Way*. New York: Bantam Books, 1990.

Rothbard, Murray. "Concepts of the Role of Intellectuals in Social Change Toward Laissez Faire." *The Journal of Libertarian Studies* 9, no. 2 (Fall, 1990).

Schwartz, Benjamin. *The World of Thought in Ancient China*. Cambridge, MA: Harvard
    University Press, 1985.
Waley, Arthur. *The Way and Its Power: A Study of the Tao Te Ching and Its Place in
    Chinese Thought*. New York: Grove Press, 1958.
Welch, Holmes. *Taoism: The Parting of the Way*. Boston: Beacon Press, 1996.
Welch, Holmes, and Anna Seidel, eds. *Facets of Taoism*. New Haven, CT: Yale Univer-
    sity Press, 1979.

Chapter 2

Aristotle and Human Flourishing

What is the Good for man? It must be the ultimate end or object of human life: something that is in itself completely satisfying. Happiness fits this description. But what is happiness? If we consider what the function of man is we find that happiness is a virtuous activity of the soul.

—Aristotle

Aristotle (384-322 B.C.) is the most significant thinker and the most accomplished individual who has ever lived. Every person currently living in Western civilization owes an enormous debt to Aristotle, who is the fountainhead behind every achievement of science, technology, political theory, and aesthetics (especially Romantic art) in today's world. Aristotle's philosophy has underpinned the achievements of the Renaissance, the birth of America itself, and all scientific advances and technological progress to this very day.

Aristotle, the teacher of those who know, defended reason, invented logic, focused on reality, and emphasized the importance of life on earth. The importance of reality, reason, and logic in Aristotelian philosophy has enabled science and technology to develop and flourish.

His philosophy of reason embodied a primacy of existence approach that states that knowledge of the world commences by looking at and examining what exists. Recognizing the validity of man's senses, Aristotle taught that men can increase their knowledge by augmenting the evidence of the senses through reason (i.e., through logic and the formulation of abstractions). He explained that conceptualization should be preceded by inductive observation in our efforts to understand the world. Reason is competent to know reality but it is necessary to begin with what exists in the world.

Aristotle teaches that each man's life has a purpose and that the function of one's life is to attain that purpose. He explains that the purpose of life is earthly happiness or flourishing that can be achieved via reason and the acquisition of virtue. Articulating an explicit and clear understanding of the end toward which a person's life aims, Aristotle states that each human being should use his abilities to his fullest potential and should obtain happiness and enjoyment through the exercise of his realized capacities. He contends that human achievements are animated by purpose and autonomy and that people should take pride in being excellent at what they do. According to Aristotle, human beings have a natural desire and capacity to know and understand the truth, to pursue moral excellence, and to instantiate their ideals in the world through action.

Metaphysics and Epistemology

Aristotle espouses the existence of external objective reality. For Aristotle, the existence of the external world and of men's knowledge of it is self-evident. He contends that the basic reality upon which all else depends is the existence of individual entities. He insists upon an independent existing world of entities or beings and that what exists are individuals with nothing existing separately from them. For Aristotle, the ontologically ultimate is the individual.

The basic laws of being, or first principles of reality, in Aristotle's metaphysics, are the philosophical axioms or laws of non-contradiction, identity, and excluded middle. According to Aristotle, these presuppositions or assumptions govern, direct, or command scientific explanation.

For Aristotle, causality is a law inherent in being *qua* being. To be is to be something with a specific nature, and to be something with a specific nature is to act according to that nature. The ideas of identity, non-contradiction, and causality underpin the fundamentals of science and are basic principles of Aristotelian philosophy.

Aristotle heralds the role of reason in a proper human life. He examines the nature of man and his functions and sees that man survives through purposeful conduct which results from the active exercise of man's capacity for rational thought. The ability to reason separates man from all other living organisms and supplies him with his unique means of survival and flourishing. It is through purposive, rational conduct that a person can achieve happiness. For Aristotle, a being of conceptual consciousness must focus on reality and must discover the knowledge and actions required if he wants to fully develop as a human person.

Aristotle is a this-worldly metaphysician who avowedly rejects mysticism and skepticism in epistemology. His view is that human nature is specific and definite and that there is some essence apparent in each and every person and object.

An advocate of this-worldly cognition, Aristotle's theory of concepts is reality-oriented. It follows that Aristotle considers essences to be metaphysical and every entity to be made up of form, the universalizing factor, and matter, the particularizing factor.

Aristotle was a this-worldly philosopher and scientist whose observations of the biological world led him to endorse realism, knowledge based on experience, and experience-based reasoning. For Aristotle, an immanent (or naïve) realist, what is general does not exist in isolation from what is individual. The existence of universals is thus dependent on the existence of particulars. Universals exist in the particulars that instantiate them. Aristotle holds that universals do exist, but not separately from the particulars. His view is that the one exists only as instantiated in the many. For Aristotle, the immanent realist, both universals and particulars are real. Individual concrete entities exist in reality and universals exist only in particulars in the form of essences. In this way, Aristotle wedded universals to objects. The universal and the particular are indivisible in reality and are separable only in analysis and thought. All things are a composite of a "this" and a "such." Each object is an individual of a certain class. Aristotle distinguishes between matter and form. The matter is the individualizing and unique-making element or aspect. The form is the universalizing element that makes it a member of a particular class. Forms are joined to objects.

Aristotle's view is that concepts refer to essences that are within the concretes of the external world. An essence is an object's nature. It is made up of the invariant characteristics inherent in a thing. An essence is in an object from the time the entity is a potentiality all the way to its becoming and being an actuality. Aristotle explains change as matter getting restructured and as requiring identity. An object that changes is what it is, the thing that it changes into is what it is, and the change process itself is what it is. Change is the actualization of potential. It follows that the world of particulars and changes in particulars is rationally explainable. Change is the capacity to grow into something and is thus the actualization of potential.

Aristotle explains that a thing's essence is in the object from the time an entity is a potentiality all the way to its actuality. Since universals exist only in particulars, we cannot apprehend the universal except through apprehension of the concrete. Matter is the underlying substratum in which development of form occurs. Aristotle is an "ontological essentialist" who defines essence as embodying the actual metaphysical nature of things. Essences exist in the world independent of the mind and are what a person's mind refers to when it forms concepts.

Knowledge is a natural process in the real world. Aristotle explains that it is natural for an animal with rational consciousness (i.e., man) to actualize its potential. This potential involves the ability to understand intelligible or law-governed structures and changes. It also includes the ability to apprehend that there are intelligibly impossible changes. Aristotle taught that the world encompasses both material and mental aspects and that it exists independently of our reasoning and thinking activities. In addition, there are certain essences in the world as well as knowable laws, structures, and connections governing them. He explains that there are no contradictions in nature (i.e., in reality). By a contradiction he means being both x and not x at the same time and in the same respect. Also, Aristotle emphasized individual human action in his *Nicomachean Ethics*, thus inventing the concept of methodological individualism—the notion that collective entities such as states, communities, or classes are reducible to individuals in relation with one another. Furthermore, he emphasized deductive reasoning in which a person begins with self-evident axioms and deduces from them.

For Aristotle, essences or universals are phenomena intrinsic in reality and that exist in particulars. It follows that to comprehend essences or universals may, at root, be a passive intuition or receptivity. Aristotle, the naturalistic realist, explains that knowledge begins and arises out of our sense experiences which are valid. It follows that a man can build on the evidence of the senses through reason, which includes logic and the formation of abstractions.

Some contemporary thinkers find fault in Aristotle for viewing essences as metaphysical rather than as epistemological. They oppose Aristotle's apparent intuitionist view that essences are simply "intellectually seen." They contend that universals or concepts are the epistemological products of a classification process that represents particular types of entities. Whereas some think that Aristotle relied too heavily on intellectual intuition, others believe that he was emphasizing the mental effort necessary to distinguish certain attributes that something has in common with other objects, setting aside those characteristics not shared.

Individuals, Communities, and the State

The highest or most general good to which all individuals should aim is to live most fully a life that is proper to man. The proper function of every person is to live happily, successfully, and well. This is done through the active exercise of a man's distinctive capacity, rationality, as he engages in activities to the degree appropriate to the person in the context of his own particular identity as a human being. Recognizing the diversity of human capabilities and circumstances, Aristotle allows for specific interpretations.

Because man is naturally social, it is good for him to live in a society or *polis* (i.e., a city-state). When civil society is governed by nature, the result is a good community that could activate men's many natural capacities. Aristotle emphasizes the individuating characteristics of human beings when he proclaims that the goodness of the *polis* is inextricably related to those who make it up. For Aristotle, social life in a community is a necessary condition for a man's complete flourishing as a human being.

Aristotle explains that friendship, the mutual admiration between two human beings, is a necessary condition for the attainment of one's *eudaimonia*. Because man is a social being, it can be maintained that friendship has an egoistic foundation. It follows that authentic friendship is predicated upon one's sense of his own moral worth and on his love for and pride in himself. Moral admiration, both of oneself and of the other, is an essential component of Aristotelian friendship. Self-perfection means to fulfill the capacities that make a person fully human, including other-directed capacities such as friendship. Aristotle explained man's social nature by referring to his potential to learn from other people and the contribution of such learning to each person's happiness.

Noting that individuals form communities to secure life's necessities, Aristotle also emphasizes the importance of active citizen participation in government. He views the proper end of government as the promotion of its citizens' happiness. It follows that the goodness of the *polis* is directly related to the total self-actualization of the individuals who comprise it. Aristotle has tendency to sometimes confuse the human community (i.e., the *polis*) and the government.

Aristotle contended that the state exists for the good of the individual. He thus preferred the rule of law over the rule of any of the citizens. This is because men have private interests whereas laws do not. It follows that the "mixed regime" advocated by Aristotle was the beginning of the notion of constitutionalism, including the separation of powers and checks and balances. He was the first thinker to divide rulership activities into executive, legislative, and judicial functions. Through his support for a mixed political system, Aristotle was able to avoid and reject both Platonic communism and radical democracy.

Human Flourishing

For Aristotle, an entity that fulfills its proper (i.e., essential) function is one that performs well or excellently. He explains that the nature of a thing is the measure or standard in terms of which we judge whether or not it is functioning appropriately or well. Things are good for Aristotle when they advance their specific or respective ends.

Aristotle bases the understandability of the good in the idea of what is good for the specific entity under consideration. For whatever has a natural function, the good is therefore thought to reside in the function. The natural function of a thing is determined by its natural end. With respect to living things, there are particular ways of being that constitute the perfection of the living thing's nature.

According to Aristotle, there is an end of all of the actions that we perform which we desire for itself. This is what is known as *eudaimonia*, flourishing, or happiness, which is desired for its own sake with all other things being desired on its account. *Eudaimonia* is a property of one's life when considered as a whole. Flourishing is the highest good of human endeavors and that toward which all actions aim. It is success as a human being. The best life is one of excellent human activity.

For Aristotle, the good is what is good for purposeful, goal-directed entities. He defines the good proper to human beings as the activities in which the life functions specific to human beings are most fully realized. For Aristotle, the good of each species is teleologically immanent to that species. A person's nature as a human being provides him with guidance with respect to how he should live his life. A fundamental fact of human nature is the existence of individual human beings, each with his own rational mind and free will. The use of one's volitional consciousness is a person's distinctive capacity and means of survival.

One's own life is the only life that a person has to live. It follows that, for Aristotle, the "good" is what is objectively good for a particular man. Aristotle's *eudaimonia* is formally egoistic in that a person's normative reason for choosing particular actions stems from the idea that he must pursue his own good or flourishing. Because self-interest is flourishing, the good in human conduct is connected to the self-interest of the acting person. Good means "good for" the individual moral agent. Egoism is an integral part of Aristotle's ethics.

Ethics, Virtue, and Self-Interest

In his ethical writings, Aristotle endorses egoism, rationality, and the value of life. He insists that the key idea in ethics is a human individual's own personal happiness and well-being. Each man is responsible for his own character. According to Aristotle, each person has a natural obligation to achieve, become, and make something of himself by pursuing his true ends and goals in life. Each person should be concerned with the "best that is within us" and with the most accomplished and self-sufficient success and excellence.

According to Aristotle, the "moral" refers to whatever is related to a person's character. He taught that the value of virtuous activity resides in realizing a state of *eudaimonic* character. Such a state must be achieved by a man's own efforts. A person needs to pursue rational or intelligent efforts in pursuing goods and in otherwise taking control of his own life. Because a man might fail or be thwarted in his efforts, Aristotle explained that a person should be more concerned with his fitness to achieve success than with the existential attainment of the success itself.

Aristotle insists that ethical knowledge is possible and that it is grounded in human nature. Because human beings possess a nature that governs how they act, the perfection or fulfillment of their nature is their end. A human being is ordered to self-perfection and self-perfection is, in essence, human moral development. The goal of a person's life is to live rationally and to develop both the intellectual and moral virtues. There are attributes central to human nature the development of which leads to human flourishing and a good human life. According to Aristotle, the key characteristics of human nature can be discerned through empirical investigation.

Aristotle teaches that ethical theory is connected to the type of life that is most desirable or most worth living for each and every human being. It follows that human flourishing is always particularized and that there is an inextricable connection between virtue and self-interest. He explains that the virtuous man is constantly using practical wisdom in the pursuit of the good life. A man wants and needs to gain a knowledge of virtue in order to become virtuous, good, and happy. The distinction of a good person is to take pleasure in moral action. In other words, human flourishing occurs when a person is concurrently doing what he ought to do and doing what he wants to do. When such ways of being occur through free choice, they are deemed to be choice-worthy and the basis for ethics.

The purpose of ethical inquiry is a practical matter according to Aristotle. He explains that practical wisdom is not only concerned with universals (such as good or value), but also with particulars which became known through experience in the choices and activities of life. He states that it is important to have practical experience with particulars if one is to optimally benefit from philosophical inquiry into ethics. Aristotle thus emphasizes the power of judgment beyond the guidance of general theory. Experience helps to perfect a person's power of moral judgment. He notes that one's facticity, including his past choices, and the contingent situations are relevant considerations in determining a correct choice. Proper actions are in the particulars that differ considerably from case to case.

Aristotle's this-worldly intrinicism says that universals exist in particulars and that men can abstract or intuit the essences or universals out of the particulars. Aristotle wants to ground his theory of concepts in the facts of reality but is not fully explicit with respect to methods by which essences get imprinted on a man's mind. He does see man as scientifically looking at reality, gathering instances, isolating and classifying phenomena, detecting similarities, discerning patterns and regularities, and obtaining essences upon which concepts and laws are constructed. Aristotle refers to this process as intuitive induction.

Aristotle saw a universal teleology or purposiveness in which everything in the universe was goal-directed and striving to actualize its essence. For Aristotle, an object actualizes its distinctive essence when it achieves an identity of formal and final causation. Man, as a rational being with free will, should strive for his own perfection. By achieving his fulfillment and all-around development he would attain happiness or *eudaimonia*. It follows that in ethics a man should choose actions that are proper to man *qua* man.

Aristotle thought that it was possible to conduct rational research with respect to value. He saw practical science as an essentially evaluative or moral science. A practical science is ethical to the extent that it takes into account the ethical aspects of the subject being studied.

Aristotle regarded reality as ordered and taught that order with respect to human affairs is a project or effort through which people aspire to happiness through the cultivation of virtues. He asserts that the end of politics is the good for man. According to Aristotle, the virtue of prudence is personal, freely pursued, and changeable according to situations. A prudent action for one individual may not be a prudent action for another person. Nevertheless, according to Aristotle, the integration of freely made prudent and varying actions results in social coordination. He believed that economic coordination is attainable when persons prudently choose and undertake economic transactions with others. Aristotle believed that human flourishing requires a life with other people.

Aristotle taught that people acquire virtues (i.e., good habits) through practice and that a set of concrete virtues could lead a person toward his natural excellence and happiness. Aristotle viewed economic activity as a means of coordination through which persons would have the opportunity to obtain the external goods necessary to attain happiness. Morally good habits promote stable and predictable behavior and foster coordination in an imperfect world. Habits, natural dispositions created through the repetition of actions, underpin virtues.

Aristotle did not regard ethics as an exact science. He said that matters of conduct are not found in an exact system, not only in dealing with specific cases of conduct, but also with respect to the general theory of ethics. He explains that a person must both investigate the nature of virtue and learn through experience to discern, consider for himself, and competently judge the particulars of the circumstances of each situation. Aristotle thus emphasizes both the difficulty of devising general principles of moral action and the importance of perception and judgment in practical decisions. One's practical wisdom is a kind of insight, perception, or sense of what to do.

Aristotle tells us that virtues, as constituents of happiness, are acquired through habituation. He also explains that virtue can be understood as a moral mean between two vices—one of excess and one of deficiency. Such a mean is not scientific or easy to calculate. Aristotle's moral virtues are desire-regulating character traits which can be found at a mean between extreme vices. For example, courage is the virtuous mean between rashness as a vice of excess and cowardice as a vice of deficiency.

With respect to ethical judgments, Aristotle expounds that a person should not expect more certainty in methods or results than the nature of the subject matter permits. It is obvious then that Aristotle did not regard ethics as an exact science. His modern critics' explanation of Aristotle's position on ethical exactness is that it was a consequence of the intrinsicist elements of his epistemology. Because Aristotle considers universals, concepts, or essences as metaphysical rather than as epistemological, it is difficult, if not impossible, for him to explain how one sees or intuits "good," "value," "ethical," and so on when he is confronted with various optional actions or objects.

Ayn Rand's Aristotelian Philosophy and Sense of Life

Ayn Rand, whose philosophy is a form of Aristotelianism, had the highest admiration for Aristotle. She intellectually stood on Aristotle's shoulders as she praised him above all other philosophers. Rand acknowledged Aristotle as a genius and as the only thinker throughout the ages to whom she owed a philosophical debt

As naturalistic realists, Aristotle and Ayn Rand are the philosophical champions of this world. Both appeal to the objective nature of things. They agree that logic is inseparable from reality and knowledge. Affirming reality, reason, and life on earth, they concur that a man can deal with reality, attain values, and live heroically rather than tragically. Men can grasp reality, establish goals, take actions, and achieve values. They view the human person as a noble and potentially heroic being whose highest moral purpose is to gain his own happiness on earth. Their shared conception of human life permits a person to maintain a realistic moral vision that has the potential to inspire men to greater and greater heights. Rand follows the Aristotelian idea of *eudaimonia* as the human entelechy.

Like Aristotle, Rand ascribes to only a few basic axioms: existence exists, existence is identity, and consciousness is identification. Aristotle and Rand agree that all men naturally desire to know, understand, and act on the knowledge acquired. For both, all knowledge is arrived at from sensory perception through the processes of abstraction and conceptualization. They each see rationality as man's distinctive capacity. Both develop virtues and concrete normative behavior from man's primary virtue of rationality.

For both Aristotle and Rand, the issue of how a person should live his life precedes the problem of how a community should be organized. Whereas Aristotle sees a social life as a necessary condition for one's thoroughgoing *eudaimonia*, Rand emphasizes the benefits accruing to the individual from living in society as being knowledge and trade. Although Rand does not expressly discuss the human need for community in her non-fiction writings, her portrait of Galt's Gulch in *Atlas Shrugged* closely approximates Aristotle's community of accord between good men. Of course, the organization of Galt's Gulch is along the lines of anarcho-capitalism rather than the minimal state political system of capitalism advocated by Rand or the somewhat paternalistic ideal of Aristotle's polity.

Viewing human life in terms of personal flourishing, both Aristotle and Rand teach that we should embrace all of our potentialities. Their similar visions of the ideal man hold that he would have a heroic attitude toward life. The ideal man would be both morally and rationally heroic. They both saw pride (or moral ambitiousness, according to Rand) as the crown of the virtues.

So, where do Rand and Aristotle most differ? Rand argues that her philosophy diverges from Aristotle's by considering essences as epistemological and contextual instead of as metaphysical. She envisions Aristotle as a philosophical intuitivist who declared the existence of essences within concretes.

Whatever their differences, it is clear that Rand's philosophy of Objectivism is within the Aristotelian naturalistic tradition. Rand inherited significant elements of the Aristotelian *eudaimonic* tradition. Rand, like Aristotle, recognized her task as helping people to know. Because of Rand, we have had a rebirth of Aristotelian philosophy with its emphasis on reason and on man, the thinker and doer.

Self-Perfection, Self-Direction, and the Limited State

An Aristotelian self-perfectionist approach to ethics can be shown to complement the natural right to liberty which itself provides a solid foundation for a minimal state. This approach gives liberty moral significance by illustrating how the natural right to liberty is a social and political condition necessary for the possibility of human flourishing—the ultimate moral standard in Aristotelian ethics interpreted as a natural-end ethics. A foundation is thus provided for a classical liberal political theory within the Aristotelian tradition. Modern proponents of this approach include Tibor R. Machan, Douglas B. Rasmussen, Douglas J. Den Uyl, and others.

Human flourishing (also known as personal flourishing) involves the rational use of one's individual human potentialities, including talents, abilities, and virtues in the pursuit of his freely and rationally chosen values and goals. An action is considered to be proper if it leads to the flourishing of the person performing the action. Human flourishing is, at the same time, a moral accomplishment and a fulfillment of human capacities, and it is one through being the other. Self-actualization is moral growth and vice-versa.

Not an abstraction, human flourishing is real and highly personal (i.e., agent relative) by nature, consists in the fulfillment of both a man's human nature and his unique potentialities, and is concerned with choices and actions that necessarily deal with the particular and the contingent. One man's self-realization is not the same as another's. What is called for in terms of concrete actions such as choice of career, education, friends, home, and others, varies from person to person. Human flourishing becomes an actuality when one uses his practical reason to consider his unique needs, circumstances, capacities, and so on, to determine which concrete instantiations of human values and virtues will comprise his well-being. The idea of human flourishing is inclusive and can encompass a wide variety of constitutive ends such as knowledge, the development of character traits, productive work, religious pursuits, community building, love, charitable activities, allegiance to persons and causes, self-efficacy, material well-being, pleasurable sensations, etc.

To flourish, a man must pursue goals that are rational both for him individually and also as a human being. Whereas the former will vary depending upon one's particular circumstances, the latter are common to man's distinctive nature—man has the unique capacity to live rationally. The use of reason is a necessary, but not a sufficient, condition for human flourishing. Living rationally (i.e., consciously) means dealing with the world conceptually. Living consciously implies respect for the facts of reality. The principle of living consciously is not affected by the degree of one's intelligence nor the extent of one's knowledge; rather, it is the acceptance and use of one's reason in the recognition and perception of reality and in his choice of values and actions to the best of his ability, whatever that ability may be. To pursue rational goals through rational means is the only way to cope successfully with reality and achieve one's goals. Although rationality is not always rewarded, the fact remains that it is through the use of one's mind that a man not only discovers the values required for personal flourishing, he also attains them. Values can be achieved in reality if a man recognizes and adheres to the reality of his unique personal endowments and contingent circumstances. Human flourishing is positively related to a rational man's attempts to externalize his values and actualize his internal views of how things ought to be in the outside world. Practical reason can be used to choose, create, and integrate all the values and virtues that comprise personal flourishing.

Virtues are the means to values and goods and the virtues, values, and goods together enable us to achieve human flourishing and happiness. The constituent virtues such as rationality, independence, integrity, justice, honesty, courage, trustworthiness, productiveness, benevolence, and pride (moral ambitiousness) must be applied, although differentially, by each person in the task of self-actualization. Not only do particular virtues play larger roles in the lives of some men than others, there is also diversity in the concrete with respect to the objects and purposes of their application, the way in which they are applied, and the manner in which they are integrated with other virtues and values. Choosing and making the proper response for the unique situation is the concern of moral living—one needs to use his practical reason at the time of action to consider concrete contingent circumstances to determine the correct application and balance of virtues and values for himself. Although virtues and values are not automatically rewarded, this does not alter the fact that they are rewarded. Human flourishing is the reward of the virtues and values and happiness is the goal and reward of human flourishing.

Self-direction (i.e., autonomy) involves the use of one's reason and is central and necessary for the possibility of attaining human flourishing, self-esteem, and happiness. It is the only characteristic of flourishing that is both common to all acts of self-actualization and particular to each. Freedom in decision making and behavior is a necessary operating condition for the pursuit and achievement of human flourishing. Respect for individual autonomy is essential to human flourishing. This logically leads to the endorsement of the right of personal direction of one's life, including the use of his endowments, capacities, and energies.

These natural (i.e., negative) rights are metanormative principles concerned with protecting the self-directedness of individuals, thus ensuring the freedom through which individuals can pursue their flourishing. The goal of the right to liberty is to secure the possibility of human flourishing by protecting the possibility of self-directedness. This is done by preventing encroachments upon the conditions under which human flourishing can occur. Natural rights impose a negative obligation—the obligation not to interfere with one's liberty. Natural rights, therefore, require a legal system that provides the necessary conditions for the possibility that individuals might self-actualize. It follows that the proper role of the government is to protect man's natural rights through the use of force, but only in response, and only against those who initiate its use. In order to provide the maximum self-determination for each person, the state should be limited to maintaining justice, police, and defense, and to protecting life, liberty, and property.

The negative right to liberty, as a basic metanormative principle, provides a context in which all the diverse forms of personal flourishing may coexist in an ethically compossible manner. This right can be accorded to every person, with no one's authority over himself requiring that any other person experience a loss of authority over himself. Such a metanormative standard for social conduct favors no particular form of human flourishing while concurrently providing a context within which diverse forms of human flourishing can be pursued.

Recommended Reading

Ackrill, J. L., ed. *A New Aristotle Reader.* Oxford: Oxford University Press, 1987.
Annas, Julia. *The Morality of Happiness.* New York: Oxford University Press, 1993.
Aquinas, T. *Commentary on the Nicomachean Ethics.* Translated by C. I. Litzinger. Chicago: St. Augustines Dumb Ox Books, 1993.
Barnes, Jonathan. *Aristotle.* Oxford: Oxford University Press, 1982.
Blaug, M., ed. *Aristotle (384-322 B.C.)* Aldershot, 1991.
Brakas, George. *Aristotle's Concept of the Universal.* Hildesheim and New York: Georg Olms, 1988.
Broadie, Sarah. *Ethics With Aristotle.* New York: Oxford University Press, 1991.
Cooper, John. *Reason and Human Good in Aristotle.* Cambridge, MA: Harvard University Press, 1975.
Gotthelf, A., ed. *Aristotle on Nature and Living Things.* Pittsburgh, PA: Mathesis Publications Inc., 1985.
Gotthelf, Allan, and James G. Lennox, eds. *Philosophical Issues in Aristotle's Biology.* Cambridge: Cambridge University Press, 1987.
Hardie, W.F.R. *Aristotle's Ethical Theory.* Oxford, 1968.
Hurka, Thomas. *Perfectionism.* New York: Oxford University Press, 1993.
Irwin, Terence. *Aristotle's First Principles.* Oxford: Clarendon, 1988.
Kelley, David. *Unrugged Individualism.* Poughkeepsie, NY: Institute for Objectivist Studies, 1996.
Kenny, A. J. P. *The Aristotelian Ethics: A Study of the Relationship between the Eudemian and Nicomachean Ethics of Aristotle.* Oxford: Oxford University Press, 1978.
———. *Aristotle on the Perfect Life.* Oxford: Clarendon Press, 1996.
Keyt, David, and Fred Miller, eds. *A Companion to Aristotle's Politics.* Oxford: Basil Blackwell, 1990.
Kraut, Richard. *Aristotle on the Human Good.* Princeton, NJ: Princeton University Press, 1989.
Lear, Jonathan. *Aristotle: The Desire to Understand.* Cambridge: Cambridge University Press, 1988.
Leyden, W. von. *Aristotle on Equality and Justice.* New York: Palgrave Macmillan 1985.
Machan, Tibor R. *Human Rights and Human Liberties.* Chicago, IL: Nelson-Hall, 1974.
———. *Individuals and Their Rights.* LaSalle, IL: Open Court, 1989.
———. *Capitalism and Individualism.* London: Harvester Wheatsheaf, 1990.
Mayhew, Robert. *Aristotle's Criticism of Plato's Republic.* Rowman & Littlefield, 1997.
McKeon, Richard, ed. *The Basic Works of Aristotle.* New York: Random House, 1941.
Meikle, Scott. *Aristotle's Economic Thought.* Oxford: Oxford University Press, 1995.
Miller, Fred D. *Nature, Justice, and Rights in Aristotle's "Politics."* Oxford: Clarendon Press, 1995.
Mulgan, R. G. *Aristotle's Political Theory.* Oxford: Oxford University Press, 1977.
Nichols, M. P. *Citizens and Statesmen: A Study of Aristotle's Politics.* Lanham, MD: Rowman & Littlefield, 1992.
Norton, David. *Personal Destinies.* Princeton, NJ: Princeton University Press, 1976.

Nussbaum, M.C. *The Fragility of Goodness*. Cambridge, 1986.

Randall, John H., Jr. *Aristotle*. New York: Columbia University Press, 1960.

Rasmussen, Douglas B., and Douglas J. Den Uyl. *Liberty and Nature*. LaSalle, IL: Open Court, 1991.

———. *Liberalism Defended*. Cheltenham, UK: Edward Elgar, 1997.

———. *Norms of Liberty*. University Park: Pennsylvania State University Press, 2006.

Rorty, Amelie. *Essays on Aristotle's Ethics*. Berkeley: University of California Press, 1980.

Ross, Sir David. *Aristotle*, 5th ed. London: Methuen, 1949.

Ross, W. D. and J. A. Smith, eds. *The Works of Aristotle Translated into English, 12 vols.* Oxford: Clarendon Press, 1912-52.

Rowe, C. J. *The Eudemian and Nicomachean Ethics: A Study in the Development of Aristotle's Thought*. Proceedings of the Cambridge Philological Society, supp. 3; Cambridge, 1971.

Veatch, Henry B. *Rational Man: A Modern Interpretation of Aristotelian Ethics*. Bloomington: Indiana University Press, 1962.

———. *For an Ontology of Morals*. Evanston, IL: Northwestern University Press, 1971.

Chapter 3

Aristotle and Economics

It is in justice that the ordering of society is centered.

—Aristotle

Aristotle (384-322 B.C.), the most important thinker who has ever lived, advanced a body of thought with respect to the development of the components of a market economy. He analyzed the economic processes surrounding him and endeavored to delineate the place of economy within a society that included commercial buying and selling. It follows that Aristotle's economic writings continue to attract the interest of contemporary thinkers. His economic thought (especially his value theory) is insightful but occasionally contradictory and inconsistent.

The particular objective of this chapter is to present, outline, reorganize, and elucidate through rewording the economic ideas found in Aristotle's *Nicomachean Ethics* and *Politics*. This chapter is designed to provide a background for readers who wish to study Aristotle's economic thought in greater detail. As such, it can be viewed as a much shorter and less technical and detailed source of much the same material found in the works of Mark Blaug, Michael Finley, Barry Gordon, Todd Lowry, and Scott Meikle, among others. Interested readers are encouraged to consult the writings of these fine thinkers.

Human Action and Political Economy

In the *Topics*, Aristotle provides his philosophical analysis of human ends and means. He explains that means or instruments of production are valuable because their end products are useful to people. The more useful or desirable a good is, the higher the value of the means of production is. Aristotle then goes on to derive a number of economic ideas from axiomatic concepts, including the necessity of human action, the pursuit of ends by ordering and allocating scarce means, and the reality of human inequality and diversity.

Aristotle explains that actions are necessarily and fundamentally singular. For Aristotle, the individual human action of using wealth is what constitutes the economic dimension. The purpose of economic action is to use things that are necessary for life (i.e., survival) and for the Good Life (i.e., flourishing). The Good Life is the moral life of virtue through which human beings attain happiness.

Given that human actions are voluntary and intentional, it follows that action requires the prior internal mental acts of deliberation and choice. Human beings seek to fulfill their perfection via action. Observing that human nature has capacities pertaining to its dual material and spiritual character, Aristotle explains that economics is an expression of that dual character. The economic sphere is the intersection between the corporeal and mental aspects of the human person.

Aristotle makes a distinction between practical science and speculative science. He states that practical science is concerned with knowledge for the sake of controlling reality. It studies knowledge that may be otherwise (i.e., contingent knowledge). Practical science studies relationships that are not constant, regular, or invariable. Aristotle classifies economics as a practical science. On the other hand, Aristotle sees speculative science as yielding necessary, universal, noncontingent truths. Speculative science generates universal truths deduced from self-evident principles known by induction. The goal of speculative science is knowledge for its own sake. Mathematics and metaphysics would be speculative sciences for Aristotle.

Aristotle taught that economics is concerned with both the household and the *polis* and that economics deals with the use of things required for the good (or virtuous) life. As a pragmatic or practical science, economics is aimed at the good and is fundamentally moral. Because Aristotle saw that economics was embedded in politics, an argument can be made that the study of political economy began with him.

For Aristotle, the primary meaning of economics is the action of using things required for the Good Life. In addition, he also sees economics as a practical science and as a capacity that fosters habits that expedite the action. Economics is a type of prudence or practical knowledge that aids a person in properly obtaining and using those things that are necessary for living well. The end of economics as a practical science is attaining effective action.

Aristotle explains that ontologically the operation of the economic dimension of reality is inextricably related to the moral and political spheres. The economic element is integrated in real action with other realms relating to the acting human person. The various domains mutually influence one another in an ongoing dynamic fashion.

Aristotle explains that practical science recognizes the inexact nature of its conclusions as a consequence of human action which arises from each person's freedom and uniqueness. Uncertainty emanates from the nature of the world and the free human person and is a necessary aspect of economic actions that will always be in attendance. Aristotle observes that a practical science such as economics must be intimately connected to the concrete circumstances and that it is proper to begin with what is known to us.

The Theory of Value

In the *Politics*, Aristotle views labor as a commodity that has value but does not give value. Rejecting labor as the source of wealth, Aristotle did not formulate the labor theory of value but instead held a theory of the value of labor. Aristotle observed that labor skill is not a determinant of exchange value. Instead, the value of labor skills is given by the goods they command in the market. He maintained that value is not created solely by the expenditure of labor in the production process. Noting that labor skill is a necessary, but not a sufficient, determinant of value, he explains that both utility and labor skills are pertinent to the determination of exchange values and exchange ratios. He says that, in the end, the basic requirement of value is utility regarding a person's desires. Value is the ability to satisfy wants. Demand is governed by the desirability of a good (i.e., its use value). According to Aristotle, exchange value is derived from use value as communicated through market demand.

In Book I of the *Politics*, Aristotle distinguishes between use value and exchange value. It was Aristotle who created the concept of value in use. The use value or utility of a good or service depends upon its being productive of an individual person's good. He explains that the use value of a given article can vary among individuals and that the demand for the item is a function of its use value. Aristotle observes that, as the quantity of the good possessed increases, the use value of that good will begin to decline at some threshold point. He also holds that the use value of a good or service will be increased if it can be consumed conspicuously; that demand will fluctuate as the extent of the use of the item is limited or wide-ranging; and that exchange value and demand are affected by the circumstances of rarity or scarcity. In addition, Aristotle distinguished between one's possessions (i.e., final goods) and instruments (i.e., factors) of production and noted that the desirability of means to an end will vary in accordance with the desirability of the end itself. In the *Topics* and in the *Rhetoric* he says that the instruments of production derive their value from the instruments of action (i.e., the final products).

Observing that economic goods derive their value from individual utility, Aristotle glimpsed the role of diminishing marginal utility in price formation. He recognized that the value of something could be established by discovering what its addition to (or subtraction from) a group of commodities did to the total value of the group. In the *Topics* he stated that the value of one good could be determined if we add it or lose it to a given complex of things. The more we gain by the addition of the good, the higher its value and the greater the loss from the absence of the good, the more desired the commodity is assessed to be. He also says that we judge between commodities by means of an addition to see whether the addition of commodity A or the addition of commodity B to a group makes the whole group more desirable. According to Aristotle, the quantity of a good reaches its saturation point when the use value plunges and becomes immaterial. In Book I of the *Politics* he points out that natural pressures of diminishing utility for goods direct remaining human energy toward moral self-improvement.

The Problem of Commensurability

Aristotle discovered, formulated, and analyzed the problem of commensurability. He wondered how ratios for a fair exchange of heterogeneous things could be set. He searched for a principle that makes it possible to equate what is apparently unequal and noncomparable. Because each thing has a substance or *telos*, it is by nature different from any other thing. His challenge was to discover how diverse products can be commensurable and thus have an exchange value or price. Aristotle's objective was to prove that every exchange of goods has to be an exchange of equivalents. How can goods of different quality, which are exchanged because of these qualitative differences, be compared with each other and be equalized? Aristotle says they must be equalized somehow by some common measure. There must be some dimension in which they are comparable if the goods are to be equalized. Aristotle was thus working from the premise that there will be no exchange without equality and that there can be no equality without commensurability. In other words, when people associate for the exchange of goods each must be satisfied that both utilities and costs are equalized before exchange takes place. Persons stand as equals in exchange as soon as their commodities are equalized. Aristotle makes several attempts to solve this paradox.

In his first effort at solving this paradox, Aristotle says that money, as a common measure of everything, makes things commensurable and makes it possible to equalize them. He states that it is in the form of money, a substance that has a *telos*, that individuals have devised a unit that supplies a measure on the basis of which just exchange can take place. Aristotle thus maintains that everything can be expressed in the universal equivalent of money. He explains that money was introduced to satisfy the requirement that all items exchanged must be comparable in some way. His thinking was that a common standard of measurement comprises commensurability and makes the equalization of goods possible. Aristotle then realized that the possibility of a measure presumes prior commensurability with respect to the dimension by which measurement is possible. He therefore sees his idea as deficient.

He next says that goods become commensurable in relation to need—the unit of value is need or demand. Need, rather than something in the nature of goods, is what makes them epistemically commensurable. Aristotle observes, however, that although need is capable of variable magnitudes, it lacks a unit of measure until money is introduced to supply it. Ultimately, he concludes that it may be impossible for different goods and services to be strictly commensurable. In his idea of commensurability Aristotle was the first to identify a serious and authentic problem of economics. Perhaps he was searching for a way of setting justifiable ratios for fair exchange so that products could be treated as "commensurable enough" to permit the exchange. The good must be an object of need that is expressible as money and the ratios must be quantitative and "precise enough."

In Book V of the *Nicomachean Ethics* and Book I of *Politics,* Aristotle distinguishes between universal justice and particular justice. Economic dealings are subject to the rules of particular justice. Particular justice involves quantitative relationships. Many writers say that Aristotle only includes distributive and corrective (i.e., rectificatory) justice under this category but other scholars say that he also means to include commutative (i.e., reciprocal) justice under this classification.

He says that distributive justice is natural justice and involves balancing shares with worth. In turn, rectificatory justice involves straightening out by removing unjust gain, restoring unjust losses, and other forms of retribution for loss and/or damages. Reciprocity involves the interchange of goods and services and does not coincide with either distributive or corrective justice. Reciprocal justice involves comparative advantages and is concerned with particularized mutual benefits derived from specialization of function.

In the *Nicomachean Ethics* Aristotle states that exchange depends on equality of both persons and commodities. It is in this work that he concentrates on the problem of commensurability. Aristotle uses artisans as examples for his general and abstract discussions found in this work. In Book V of the *Nicomachean Ethics* he deals with justice, is concerned with determining proper shares in various relationships, analyzes the subjective interactions between trading partners looking for mutual benefit from commercial transactions, develops the concept of mutual subjective utility as the basis of exchange, and develops the concept of reciprocity in accordance with proportion. In the *Nicomachean Ethics*, Aristotle, in his treatment of justice, applies the concepts of ratio and proportion to explain just distribution.

Aristotle states that fair exchange is a type of reciprocity, not of equality, but rather of proportion. This is achieved by equalizing proportions of products. His concern here is with the ratios in which goods are exchanged. Individuals create products of different value and unequal creators are made equal through the establishment of proportionate equality between the products. This led Aristotle to the consideration of commensurability and to inquire into the notion of exchange values.

According to Aristotle, value is assigned by man and is not inherent in the goods themselves. He says that exchange occurs because what the participants want is different from what they have to offer. Need plus demand is what goes into determining proportionate reciprocity in a given situation. Aristotle explains that the parties form their own estimations, bargain in the market, and make their own terms and exchange ratios. The exchange ratio is simply the price of things. For Aristotle, voluntary is presumed just. Exchange must be mutually satisfactory. He sees mutuality as the basis for exchange and the equating of subjective utilities as the precondition of exchange. There is a range of reciprocal mutuality that brings about exchange. The actual particular price is determined by bargaining between the two parties, who are equal as persons and different only with respect to their products.

Aristotle appears to have recognized the subjective and relational nature of an exchange ratio. He observed that an exchange ratio is not a ratio of goods alone nor merely a ratio of people exchanging the goods involved in the transaction. Rather, it is simultaneously a ratio reflecting the interrelationships among and between all of the people and all of the goods involved in this transaction. This ratio of proportionate reciprocity is used to equalize both goods and persons.

For Aristotle, money is a medium of exchange that makes exchange easier by translating subjective qualitative phenomena into objective quantitative phenomena. Although subjective psychological want satisfaction cannot be directly measured, the approximate extent of want satisfaction can be articulated indirectly through money. Not only does money eliminate the need for a double coincidence of wants, it also supplies a convenient and acceptable expression for the exchange ratio between various goods. Money, as an intermediate measure of all things, is able to express reciprocity in accordance with a proportion and not on the basis of a precisely equal ratio. Money, according to Aristotle, has become a convention or type of representation, by which all goods can be measured by some one thing. Money, as a modulating element and representation of demand, becomes a useful common terminological tool in the legal stage of the bargaining process.

The Household and the *Polis*

In the *Politics*, Aristotle discusses exchange, barter, retail trade, and usury. He explains that exchange takes place because of natural needs and the fact that some people have more of a good and some have less of it. He says that natural exchange redistributes goods to supply deficiencies out of surpluses. Voluntary exchange occurs between self-sufficient citizens who exchange surpluses, which they value less, for their neighbor's surpluses, which they value more.

For Aristotle, true wealth is the available stock of useful things (i.e., use values). He is concerned with having enough useful things to maintain the needs of the household and the *polis*. He says that wealth-getting that aims at use-value is legitimate. Use-value or true value involves goods that are necessary for life and for the household or the community of the city. Aristotle considers both the household and the *polis* to be natural forms of association. It is not against nature when individual households mutually exchange surpluses to satisfy the natural requirement of self-sufficiency. Aristotle considers friendship to be a necessary condition for natural exchange.

Aristotle maintains that property must be used in a way that is compatible with its nature. Its use must benefit the owner by also being a necessary means of his acting in correspondence with his own nature. In the *Politics*, Aristotle distinguishes between natural and unnatural acquisition and discusses the problem of excess property. He says that the right to property is limited to what is sufficient to sustain the household and the *polis* life of the city. He explains that exchange between households requires mutual judgments of equal participants in the life of the *polis*. The life of the household is a sound and productive means to *polis* life if it produces only the necessary goods and services that provide a setting for the exercise and development of the potentialities required for *polis* life.

Aristotle emphasizes the importance of natural limits in a system of natural relationships. He says that natural exchange has a natural end when the item needed is acquired. Production is the natural process of obtaining things for life's needs. Aristotle maintains that there is a limit to the amount of property that can be justifiably acquired as well as a limit to the ways in which it can be legitimately acquired.

According to Aristotle, a household relies on exchange to supply property necessary to the household so that the citizen can develop his humanity. Natural exchange operates within an environment of friendship and mutual concern to complement the basic self-sufficiency of the household. Natural exchange between households requires the exercise of virtues and furnishes a bridge between one's work and well-being. A wide range of material goods is needed to attain a person's moral excellence. Economic activity is necessary to permit leisure and the material instruments necessary for a person to develop the full range of his potential and thereby flourish. Aristotle teaches that *eudaimonia* involves the total spectrum of moral and intellectual excellences.

Aristotle explains that wealth derives its value from its contribution to the acquisition of other goods desirable for their own sake. Wealth and external or exterior goods are instruments that facilitate virtuous activity and *eudaimonia*, are means to an end, and have some natural limit with respect to each individual.

Aristotle says that the *polis* exists for the sake of the good life, that the *polis* is a partnership in living well, and that mutual interaction is the bond that holds society together. He observed that people are related to each other through the medium of goods but that acquisition beyond the necessary diverts the citizen's capacities from the sphere of *polis* life. Advocating an inclusive-end teleology, Aristotle endorsed an active life devoted to a wide range of intellectual and moral perfections including the active engagement in civic affairs.

In the *Politics*, Aristotle advanced the synergistic idea of social aggregation with the aggregate benefits to people exceeding the objective total of the benefits to individuals *qua* individuals. He sees this excess amount of benefits as a positive measurement of the goodwill created through association and as a reflection of the unifying strength of a society. In part, it is the mutual benefits of exchange which bring people together, with one desiring another's goods more than he desires his own and vice versa.

Types of Exchange

In the *Politics*, Aristotle delineates the historical development of money from its initial existence as a commodity. He also discusses the entire range of commodity exchange including barter, retail trade, and usury.

Aristotle declares that the first type of exchange, barter, the direct non-monetary exchange of commodities, is natural because it meets the natural requirement of sufficiency. After direct working of the land, barter between households is the next most natural means of wealth acquisition. For Aristotle, natural exchange is based on the right to property being determined by the capacity for its proper use. He sees barter as natural but inadequate because of the difficulty of matching households with complementary surpluses and deficiencies. The concepts of surplus and deficiency are normative and derive from the right of property.

Aristotle is irresolute and ambivalent regarding the second form of exchange which involves the transferring of goods between households but mediated by money. Here each participant starts and ends with use value which he approves of but the item is not being used in its natural aim or function because it was not made to be exchanged. Aristotle observes that what is natural is better than what is acquired and that an item that is final is superior to another thing that is wanted for the sake of this item.

The introduction of money eliminates the problem of the double coincidence of wants. For Aristotle, the legitimate end of money is as a medium of exchange but not as wealth or as a store of value. He observed that money became the representation of want by agreement on law. A currency acceptable within the *polis* permits the full potential to be realized.

Aristotle thought that money departs from its natural function as a medium of exchange when it becomes the beginning and end of exchange with no limit to the end it seeks. The ease of exchange permitted by the use of money makes it possible to engage in large production projects for exchange purposes instead of for direct household use. This can corrupt natural exchange for which money is a valuable instrument. Money, rather than serving simply to facilitate commodity exchange, can become the goal and end in itself.

In the third form of exchange, retail trade, a person purchases in order to sell at a profit. Retail trade is concerned with getting a sum of money rather than acquiring something that is needed and therefore consumed. Whereas Aristotle views household management as praiseworthy and as having a natural terminus, he is skeptical about retail trade because it has no natural terminus and is only concerned with getting a sum of money. Retail trade knows no limits. When money becomes an intermediate element in exchange, the natural limits on physical wants no longer exercise restraints on a person's desires. The lack of effective natural restraints leads to the unlimited desire for wealth. There exist no natural conditions restricting a person's desire to acquire money wealth.

For Aristotle, retail trade is not a way of attaining true wealth because its goal is a quantity of money. He criticizes money-making as a way of gaining wealth. The end of retail trade is not true wealth but wealth as exchange value in the form of a sum of money. Aristotle observes that exchange value is essentially a quantitative matter that has no limit of its own. He says that it is from the existence of wealth as exchange value that we derive the idea that wealth is unlimited.

In Book V of the *Nicomachean Ethics*, Aristotle states that commodity exchange between craftsmen is a natural but inferior form of exchange that is not closely connected to *polis* life. He says that craftsmen are involved with specialized production based on unlimited and unnatural acquisition, are not the equals of household heads, and are therefore unsuited for citizenship and for *polis* life.

The fourth form of trade is usury—the begetting of money from money. Aristotle says that the usurer is the most unnatural of all practitioners of the art of money-making. The lending of money at interest is condemned as the most unnatural mode of acquisition. Aristotle insists that money is barren. He did not comprehend that interest is payment for the productive use of resources made available by another person.

Aristotle's economic criticisms are directed at wealth-getting in the sense of money-making. He disregards the fact that men were able to search for unlimited wealth even before money came into existence. Although he realized that wanting too much is a human failing, he placed a great deal of blame on money because it had no natural terminus. Aristotle taught that when a man pursues wealth in the form of exchange value he would undermine the proper and moral use of his human capacities. He fails to mention that men of commerce provide useful public service and make money only if they do so.

An Originator of Economic Analysis

Aristotle saw so much, even in the field of economics. He foresaw significant elements of Austrian value theory. For example, he glimpsed the concept of diminishing utility and its application to exchange value (i.e., price) determination. He held a theory of the importance of value determination in evaluating the efficiency of means in attaining human objectives. He also anticipated the Austrian theory of imputation that holds that the value of productive factors can be obtained via imputation from the market values of final products. Aristotle was the first to draw a distinction between value in use and exchange value. His premarginal utility theory also rejected the labor theory of value that later was held by many of the classical economists. In addition, he was the first thinker to analyze the problem of commensurability. Additionally, Aristotle recognized the paradox of value and the operation of the principle of scarcity. Although Aristotle's economic insights and influence on the development of economic thought were considerable, he did make some errors and failed to fully appreciate that markets and money-making activities could provide a mechanism through which order in society could be produced through individuals pursuing their own ends. Nevertheless, Aristotle is one of the great thinkers in the history of economic thought.

Recommended Reading

Ambler, W. "Aristotle on Acquisition" *Canadian Journal of Political Science* 17 (1984): 487–502.

Ashley, W. J. "Aristotle's Doctrine of Barter." *Quarterly Journal of Economics* 9 (1895): 333–41.

Austin, M. M., and P. Vidal-Naquet. *Economic and Social History of Ancient Greece: An Introduction.* Berkeley: University of California Press, 1980.

Barker, E. *The Politics of Aristotle.* Oxford: Oxford University Press, 1946.

Blaug, M., ed. *Aristotle (384–322 BC).* Aldershot, UK: Edward Elgar, 1991.

Bolkestein, H. *Economic Life in Greece's Golden Age.* Edited by E. J. Jonkers. London,: F.J. Brill, 1975.

Cashdollar, S. "Aristotle's Politics of Morals." *Journal of the History of Philosophy* 11 (1973): 145–60.

Clark, S. R. L. *Aristotle's Man: Speculations upon Aristotelian Anthropology.* Oxford: Oxford University Press, 1975.

Cooper, J. M. "Aristotle on the Goods of Fortune." *Philosophical Review* 94/2 (1985): 173–96.

Ferguson, J. "Teleology in Aristotle's *Politics.*" Pp. 259–73 in *Aristotle on Nature and Living Things,* edited by A. Gotthelf. Bristol: Mathesis Publications, 1985.

Finley, Moses L. "Aristotle and Economic Analysis." Pp. 32–40 in *Studies of Ancient Society.* London: Routledge and Kegan Paul, 1974.

Gordon, Barry. *Economic Analysis Before Adam Smith.* New York: Barnes & Noble, 1975.

Gordon, B. J. "Aristotle, Schumpeter and the Metalist Tradition," *Quarterly Journal of Economics* 75 (1961): 608–14.

———. "Aristotle and the Development of Value Theory." *Quarterly Journal of Economics* 78 (1964): 115–28. Reprinted pp. 113–26 in *Aristotle (384–322 BC),* edited by M. Blaug. Aldershot: Edward Elgar, 1991.

———. "Aristotle and Hesiod: The Economic Problem in Greek Thought." *Review of Social Economy* 21 (1963): 147–56. Reprinted on pp. 113–26 in *Aristotle (384–322 BC),* edited by M. Blaug. Aldershot: Edward Elgar, 1991.

Gotthelf, A., ed. *Aristotle on Nature and Living Things.* Bristol: Mathesis Publications, 1985.

Irwin, T. H. *Aristotle: Nicomachean Ethics.* Indianapolis, IN: Hackett, 1985.

———. "Moral Science and Political Theory in Aristotle." In P. A. Cartledge and F. P. Harvey, eds. *Crux: Essays Presented to G. E. M. de Ste. Croix on his 75th Birthday, History of Political Thought* 7, no. 1–2 (1985). Duckworth.

———. "Generosity and Property in Aristotle's Politics." *Social Philosophy and Policy* 4 (1987).

Joachim, H. H. *The Nicomachean Ethics*. Oxford: Clarendon Press, 1951.

Johnson, V. "Aristotle's Theory of Value." *American Journal of Philology* 60 (1939): 445–51.

Kauder, E. "Genesis of the Marginal Utility Theory from Aristotle to the End of the Eighteenth Century." *Economic Journal* 63 (1953): 638–50. Reprinted on pp. 42–54 in *Aristotle (384–322 BC)*, edited by M. Blaug. Aldershot: Edward Elgar, 1991.

Kenny, A. J. P. *Will, Freedom and Power*. Oxford: Blackwell, 1975.

Keyt, D., and F. D. Miller, Jr., eds. *A Companion to Aristotle's Politics*. Oxford: Blackwell, 1991.

Langholm, O. *Wealth and Money in the Aristotelian Tradition: A Study in Scholastic Economic Sources*. Oslo: Oxford University Press, 1983.

Leyden, W. von. *Aristotle on Equality and Justice*. London: Macmillan, 1985.

Lord, C. *Aristotle: The Politics*. Chicago: University of Chicago Press, 1984.

Lowry, Todd S. "Aristotle's 'Natural Limit' and the Economics of Price Regulation." *Greek, Roman, and Byzantine Studies* 15 (1974): 57–63.

———. "Recent Literature on Ancient Greek Economic Thought." *Journal of Economic Literature* 17 (March 1979): 65–86.

McNeill, D. "Alternative Interpretations of Aristotle on Exchange and Reciprocity." *Public Affairs Quarterly* (1990): 55–68.

Meikle, Scott. "Aristotle and the Political Economy of the Polis." *Journal of Hellenic Studies* 99 (1979): 57–73.

———. "Aristotle on Equality and Market Exchange." *Journal of Hellenic Studies* 111 (1991): 193–96.

———. "Aristotle and Exchange Value." Pp. 156–81 in *A Companion to Aristotle's Politics*, edited by D. Keyt and F. D. Miller, Jr. Oxford, 1991. Reprinted on pp. 195–220 in *Aristotle (384–322 BC)*, edited by M. Blaug. Aldershot: Edward Elgar, 1991.

———. "Aristotle on Money." *Phronesis* 39/1 (1994): 26–44.

———. *Aristotle's Economic Thought*. Oxford: Clarendon Press, 1995.

———. "Aristotle on Business." *Classical Quarterly* NS 46 (1996): 138–51.

Mulgan, R. G. *Aristotle's Political Theory*. Oxford: Oxford University Press, 1977.

Nussbaum, M. C. *The Fragility of Goodness*. Cambridge: Cambridge University Press, 1986.

———. "Nature, Function and Capability: Aristotle on Political Distribution." *Oxford Studies in Ancient Philosophy*, suppl. vol. (1988): 145–84.

Polanyi, K. "Aristotle Discovers the Economy." In *Primitive, Archaic and Modern Economies*, edited by G. Dalton. New York: Anchor Books, 1968.

Ritchie, D. G., "Aristotle's Subdivisions of Particular Justice." *Classical Review* 7 (1894): 185–92.

Rosen, F. "The Political Context of Aristotle's Categories of Justice." *Phronesis* 20 (1975): 228–40.

Ross, W. D. *Ethica Nicomachea*. Oxford: Oxford University Press, 1925.

Rothbard, Murray. *Economic Thought Before Adam Smith: Austrian Perspective on the History of Economic Thought*. Cheltanham, UK: Edward Elgar Publishing Ltd., 1995.

Singer, K. "Oikonomia: An Inquiry into the Beginnings of Economic Thought and Language." *Kyklos* 11 (1958).

Smith, B. "Aristotle, Menger, Mises: An Essay in the Metaphysics of Economics." *History of Political Economy*, suppl. to vol. 22 (1990): 263–88. Reprinted on pp. 263–88 in *Carl Menger and his Legacy in Economics*, edited by B. Caldwell. Durham: Duke University Press, 1990.

Soudek, J. "Aristotle's Theory of Exchange: An Inquiry into the Origin of Economic Analysis." *Proceedings of the American Philosophical Society* 96 (1952): 45–75. Reprinted on pp. 11–41 in *Aristotle (384–322 BC)*, edited by M. Blaug. Aldershot: Edward Elgar, 1991.

Spengler, J. J. "Aristotle on Economic Imputation and Related Matters." *Southern Economic Journal* (1955): 371–89.

Springborg, P. "Aristotle and the Problem of Needs." *History of Political Thought* 5 (1984): 393–424.

Worland, S. T. "Aristotle and the Neoclassical Tradition: The Shifting Ground of Complementarity." *History of Political Economy* 16 (1984): 107–34. Reprinted in *Aristotle (284–322 BC)*, edited by M. Blaug. Aldershot: Edward Elgar, 1991.

Chapter 4

Epicurus on Freedom and Happiness

*It is impossible to live a pleasant life without living wisely and well and justly.
And it is impossible to live wisely and well and justly without living a pleasant
life.*

—Epicurus

Epicurus (341–270 BC), a major philosopher of the Hellenistic period, largely
relied upon Democritus for his materialistic and atomistic theory of nature.
However, he does modify Democritus's metaphysics because of its skeptical and
deterministic implications. Epicurus founded his physics based upon Democritus
but discovered that Democritus had no distinguishing ethical doctrine and, therefore, had to formulate his own objective ethics. Epicurus went on to formulate a
self-centered moral philosophy in which the individual person is the realm of
moral enterprise.

Metaphysics

Epicurus held that the only things that exist are corporeal bodies and void. He
taught that the elementary constituents of nature were discrete, solid, and indivisible material particles (i.e., atoms) and empty space. He said that everything
that exists is made up of eternal atoms separately falling in space. The atoms are
of different shapes and sizes and have weight. He taught that atomic motion is
not solely the result of past motion and weight. Although subject to their past
motion and weight, occasionally and randomly atoms swerve to the side, resulting in atomic collisions. This lateral swerve involves a small angle of deviation
from the original path. Objects in the world are therefore conglomerations of
atoms or macroscopic bodies that can be explained in terms of collisions, re-
boundings, and combinations of atoms. According to this accidentalist atomism,

worlds spontaneously emerge from the interaction of innumerable small particles. Epicurus attempted to explain all natural phenomena in atomistic terms through a naturalistic account of evolution from the formation of the world to the emergence of human societies. Some thinkers interpret this to mean that he would have a difficult, but not impossible, task in accounting for the persistent nature of objects and species (e.g., man). Other thinkers interpret Epicurus as maintaining that atoms do randomly bump into each other, and so eventually, given the laws of nature that allow for order to appear and persist, it can be inferred that in the infinite time and space of the universe order will indeed appear in various places. In other words, nature randomly tries all kinds of combinations, but only those that accord to the laws of nature emerge and persist.

Epicurus believed that all that exists is corporeal and that the universe has no beginning, has always existed, and will always exist. He wanted to eliminate the idea that God created everything and that human behavior should be based on obedience to God-given principles. He also wanted to dispense with transcendent entities such as Platonic Forms existing in themselves in some supernatural world. His goal was to liberate mankind from the fear of God and from the fear of death. Epicurus taught that fear of the gods and fear of death can be eliminated by right doctrine.

Death and the Soul

He used his radical, atomistic, and materialistic metaphysics to deny the possibility of the soul's survival after death and its possible punishment in the afterlife. Epicurus taught that soul atoms become disarranged at death and therefore could no longer support conscious life. Upon death, the body decomposes, and all of its atoms become dispersed throughout the air. At death, a particular body, including the soul (or mind), becomes a number of distinct atoms. The soul does not survive the death of the body. This is because a person is an inextricable union of an atomistic body and an atomistic soul (or mind). Epicurus is obviously the arch-enemy of any type of Cartesian dualism.

According to Epicurus, the human person is composed of atoms of different sizes and shapes. Soul atoms are particularly fine, the most easily moving, distributed throughout the body, and are the means by which persons have sensations and experience pleasure and pain. A major part of the soul is concentrated in the chest and is the central location of higher intellectual functions. Epicurus's Identity Theory of Mind (or Soul) holds that the mind proper resides in the chest and is primarily responsible for sensation and thought. Other soul atoms are spread throughout the remainder of the body permitting the mind to communicate with it. Epicurus explains that the mind is able to engage in sensation and thought only when it is a part of a living body and only when the atoms that comprise it are correctly arranged.

Removing Sources of Anxiety

Epicurus maintains that gods exist and that they too must be material beings and the result of purposeless and random events. These gods do not concern themselves with human beings. Only discontented beings act, and because gods are perfect and totally contented they are not involved in any manner in human affairs.

Epicurus contends that fear of death and punishment in the afterlife are primary causes of anxiety that itself is the source of irrational desires. He states that the most preeminent negative mental state is the fear of irrational dangers such as death. Death is nothing to us while we are alive and when death occurs we no longer exist. Epicurus says that death need not worry anyone because only a living being has sensations of either pain or pleasure. The time before a person was born (i.e., the preceding infinity of pre-natal nonexistence) is like the subsequent eternity of after-death nonexistence. He explains that, in the absence of fear of God or of death, a man's life is totally under his control. Because he denied immortality, Epicurus apprehended that all values must occur during the span of one's life and that life itself was the greatest good. He contended that the only thing that is intrinsically good is one's own pleasure or happiness. His focus was on the individual search for happiness. He emphasized the individual's desires for bodily and mental pleasure rather than upon God's commandments or abstract principles of proper conduct.

According to Epicurus, the goal of human life is happiness that results from the absence of physical pain (*aponia*) and the absence of mental disturbances (*ataraxia*). He says that the attainment of pleasure is the aim of all human action. Pleasure, the standard of goodness, is the beginning and end of a happy life. Epicurus employed integrative induction and deduction to discover the goal of pleasure for human beings. He observed reality and abstracted to reach this fundamental conclusion. Epicurus asserts that the pursuit of pleasure must be guided by reason, that a man should make sober calculations with respect to the motives and rationale for his every choice and avoidance, and that simplicity is the key to pleasure. He recommends a virtuous, somewhat ascetic life as the best means to gain pleasure.

The Swerve

Epicurus observed spontaneity and the ability to originate action in human beings, was concerned with rational agency, and wanted to defend and preserve a person's ability to use his reason to control his actions and to shape his character. He therefore advanced the idea of the swerve in order to provide space for voluntary undetermined action. Epicurus's notion of the swerve introduces indeterminacy into the universe and argues for the possibility of action not wholly deriving from the positions of the soul's constituent atoms. He says that the

swerve is necessary to preserve human freedom and to break the bonds of determinism. The swerving of atoms to the side at uncertain times is thought by
Epicurus to save us from determinism. He maintains that the mind is undetermined and capable of any motion up to the time when it actually moves. Free
volition permits each of us to move ourselves as we choose. Unfortunately, Epicurus does not provide a detailed explanation on how the swerve actually does
preserve human freedom. It is problematic how the swerve can explain free will.

Epicurus provides no explanation of if, and how, the swerve is involved in
the production of every free action. He does not tell clearly, and in detail, how
the swerve is supposed to effect human choices. In addition, upon analysis, it
appears that the atomic swerve, as he described it, would only effect a random
change and therefore not have any connection with morality. Of course, on the
positive side, Epicurus did at least recognize the free will problem and ingen-
iously used the idea of the swerve to "solve" the problem of free will.

Ethics

Epicurus's ethics can be viewed as a form of egoistic hedonism (or hedonistic
egoism). He states that nature compels all human beings to search for pleasure
and to avoid pain. Epicurus thus approached ethics from a biological (and psychological) perspective. He said that human beings need health of the body and
calm of the soul and that freedom from pain and peace of mind imply a state of
rest and tranquility. It follows that the true test of pleasure is the removal of all
that gives pain. When a person reaches that goal he is in a state of contentment
and rest called happiness, *eudaimonia*, or tranquility of mind (*ataraxia*).

It follows that ethical evaluations of good and bad can be applied only with
regard to the end (i.e., one's individual pleasure) toward which the contemplated
action aims. But how does a person know what is good and bad? Epicurus's
empiricist theory of knowledge begins with the testimony of the senses, including sensations and perceptions of pleasure and pain. His anti-skeptical empiricist
epistemology states that a person can gain knowledge by relying on the senses.
Epicurus states that in addition to sensations, we learn truth and reality through
one's preconceptions—ideas resulting from previous impressions. These preconceptions are formed in our material minds as the result of repeated sense
experiences of similar objects or events.

Reason and the Virtues

For Epicurus, reason is an instrument to help us live pleasurably. He taught that
not every pleasure has the same value or is choiceworthy. It follows that the
popular notion that Epicurean hedonism advocates a life of sensual delights is
incorrect. Epicurus said that a person must use his reason to calculate what is in

his best long-term self-interest and that prudence was the only real guide to happiness. He held that philosophy is essential for successful human living and that tranquil pleasures are superior to active ones. He also maintained that the standard for determining and arranging one's values is the application of reason to one's own life.

According to Epicurus, virtues are rational behaviors that lead to *eudaimonia*. Virtues are desirable purely as instrumental means to happiness and are chosen because of pleasure and not for their own sake. He links virtues with living pleasurably and states that having positive character traits is a good strategy for an individual to attain happiness. For Epicurus, all virtues (including courage, self-sufficiency, integrity, justice, honesty, pride, and generosity) are ultimately forms of prudence. To be happy, a man must live prudently, well, and justly. Prudence is the greatest of the virtues and the source of all the other virtues.

Pleasures and Desires

Epicurus distinguished between kinetic (moving or process) pleasures and static pleasure. Kinetic pleasures arise from movement and static pleasure involves the state of satiety and involves rest. Kinetic pleasure is what we experience when we are in the process of satisfying our desires and static pleasure is the state of having satisfied our desires. Kinetic pleasures (*aponia*) are physical and deal with the present and static pleasure (*ataraxia*) involves an internal mental state in which fear, suffering, and agitation are absent or removed and the soul is at rest.

Aponia can refer to active or lively pleasures that stem from motion and activity. It can also mean painlessness or physical health. *Ataraxia* can mean a quiet, calm, sedate, or tranquil state of mind. *Ataraxia* refers to a state of mind that is rational, focused, clear, and without inner conflict or confusion. In *ataraxia* nothing is interfering with the natural state of the particular individual person.

Epicurus divides pleasures and desires into (1) natural and necessary (i.e., needs), (2) natural but unnecessary (i.e., wants), and (3) unnatural and unnecessary (i.e., vain and empty) ones. He believes that the more we can limit our pleasures and desires, especially to those that are the most necessary and most natural, the more likely we are to attain sustainable pleasure and happiness. The internal and external conditions required for each person's survival are the components of Epicurus's idea of natural and necessary pleasure or desire. Certain things are needed for a man's freedom from disturbances and necessary for the individual's life itself. According to Epicurus, pleasure is objective to the degree that it results from satisfying the natural and necessary desires.

We could say that natural and necessary desires are foundational and that natural but non-necessary ones are derivative and optional. Epicurus emphasizes the life of voluntary simplicity with few or no civic obligations and with inconsiderable material possessions. Of course, because we are individuals, the idea of *ataraxia* permits variations for meeting people's needs According to Epicurus, a person can attain *ataraxia* only through the exercise of dispassionate reason.

Active Pleasure versus Static Pleasure

The relationship between active pleasures and static pleasures can be debated. It is not clear if a kinetic activity can lead to tranquility or vice versa or if a lively pleasure such as work or sex can be of value and lead to *ataraxia*. In order to look at this question I would like to begin by reproducing something I wrote regarding happiness several years ago on pages 47–48 of my 2002 book, *Capitalism and Commerce*. The following was written before I encountered Epicurus's teachings:

> Happiness in a comprehensive sense applies to one's life taken as a whole and thus arises from having a coherent, rationally chosen stance regarding the proper way to spend one's life. This is not the happiness we experience when we have obtained a particular goal or object. Rather, such metalevel happiness is evident through the holding of rational values with respect to the kind of life that is worth living and is characterized by a feeling of tranquility regarding the way one has lived and will continue to live his life. Metalevel happiness and object-level perturbation are compatible. Happiness at a metalevel provides a stable framework within which activity and striving are situated. A man who holds rational values and who selects ends and means consonant with the nature of existence and with the integrity of his own consciousness has achieved his values—not his existential values, but the philosophical values that are their precondition.
>
> Metalevel happiness requires a proper perspective that comes from the serenity or peace of mind one gets from knowing that one is free to rationally choose among alternatives. . . .
>
> Metalevel happiness provides the confidence and peace of mind that enables us to enjoy our everyday pursuits (i.e., our passions). Whereas the serenity of metalevel happiness is unitary, our projects are many, diverse, and complex. Unlike metalevel tranquility that potentially can be the same for all, passions are different and unique for each person. Serenity results from the possession of a consistent and hierarchical system of beliefs, values, and emotions. Our passions involve our desires to satisfy, through action, the values to which we are committed. There are reciprocal and synergistic effects between one's metalevel happiness and happiness that is experienced when one has achieved or passionately attempted to achieve a particular goal.

Could Epicurus have meant something like the above? Static pleasure can be viewed as: (1) the pleasure of being in a state of having satisfied one's desires, (2) the pleasure of being in a state of not having certain types of desires, and (3) the pleasure one has when functioning in the natural state without interference. Given the third viewpoint, we could say that a person's projects are significant and may involve static pleasure if they engage the natural capacities of the unencumbered individual.

Epicurus' idea of *ataraxia* implies an occurrent end state in which greater pleasure (i.e., tranquility) is not possible. Accordingly, one is either in that complete state or is not in that complete state. A person can be tranquil in degrees but cannot be completely tranquil in degrees. I believe that it follows that success in one's life projects and the extent of one's tranquility can have a positive and reciprocal relationship with one another. In other words, it may be possible to incrementally work up to the point of *ataraxia*. It is possible for a person to be living completely and fully without fear when he is totally engaged in his projects without being worried about finishing them, about how long it my may take to complete them, or about what comes next after they are realized. If a person's natural capacities are engaged by the projects he chooses and he pursues these without disturbances then during that time we could say that he has achieved *ataraxia*.

Friendship, Justice, and Politics

Epicurus values friendship highly as one of the best means of attaining pleasure. He said that men are oftentimes troubled by fear of other men and that friendship, which includes trust, helps to lessen the problem of hostility of other men. In human friendships there exist elements of protection, support, and help when needed. According to Epicurus, friendships develop so that definite and concrete benefits can be obtained in our efforts to maximize our pleasure. He states that although friendships arise because of our desire for pleasure, our love for our friends increases as our friendships advance and evolve. No life can ultimately be satisfying unless it includes friends. Friendship is thus a kind of quasi-contractual relationship by which we love, and are loyal to, our friends. Epicurus understands that friendship involves both its intrinsic attractiveness and the commitment of loyalty founded upon a realistic assessment of security, tangible and intangible gains, and rewards that friendship confers to an individual. Life with, and among, others can be expected to be good in Epicurus' benevolent universe. It follows that friends should only ask one another to do what is just and honorable.

Epicurus has a well-developed contractarian theory of justice in which justice is seen as instrumental and laws are viewed as useful. Natural justice is a reciprocal and advantageous pledge neither to harm others nor to be harmed by them. For Epicurus, the necessary and sufficient condition for the formation of civil society is the invalidation of the initiation of force. He teaches that a function of civil society is to deter those who might coerce and inflict pain upon other individuals.

Epicurus explains that it is in one's self-interest to be just because no pleasure gained by injustice could repay the prudent man for his loss of *ataraxia*. The wise man avoids wrongdoing because he has no interest in the inferior pleasures that are attained through injustice. Such unnatural and unnecessary pleasures would diminish the individual's security, self-sufficiency, and *ataraxia*.

Epicurus cautions the wise man not to get involved in politics because of the personal perturbation it brings. He offered no political program and said that political power is inessential, irrelevant, and likely to be detrimental to a person's efforts to lead a happy life. Epicurus wanted each individual to be as free as possible to plan his own life. For Epicurus, the moral is what provides pleasure to individuals in a context in which there is no social discord. Given the above, it certainly sounds as if Epicurus was one of the world's first libertarians.[1]

Note

1. For more on this, see Martin Masse, "The Epicurean Roots of Some Classical Liberal and Misesian Concepts," *Le Québécois Libre* no. 153 (April 15, 2005).

Recommended Reading

Annas, Julia. "Epicurus on Pleasure and Happiness." *Philosophical Topics* 15 (1987): 5–21.
———. "Free Action and the Swerve." Review of Walter G. Englert, "Epicurus on the Swerve and Voluntary Action." *Oxford Studies in Ancient Philosophy* 8 (1990): 257–91.
———. *The Morality of Happiness*. Oxford: Oxford University Press, 1993.
Armstrong, John M. "Epicurean Justice." *Phronesis* 42 (1997): 324–34.
Asmis, Elizabeth. *Epicurus' Scientific Method*. Ithaca, NY: Cornell University Press, 1984.
Bailey, Cyril B. *The Greek Atomists and Epicurus*. Oxford: Clarendon Press, 1928.
Bobzien, Susanne. "Did Epicurus Discover the Free-Will Problem?" *Oxford Studies in Ancient Philosophy* 19 (2000): 287–337.
Brown, E. "Epicurus on the Value of Friendship (Sententia Vaticana XXIII)." *Classical Philology* 97 (2002): 68–80.
Clay, Diskin. *Lucretius and Epicurus*. Ithaca, NY: Cornell University Press, 1983.
Cooper, John M. "Pleasure and Desire in Epicurus." Pp. 485–514 in *Reason and Emotion*, edited by John M. Cooper. Princeton, NJ: Princeton University Press, 1999.
DeWitt, N. W. *Epicurus and His Philosophy*. Minneapolis: University of Minnesota Press, 1954.
Englert, Walter G. "Epicurus on the Swerve and Voluntary Action." Atlanta: Scholars Press, 1987.
Everson, Stephen. "Epicurus on the Truth of the Senses." Pp. 161–83 in *Epistemology*, edited by Stephen Everson. Cambridge: Cambridge University Press, 1990.
Furley, David. *Two Studies in the Greek Atomists*. Princeton: Princeton University Press, 1967.

Gabb, Sean. "Epicurus: Father of the Enlightenment." *Le Quebecois Libre* 241 (November 11, 2007).

Huby, P. M. "Epicurus' Attitude to Democritus." *Phronesis* 23(1) (1978): 80–86.

Jones, Howard. *The Epicurean Tradition*. London: Routledge, 1989.

Konstan, David. "Epicurus on Up and Down (Letter to Herodotus sec. 60)." Phronesis 17 (1972): 269–78.

———. *Some Aspects of Epicurean Psychology*. Leiden: E.J. Brill, 1973.

———. "Problems in Epicurean Physics." *Isis* 70 (1979): 394–418.

Laertius, D. *Lives of Eminent Philosophers*. Translated by R. D. Hicks. Cambridge, MA: Harvard University Press, 1991, [1926, A.D. third century].

Lesses, Glenn. "Happiness, Completeness, and Indifference to Death in Epicurean Ethical Theory." *Aperion* 35 (2002): 57–68.

Long, A. A. *Hellenistic Philosophy*. 2nd ed. Avon: Bath, [1974] 1986.

Masse, Martin. "The Epicurean Roots of Some Classical, Liberal and Miseasian Concepts." *LeQuébécois Libre*, 153 (April 15, 2005).

Miller, F. D. "Epicurus on the Art of Dying." *Southern Journal of Philosophy* 14, no. 2 (1976): 169–77.

Mitsis, Phillip. *Epicurus' Ethical Theory: The Pleasures of Invulernability*. Ithaca, NY: Cornell University Press, 1988.

———. "Happiness and Death in Epicurean Ethics." *Apeiron* 35 (2002): 41–55.

Obbink, Dirk. "The Atheism of Epicurus." *Greek, Roman and Byzantine Studies* 30 (1989): 187–223.

O'Connor, E., translator. *The Essential Epicurus*. Buffalo, NY: Prometheus Books.

O'Keefe, Tim. "Does Epicurus Need the Swerve as an Archê of Collisions?" *Phronesis* 41 (1996): 305–17.

———. "Is Epicurean Friendship Altruistic?" *Apeiron* 34 (2001): 269–305.

———. *Epicurus on Freedom*. Cambridge: Cambridge University Press, 2005.

Preuss, P. *Epicurean Ethics*. Lewiston, ID: Edwin Mellen, 1994.

Purinton, Jeffrey S. "Epicurus on the Telos." *Phronesis* 38 (1993): 281–320.

———. "Epicurus on 'Free Volition' and the Atomic Swerve." *Phronesis* 44 (1999): 253–99.

———. "Epicurus on the Nature of the Gods." *Oxford Studies in Ancient Philosophy* 21 (2001): 181–231.

Rist, John. *Epicurus: An Introduction*. Cambridge: Cambridge University Press, 1972.

Rosenbaum, S. E. "Epicurus on Pleasure and the Complete Life." *Monist* 73, no. 1 (1990): 21–41.

Russell, Daniel Charles. "Epicurus and Lucretius on Saving Agency." *Phoenix* 54 (2000): 226–99.

Schofield, M., and G. Striker, eds. *Studies in Epicurus and Aristotle*. Weisbaden: Otto Harrassowitz, 1960.

Warren, James. "Epicurean Immortality." *Oxford Studies in Ancient Philosophy*, 18 (2000): 231–61.

Wheeler, C. J. *Ethical Egoism in Hellenic Thought*. Los Angeles: University of Southern California, Doheny Library, 1976.

Chapter 5

Thomas Aquinas's Christian Aristotelianism

*All things participate to some degree in the eternal law insofar as they derive
from it certain inclinations to those actions and aims which are proper to them.
But, of all others, rational creatures are subject to divine providence in a very
special way; being themselves made participators in providence itself, in that
they control their own actions and the actions of others.*

—Thomas Aquinas

Thomas Aquinas (1225–1274), the dominant thinker of the Middle Ages, combined the science and philosophy of Aristotle with the revealed truths of Christianity. Holding that Aristotelianism is true but is not the whole truth, he reconciled the philosophy of Aristotle with the truth of Christian revelation. Aquinas
was a committed disciple of Aristotle but was an even more sincere disciple of
the Church. He reconceived Aristotle's ideas to a new context, was able to make
distinctions that Aristotle did not formulate, and never hesitated to go beyond
Aristotle. The thirteenth-century rediscovery and revival of the corpus of Aristotle's teaching and Aquinas's synthesis of it with the tenets of Christian faith
effected a dramatic change in medieval political thought. Through his writings,
Aquinas provided a solid bridge from the ancients.

Reason and Faith

According to Aquinas, philosophy and theology do not contradict one another
and play complementary roles in the quest for truth. For Aquinas, the whole of
human knowledge forms one all-encompassing, orderly, hierarchical system
with sciences at the base, philosophy above them, and theology at the top. It
follows that human values and truths are not eradicated by the revelation of
higher ones. Faith does not contradict nature, human knowledge, or science.

Philosophy proceeds from principles discovered through the use of human rea-son and theology emanates from authoritative revelation. Philosophy and relig-ion are equally valid in their respective spheres and reason and faith cooperate in advancing the discovery of truth. Aquinas emphasizes that divine revelation in no way contradicts that which men discover by the use of natural reason.

Aquinas taught that the universe is an orderly and integrated hierarchy that can only be fully understood when seen in relationship to God. In fact, Aquinas promulgated a fourfold classification of law in which only one category is hu-man. Eternal law is practically identified with the divine reason of God that gov-erns and orders the entirety of creation. The eternal law is "imprinted" on all things, including men. Natural law is that part of the eternal law that is presented to the reason of man. Natural law is absolute and unalterable because it is de-creed by God. Men are guided by a rational apprehension of the eternal law which is imprinted as precepts, rules of behavior, or broad principles of natural law. Because men are autonomous beings they must choose to observe the law of nature through acts of free will. Natural law is a product of unaided reason. Human laws are positive laws that are, or should be, derived from natural law. It is the correlation between natural law and human law that determines the moral validity of the latter. The divine law, the law of grace, is the portion of the eter-nal law that God has revealed to man through the Old and New Testaments, the law of Moses, the Decalogue, and in Church dogma. Divine law is a gift rather than a discovery of natural reason. Revelation adds to reason but does not over-turn it. Divine law supplements natural law and corrects its human misinterpre-tations. It is needed because natural law cannot direct man to his transcendent end.

Aquinas's thorough, provocative, and nuanced philosophy can be referred to as natural theology. As a philosopher, he begins with sense experience and reasons upward, culminating in the idea of God, but as a theologian, he begins with faith in God. Aquinas describes natural law in metaphysical and theological terms and explains that natural law and human nature can be but understood as products of God's wisdom. Because God governs the world as the universal first cause, it follows that human acts are praiseworthy only insofar as they promote God's purposes. His organic metaphysical and theological synthesis considers what belongs to man's proper nature and regards what is true and good about men insofar as they are related to God.

For Aquinas, the human person is made in the image of the Creator and is endowed with inalienable responsibilities. The human person is the only living thing created as an end in himself. It is in his liberty that the person is made in the image of the Creator. Aquinas understood that a person, as opposed to a mere individual, has the capacity for insight, choice, and responsibility, in addi-tion to being free and independent of every other member of his species. A hu-man being is free because he can reflect, choose, and be responsible. It follows that the human act is a combination of will plus reason and knowledge. Aquinas distinguishes between acts of a man and human acts, identifies the liberty of human understanding to focus on relevant factors (i.e., the liberty of specification), and emphasizes the liberty to reach a determination and judgment (i.e., the liberty of exercise).

Aquinas built on and further developed Aristotle's theory of ethics. Both maintained that happiness is related closely with a person's purpose or end. However, Aquinas added his idea of a supernatural end to Aristotle's naturalistic morality in which you attain virtue and happiness through the fulfillment of your natural capacities. For Aquinas, human nature does not embody its own standards for achievement. Discerning that Aristotelian ethics was incomplete, Aquinas was concerned with both a person's natural end and his supernatural end. He concludes that human perfection is the work of two societies—one concerned with immanent good and the other with transcendent good.

Aquinas held the concept of twin authorities—temporal and spiritual with each being supreme in its own sphere. This is because man possesses both a bodily nature and a rational and spiritual soul. Value and power are thus bifurcated into temporal and eternal spiritual ones. Of course, he views the Church as the crown of social organization and the creation of human law as one of the most important tasks that God has entrusted to his image-bearer. According to Aquinas, the state is willed by God, has a God-given function, is needed to attend to the common good, and is ultimately subordinate to the Church.

Political Thought

Aquinas frequently turns to public authorities as the chief guardians of the common good. He says that the state's function is to secure the common good by keeping the peace, by organizing and harmonizing the activities of citizens, by providing for the resources to sustain life, and by precluding or thwarting obstacles and hindrances to the good life. The purpose of authority is to provide for the common good, which Aquinas maintains must be the good of the concrete person. The term, common good, has no meaning for Aquinas unless it produces the good of the individual. He states that the common good results from a brotherhood of insight, choice, freedom, and responsibility, and that people in society must define and implement this common good through the government.

Aquinas accepted the Aristotelian idea that the state springs from the social nature of man rather than from his corruption and sin. He sees the state as a natural institution that is derived from the nature of man. Man is naturally a social and political animal whose end is fixed and determined by his nature. Aquinas explains that social living requires some form of civil authority and that the notion of ordering toward an end implies a directing authority. He says that the state preserves an orderly society by maintaining internal and external peace and by ensuring the satisfaction of man's material necessities. He believes that government is needed to regulate the economic activities of individuals but thinks that such regulation should be the exception rather than the rule and should be used only in emergencies and to prevent chaos. According to Aquinas, the common good requires that the social system have a ruling sector, that rulership is a trust for the entire community, and that the duty of the ruler is to direct action in order for men to live a happy and virtuous life. The multitude must be directed in acting well and living virtuously.

Recognizing that natural law is prior to any civil jurisdiction, Aquinas taught that the inherent end of personhood is communion with others and that the inherent end of a true community is full respect for the personhood of each of its members. He knew that civilization is constructed through reasoned discourse and rational persuasion and that civilized institutions need to respect the human person's capacity to reflect and to choose. Because humans are self-determined persons (not merely individuals), it follows that political legitimacy comes from the participation of all citizens in choosing their leaders.

Aquinas was concerned with the liberty of autonomous persons to conduct their affairs through civil conversation and rational persuasion. He valued highly the practical order of civil society through which each individual gains mastery of his own liberty through the cultivation of habits and virtues. Although it is not likely that Aquinas had formed the idea of natural rights, he did recognize that all men are equal in liberty even though there are wide inequalities and differences with respect to their talents, capacities, and callings. Aquinas spoke of indelible laws in man's being that command the respect of everyone. Society involves the mutual exchange of ideas, products, and services for the sake of a good life to which its many individual members contribute.

Aquinas explained that government agents had certain limits beyond which they could not function. They are bound by laws of human nature that emanate from the act of God's creation. It follows that positive laws that are inconsistent with man's nature should not be enacted or should be overturned. Positive laws must be just and must be derived from general principles of natural law. An ordered society under human laws applies to people at their natural level. Therefore, to ensure an ordered society, human laws must be constructed.

According to Aquinas, a ruler is needed even in the state of perfection or innocence in order to provide direction and guidance. He adds that, although people require an orderly political life, the authority of government agents ought to be limited. Tyranny is illegitimate and justice demands that a tyrant be deposed. Aquinas explains that public action, rather than individual violence, is the proper remedy against tyranny. Justifiable resistance is a public act of the whole people. He observes that political authority exists originally in the whole people organized as a civic community. It follows that there is no power to frame laws except as representing the people and that legitimate title to power is the result of a transfer by the rational act and consent of the community.

Aquinas held the idea of the limited scope of government authority. Although he posited no real theory of the hypothetical best regime for the ideal community, he favored a mixed regime for the real world. He says that the regime worthiest of the human person mixes the best elements of monarchy, aristocracy, and democracy. This mixed regime would be limited by moral law and legal or constitutional devices to prevent arbitrary use of power. Realistic and pragmatic in his thinking, he saw that a mixed government would be the best practical type, would require consent and permit moral freedom, would minimize the danger of tyranny, and would allow people to believe that they had a say and a stake in the community.

For Aquinas, the political community is the sovereign construction of reason. He says that the political sovereign has authority to legislate from God and is therefore responsible to God. Accordingly, law should advance the common good. In his writings, Aquinas linked ethics to politics and the individual human person to the common good. He also emphasized that civilized political institutions respect the human capacity for reflection and choice, which provide the foundation of law.

Aquinas, in the Aristotelian tradition, emphasizes the inexact character of ethics and the mutability of law due to the contingency of specific circumstances. He explains that law can be adapted to time and place and properly changed due to changed conditions of men. What is just depends upon the circumstances. He adds that legislators must also consider and test the usefulness of possible rules to determine that which is most appropriate to be law. Aquinas maintains that utility is an important standard or criterion for ascertaining the justice of legal rules. Usefulness is a standard for discerning when a law should be changed. Law is not to be imposed once for all time. Observing that moral and legal reasoning is an inexact science, Aquinas states that good law is created through past experience and the consideration of pertinent social circumstances.

According to Aquinas, the function of positive law is mainly to embody and give coercive force to the principles of natural law in the form of authoritative direction. Recognizing the limits of law in the production of virtuous citizens, Aquinas teaches that law should not directly dictate the exercise of all the virtues nor directly forbid the exercise of every vice. Aquinas distinguishes between matters of justice that are morally required and those that are both morally and legally binding, and states that the common good of the political community should only prohibit vices that threaten social life itself such as theft and murder. True virtue consists in using one's reason and free will in making the right choices. For Aquinas, the primary practical problem of an individual's moral life is to decide what to do in the unique circumstances in which each unique person finds himself.

He stressed that political authorities should be concerned with broad matters of general interest rather than with small details of individual conduct. No laws are capable of anticipating every particular circumstance to which a law could be applied. It follows that laws should be stated in general terms, expressing what is proper for cases of most frequent occurrence. There may be situations in which a law that is applicable to most cases would produce an injustice if rigidly applied. Aquinas, therefore, suggests permitting the judge to have the power of equity that allows him to moderate promulgated law in order to achieve a just outcome.

Aquinas understood that custom can create, abolish, or amend law. He favored law that was consistent with prevailing customary practices. Custom is an expression of widespread human rationality and not just the product of the articulated rationality of a select few. Aquinas was committed to liberty, loved tradition, and had a sense of realistic hope and moderate institutional progress.

Economic Thought

Aquinas addressed a number of economic questions particularly in *Summa Theologica* II. Among the topics covered are the division of labor, property rights, the just price, value theory, insider trading, and usury, among others. Although he said there was something ignoble about trade, he also recognized the usefulness of merchants whose activities were to the community's advantage. Aquinas taught that the operational principles of the economic order are subordinate to the moral and political ends of the city. His justification of mercantile profits offered many examples of the benefits that commerce could bring to society.

Foreseeing Adam Smith's division of labor theory, Aquinas explained that diversification of men for diverse tasks is the work of divine providence and stems from natural law, with different men possessing abilities and inclinations for different occupations and functions. He recognized the benefits of exchange and the division of labor in satisfying the needs and wants of individuals.

Aquinas views private property as necessary for human life and as an extension of natural law. He acknowledges that under natural law all property is communal, but also contended that the addition of private property was an extension, and not a contradiction, of natural law. Aquinas explains that human reason derives the notion of distinction of possession for the benefit of individual human lives. He states that possession of private property is necessary because: (1) men will more resolutely and attentively take care of things if they possess them instead of the goods being held in common by all or many others; (2) possession advances order rather than chaos and confusion as responsibility can be determined; and (3) private possession promotes a more peaceful state. Aquinas realized that, not only does creativity require property, without property under the dominion of every person the individual's liberty of action is diminished. He accepted an unequal distribution of private property but also approved of the regulation of private property by the state. He also said that while the ownership of goods should be private, the use of goods must be in common (so that the poor and needy can have their share) or must be in service of the common good.

It is difficult to judge precisely what Aquinas meant by the term "just price." The various interpretations of what he meant by just price include, but are not limited to: (1) an equivalence in terms of labor cost; (2) an equivalence in terms of utility; (3) an equivalence in terms of total cost of product; and (4) market price.

When speaking of the "just price" in an organized exchange, Aquinas often appears to mean the price that is paid in a more or less competitive market. Noting that exchange takes place for the utility of both parties, Aquinas states that the norm of commutative justice is expressed in the principle of equivalence between reciprocal contributions. Accordingly, there needs to be a certain equivalence or proportion between what is given and what is received. Aquinas describes commutative justice as the principle of absolute equality in exchanges of goods and services among individuals. He explicitly repudiated the notion that prices should be determined by one's position or station in life, noting that the selling price of any commodity should be the same whether or not the buyer or seller is poor or wealthy.

For Aquinas, the valuation of goods does not seem to depend upon any intrinsic property of the goods themselves. The equality to which Aquinas frequently refers appears to be the mutual satisfaction gained by each contracting party in an exchange. Aquinas also observes that the one element that measures all products and services is the need that involves all exchangeable goods because all things can be related to human needs. It is apparent that Aquinas was certainly not reducing the value of a good to labor by itself. Recognizing that market forces affect the value that is placed on goods and services, Aquinas is clearly not subscribing to the labor theory of value.

Aquinas wrote that buying and selling seem to have been introduced for the mutual advantages of the involved parties because one needs something that is possessed by the other and vice versa. He states that when market exchanges occur to meet the needs of the trading partners then there is no question of unethical behavior. However, if one produces for the market in expectation of gain then he is acting rationally only if his prices are just and his motives are charitable. The prices are just if both the buyer and seller benefit and the motives are charitable if the profits are to be used for self-support, charitable purposes, or to contribute to public well-being.

Aquinas presented a mixed but somewhat benevolent view of trade. He said that while trade may present opportunities for sin, it is not sinful by its nature. Aquinas denounced covetness, love of profit, and avarice but said that mercantile gain was justified when directed toward the good of others.

The just price for Aquinas is the one that, at a given time, can be received from the buyer, assuming common knowledge and the absence of fraud and coercion. Aquinas anticipates the problem of "insider trading" when he observes that a person may sell a scarce product at the prevailing market price although he knows that more of the product is on the way and will be available shortly. The implication is that there is no moral duty to inform a potential customer that the price of the product that one is attempting to sell is probably going to be lower in the near future.

It appears that Aquinas, at least implicitly, anticipated the concept of opportunity cost. He explains the idea of price as just compensation to the seller for the utility lost when he becomes detached from the item sold. Aquinas also mentions the benefits supplied by men of commerce when they conserve and store goods, import goods that are necessary for the republic, and transport goods from geographical areas where they are in great supply to places where they are scarce.

Aquinas, like the Bible and Aristotle, wrongly condemned the practice of charging interest for the lending of money. All fail to see that borrowers are not injured when they take out a loan and, in fact, are likely to benefit fit they can invest in a project that yields a return greater than the interest paid. Aquinas says that usury, the charging of money on loans, is sinful and unnatural because money is barren and was simply invented for the purpose of exchange.

Recommended Reading

Aertsen, Jan. *Nature and Creature: Thomas Aquinas' Way of Thought.* Leiden: E.J. Brill, 1988.

Aquinas, St. Thomas. *Summa Theologica.* Translated by Fathers of the English Dominican Province. New York: Benziger Bros, 1947.

Bigongiori, Dino, ed. *Political Ideas of St. Thomas Aquinas: Representative Selections.* New York: Hafner, 1953.

Bourke, Vernon J. *Aquinas's Search for Wisdom.* Milwaukee, WI: Bruce, 1965.

Bradley, Denis. *Aquinas on the Twofold Human Good: Reason and Human Happiness in Aquinas' Moral Science.* Washington, DC: Catholic University of America Press, 1997.

Brock, Stephen. *Action and Conduct: Thomas Aquinas and the Theory of Action.* Edinburgh: T&T Clark, 1998.

Burrell, David. *Aquinas: God and Action.* Notre Dame, IN: University of Notre Dame Press, 1979.

Chenu, Marie-Dominique. *Toward Understanding St. Thomas.* Chicago, IL: Regnery, 1964.

Chesterton, G. K. *St. Thomas Aquinas.* New York: Sheed and Ward, 1933.

Conover, Milton. "St. Thomas Aquinas as a Social Realist," *Social Science* (June 1954).

Copleston, F. C. *Aquinas.* London: Penguin Books, 1955.

Davies, Brian. *The Thought of Thomas Aquinas.* Oxford: Clarendon Press, 1992.

D'Entreves, Alexander P. *The Medieval Contribution to Political Thought.* Oxford: Oxford University Press, 1939.

Elders, Leo. *The Philosophical Theology of St. Thomas Aquinas.* New York: E.J. Brill, 1990.

Dougherty, George V. *The Moral Basis of Social Order According to St. Thomas.* Washington, DC: Catholic University Press, 1941.

Farrell, Walter. "Natural Foundations of the Political Philosophy of St. Thomas." Proceedings of the American Catholic Philosophical Association, 1931.

Finnis, John. *Aquinas: Moral, Political, and Legal Theory.* Oxford: Oxford University Press, 1998.

Flannery, Kevin. *Acts Amid Precepts: The Aristotelian Logical Structure of Thomas Aquinas' Moral Theory.* Washington, DC: Catholic University of America Press, 2001.

Gilby, Thomas A. *The Political Thought of Thomas Aquinas.* Chicago: University of Chicago Press, 1958.

Gilson, Etienne. *Reason and Revelation in the Middle Ages.* New York: Scribners, 1938.

———. *Thomism: The Philosophy of Thomas Aquinas.* Translated by L. K. Shook and A. Mauer. Toronto: Pontifical Institute of Medieval Studies, 2002.

Gordon, Barry. *Economic Analysis before Adam Smith*. London: Macmillan, 1975.

Hankley, W. J. *God in Himself: Aquinas' Doctrine of God as Expounded in the Summa Theologicae*. Oxford: Oxford University Press, 1987.

Hearnshaw, F. J. C., ed. *The Social and Political Ideas of Some Great Medieval Thinkers*. London: Harrap, 1923.

Jaffa, Harry V. *Thomism and Aristotelianism: A Study of the Commentary by Thomas Aquinas on the Nicomachean Ethics*. Chicago: University of Chicago Press, 1952.

Jenkins, John. *Knowledge and Faith in Thomas Aquinas*. Cambridge: Cambridge University Press, 1997.

Langholm, Odd. *Wealth and Money in the Aristotelian Tradition: A Study in Scholastic Economic Sources*. Bergen: Universitetsforlaget, 1983.

Lowry, S. Todd. *The Archaeology of Economic Ideas: The Classical Greek Tradition*. Durham, NC: Duke University Press, 1987.

Maritain, Jacques. *St. Thomas Aquinas*. New York: Meridian Books, 1964.

Martin, Christopher. *Thomas Aquinas: God and Explanations*. Edinburgh: Edinburgh University Press, 1997.

———. *The Philosophy of Thomas Aquinas: Introductory Readings*. London: Routledge Kegan & Paul, 1988.

Martinez, Marie L. "Distributive Justice According to St. Thomas." *Modern Schoolman* (May 1947).

McDermott, Timothy. *Aquinas Selected Writings*. New York: Oxford University Press, 1993.

McInerny, Ralph. *Aquinas on Human Action*. Washington, DC: Catholic University of America Press, 1992.

———. *Thomas Aquinas Selected Writings*. London: Penguin Classics, 1998.

———. *Aquinas*. Cambridge: Polity Press, 2004.

Murphy, Edward F. *St. Thomas' Political Doctrine and Democracy*. Washington, DC: Catholic University Press, 1921.

Parsons, W. R. "Medieval Theory of the Tyrant." *Review of Politics* (April 1942).

Pieper, Josef. *Guide to Thomas Aquinas*. New York: Pantheon, 1962.

Roover, R. de. "The Concept of the Just Price: Theory and Economic Policy." *Journal of Economic History* 18 (December 1958): 418–34.

Stump, Eleonore. *Aquinas*. London: Routledge, 2003.

Ward, L. R. "St. Thomas' Defense of Man." Proceedings of the American Catholic Philosophical Association (1945).

Weisheipl, James A. *Thomas D'Aquino: His Life, Thought and Work*. Washington, DC: Catholic University of America Press, 1974.

Wippel, John. *The Metaphysical Thought of Thomas Aquinas: From Finite Being to Uncreated Being*. Washington, DC: Catholic University of America Press, 2000.

PART II

EARLY MODERN AND RENAISSANCE PERIODS

Chapter 6

Spinoza on Freedom, Ethics, and Politics

The highest activity a human being can attain is learning for understanding, because to understand is to be free.

—Baruch Spinoza

If one mentions the name Spinoza, he is likely to get a response something like "Oh, wasn't he the pantheist philosopher who lived around the time of Hobbes and Locke?" Of course he was, but he was also much more than that. Baruch (Benedict de) Spinoza (1632-1677) promulgated a deductive, rational and monist philosophy that exhibited a mathematical appreciation of the universe and that held that things can only be understood when viewed in relation to a total structure. Spinoza's thought is still extremely relevant to twenty-first-century thinkers in areas such as methodological individualism, value theory, ethical naturalism, self-perfectionism, and political philosophy. For example, many of Spinoza's ideas are reflected in the works of contemporary philosophers such as Douglas Den Uyl, Douglas Rasmussen, and Tibor Machan.

Metaphysics

There is no ontological hierarchy for Spinoza. For him, the transcendent world does not exist. He proclaims there is no world except the existing one. In Spinoza's pantheistic notion there is only one substance (God), an absolutely infinite being made up of infinite attributes of which only two, thought and physical extension, are known by man. He states that God's existence is necessary and that, because there is nothing other than the divine substance and its modifications, there is nothing that is contingent. All entities, including man, are determined by universal natural laws to exist and to act in a given definite and fixed manner. Spinoza maintains that all things in the universe are modifications of the same single substance and, therefore, not totally free in the sense in being able to do anything whatsoever.

Man is a modification (or mode) of the unique, infinite substance that is God or Nature. Nature is an indivisible, uncaused, and substantial whole and is the only substantial whole. God is simply nature under another attribute. Every single mode is caused by God's infinite power that necessarily creates the whole of nature. Spinoza thus conceives of God as the immanent cause of Nature. Spinoza's God is the cause of all things because all things follow necessarily and causally from his divine nature. This is in contrast to the Judeo-Christian idea of God as a transcendent being who causes a world separate from himself to exist by creating it out of nothing.

Man is a composite mode of the attributes of thought and extension and therefore man only knows two attributes of God or Nature—mind and body. Mind and body are different aspects of a single substance that Spinoza calls alternately God and Nature. For Spinoza, man is non-durational and rooted in the timeless essence of God, expressly as one of the innumerable specific ways of God being externalized. The mind and the body are different expressions under thought and under extension of the same existent—the human person.

Human Nature

Human beings are bound by the same natural laws as are all other segments of the universe. Man is an integral part of nature and therefore subject to its laws. In Spinoza's system, men are undisputably part of nature, a domain governed by cause and effect. However, the human body, including its corresponding mind, is significantly more complex than other entities with respect to its composition and in its dispositions to act and to be acted upon. For Spinoza, action refers to the human power to influence causal chains. He explains that all thinking is action and that all action has its concomitant in thought.

According to Spinoza, primacy of self-interest is a basic law of human nature. He says that human beings share a common drive for self-preservation and seek to maintain the power of their being. *Conatus* is the power to preserve in being. Spinoza's *conatus* principle states that human individuals aim to persist in being in order to assert themselves in the world in their distinct individuality. Like all things in nature, man through his body and through his mind strives to persevere in his being and his mind is conscious of this striving. It is in man's capacity to think that he differs from all other natural entities.

Spinoza explains that all things in nature proceed from an eternal necessity. Viewing cause and reason as equivalent terms, Spinoza says that there is no freedom if we understand freedom to be to the power of performing an action without cause or reason. Everything, including man, is bound by laws of nature and other natural constraints. Human beings have a caused nature and are not outside nature. Nature's bounds are set by laws which have attachment to the eternal order of the whole of Nature, of which man is but a part. Man functions as an individual relative to other entities, and, at the same time, he is part of the universe.

Freedom and Ethics

How can freedom exist in Spinoza's "deterministic" universe? According to Spinoza's definition of freedom, a thing is said to be free which exists by the mere necessity of its own nature and is determined in its actions by itself alone. Like Aristotle, Spinoza values something as terms to the extent to which it realizes its nature. Real freedom, for Spinoza, means acting according to the necessary nature of man. Freedom means to follow the determined *conatus*, which is man striving to persist in his own being. When applied to human beings, the general law of self-preservation has distinctive importance to Spinoza's concept of freedom.

Spinoza's ethics is based on ontology of man whose moral condition can only be accounted for by his own existential condition. Spinoza's moral philosophy has a definite naturalistic character. He sees the foundation of virtue as the endeavor a person makes to preserve his own being. It follows that the basic unit of Spinozist ethics is the individual human person. The attainment of virtuous beliefs is a legitimate end, the acquisition of which is something for each individual to achieve if he can. It is in a person's interest to be moral and virtuous. For Spinoza, virtue involves the fuller development of one's individuality.

If ethics is possible, there must be a mode in which determinism is combined with freedom. Spinoza notes that people experience and distinguish between good affects that favor the originating *conatus* of life and bad ones that do not. He explains that in a totally determined system there would be no reason for such qualitative distinctions. He concludes that people live in a universe determined by a type of relative necessity in the circumstances and not in one of absolute necessity. According to Spinoza, man's necessary nature (i.e., to persist in his own being) is not absolutely necessary. Instead, it is possible, contingent, and voluntarily acquired depending upon an effective person's chosen activities. For Spinoza, freedom means the existence of options and the ability to make value judgments and decisions. He says that a human being has the power to act and is the origin of the impulse to act.

Spinoza teaches that to behave virtuously is to act, live, and preserve one's being in accordance with reason and on the basis of what is in our own interest and is useful to us. He views freedom as the positive intellectual capacity to act in order to attain our own ends with the knowledge that our actions are always limited by natural law. For Spinoza, power is the knowledge of necessity. He explains that powerful (i.e., virtuous) persons act because they understand why they must act. To be free is to be guided by the law of one's own nature which, according to Spinoza, is never inconsistent with the law of another's nature. He explains that a person's interactions with the rest of nature can either increase his ability or power to preserve in his existence or decrease his ability to do so.

It follows that we should pursue what we believe will benefit us by increasing our power to act.

The *conatus* is a potency which requires human effort. According to Spinoza, ideas are active and prompt people to act. He explains that the failure to act may indicate an absence of insight. He says that insight into a man's relation to God is the initial step toward virtue. Virtue consists in the pursuit of knowledge and the understanding of adequate ideas. Spinoza sees rationality as an essential means of attaining the good life. Man reaches happiness through understanding. Happiness and well-being lie in the life of reason.

Spinoza describes perfection of the human mind in terms of its power of thinking and freedom in terms of not being controlled completely by external forces. We are free when the causes of our action are internal to us and we are unfree when those causes are external to us. Bondage means acting because of forces external to the actor or being moved by causes of which the person is unaware. We are not free to the extent that we act because something beyond our control causes us to act. When the cause of something lies in our own nature, it is a matter of the mind acting. When the cause is external to our nature, then we are passive and being acted upon. Things that happen to us tend to produce joy or sadness. It follows that people should attempt to understand the reasons they are affected by the outside world in the ways that they are affected. Reason helps individuals to understand the causes in the form of external forces that limit their power to act. Once understanding is achieved people are able to overcome their sadness. In addition, the act of understanding the cause or nature of anything naturally leads to joy.

Spinoza maintains that emotions may be the most serious threat to a person's freedom and that it takes a man of wisdom to break the chains that enslave him to his passions. An individual is capable of controlling his passions by attaining insight into the nature and causes of his emotions. A man should endeavor to free himself from his passions, or at the minimum try to restrain or moderate them, thus becoming an active autonomous person. If this freedom can be achieved, a person will be free in the sense that whatever happens to him results from his own nature rather than from things external to himself. Spinoza teaches that a man can moderate and restrain the affects via virtue. A person should free himself from reliance on the senses and imagination and rely as much as he can on his rational faculty. Liberation lies in acquiring knowledge which empowers the mind, thus making it less susceptible to external circumstances. Knowledge, virtue, power, and freedom are one.

Ethics, for Spinoza, is a matter of liberation from the bondage to passive affects through the cultivation of reason. He says that the mind is able to weaken the hold passions have over an individual. This is accomplished by acquiring adequate ideas of the affects. To reach higher intelligent expressions of human power, reason must regulate passion. As we gain more adequate understanding of the causes acting on us, our power (or freedom) increases. Such freedom is realizable through the exercise of reason and reflection. A person's goal is to attain a relative adequacy that will increase his powers of intellectual and physical self-determination in place of passive, self-enslaving passions. This involves acting to escape the constraints and to embrace the possibilities and necessitates an enactive enhancement of individual power and autonomy. The mind is active only insofar as it understands adequate ideas. This understanding is the basis of virtue. In fact, the effort to understand is the primary and sole foundation of virtue.

According to Spinoza, adequate ideas are formed in an orderly and rational manner in three stages including sense experience (and imagination), reason, and intuition. If a mind reaches the level of *scientia intuitiva* it realizes its actual nature and sees individual things for what they truly are. Understanding through this type of knowledge is under the aspect of eternity and in relation to God. Spinoza was optimistic with respect to the cognitive powers of human beings for understanding the nature of the individual human person and other organisms and their place in the natural order of the world. Spinoza explains that a person whose mind is made up mainly by adequate ideas participates more fully in eternity than a man whose mind is constituted largely by inadequate ideas. He says that a man's intellect is eternal as part of God's infinite intellect.

Genuine understanding of the universe is the form of a person's participation in the absolute and eternal God-substance. The human mind is part of the infinite intellect of God, and, when the mind knows, it is God who knows and who is known to the extent that he can be explained through the nature of the human mind. A person of higher understanding is aware of a certain eternal necessity of himself, of objects, and of God. As a result, he enjoys peace of mind and self-control.

Spinoza's free person experiences calmness of mind and experiences good and bad events with equanimity. By living under the guidance of reason, a person will enjoy the pleasure of self-contentment. He will concentrate on doing those things that are most important to him and he will take care of others. For Spinoza, virtue involves the seeking of one's own advantage. The virtue of courage is the desire of an individual to endeavor to preserve his own being according to the dictates of reason alone. In addition, nobility is the virtue of a person to attempt to help others and to be friends with them. Man is aware of his kinship with, and similarity to, others. Recognizing man's natural sociality, Spinoza states that it is natural to pursue the happiness of our fellow men.

According to Spinoza, the free individual does not fear eternal punishment nor does he expect eternal rewards in some after-life. He is not concerned with notions such as apocalypse, redemption, and so on. Such a man realizes that the mind (or soul) is not immortal in any personal sense but that it does have a particular type of eternity. The human mind, being part of the intellect of God, cannot be destroyed absolutely with the body. There is something of it that remains which is eternal. Although Spinoza holds a doctrine of personal identity, he does not hold a doctrine of personal immortality.

Spinoza provides the moral world with an immanent basis. His metaphysics and ethics are inextricably connected. He says that to act in accordance with our nature is to act virtuously. The purpose of his ethics is to free people to live in the world as it is without distracting themselves by appealing to a transcendent divine providence. In his ethical naturalism, ethical propositions are explainable in terms of natural propositions. Spinoza's goal was to bridge gaps and reconcile schisms such as God versus Nature, determinism versus freedom, fact versus value, mental versus physical, eternity versus temporality, reason versus passion, objective versus subjective, etc.

Spinoza explains mental phenomena as grounded in the objective natural world and moral values as rooted in the objective characteristics of the universe. He views the study of the mind and the study of ethics to be deeply intertwined—ethics is a function of the understanding mind. By nature, the domain of the mind is ethical in character.

Spinoza's ethics is organized around the search for the highest good, the achievement of the highest human perfection, which once attained will guarantee happiness. The good is whatever makes a person more perfect and it is up to each individual to evaluate or judge what is good and what is bad. For Spinoza, something is useful and, therefore, valuable if it increases a person's power of action. It is obvious that Spinoza's value theory is connected to his metaphysics. He says that if something agrees with our nature then it cannot be bad and that a useful thing is valuable in relation to a particular agent. Although value is relative to a man's essence as a rational being, it is also objectively valuable because it is grounded on a standard independent of subjective attitudes.

Although maintaining that goods are only valuable relative to particular individuals, Spinoza argues that some goods have value which does not change with the person or the circumstances. He differentiates between circumstantially valuable goods and non-circumstantially valuable goods. According to Spinoza, goods pertaining to the body can be authentically valuable and good, but what leads to understanding is certainly valuable and good. He says that knowledge of God is the mind's most important good. Knowledge of God is always useful and is thus non-circumstantially valuable. Whereas some knowledge is useful in some circumstances and for some persons but not for other persons, knowledge of God is always advantageous to every individual. Knowledge of God is knowledge of nature, including the principles, laws, and rules by which nature operates.

Politics

According to Spinoza, the state of nature is characterized by the primacy of the individual. Civil society arises when men recognize the advantages of society with respect to the enhancement of their power as individuals. Spinoza emphasizes that the individual retains his natural right when he enters civil society. These free individuals will comprise a harmonious society as long as men live according to the guidance of reason rather than according to their passion. In a society in which all persons live by the direction of reason there will be no need for a political authority to restrict people's actions. Unfortunately, human beings do not always live under the guidance of reason. It follows that a sovereign or state is necessary in order to ensure through the threat of force that individuals are protected from the unrestrained forceful pursuit of self-interest on the part of other individuals.

Spinoza teaches that the state must be deduced from the common nature of man. He sees the real purpose of the state as freedom. He conceives of the state as an expression of the rational order of the universe. As an institution, the state is the rational embodiment of checks upon the irrational power of the populace. Spinoza explains that sovereign authority is required to maintain stability for the sake of its citizens' potential flourishing. Holding that the origin and purpose of the state is security, he emphasizes that morality is not the concern of the state. The state has no moral foundation. It is devoid of normative principles. Spinoza understood that the scope of morality was deeper and wider than the scope of politics. The state comes into being because social order (i.e., peace) is a necessary condition for the exercise of individuals' power of self-preservation. A person is free to the degree that he rationally decides what ends are in his interest.

Spinoza explains that a person is free in society whenever the state is ruled by reason. In such a state, political freedom involves the least possible encroachment on personal freedom, including the exercise of one's judgment. Spinoza's prescriptive political philosophy suggests that state force be limited to providing peace and social order. Such a minimalist state would leave people free to pursue their own projects. The sovereign's power does not extend to all aspects of an individual's life.

For Spinoza, the proper objects of desire are: (1) to know things by their primary or first causes; (2) to control one's passions (or to acquire virtuous habits); and (3) to live one's life in safety, security, and physical well-being. The means of attaining the first two reside in the nature of man himself and depend solely upon the laws of human nature. Politics applies to only the third classification because the means to ensure security of life and conservation of the body lie mainly in external circumstances. This implies the need for a society with definite and uniform laws.

Morality is excluded from Spinoza's political theory. He understood that politics is not appropriate for the production of virtue. Morality surpasses the political. Politics is pertinent to providing security and physical well-being and not to ethical matters. Politics is concerned with peace and commodious living which are necessary, but not sufficient, conditions for attaining the good. However, their achievement is far removed from, and has little to do with, character development and substantive morality. According to Spinoza, political theory should not be concerned with morality and morality cannot be reduced to a matter of rights nor to the operation of the state, which comes about through social cooperation and agreement as a means of attaining social order.

Social contract, for Spinoza, is based on the desire for individual freedom. People desire a stable political community to provide a substantial degree of personal freedom, particularly regarding freedom to philosophize and on freedom of religious expression. Spinoza argues that the security and stability of society is enhanced by freedom of thought. He explains that individuals exercise their judgment by natural right and that no one, including the state, has the power to command the thoughts of another person.

Spinoza states that the expression should be limited only when it directly obstructs the main purpose of the state. It is only in the most extreme cases that the state has the right to restrict expression. It is permissible to express different and conflicting opinions up to the point of defiance of all law and order (i.e., sedition). It is acceptable to speak against particular state actions but not against the state's right to make and enforce laws. Spinoza explains that broad toleration of expression is a basic component of any social contract. According to his perfectionist concept of toleration, the more the state is tolerant, the more likely and more readily it will be for individuals to be tolerant in their lives. Spinoza's argument for tolerance is integral to his more comprehensive idea of human flourishing.

Spinoza maintains that the main threat to freedom comes from church ministers who depend upon fear and superstitions to gain and to keep power. He explains that some clergy want to use politics as a means for resolving theological disputes or for seeking dominance. He wanted to free the public square of clerical politician-preachers overwhelmed with their own holiness. Some clergy advance claims as a means to divide government and pave the way to their own ascendancy to power. Spinoza, like Epicurus, saw religion as a major source of the world's problems as religious claims and doctrinal differences often intensify into religious wars. He observes that legislation of beliefs was a major source of religious schisms. Schisms emerge from efforts of authorities to decide through law the intricacies of theological controversies. He also emphasizes the danger to public stability from the existence of a diversity of religious sects and ceremonial rites of worship. Spinoza wanted the state to have sufficient power to effectively battle the clergy and their various brands of intolerance. Desiring to remove religion as a disturbing factor in politics, Spinoza advocated the subordination of religion to politics. This, he said, would prevent sectarianism and the multiplication of religious battles.

Spinoza's goal was to divest the clergy of all political power by placing authority over the practice of religion in the hands of the state. He did not want to abolish religion but he did want to protect the state from the diverse judgments of the many. Spinoza suggests that the sovereign should have total dominance in all secular and spiritual public matters. The state is thus charged with keeping all members of society to the agreement of the social contract through its absolute powers with respect to public affairs. Spinoza emphasizes the need for the preservation of unity within the state. He thus calls for rights of the sovereign free of restriction so that the sovereign may be strong enough to protect individuals from both social and clerical intolerances.

Spinoza's position is that the state has the same absolute right to command regarding spiritual rights as it does with respect to temporal rights. By spiritual rights, Spinoza refers to outward observances of piety and external religious rites and not to the inward worship of God nor to piety itself. His goal is to secure freedom from speculative doctrines and ceremonial practices. He therefore places all questions regarding external ceremonies and rites in the hands of the state. Spinoza subordinates religious authority and activities to political authority. Outward religious practices encroach upon the beliefs and relationships of citizens and thus fall under state interests. Freedom of religious diversity is to be permitted among the citizens but this liberty is limited to private worship and belief. Spinoza's goal is to divorce politics from the traditional types of religious authority.

Spinoza argues for a minimal rational religion determined by the state. There is to be no church separate from the religion instituted by, and regulated by, the state. He had studied scripture in a similar way as he studied nature and concluded that the Bible and other religious texts were filled with speculative and inadequate views. He saw no legitimate purpose in arguing from authority, opinion, or superstition. Desiring a minimal number of theoretical propositions for religion, he looked for a form of rational religion that was in accord with the requirements of universal human morality. Spinoza concludes that the sovereign should require adherence to no more than a minimal creed that was neutral regarding competing sects. He therefore interprets and boils down all religions to the ideas of justice and charity. He maintained that just and kind behavior were to be the pillars of religious belief. Spinoza says that the only moral lesson that we should take from the Bible is to obey God, which he interprets to mean to love one's neighbor as oneself. The universal message of scripture is that the law of God commands only that we know and love God and take the actions necessary for achieving that condition.

According to Spinoza, to love one's neighbor is to respect his rights. By restricting the authority of organized religion to precise rules defined by the sovereign, Spinoza believes he has liberated reason from the perils of superstition without eradicating the valuable effects of faith. The universal covenant he suggests would take the place of various special covenants and would have been deduced from the principles of morality.

On the other hand, Spinoza says that inward worship of God would be exempt from the authority of the state. Inward piety belongs exclusively to the individual. He observes that a person's inward opinions and feelings are not directly available to the sovereign. It follows that the best approach for the sovereign is to establish the rule that religion is comprised only of justice and charity and that the rights of the sovereign in religious matters (as well as in secular ones) will simply pertain to actions.

Spinoza states that freedom of thought and speech must be sustained. No one can control or limit another person's thoughts. He adds that it is risky for the state to attempt to exercise rights over speech. It is also impossible to achieve. In addition, as an advocate of democracy, Spinoza contends that freedom of speech must be allowed in order to express the natural differences among men. Spinoza suggests a self-limitation of the sovereign regarding religious speech. The state's toleration of nonestablished religions would be viewed as a discretionary matter instead of as toleration of religious speech.

Spinoza preferred democracy over monarchy as the best form of government. He understood that democratic power was the best political foundation for the realization of individual freedom. It distributed power with respect to public affairs as widely as possible. Democracy is congruent with Spinoza's horizontal metaphysics. Democracy reflects the state of nature by restricting the right of elected officials to the amount of their individual power. In addition, the natural heterogeneity of human beings underpins the heterogeneity of their individual amounts of power. Democracy mirrors the state of nature as it recognizes in its structure the differences among individuals. Spinoza also says that it is proper to treat all citizens as equals because the power of each, in regard to the entire state, is negligible. His defense of democracy is a defense of the conditions that make philosophy possible. By philosophy he means the then-new materialist science and secular study. Spinoza wanted to preserve philosophy from the superstitious corruptions of competing organized religions. He did not want to confound philosophy and theology.

Recommended Reading

Allison, Henry. *Benedict de Spinoza: An Introduction*. New Haven, CT: Yale University Press, 1987.

Balibar, Etienne. *Spinoza and Politics*. London: Verso, 1998.

Bennett, Jonathan. *A Study of Spinoza's "Ethics."* Indianapolis, IN: Hackett, 1984.

Chappell, Vere, ed. *Baruch de Spinoza*. New York: Garland Publishing, 1992.

Curley, Edwin. *Spinoza's Metaphysics: An Essay in Interpretation*. Cambridg, MA: Harvard University Press, 1969.

Curley, Edwin, and Pierre-François Moreau, eds. *Spinoza: Issues and Directions*. Leiden, Neth.: E.J. Brill, 1990.

De Dijn, Herman. *Spinoza: The Way to Wisdom*. West Lafayette, IN: Purdue University Press, 1996.

Delahunty, R. J. *Spinoza*. London: Routledge & Kegan Paul, 1985.

Della Rocca, Michael. *Representation and the Mind-Body Problem in Spinoza*. Oxford: Oxford University Press, 1996.

Den Uyl, Douglas J. *Power, State and Freedom: An Interpretation of Spinoza's Political Philosophy*. Assen, Neth.: Van Gorcum, 1983.

Donagan, Alan. *Spinoza*. Chicago: University of Chicago Press, 1988.

Freeman, Eugene, and Maurice Mandelbaum, eds. *Spinoza: Essays in Interpretation*. LaSalle, IL: Open Court, 1975.

Garrett, Don, ed. *The Cambridge Companion to Spinoza*. Cambridge: Cambridge University Press, 1996.

Grene, Marjorie, ed. *Spinoza: A Collection of Critical Essays*. Garden City, NY: Doubleday/Anchor Press, 1973.

Grene, Marjorie, and Debra Nails, eds. *Spinoza and the Sciences*. Chicago: University of Chicago Press, 1986.

Hampshire, Stuart. *Spinoza*. London: Penguin, 1951.

Kennington, Richard, ed. *The Philosophy of Baruch Spinoza*. Washington, DC: Catholic University Press, 1980.

Lloyd, Genevieve. *Part of Nature: Self-Knowledge in Spinoza's Ethics.* Ithaca, NY: Cornell University Press, 1994.

———. *Spinoza and the "Ethics."* London: Routledge, 1996.

———, ed. *Spinoza Critical Assessments.* 4 vols. London: Routledge, 2001.

Mark, Thomas Carson. *Spinoza's Theory of Truth.* New York: Columbia University Press, 1972.

Mason, Richard. *The God of Spinoza: A Philosophical Study.* Cambridge: Cambridge University Press, 1997.

Nadler, Steven. *Spinoza: A Life.* Cambridge: Cambridge University Press, 1999.

Popkin, Richard. *Spinoza.* Oxford: One World, 2004.

Preus, J. Samuel. *Spinoza and the Irrelevance of Biblical Authority.* Cambridge and New York: Cambridge University Press, 2001.

Shanan, Robert, and J. I. Biro, eds. *Spinoza: New Perspectives.* Norman, OK: University of Oklahoma Press, 1978.

Smith, Steven B. *Spinoza, Liberalism and the Question of Jewish Identity.* New Haven, CT: Yale University Press, 1997.

———. *Spinoza's Book of Life.* New Haven, CT: Yale University Press, 2003.

Spinoza, Baruch. *Spinoza Opera.* 4 vols. Edited by Carl Gebhart. Heidelberg: Carl Winter, 1925.

———. *The Collected Works of Spinoza.* Vol. 1. Edited and translated by Edwin Curley. Princeton: Princeton University Press, 1985.

———. *Theological-Political Treatise.* Translated by Samuel Shirley. Leiden, Neth.: Brill, 1989.

———. *A Spinoza Reader: The Ethics and Other Works.* Edited and translated by Edwin Curley. Princeton, NJ: Princeton University Press, 1994.

———. *Baruch Spinoza: The Complete Works.* Edited by Michael L. Morgan and translated by Samuel Shirley. Indianapolis: Hackett, 2002.

Steinberg, Diane. *On Spinoza.* Belmont, CA: Wadsworth, 2000.

Verbeek, Theo. *Spinoza's Theologico-Political Treatise: Exploring the "Will of God."* London: Ashgate, 2003.

Wolfson, Harry Austryn. *The Philosophy of Spinoza.* 2 vols. Cambridge, MA: Harvard University Press, 1934.

Chapter 7

John Locke's Limited State

To understand political power right, and derive it from its original, we must consider what state all men are naturally in.

—John Locke

John Locke (1632-1704) connected with the long tradition of medieval political thought going back to Thomas Aquinas. His philosophical writings led to the great revolutions toward the end of the eighteenth century. Locke is America's intellectual Founding Father. Especially in his *A Letter Concerning Toleration* (1689) and *The Second Treatise of Civil Government* (1690), he created what would become the philosophical source for the founding principles of the United States as expressed in The Declaration of Independence and in the Constitution of the United States. In his writings, Locke established a theory that reconciled the liberty of the individual citizen with political order.

Epistemology

In order to understand Locke, we must begin with his epistemology as put forth in his *An Essay Concerning Human Understanding* (1690), a work that took him twenty years to complete. The underpinning philosophical foundations of Locke's political thought are found in this work in which he discusses the nature of the world as it is known to us and the ways whereby we come to know it. Locke set out to inquire into the nature, origin, sources, certainty, and extent (or limits) of human knowledge. In this essay, Locke's interest centers on the nature of reality, God, and the grounds of our knowledge of them.

Locke agrees with Descartes's *cogito* that the existence of the self is implied in every state of consciousness. The notion that "I think, therefore, I am" implies the prior certainty of consciousness (i.e., that consciousness precedes consciousness of objects). What both mean to say is that every idea of which a person is conscious is an affirmation of his existence as the subject of that experience. Although consciousness is an axiom, it is not the primary one that the above inversion appears to make it. The irreducible foundational axiom is that there must first be something that exists of which a person can be aware. It would have been better if Locke had written that consciousness, the second axiom, is the faculty of perceiving that which exists. There must first be something. If nothing exists, then there is nothing about which to be conscious.

Expressing humility about what men are capable of knowing, Locke states that our knowledge extends no further than our ideas. He teaches that our knowledge is bounded and that some things exceed the mind's comprehension. According to Locke, knowledge is restricted to ideas, no ideas are innate, and ideas originate from sense experience. The mind is *tabula rasa* (blank sheet) until a person experiences the external world. Without experience, nothing is written on the "tablets" of the mind. Being originally blank, the human mind gains knowledge through the use of the five senses and a process of reflection. It is data from the external world that triggers the operations of the mind.

A notable exponent of empiricism, Locke attacks Descartes's doctrine of innate ideas and ridicules the view that ideas can be antecedent to experience. Ideas produced by sensations are in the mind and are indications in us of an external reality. A sensation is the product of a man's experience with the external world. Locke makes sensations (like tall, brown, and solid) prior to percepts. He says that the mind brings the sensations together to form the percept "tree." Attributes, rather than entities, are thus primary for Locke. Locke explains that when we observe an object, ideas enter our minds single file, and that ideas of different qualities of an object enter through different senses.

Sensations tell us about things and processes in the external world. Locke says that ideas are caused by the real world but they do not permit us to see that world as it is in itself. External experiences, called sensations, give us ideas of supposed external objects. He explains that we know ideas but we really do not know objects or things-in-themselves. What is known by one's mind is not the thing-in-itself but rather the representation of the thing that the mind was able to assemble. Holding a representationalist theory of perception, Locke contends that the mind perceives ideas and ideas are caused by and represent the objects that cause them. He states that consciousness is the perception of what passes in a man's own mind and what the mind grasps is not reality but ideas of reality. It follows that we are aware of the idea that is between consciousness and existence.

Locke speaks of all the objects of understanding (i.e., the ideas) as being in the mind. He uses the term, idea, so vaguely and broadly that it includes, at various times, sensations, percepts, representations, images, concepts, and notions. Locke explains that there are innate faculties through which the mind perceives, remembers, and combines ideas that come to it from without. He says the mind is also capable of desiring, deliberating, and willing. Our faculties of knowing are thus innate although our ideas are not. The processes which transform the material provided by the senses into knowledge are activities of the mind which themselves cannot be reduced to ideas. These mental activities are the source of a new class of ideas. These are ideas of an internal reality—ideas about the activity of our minds which are the product of reflection. Ideas of reflection involve perceiving, thinking, believing, reasoning, knowing, doubting, willing, and so on.

In Locke's theory of knowledge, which is limited to mental content, it is impossible to prove the actual existence of supposed objects. Locke admits the existence of substances but claims they are unknowable. By asserting that phenomena alone are knowable, he distanced the realm of the known with the realm of the knower. Locke's theory of knowledge is isolated from reality and unable to break through the phenomenalism in which it is encompassed to reach metaphysical data. For example, Locke refers to and uses the principle of causality while denying its validity because it exists in the real world of real objects and beings outside of one's mind. We could say that Locke is an empirical phenomenalist.

Locke's notion of ideas as intermediary and representational ultimately became for Kant the phenomenal world. Locke's view led to the skepticism of Hume and Kant's two-world dualism. Locke unintentionally opened the door and paved the way for Kant's epistemological dualism, which constituted an all-out attack on the mind's ability to know reality.

According to Locke, there are two types of experience (sensation and reflection) and ideas are either simple or complex. Simple ideas are obtained from sense experience and through reflection the mind can combine simple ideas into complex ones. Reflection tells us about the operations of our own minds. We cannot have the experience of reflection until we have already had the experience of sensation. Simple ideas comprise the source of the raw materials out of which our knowledge is constructed. Complex ideas are built by the mind as a compound of simple ideas. The mind is able to bring ideas together, combine them, and abstract from them.

Both sensation and reflection can produce simple ideas. For sensation, simple ideas are referred to as sensible qualities and can be divided into primary and secondary ones. According to Locke, primary qualities really do exist in the objects themselves and secondary qualities produce ideas that have no counterpart in the objects. He distinguishes between the primary qualities, which are objective, and the secondary qualities, which are subjective. Primary or mathematically determinable qualities of an object actually exist in the world and secondary qualities do not exist in objects as they exist in ideas. Primary qualities include solidity, extension, figure, motion or rest, and number. Examples of secondary qualities are colors, sounds, tastes, odors, and so on. Locke sees these qualities as attributes as stuck into a substratum which he calls "something I know not what." The substratum is a substance in which qualities are said to subsist. Of course, we know that this view is wrong and that an entity is simply the sum of all of its attributes.

Complex ideas are said to be either ideas of substances or ideas of modes. Substances are independent existences such as God, angels, human beings, animals, plants, and constructed things. Mixed modes are dependent existences such as moral and mathematical ideas and the languages of religion, politics, and culture. Locke explains that ideas of substances are compounded from simple ideas but which are intended to represent real objects rather than abstractions. These ideas of substances name the objects of our concern as the underlying realities that support the qualities known to us through sensations. Locke says that these ideas of substances are real because they are combinations of simple ideas as really co-existing and united in things outside of us. On the other hand, mixed modes refer to abstract ideas that have no counterpart in external reality and have only a purely intellectual existence. Mixed modes include ideas put together at the pleasure of the mind. Example of mixed modes are ideas of justice, obligation, liberty, and so on. Locke explains that mixed modes are identical with archetypes within our own minds and created by our minds out of simple ideas.

In a similar manner, Locke goes on to complete his classification of ideas with ideas of relation. Locke explains that knowledge involves relations and relations are the work of the mind. He gives the example of the notion of moral relations arising from the idea of God compounded with ideas of pleasure and pain. He explains that from the constant association of pleasure and pain with our actions we recognize rules of behavior that specify what is good and bad. Locke will later go on to determine rights from the relations that exist between God and man.

According to Locke, we know that we exist with the highest degree of certainty and we know that God exists with the second highest degree of certainty. The notion of God is an idea of substance constructed from simple ideas such as existence, knowledge, duration, pleasure, pain, happiness, power, and infinity. The idea of God is deduced from a person's intuitive knowledge that he exists as a conscious human being and that something greater must have caused him. By inference, he has the idea of an eternal, most knowing, most powerful being of pure consciousness. The idea of God as creator, the first efficient cause of everything that exists, leads Locke to the conclusion that God is the legislator of the rules of behavior. Locke's notion of the moral good is inextricably tied to the idea of a God who is greatly concerned with our happiness. He says that through our reason we can discover the moral rules that conform to God's law. Although we cannot know the mind and reasons of God or the ultimate why and wherefore of things, we can understand the how of things as revealed in the processes of the world.

With respect to free will, Locke explains that the mind has the power to suspend the execution and satisfaction of its desires and is free to consider, examine, and weigh them alongside others. Men can voluntarily control their thinking. They can choose to employ or to withhold their conceptual faculty. Locke says that people are able to control their passions. Because men can exercise their freedom by thinking about the consequences of their actions and then deciding what to do, they can be held morally and legally responsible for their actions. Locke views each person as a free moral agent who possesses sufficient reason to guide and order his own life.

Political and Ethical Theory

Locke's *First Treatise of Government* was a polemical work refuting the doctrine of the Divine and Absolute Right of Kings that was supported by Sir Robert Filmer. Locke systematically attacks Filmer's thesis that royal power is similar to parental authority, that is predicated upon, and descended from, the power of the first king, Adam.

Locke's *The Second Treatise of Government* contains the key elements in Locke's political theory, including the state of nature, natural law, natural rights, social contract, government consent, and the right of property ownership. It is in this work that Locke explains that the function of legitimate civil government is to preserve the rights of life, liberty, health, and property of citizens and to prosecute and punish those who violate the rights of others. The *Second Treatise* is by far Locke's most influential work.

Locke's political theory builds upon and improves upon the work of Thomas Hobbes (1588-1679). Hobbes maintained that man is determined to do what he does by the passions innate in his person. Rejecting free will, he views reason as a calculating mechanism sparked into action by the passions. The biological passions, especially the drive for self-preservation, provide the force that incites all human behavior. When men are outside of civil society and have no legal system it is proper for a man to do whatever he does. Hobbes thought that people are driven to act and will act according to their passions. He thought that a state of war would, by necessity, encourage people to form social units and to form social contracts through which peace would be maintained. He says that in civil society the unlimited rights all men have will have to be forfeited. Hobbes recommends an absolute monarchy in which only positive laws exist. He believed that warlike conditions required absolute rule to establish law and attain peace.

For Locke, the state of nature is not Hobbes's "war of all against all." Unlike Hobbes, Locke does not equate the state of nature and the state of war. Locke refers to the original state of nature as the great natural community of mankind. This state of nature is a state of freedom where men are able to order their actions and dispose of their possessions as they see fit. He maintained that the original state of nature was generally pleasant and characterized by reason and tolerance. In this pre-political society men are free, independent, and the equal of every other human being. The state of nature is one of peace, good will, mutual assistance, and preservation in which all power and jurisdiction is reciprocal. In this state, there is no natural superior or inferior and a man must protect himself and his own the best he can. Natural freedom derives from natural equality.

Locke explains that men in the state of nature know the moral law through reason and that the state of liberty is not a state of license. He says that the natural liberty of man is to have only the law of nature for his rule. The state of nature is not devoid of law. Everything that is ever right or wrong is so eternally. A person's freedom and actions are regulated by natural law which obliges everyone. Reason teaches all mankind that, being all-equal and independent, no one ought to harm another in his life, health, liberty, or possessions. Nature makes every man an executioner of the law with authority to punish wrongdoers. Locke observed that men have an innate desire for self-preservation and happiness. Locke says that everyone is bound to preserve himself and that natural man, being social, ought to preserve the rest of mankind. The law of nature needs an executor. Because there are aggressors, even in the state of nature, this executive power is given to every man who has the right and obligation to restrain offenders and to protect the innocent. In the state of nature, everyone has the executive power of the law of nature and is obliged to preserve himself and to preserve all mankind. An aggressor is to be treated as an individual unfit to associate with human beings and as a threat to all mankind. Despite the presence of aggressors, we can safely say that Locke's state of nature is not nearly as violent as Hobbes's. In Locke's state of nature, a sometimes precarious peace prevails.

The state of nature involves men living together according to reason without a common superior with authority to judge among them. In the state of nature there is an absence of a common judge and the absence of any law except the law of nature. A state of peace exists when men live together and there is no use of force without right. The state of war involves the use of force without right, justice, or authority. In civil society there exists a common judge with authority to enforce civil laws. Both in the state of nature and in civil society sometimes a state of peace may dominate and at other times a state of war may prevail. Whenever force is instituted, a state of war exists. They can occur in either the state of nature or in civil society.

The state of nature involves the state of war because of the passionate nature of man. According to Locke, the moral law, the law of God, is always valid but it is not always kept. Natural justice exists even if the state does not exist. Moral rights and duties are intrinsic and prior to positive law. Positive laws add nothing to the ethical nature of conduct but simply provides a mechanism for effective enforcement. The moral rules established by God are valid whether observed by government or not. Locke says that men recognize that the laws of nature constitute moral obligations for them.

Locke teaches that morality needs a lawgiver and that the lawgiver is God. If one obeys or breaks God's law then pleasure and pain, respectively, will be experienced in this world and in the next life. Locke believes that ethics can be made a deductive and demonstrable science like mathematics. He contended that his political theory was underpinned by self-evident truths of a demonstrable science of ethics. He says that morality is scientific, rational, provable, and a deductive certainty. Unfortunately, he never gave the proof for this deductive ethics. Nowhere does he endeavor to deduce such a systematic code.

Locke explains that natural rights exist in the state of nature before the introduction of civil government. He interpreted natural law as a claim to innate, indefeasible rights inherent in each individual. These natural rights are attributes of the individual person. He says that natural law implies natural rights and correlative duties. Locke explains that all individuals are endowed by their creator with a right to life, liberty, and estate. Men are all the workmanship of one omnipotent and omniscient Maker. Because men are God's property to be morally used by God for his purposes, it is wrong to injure God's property. It follows that Locke's ultimate validation of rights is based on religion. All human beings have natural rights inherent in their created nature and have moral obligations to respect the rights of others.

The purpose of natural rights is to sanction the sovereignty of the choices of each individual person. Individual rights imply a sphere where one is free from force. Locke understood that only individuals think, judge, will, and act. He knew that reason is an attribute of the individual and that each individual has free-will control of his reason. Locke also realized that men are metaphysically equal, not in their talents, but in the fact that a man's life is a gift from God and that he has right to use his life as he chooses. Rights are possessed by all men by virtue of being human and there is no right to violate rights. Locke had the insight that, in order to discern what human nature requires in a social context, it was necessary to analyze human nature independently of that social context.

Locke recognized that the natural right to freedom is necessary for the possibility of moral action. It follows that the purpose of natural rights is to protect individual autonomy and accountability. He saw that it is illegitimate to use coercion against a man who does not first undertake the use of force. It follows that in the state of nature all men equally have the legitimate right to punish transgressors. It is proper to use force in self-defense against unjust violence. In other words, victims can enforce the law of nature in the state of nature. When the law of nature is violated the result is a state of war in which an unjust aggressor has violated someone's rights.

Locke explains that the defect of the state of nature is that it has no organization to give effect to the rules of right. He says that there are deficiencies in a system that must depend upon self-execution of the natural law. It follows that men would seek an institutional device that would make more secure the rights they already possess. The political power of such an institutional device would be derived from the transfer of individuals to enforce the law of nature. Locke says that civil power can have no right except as derived from the individual right of each man to protect himself and his property. He explains that the individual does not surrender his substantive natural rights, but only his right of executing the law of nature. Men are said to leave the state of nature when they voluntarily give their natural right to self-defense to a common public authority. The power of the government is nothing except the natural power of each person resigned into the hands of the community. This is a better way of protecting natural rights than the self-help to which each person is naturally entitled. Locke states that any number of persons can make a compact to leave the state of nature. He explains that the individual is driven into political society by inconveniences of his natural conditions rather than by nature itself. Men are motivated to form a civil society by their desire to avoid the annoyances of the state of nature and not by the fear of destruction. A government might better guard natural justice and avoid the inconveniences that disorder men's properties in the state of nature.

Civil society originates when, for the better administration of the law, people agree to delegate that function. In order to acquire mutual protection, men place the retaliatory use of force under established, settled, objective, known law interpreted by an impartial judge. In addition, the combined force of individuals helps to overcome the strength of rights violators. Men form into societies in order to have the united strength of the entire society to secure and defend their properties and to have standard rules by which everyone may know what is properly his. Power is needed to back and support these standard rules, to give them due execution, and to punish the crimes committed against them. Of course, the power is limited by the purposes for which it was made.

The law should be received and permitted by common consent to be the standard of right and wrong and the common measure to settle all controversies. In order to have objective administration of the law, society requires a known and impartial judge with authority to determine all differences according to the established law. Locke explains that it is unreasonable for men to be judges in their own cases because self-interest will be apt to make them partial to themselves and their friends.

Locke's social contract theory sees the establishment of a government as a two-step process. The original compact by which men incorporate into society is one to form a civil society. Once this society is established, the people must then proceed to set up a government. Civil society is derived from the consent of its members. No man, without his consent, can properly be subjected to the political authority of another. Through the social contract, men transfer to the newly created community the power to execute the natural law which is the power they held in the state of nature. The people are the parties to the social compact, with each person agreeing with all the others to form one society. Locke states that unanimity is necessary to form the social compact to make an individual a member of civil society. Consent to join a community is binding and cannot be withdrawn. Anyone who refuses to join may go his own way and provide for himself elsewhere.

Locke says that by consenting to the agreement to form a political body, each man obligates himself to acquiesce to majority rule. Once an individual has agreed to the original contract he is bound thereafter to accept the decisions of the majority. Why is it that in the original contract unanimous consent is required and in subsequent acts of government only majority approval is necessary? Can't the majority occasionally exploit its greater power to violate individual rights?

The principle of majority rule does not have the immediate and obvious validity that Locke thought it had. Perhaps he considered the establishment of a government as less important than the original agreement that makes a civil society. Of course, he did argue that an individual's rights are less severely threatened by majority rule than by monarchist absolutism. He wanted political society to be constructed so that it would be unable to oppress its citizens. Locke attributes no special wisdom to the majority and seems to base his argument on expediency and the law of the greater force. In a democracy the majority will have the greater force and will prevail.

Locke furthers the fiction of a social contract with the additional fictions of unanimous consent and tacit consent. He explains that if anyone accepts the benefits of a government he has tacitly consented to the conditions the government imposes on him. Locke understood that most people live under a government that they never explicitly authorized to make decisions for them but have given their tacit consent. He says that a government is legitimate because its power derived from the people who gave their consent at its formation and that any person who is born within a particular government and accepts the protection supplied by it gives tacit consent as to the government's legitimacy.

Locke realizes that the main powers of a government ought to be separated because it may be too great a temptation for the same individuals who have the power of making laws to also have the power to execute them. He explains that legislative power is superior to executive power and that the power of the government must be limited by law. Limited rule is justified under a government that gains its authority from the people and holds its power in trust for their benefit. Being responsible to the people, the government's power is limited by moral law and by constitutional traditions and conventions. Locke states that the legislature should be a representative body subject to periodic re-election. He says that federative power, as a member of the international community, should be in the same hands as executive power which achieves peace, order, and security of property. According to Locke, the protection of property is the principal business of the government because there is a natural right to property that antedates the establishment of civil society.

Private Property

The survival of each person requires that he be able to use material objects to sustain his life. Because God wants each individual person to live and prosper, he instituted the right to property as a corollary to the right to life. Locke's supposition is that God gave the earth and its fruits to all men in common. It follows that in the state of nature property was common in that every person had the right to gain subsistence from whatever nature provided. Originally, nobody had a private domain exclusive of the rest of mankind. God not only gave the world to men in common, he also gave them reason to make use of it. The problem that Locke faced was to explain how commonly available resources can become legitimate private property to the exclusion of the right of other men. Locke employs the principle of individuation in the world to explain how collective property can become individual private property. He says that a person transfers his individuality into matter through his own labor. This individuates and decommunalizes property.

Private property does not and cannot come about by universal consent. According to Locke, natural man enjoys property in his own person which is the foundation of all other property. This concept of self-ownership is the cornerstone of individualism and personal freedom. Every man owns not only his own person but also his own labor. It follows that people can legitimately turn common property into private property by mixing their labor with it, thereby using and improving it. Because individuals mixed their bodies in the form of their labor with unowned (free) resources, they created something new that was their property. What a person does when he applies his labor to a natural object is to endow it with certain attributes belonging to one's own mode of existence. The Lockean view is that the quality of the owner's very personality is embodied in his property. The right to private property arises because by labor man can extend his own personality into the objects created. This natural right to private property exists even in the primitive society of the state of nature. The right to private property precedes civil law and is grounded in natural moral law.

Nature itself severely limits property in the state of nature. The natural fact of spoilage drastically limits property in the state of nature and acts as a type of rule to maintain a fair distribution of goods in the state of nature. This leads Locke to proclaim that spoilage limits the right of clear and exclusive acquisition in the state of nature. Private property is thus limited to as much as anyone can make use of before it spoils. Men should not allow things to go to waste in the state of nature. We could say that nature has put both a moral and a practical limit on the amount of property that anyone can accumulate. The limit is not defined by the amount of what is owned but only by the consequences of the ownership. As long as nothing spoils in one's possession, it makes no difference how much property he owns. Property ownership is thus qualified to as much as anyone can make use of to any advantages of life before it spoils. This is known as the "Lockean proviso."

Locke believed that greater productivity of some would raise the general standard of living. He says that a person is wrong to think that a man deprives others by enclosing land and cultivating it for his own use. It follows that all his neighbors benefit because cultivated land is more productive. The poor frequently gain as an unintended consequence of the acquisitive actions of others. Because the productive use of resources by one person tends to enrich everyone, we could say that men's interests are not in conflict and that wealth is not a static quantity—one man's gain is also everyone else's gain.

Locke recognized that spoilage is a necessary, applicable, and effective means toward fair distribution only in the case of a scarcity of perishable goods. The invention of money renders the accumulation of property essentially harmless and avoids the disadvantages inherent in the original natural limits to property ownership in the state of nature. The invention of money, which does not spoil, made it desirable and reasonable for a person to produce more than was required for his family's immediate needs (i.e., more than they could consume before it spoiled). Men could exchange money for perishable and other goods. There would be no limit to the private acquisition of wealth if held in the form of money. Without money, a person had no incentive to expand his holdings and produce a surplus.

Money came into existence through a natural mutual consent process in the state of nature. Through this process the most durable and easily tradable commodity ultimately becomes acceptable as a money commodity. Locke's theory of the origins of social institutions provided the framework for his consent theory of money. Money allows the more talented, rational, and industrious to create more, to accumulate the products of their labor, and to increase their wealth relative to others. According to Locke, money makes possible a benevolent form of property accumulation that enriches some without making others poorer.

Locke thought that labor was the major creator of economic value but that the market or relative value or the price of an object depended upon its usefulness and scarcity rather than the amount of labor embodied in it. In Locke's system, one earned property through his own efforts but the value of that property was determined by the market. It follows that Locke's writings implied no theory of labor exploitation. There is no evidence that Locke believed there would be a relationship between the amount of labor that goes into a product and its market price.

Locke explains that money so transformed the conditions of the state of nature that it was no longer desirable for men to live together without greater protection for their possessions. Lockean man therefore quits the state of nature and forms into civil society for the protection of his life, liberty, and estate. Locke sees the economy as logically prior to government and explains that government arises to remedy inconveniences that occur in the state of nature. The purposes of the government are to protect property, to keep order, and to provide a peaceful environment in which each person can freely pursue his own ends. Locke says that some government regulation of trade is necessary to protect and foster commercial interests. Here he is talking about procedural rather than substantive regulation. Permissible regulation for Locke includes contract enforcement, dispute adjudication, and the registration of deeds and titles. As an advocate of free markets, he is against the regulation of interest rates on both economic and moral grounds. Locke's reflections on the interest rate show that he is strongly against fixing the rate of interest by law.

Tyranny and Toleration

At the end of the *Second Treatise* Locke speaks about the nature of illegitimate governments and the conditions under which rebellion is legitimate and appropriate. He says that an illegitimate civil government violates the natural rights of its citizens and puts itself into a state of war with them. Whenever legislation attempts to take away or destroy people's property or reduces them to slavery the government puts itself into a state of war with the people. In such cases Locke defended the moral right of revolution to resist tyranny.

In his writings on toleration, Locke teaches that religious persecution by the state is wrong and that the use of force to get people to hold certain beliefs is illegitimate. He says that the persecution of religious diversity generates turmoil and that religion should be treated as a purely private and individual matter. Churches are said to be voluntary private organizations with equal legitimacy before the law. Boundaries separating church and state should be fixed and immovable. A secular state provides for peace, order, and safety. Public force can protect life and property but it cannot persuade one's conscience. Eternal salvation cannot be forwarded through coercive measures. Government force must be separated from the mind—ideas cannot be forced.

Locke says that because the mind is fallible we ought to tolerate one another's opinions. Religion is a matter of faith and faith is a matter of inner conviction. The purpose of religion is to help people attain salvation in the hereafter. He explains that "social justice" is not a concern of the church but rather is the business of the civil society only. Locke contends that religion is entirely outside the jurisdiction of the state but he does also say that atheists and Catholics are not to be tolerated! The exception to his support of religious toleration with regard to atheists is based on the idea that the existence of the state depends on a contract, and the obligation of that contract (like all moral law) depends upon the will of God. Locke explains that promises, covenants, and oaths, which constitute the bounds of civil society, can have no hold on atheists. He is also concerned that members of the Catholic Church are potentially dangerous and may pose an additional threat to the social order.

Recommended Reading

Aaron, Richard. *John Locke*. Oxford: Oxford University Press, 1937.

Ashcraft, Richard. "Locke's State of Nature: Historical Fact or Moral Fiction." *American Political Science Review* 62 (1968): 898–915.

———. *Locke's Two Treatises of Government*. London: Allen and Unwin, 1987.

Ayers, Michael. *Locke: Epistemology and Ontology*, 2. London: Routledge, 1991.

Cherno, M. "Locke on Property: A Reappraisal." *Ethics* (October 1957).

Cranston, Maurice. *Locke*. London: Longmans, Green and Company, 1961.

Czajkoroski, Casimir J. *The Theory of Private Property in John Locke's Political Philosophy*. Notre Dame, IN: Edwards Brothers, Inc., 1941.

Dunn, John. "Consent in the Political Theory of John Locke." *The Historical Journal* 10 (1967): 153–82.

———. "Justice and Locke's Political Theory." *Political Studies* 16 (1968): 68–87.

———. *The Political Thought of John Locke*. Cambridge: Cambridge University Press, 1969.

———. *Locke*. New York: Oxford University Press, 1984.

Gibson, James. *Locke's Theory of Knowledge and Its Historical Relations*. Cambridge: Cambridge University Press, 1968.

Glenn, Gary D. "Inalienable Rights and Locke's Argument for Limited Government: Political Implications of a Right to Suicide." *Journal of Politics* 46 (1984): 80–105.

Gough, J. W. *Locke's Political Philosophy.* Oxford: Clarendon Press, 1950.

Grant, Ruth. *John Locke's Liberalism.* Chicago: University of Chicago Press, 1987.

Hamilton, W. H. "Property—According to Locke." *Yale Law Journal* (April 1931).

Hobbes, Thomas. *Leviathan.* Edited by C.B. Macpherson. Baltimore: Penguin Books, [1651] 1975.

Hundert, E. J. "Market Society and Meaning in Locke's Political Philosophy." *Journal of the History of Philosophy* 15 (1977): 33–44.

Johnston, H. "Locke's Leviathan." *Modern schoolman* 26, (1948/49): 201-210.

Jolley, Nicholas. *Locke, His Philosophical Thought.* Oxford: Oxford University Press, 1999.

Kendall, Willmoore. *John Locke and the Doctrine of Majority Rule.* Urbana: University of Illinois Press, 1941.

———. "John Locke Revisited." *The Intercollegiate Review* 2 (January-February 1966): 217–34.

Krause, John L. *John Locke: Empiricist, Atomist, Conceptualist, and Agnostic.* Philosophical Library, 1969.

Lamprecht, Sterling. *Moral and Political Philosophy of John Locke.* New York: Columbia University Press, 1918.

Lemos, R. M. "Locke's Theory of Property." *Interpretations* 5 (1975): 226–44.

Leyden, W. von. "John Locke and Natural Law." *Philosophy* 31 (January 1956): 23–35.

Locke, John. *Essays on the Law of Nature.* Edited by W. von Leyden. Oxford: Clarendon Press, 1954.

———. *Locke's Two Treatises of Civil Government.* Edited by Peter Laslett. 2nd ed. Cambridge: Cambridge University Press, 1960.

———. *An Essay Concerning Human Understanding.* Amherst, NY: Prometheus Books, [1689] 1989.

———. *Two Treatises of Government.* Edited by Peter Laslett. Cambridge: Cambridge University Press, [1690] 1989.

Lowe, E. J. *Locke on Human Understanding.* London: Routledge Publishing Co., 1995.

MacPherson, C. B. *The Political Theory of Possessive Individualism: Hobbes to Locke.* Oxford: Clarendon Press, 1962.

Marshall, John. *John Locke: Resistance, Religion and Responsibility.* Cambridge University Press, 1994.

Marshall, Paul. "John Locke: Between God and Mammon." *Canadian Journal of Political Science* 12:1 (1979): 73–96.

Mendus, Susan. *Locke on Toleration in Focus.* London: Routledge Publishing Co., 1991.

Neilson, F. "Locke's Essays on Property and Natural Law." *American Journal of Economics and Sociology* (April 1951).

Riley, Patrick. "Locke on 'voluntary agreement' and political power." *Western Political Quarterly* 29 (1976): 136–45.

Rowen, H. H. "Second Thought on Locke's First Treatise (Confusion of Property and Political Power)." *Journal of the History of Ideas* (January 1956).

Ryle, Gilbert. *Locke on the Human Understanding.* Oxford University Press, 1933.

Schochet, Gordon, ed. *Life, Liberty and Property: Essays on Locke's Political Ideas.* Belmont, CA: Wadsworth, 1971.

Schouls, Peter. *Reasoned Freedom: John Locke and the Enlightenment.* Ithaca, NY: Cornell University Press, 1992.

Seliger, Martin. *The Liberal Politics of John Locke*. New York: Frederick A. Praeger, 1969.

Simmons, A. John. *The Lockean Theory of Rights*. Princeton, NJ: Princeton University Press, 1992.

Simon, W. M. "John Locke: Philosophy and Political Theory." *American Political Science Review* (June 1951).

Strauss, Leo. "Locke's Doctrine of Natural Law." *American Political Science Review* (June 1958).

Tipton, I. C. *Locke on Human Understanding: Selected Essays*. Oxford: Oxford University Press, 1977.

Tully, James. *A Discourse on Property*. Cambridge: Cambridge University Press, 1980.

———. *An Approach to Political Philosophy: Locke in Contexts*. Cambridge: Cambridge University Press, 1993.

Vaughn, Karen I. "John Locke and the Labor Theory of Value." *Journal of Libertarian Studies* 2, 4 (Winter 1979): 311–26.

———. *John Locke, Economist and Social Scientist*. Chicago, IL: University of Chicago Press, 1980.

Webb, T. E. *The Intellectualism of John Locke*. Dublin: np, 1857.

Wood, Neal. *The Politics of Locke's Philosophy*. Berkeley: University of California Press, 1983.

Woolhouse, R. S. *Locke's Philosophy of Science and Knowledge*. New York: Barnes and Noble, 1971.

Yolton, John. "Locke on the Law of Nature." *Philosophical Review* (October 1958).

———. *John Locke: Problems and Perspectives*. Cambridge: Cambridge University Press, 1969.

———. *Locke and the Compass of Human Understanding: A Selective Commentary on the "Essay."* Cambridge: Cambridge University Press, 1970.

Zuckert, Michael P. *Natural Rights and the New Republicanism*. Princeton, NJ: Princeton University Press, 1994.

Chapter 8

Turgot on Progress and Political Economy

There is no need to prove that each individual is the only competent judge of the most advantageous use of his lands and of his labour. He alone has the particular knowledge without which the most enlightened man could only argue blindly. He learns by repeated trials, by his successes, by his losses, and he acquires a feeling for it which is much more ingenious than the theoretical knowledge of the indifferent observer because it is stimulated by want.

—A. R. J. Turgot

Anne-Robert-Jacques Turgot (1727–1781) was a major political and intellectual figure in pre-revolutionary France. He was a man of wide-ranging intellectual interests and is considered to be a symbol or exemplar of the Enlightenment. A. R. J. Turgot was a well-respected social philosopher and political economist despite having written no books. He was a man of letters who was actively involved in pubic life. Turgot's breadth of interest, enormous erudition, and powers of analysis and synthesis were of the highest order.

Although Turgot's father was a government official, his family expected the young Turgot to enter the Church and become a priest. He enrolled in a seminary and became an Abbé but ultimately joined the royal bureaucracy first as a regional administrator as Intendant of Limoges and later as Comptroller-General (i.e., Minister of Finance) of France. Originally he was apparently destined for a clerical and academic career, but in 1751 he decided to turn from theological to legal studies and to enter a career in royal administration that entailed administrative and judicial services.

Progress

Turgot had a philosophical historian's interest in social dynamics, social change, development, evolution, and progress. In his works on philosophical history, Turgot exhibits a systematic and scientific view of society. Two of the main sources of Turgot's ideas on history and progress are the two public discourses he delivered in Latin at the opening and closing of the Sorbonne in 1750 when we has twenty-three years of age. To these he added his 1751 discourses on universal history and a project on political geography. It was after these discourses in 1751 that he decided against ordination in the Church.

Turgot begins by praising the role of divine beneficence and knowledge in human progress but moves on to extol the qualities of human nature that lead to advancement. He saw the Supreme Being not as an interventionist God, but rather as Prime Mover. Turgot viewed God not as an immanent Deity, but instead as a First Cause. Early on, he speaks about the benefits of Christianity to the progress of mankind. He noted that Christianity was the moving spirit of mankind's progress since the fall of the Roman Empire. However, Turgot mainly discussed the secular causes and stages of mankind's progress. His writings are a mixture of Christianity and humanism with greater emphasis on the latter.

Turgot saw human progress as rooted in human faculties, motivations, will, and fixed natural law. He viewed progress as a basic law of the universe that did not require divine intervention—man progresses under his own power. Turgot's ideas of world history and progress lay far outside and beyond Biblical teachings. In essence, Turgot discerned that man must learn to adjust and to adapt to the natural laws of the universe. The starting point for the human mind is nature as it is. Man's problem then is to discover the fundamental principles that underpin the workings of the world. To do this involves the study of the processes of causation through which the past causes the present and the past and present together cause the future. All ages are linked by a series of causes and effects which connects the present state of the world with all those states that have come before it. For Turgot, progress was the inevitable consequence of historical development and, at the same time, the creation of the human will acting with an understanding of the past.

Turgot believed in progress and in the perfectibility of man. The human mind, including the exercise of reason and volition, has the potential for progression. He predicted the future of reason and the inevitable advancement of the human mind. He discussed man's ability to accumulate experience by receiving impressions from the outside world, reflect upon them, combine them, and improve upon them. For Turgot, man is created by God, is subject to Lockean epistemology, and has the capacity to become a civilized moral person. He saw humanity progressing slowly but somewhat steadily toward greater perfection. Progress is found in man's singular ability to conceptualize and store knowledge, improving upon it, and making it available to each new generation. Although subject to natural law, men are able to use reason to change and reconstruct, in part, their environment. Turgot was confident and optimistic that a knowledge of the past enables man to build a better future.

Subscribing to Rousseau's idea of the natural goodness of man, Turgot believes that there is a harmony in nature. Accordingly, if men act in accordance with nature's laws, they will observe themselves to be in harmony with other people. He accepted the notion of enlightened self-interest and repudiated the idea that the origins of man's actions were solely egotistical. He saw that moral behavior was subject to improvement and that moral progress depended upon obedience to reason and natural law, the practice of tolerance, rational acceptance of law, recognition of the importance of the virtues, and utility. Turgot wanted reason to become more and more important and to diminish emotions and passions.

Turgot observed a fundamental distinction between the physical world and the moral human world. He sees recurrence in the physical order and progress in the human order. He says that the idea of progress distinguished the human order from the physical order and that men do not possess the constancy of the physical world. According to Turgot, there is a basic drive in human nature to create novelty and to innovate. The notion of innovation is the basic new idea in Turgot's view of the historical world. Mankind is distinguished by innovation, change, and progress. For Turgot, progress is the realm of human beings and constitutes a system of worldly morality.

Turgot developed the four-stage theory of economic and social development from hunter-gatherer, to pastoral, to agricultural, and finally to the peace and prosperity of commercial or market society. Turgot employs a stadial or evolutionary theory of development in which society naturally progresses, evolving in a sequence of regular stages, the last of which is the contemporary commercial world of capitalism. His idea is of the linear progressive advancement of mankind.

Turgot explains that there is a process through which each age inherits the social, political, economic, educational, institutional, artistic, and other legacies and environments of its predecessors. There is a process of acquisition, preservation, and addition to an increasing body of knowledge about man and his world. Turgot discusses an ever-growing accumulation, increasing inheritance, and eternal transmission of the world's store of knowledge as civilized man has recorded more and more information about the complex and diverse conditions of mankind. This progressive accumulation, augmentation with novel discoveries, and transmission of knowledge has been made possible by language and writing. The past is a valuable store of experience and ideas for mankind. Knowledge and progress go together.

Men are able to synthesize new combinations in order to develop novel ideas. An orderly language is required as a means for the communication of such knowledge and as a repository for the history of mankind's progress. Such a language provides adequate symbols for displaying one's ideas and transmitting them to future generations. Turgot viewed language as an index that reflects the stadial development of a given nation or region. It follows that the development of human civilization is a history of language, writing, and symbolic communication. Symbols can hold acquired and new ideas and transmit them socially to successive generations.

According to Turgot, the change process in language is vital—language should not be too rigid and static. When languages change, they are frequently made more expressive and flexible. New words are invented only when there are new ideas that need to be expressed. Turgot observes that there must be appropriate conditions of language in order for genius to ascend. A precondition of progress is that a society be open to the spirit of change in language as well as in many other areas.

Turgot envisioned inexorable progress with respect to the mathematical nature of all types of specific knowledge. His goal is to have all knowledge expressed as mathematical symbols rather than in imprecise language that can be colored by passion, personal prejudices, politics, irrationality, and imagination. Turgot was looking for a body of rational linguistic symbols and wanted to see the steady conceptualization by man at the sacrifice of his emotional and fanciful propensities. He valued strongly the superiority of the abstract over the concrete.

According to Turgot, history has demonstrated the actuality, direction, and possibility of progress but it has also shown instances in which progress is hindered by man's irrationality and by other factors. He notes that inherited ideas can sometimes be obstacles to new knowledge. In addition, he explains that human societies pass through cycles of progression and regression. On the one hand, there is a basic drive in human nature to create novelty and to innovate. On the other hand, there exists a negating principle through which institutions can keep man in a routine of repetition and sameness. Movement as a primordial force, a preference for liberty, and a creative and critical spirit raises societies into civilizations. However, these impulses are sometimes hindered by conservative institutions that become impediments to further progress. Mere repetition adds nothing to progress. World history is thus a struggle between the desire for movement and the proclivity toward quiescence. Turgot adds that men are sometimes led astray but learn from their mistakes and move forward. He did not see progress heading toward the elimination of all errors, evil, or misery, but he did say that progress involves the overcoming of impeding forces in physical nature, in society, and in man himself. According to Turgot, the human spirit will always propel a society out of stagnation. It follows that nature leads man to truth but at an uncertain and uneven pace.

Turgot did not believe that the Middle Ages were a totally dark period of detrimental impact on the human mind. He said that Christianity through medieval scholastic philosophy fostered reason and acuminated European minds. To this he added the fact that favorable linguistic conditions were developed during the Middle Ages which became essential for the Renaissance to occur. He also observed that barbarism evolved into a system of government and policies and that feudalism was at least better than anarchy. Turgot also noted that the re-awakening of speculative science during the Renaissance had been fostered by the introduction of mechanical inventions during the Middle Ages which helped to diffuse scientific knowledge and to make individuals aware of the achievements of those who came before them. He sees technology and artisanship as a foundation for science, which then brings even newer technology and products into being, and so on. Within a society, Turgot saw technical progress, as embodied in the production techniques of artisans, to be the most enduring and the hardest to destroy. He also sees technical progress occurring throughout history at a relatively stable tempo compared to other forms of progress.

Turgot explains the importance of a "social surplus" as the means by which advances of one stage of progress to the next were made possible. He said that the coming of the agricultural stage of development creates a social surplus which induces trade, tourism, the division of labor, the useful arts, educational advances, other accomplishments, and increased inequalities of life's conditions in different parts of the world. All nations do not progress regularly or at the same speed. Even at a time when most societies are declining or decaying, Turgot proclaims that there will be some society moving forward. Although he sees evil forces at work throughout history, Turgot is confident that the good will win out and that mankind will continue to grow toward perfection.

Turgot explains that differences in the world during a given time period are due to more than simply adaptations to climate and terrain. He criticizes theories of purely climatic and topographical causes of the variability among various cultures. Turgot says that these differences are better viewed as degrees of social development. However, he does acknowledge that geography is important as an environment for cultural and social processes which bring about progress. There is an infinite variety of historical conditions and circumstances (such as war, colonization, and even chance) which affect the unequal progression of nations. It is only natural that there are inequalities in the progress made by different nations. Turgot also noted that the variations in history were additive.

Turgot inquired into the causes of cultural advancement and cultural decline and asked why creative achievements are seldom found in history. He believed that the causes of creative achievements were found in environments that emphasize reason, liberty, change, mobility, and a diversity of ideas. Welcoming energy, action, and novelty, Turgot contended that the genius played a critical role as dynamic change agent. He was convinced that progress was due to the achievements of the few who were gifted with real genius. Whereas Turgot saw only small differences in the physical abilities of men, he recognized a substantial inequality in their mental capabilities and in the character of their spirits.

Turgot was interested in the contexts and factors of society that enabled genius to develop and in the distribution in time and place of such creative individuals. He assumes that geniuses in a given field are constantly present but that there needs to be a cultural context in existence that makes possible their development and appearance as creative individuals. He sees the biological presence of superior innate powers as only the beginning in the emergence of creative individuals.

Opportunities for progress are always present but they need to be perceived, reflected upon, and acted upon in order to be actualized. Turgot says that a genius grasps novel opportunities and goes forward to articulate his vision. He sees genius as the human moral force that moves world history. Genius thus explains the diversity in the rate and attributes of progress throughout time and space.

Turgot assumed that nature was similarly productive of great minds in various historical periods and that the more earthly inhabitants there were, the more potential geniuses there would be. It follows that favorable conditions in society and in politics are needed in order to promote geniuses to their full capacity. Turgot says that the maintenance of geniuses and the optimization of their potential is the principal operation of the good society. He emphasizes that the accumulation of knowledge requires freedom of inquiry and is in favor of a political structure that promotes opportunities for liberty and spontaneous action. He saw that free exercise of one's talents was good as long as there was no harm to others.

Turgot witnessed an increasing momentum of both vertical and horizontal progress. With the broadening of communication networks, the Enlightenment was about to bring the entire world into civilization thus safeguarding against degeneration. Volitional men were exerting even greater control over nature through technology. He saw mankind as embodying a law of steady perfectibility.

According to Turgot, through their actions men gained ideas of distinction and of unity. Although Turgot embraces boundless diversity, he explains that everything in nature is linked together despite the differences. All aspects of the universe are interconnected. Metaphysically, there is one universe in which every entity is related in some way to all the others. No aspect of the total can exist apart from the total. All entities are related through the inexorable laws of cause and effect. No concrete existent is totally isolated without cause and effect. Each entity potentially affects and may be affected by the others. As inhabitants of the universe, each person is linked via cause and effect, to everything that exists. It follows that all true knowledge is interrelated and interconnected, properly reflecting a unified whole that is the universe.

Statesman and Theorist

Turgot's first writing on economics came in 1749 in his *Letter to the Abbé de Cicé* in which he attacked the inflationary doctrines of Scottish financier John Law, who had moved to France. In it, Turgot took a metallist stance defending gold against the view that it was possible to replace metallic money with paper credit. In 1753, he wrote letters advocating the toleration of Protestants in France. Then, during 1755–1756, he traveled with free trade and free competition advocate and physiocrat Vincent de Gournay. In 1759, he wrote the *Elegy for Gournay*, explaining why it is impossible for government bureaucrats to direct an economy. Then, in 1761, Turgot was appointed intendant for Limoges, a poor region of France. At this point, Turgot's intellectual and practical interests turned almost exclusively in the direction of economic thought and practice. However, his later economic work, as a civil servant and statesman, occurs in the context of, and continues to develop, his theories of history and social development.

Turgot blamed much of the economic decline of Limoges on high taxation of the peasants there. Therefore, he wanted to make taxation more equitably based. The *taille* was based upon the tax collector's personal estimate of a person's ability to pay—many aristocrats and clergy were exempt from this tax, leaving the tax burden on the peasants. Unfortunately, Turgot was unable to abolish the *taille*. However, he was able to eradicate the *corvée* which consisted of unpaid forced labor on the royal roads. He was able to replace this forced labor obligation with the paid labor of proper workers, engineers, and contractors who built and improved roads and drainage.

Serving as intendant of the district of Limoges from 1761–1774, Turgot was able to turn Limoges into one of the more prosperous districts in France. During this time period, he was able to do much more than to eliminate compulsory labor for public work. He took many additional measures to save Limoges from widespread famine. Among the many problems he faced there were the unequal incidence of the tax burden, unproductive agriculture, scarcity, sporadic famine, restricted markets, inadequate poor relief, poor roads, problems in transporting troops, inadequate schools, inefficient gathering of statistics, and so on.

Turgot introduced new crops and new agricultural methods for cultivation and storage. In addition, he established agricultural and veterinary schools as a way to improve the quality of labor in the district. He also reduced tariffs, promoted local free trade, especially in corn, and used government funds in the form of loans to grain markets in order to promote imports into Limoges. Furthermore, Turgot instituted a better relief system for the poor. Not only did he provide work for the poor, he also reduced their taxes, established emergency burdens on the rich, and placed special restrictions on landowners.

In 1766 Turgot drew up a list of questions on economics for two Chinese students whom the Jesuits had sent to study in Paris. To help instruct them in understanding his interrogations, he put his ideas on paper. These fifty-three pages became his *Reflections on the Foundations and Distribution of Riches* and included the following themes: the division of labor, the origin and use of money, the improvement of agriculture, the nature of capital and the different modes of its employment, the legitimacy of interest and loans, and revenue from land. Then, in 1769, he wrote *Value and Money*, which developed an Austrian type theory beginning with Crusoe economics and moving to two-person exchange, to four-person exchange, and finally to a competitive market economy.

Turgot had a second opportunity to put free-market reforms into practice when he served as France's Minister of Finance from 1774–1776. He courageously attempted to save the French monarchy from economic disaster by keeping government spending in check and by encouraging private economic enterprise. Turgot sought a lessening of state activity in many areas. The French government had been running a deficit for years and was close to bankruptcy as a type of welfare state for various privileged and entrenched interests that obstructed change. He wanted to return the country to solvency by reducing expenditures and increasing tax revenue. Turgot expected free markets to bring about increased production, leading to lower prices for consumers and to a greater source of tax revenue for the state. He told Louis XVI to cut government spending and to make taxes more equitable or there would be a danger of revolution. As Comptroller-General, Turgot adopted the slogan "No Bankruptcy, No Increase in Taxes, No Loans."

Turgot was concerned with failure in various markets, including those in corn, labor, and land rents. He also observed administrative chaos and the proliferation of self-serving local authorities in the form of bureaus, agencies, boards, courts, and councils. There was also rampant corruption among government officials. In addition, he saw the need for practical political education of France's citizens. Turgot also looked disapprovingly upon the guild system, a carryover from medieval times, which prevented workers from entering certain occupations without permission much like contemporary occupational licensing.

To a great extent, as Finance Minister, Turgot tried to institute on a larger scale the reforms he introduced at Limoges. His highest priority was to establish freedom of the grain industry in all of France as he had done in Limoges. He said that maintaining free trade in corn is the best way to prevent scarcity in European nations. Turgot opposed strongly government intervention in the corn trade. During 1775 he attempted to reform the *taille*—a tax abuse that weighed more heavily on the poor. In 1775, he was able to gain enough support to have the controls lifted on the internal trade of grain, thus restoring the free circulation of grains sold within France. He also wanted to abolish laws restricting the wine industry. The next year Turgot, in one of his Six Edicts of 1776, officially removed the controls on the prices and transportation of grain, flour, and bread. It was with these Six Edicts that he attempted to transform and refashion the traditional monarchy of France.

A second of these edicts called for the eventual abolition of guilds which monopolized various trades. There remained only a few exceptions. Turgot viewed work as a creative act and as a key instrument of freedom. To shackle work with restrictions was to violate the right to liberty and to stifle the possibility of change. The guild system involved the use of close corporations which represented the various trades—no one could exercise such trades without going through a long list of formalities. Turgot insisted that these corporations be suppressed except in a few industries.

In another important edict Turgot abolished the *corvée*, thus furthering the freedom of work. He ended the government's policy of conscripting labor yearly to construct and maintain roads and replaced it with a more efficient tax in money. It had been the practice of the royal department of roads and buildings to conscript the labor of peasants and farm workers, without the payment of wages, in building and repairing the royal highways. Turgot intended, in place of the *corvée*, to employ a trained road-building force and to pay their wages through a moderate tax increase. Road construction and repair, along with the transportation of military stores, were to be transferred to the supervision of proper engineers. In addition, France was to have transportation of military provisions well-guarded.

The last three of the six edicts were of little consequence and dealt with the discharge of government officials who imposed restrictions on ports and docks, abolishing tax on the cattle and meat industries, and cutting the tax on suet (i.e., hard animal fat). Unfortunately, the nobility and the upper classes undermined Turgot and his Six Edicts. He ran into insurmountable opposition on the part of nobles, the clergy, and the Parliament of Paris and was dismissed from his position.

Turgot was a clearly articulated defender of individual and economic freedom who realized that interference with freedom can have systemic effects. He observed that conditions in various markets are interrelated through a reciprocal interdependence. He understood the complex interrelations of the ingredients of land, labor, capital, wages, production, consumption, and so on in the economy. He had a grand conception of an open and dynamic society. He said that government should be limited to protecting individuals against injustices and the nation against invasion. Turgot realized that free commerce was the best protection against scarcity. He wanted to abolish crushing taxes, trade restrictions, monopoly privileges, and forced labor and to reduce government expenditures and public debt. Turgot was opposed to military conscription and protectionism. Although he desired freedom in foreign commerce, he was most interested in eliminating restrictions on France's internal trade. For example, he wanted to introduce banking and taxation reforms. Turgot also wanted to create a scientific system of weights and measures.

During his two years as Minister of Finance, Turgot proposed a gradual progress of deregulation that put trust in the operation of the open market. His goal was to have general liberty in buying and selling. Moderation and gradualism were his form of tactics. His main efforts were to prepare the public for, and to institute, reasonable and incremental reforms.

Turgot wanted to see local self-government in France and ultimately a constitutional government of the nation. He desired political liberty and favored constitutional limits on royal power as well as strong regional governments. Turgot therefore proposed a hierarchy of elected assemblies going from the village up to the national level. Although he was sympathetic to American rebels, he himself would not recommend that they go to war. He also warned Americans that slavery is not in accord with a proper political constitution. Turgot also cautioned America about the danger of possible civil war.

Political Economy

Although Turgot was familiar with, and close to, the physiocrats with respect to their views on economics, he goes further than they do and in a different direction. Like the physiocrats, he promoted free trade and advocated a single tax on the net product of land. He wanted taxes to be shifted back to agriculture. Turgot agrees with the physiocrats that, because ultimately only agriculture is productive, there should be a single tax on land. Taxation of land was thus the only proper source of revenue for the state. He saw land as a unique form of wealth and presented an early view of the law of diminishing returns in agriculture. Turgot's ultimate goal was actually to eliminate taxes. Not a full-fledged physiocrat, he was more interested in abolishing taxes than exacting them on agricultural land. However, as long as taxation was a reality, his "ideal" in taxation would be a single imposition levied only on land. Turgot recommended taxing only the landowners and not the tenants.

In his writings on progress, Turgot had analyzed the relationship between agrarian and industrial organizations. He explained that the development of commercial capital activates growth both in the involved industries and in agriculture. According to Turgot, industry yields a surplus that creates a demand, not only for crafts and products created through new technology, but also for products of the soil.

According to Turgot, each person compares various economic goods, values them, forms ordinal preference scales, and then chooses among them. He does this while considering his present and future wants and needs and the potential uses of the different economic objects. Turgot saw that these values were subjective (i.e., personal) and not able to be measured in any way except ordinally. Explaining the mutual benefits of free exchange, Turgot states that exchange increases the wealth of both parties. He also notes that each transactor wants to gain as much as possible and to surrender as little as possible in a given exchange. Like the much later F. A. Hayek, Turgot spoke of the essential particular knowledge of subjective individual actors who tend to act in their perceived self-interest.

Turgot observed that the subjective utility of an economic good decreases as its supply to an individual increases—diminishing utility is a function of abundance. A forerunner of the Marginalist Revolution, Turgot conceived of the idea of diminishing marginal productivity of factor inputs. Increasing the quantity of some factors increases the marginal productivity until a maximum point is attained. Past this point, the marginal productivity will decrease, fall to zero, and ultimately will turn negative. Each increase in input would be less and less productive. Essentially, all that Turgot lacked was the idea of the marginal unit.

Concerned with the classical political economy of scarcity, Turgot saw economics as the allocation of scarce resources to a number of alternative ends. He understood that all costs are opportunity costs because in choosing to employ resources in one way, a person has to give up using specific resources in some other productive manner. Turgot views the capitalist-entrepreneur as desiring to earn his imputed salary plus the opportunity cost (today we would say lost contribution margin) that he gave up by not investing his money somewhere else.

Turgot observed that natural resources must be converted to economic products through the application of human labor and that production takes time to take place. He thus recognized the critical role of time in the production process. In addition, he noted that capital in advance is essential to the production process. The act of waiting, which is necessary in modern production processes, must be rewarded by a return to the suppliers of capital. This return is, at the minimum, equal to the market rate of interest on the capital invested in the company.

While products are being worked on, there must be advance payments to laborers, who, Turgot explains, are agreeable to paying the capitalists a discount out of production in order to be paid money in advance of the uncertain future revenues. He says that capital advances are essential in all productive enterprises. The interest return on investments can be viewed as the price labor pays to capitalist-entrepreneurs for advancing savings in the form of current money. Turgot emphasized that the time element in production is a function of the use of capital-intensive production methods, the division of labor, and the demand for capital. He apportioned the return to the capitalists into pure interest, depreciation, and entrepreneurial payment that includes a risk premium.

Turgot recognized that capital was required for economic growth and that the only way to amass capital was for individuals not to consume everything that they had produced. He illuminated the meaning of the term "surplus" and explained the link between surplus and economic growth and progress. Turgot observed that a prosperous economy depends upon the free flow of capital—capital promotes economic activity. The greater the amount of saving, the excess of income over consumption, the higher the accumulation of capital will be. Savings are accumulated in the form of money and then are invested in capital goods. He explains that the advance of savings to the factors of production is the essence of investment.

Turgot's savings and capital formation analysis is one of his greatest contributions in economics and it became the basis for the nineteenth-century classical theory of savings and investment. He demonstrated clearly the benefit of a policy of capital accumulation and explained that money was essential to the process of accumulating capital and generating economic growth. Money was the required ingredient for transferring savings into investment. Although the surplus accumulated via savings could be held in commodities or in money, Turgot explained that economic society languished before the arrival of metallic money because of the extreme difficulty of aggregating and transforming surplus production into capital. Money allowed people to more easily accumulate and employ their savings.

Money is also a commodity and is not merely a conventional symbol. Turgot explains that it is a form of wealth and has value in itself. Metallic money is more than a sign of value. He said that gold and silver are money by the nature of things and that precious metals are one of the forms of capital. For him, money was intrinsically valuable in the form of gold and silver. He explained that money had to be a commodity having intrinsic value for it to be useful as a medium of exchange. Turgot was against the perspective that the government could effectively issue paper money as a substitute for metallic money. His favored order is one in which metallic money, representing savings, is loaned to borrowers. Savings, in the form of money, are loaned to entrepreneurs who desire to invest. This money is channeled through moneylenders as intermediaries. Some people earn interest income from loans made to farmers, landowners, merchants, and industrialists. Such financiers promoted the circulation of capital. Money is vital for transferring savings into investments.

Interest, the price of borrowed money, is determined by the supply and demand for capital and is not immoral. To lend and borrow is the result of a voluntary contract by two parties, each of whom hoped to gain from the transaction. Turgot recognized that a loan is a reciprocal contract between two parties because each believed that it is advantageous to him. Because there exists no exploitation in charging interest, Turgot says that usury laws have been refuted.

Turgot understood that the explanation for interest is time preference—the phenomenon of discounting the future and of setting a premium upon the present. He explains that the present market value of a capital asset tends to equal the aggregate of the expected annual future returns from it discounted by the market rate of interest (or time preference). Turgot also emphasized that an entrepreneur's expected profits must exceed the loan rate of interest in order for a loan to have taken place—he saw the relationship between the profit rate and the interest rate.

Turgot asserted that the rate of interest was determined in the market via exchange. He perceived the relationship between the interest rate and the quantity of money. More specifically, he observed the interrelationship among the supply and demand for money and people's time preferences which come together to effect the relative amounts of spending and saving and the interest rate. Turgot saw that a decrease in thrift would raise interest rates and vice versa. He explained that a low interest rate is a function of a high savings rate and that a low interest rate propels the economy to high rates of economic growth. Turgot noted that a change in the rate of accumulated savings affects the interest rate, which changes the allocation of resources in the economy. He also talked about the difference between the natural rate of interest that would occur in a free economy and the actual interest on loans (i.e., the difference between the real and nominal rates of interest). Similarly, he distinguished between a product's natural price and its market price.

Turgot said that money can be employed to: (1) purchase land for cultivation or to lease to farmers; (2) invest in industry by acquiring buildings, materials, and tools for manufacturing; (3) invest in agriculture by renting land and purchasing stock and implements for agricultural entrepreneurship; (4) invest in trade by buying finished goods and other requirements for commercial activities; and (5) lend to others for the above purposes. According to Turgot, all these activities either directly or indirectly return money to the circular flow—there are no leakages. His analysis of savings and investment thus foretells classical analysis which denies the possibility of leakage from the exchange process and, therefore, the possibility of a general glut of products. It is clear that Turgot anticipated J. B. Say's Law of Markets.

Turgot was for the freedom of domestic and foreign trade and against mercantilist regulation, forced cartelization, and special privileges conferred by the government. He said that regulation involves expenses that become a tax on products—the result is overcharging domestic customers and discouraging foreign purchasers. He wanted sound money and warned against the dangers of fiat paper money. Turgot also explained that individual self-interest moves society forward and is in accord with the general interest. He also anticipated the diminishing marginal utility theory of Carl Menger and others. Turgot explained that a person can only pay taxes by reducing consumption and that there was no logical basis for levying different rates on different products. He, like the physiocrats, believed that the strain of taxation should fall only on the owners of land because of the very nature of the world. Turgot was a low-interest advocate who contended that money was the foundation of capital. He saw savings as a real phenomenon that facilities greater investment in the economy. For a busy man of affairs who found little time to devote to economics, he certainly has made some monumental contributions in that field.

Recommended Reading

Daire, Eugène, ed. "Notice historique sur la vie et les oeuvres de Turgot." In *Oeuvres de Turgot* 1. Two volumes. Paris: Guillaumin, 1844. Published as volumes 3 and 4 of the *Collections des principaux Economistes*.

Dakin, Douglas. *Turgot and the Ancien Régime in France*. London: Methuen, 1939.

Deloche, R. "Turgot, Condorcet et la question de l'affectation des resources." In *Condorcet: Mathematician, Economiste, Philosophe, Home Poitique*, edited by P. Crépel and C. Gilain. Paris: Minerve, 1989.

Desai, M. "A Pioneering Analysis of the Core: Turgot's Essay on Value." *Recherches Economiques de Louvain* 53 (1987): 191–98.

Faure, Edgar. *La Disgrâce de Turgot*. Paris: Gallimard, 1961.

Feilbogen, S. *Smith and Turgot*. Vienna: Holder, 1892.

Groenewegen, Peter D. "A Reappraisal of Turgot's Theory of Value, Exchange and Price Determination." *History of Political Economy* 2 (1970): 177–96.

———. "A Reinterpretation of Turgot's Theory of Capital and Interest." *Economic Journal* 81 (1971): 327–28, 333, 339–40.

———. *The Economics of A. R. J. Turgot*. The Hague: Martinus Mihjoff, 1977.

———. "Turgot's Place in the History of Economic Thought: A Bicentenary Estimate." *History of Political Economy* 115 (Winter 1983): 611–15.

Hutchison, T. W. "Turgot and Adam Smith." *Scottish Journal of Political Economy* 16 (1969): 271–87.

———. "Turgo et Smith." In *Turgot, Economiste et Administrateur*, edited by C. Bordes and J. Morange. Paris: Press Universitaire de France, 1981.

Meek, R. *Turgot on Progress, Sociology and Economics*. Cambridge: Cambridge University Press, 1973.

———. *Social Science and the Ignoble Savage*. Cambridge: Cambridge University Press, 1976.

Monjean, M. "Turgot." In *Dictionnaire de l'économie politique* 2, edited by MM. Ch. Coquelin et Guillaumin. Paris: Guillaumin, 1853. Online: vol 2 http://gallica.bnf.fr/scripts/ConsultationTout.exe?E=0&O=N024410

Nisbet, Robert. "Turgot and the Contexts of Progress." *Proceedings of the American Philosophical Society* 119, no. 3 (June 1975).

Rothbard, Murray N. *An Austrian Perspective on the History of Economic Thought (Economic Thought before Adam Smith)*. Aldershot, UK: Edward Elgar Publishing, 1995.

Schelle, Gustave. "Turgot." In *Nouveau Dictionnaire d'économie Politique* 2, edited Léon Say et Joseph Chailley-Bert. Paris: Guillaumin, [1891–1892] 1900.

Turgot, A. R. J. *Lettres dur le commerce des grains, adressées au contrôleur-général.* In *Oeuvres de Turgot*, edited by Eugène Daire. Paris: Guillaumin, [1770] 1844.

———. "Seconddiscours en Sorbonne. Sur le progress successif e l'esprit humain." In *Oeuvres de Turgot Volume 2*, edited by Eugène Daire. Paris: Guillaumin, [1750] 1844.

———. "Lettres sur la tolerance." In *Oeuvres de Turgot* 2, edited by Eugène Daire. Paris: Guillaumin, [1753] 1844.

———. *Articles from the Encylopédie.* "Foires et Marchés" In *Oeuvres de Turgot* 1, edited by Eugène Daire. Paris: Guillaumin: 1844.

———. "Déclaration du roi." In *Oeuvres de Turgot* 2, edited by Eugène Daire. Paris: Guillaumin: 1844.

———. "4 Edits du roi." In *Oeuvres de Turgot* 2, edited by Eugène Daire. Paris: Guillaumin: 1844.

———. "Lettres-patentes." In *Oeuvres de Turgot* 2, edited by Eugène Daire. Paris: Guillaumin: [1757] 1844.

———. "Eloge de Gournay." In *Oeuvres de Turgot* 1, edited by Eugène Daire. Paris: Guillaumin, [1759] 1844.

———. "Lettres sur le commerce des blés." In *Oeuvres de Turgot* 1, edited by Eugène Daire. Paris: Guillaumin, 1770.

———. *Oeuvres de Turgot et Documents le Concernant.* Edited by G. Schelle. Paris: Alcan, 1913–1923.

———. *Reflections on the Formation and Distribution of Riches.* New York: Augustus M. Kelley (online from Liberty Fund), 1921.

Weulersse, Georges. *La Physiocratie sous les ministères de Turgot et de Necker*, 1774–1781. Paris: Presses universitaires de France, 1950.

Chapter 9

Adam Smith's Moral and Economic System

Man was made for action, and to promote by the exertion of his faculties such changes in the external circumstances both of himself and others, as may seem most favourable to the happiness of all.

—Adam Smith

Adam Smith (1723-1790), moral philosopher and economist, wrote two great books, the well-known *Wealth of Nations* (1776) and *Theory of Moral Sentiments* (1759), which has been overshadowed by his treatise on economics. Contrary to popular belief, these two works do not exist in isolation from one another and *TMS* is not superseded by *WN*. Whereas *WN* is concerned more directly with economic matters, *TMS* explains a moral system that provides a general framework for the economic domain.

WN conveys a detailed understanding of why a free economy works best. In this work, Smith seeks to discover and formulate the general principles of justice and law in the economic realm. In *WN*, Smith addresses individuals' own advantages, self-interest, and self-love, which represent one aspect of human nature. Because the commercial man of *WN* is, for Smith, the virtuous man in only one of his facets, he does not proceed beyond the private virtue of prudence or the limited notion of what we would call metanormative or commutative justice to go into the positive virtue of benevolence. In *WN* Smith made economics the study of spontaneous and unintended order which arises when voluntary exchanges among individuals produce benefits for the parties involved.

In *TMS*, Smith examines the process by which individuals adopt moral standards through which they judge actions by others and by themselves. This book explains how individuals can overcome the selfish impulses of the commercial realm. Recognizing that there is more to life than economics and politics and that men possess more than self-regarding sentiments, Smith discusses the phenomena of moral sentiments and sympathetic feelings among men and their desire to please others and gain their approval.

There is a consistency in outlook and general compatibility between *TMS* and *WN* and a close relationship between Smith's moral philosophy and economics. *TMS* is concerned with the ordering of moral behavior and the maximization of virtue and *WN* is concerned with the ordering of economic behavior and the maximization of wealth as a means to a higher end. As a professor of moral philosophy at the University of Glasgow, Smith's course consisted of four parts: natural theology, ethics, justice (or jurisprudence), and political economy. His lectures on moral philosophy were the beginnings of *TMS*.

There is no discontinuity between the Smith of *TMS* and the Smith of *WN*— there are not two Adam Smiths. *WN* fits into the moral framework of *TMS*. There is a logical flow from Smith's moral philosophy to his jurisprudence and political economy. Exchange is shown to occur within the moral framework of his first book. *TMS* provides the foundational concepts of human nature and morality upon which the ideas of *WN* rest. Smith's two books provide a systematic and essentially unified whole in which moral and economic ideas are coordinated and integrated. Both are integral parts of his vision of man and society. The commercial man of *WN* and the benevolent man of *TMS* are not two different men.

Adam Smith's Moral Theory

Smith delineates two levels of virtues. His lower or commercial virtues are self-interested ones and include prudence, justice, industry, frugality, constancy, and so on. Another set of virtues, the primary or nobler virtues, includes benevolence, generosity, gratitude, compassion, kindness, pity, friendship, love, and so on. Although there is a hierarchical relationship between these sets of virtues, Smith explains that there must also be a balance or harmony between them. In the economic sphere, self-interest allows men to operate on the lower level of virtue and yet attain the greatest benefits for society as a whole. A man need not be totally virtuous for the economic system to function to maximize wealth. The lower virtues are at the base of Smith's value theory and his determination of market prices. Smith explains that, as people get beyond the level of primitive economy to enter an advanced society and civilization, there arises the opportunity to develop higher virtues.

According to Smith, the four principal virtues in a person's life are justice, prudence, benevolence, and self-command. It is through the exercise of self-command, Smith's cardinal virtue, that a man can rein in his selfish impulses, regulate his conduct, and indulge benevolence. Self-command involves the ability to control one's feelings, to restrain one's passion for his own interests, and to enhance his feelings for others.

In *TMS*, Smith explains the evolutionary process by which the virtues and moral sentiments develop. He is concerned with what produces moral behavior in man and with how man's sentimental capacity develops. He wants to understand how we progress from having virtually no such standards as children to having widely shared standards of moral judgment as adults.

Smith's moral theory relies heavily on the eighteenth-century sentimentalist school of ethics comprised of empiricists who were strongly influenced by David Hume (1711-1776). Sentiments (also known as passions, dispositions, affections, or propensities) are feelings or emotions, and according to Smith, are the basis of moral judgment. These sentiments have been implanted in human nature by a beneficent and utilitarian deity in order to bring about the happiness and welfare of mankind. For Smith, these feelings are axiomatic and are behind a man's choices and actions. Some of these passions are selfish and some are unselfish. Like Hume, Smith considers the sentiments to be more fundamental than reason and to be what reason works on or what guides reason. The moral sentiments include approval, disapproval, gratitude, resentment, etc.

Although Hume did not systematically formulate a political or an economic philosophy, his work does represent a subtle effort to build a system of liberal values based on skeptical and anti-rationalist foundations. In turn, the writings of Smith, who was also an anti-rationalist, provided an overarching general theory and a much more extensive discussion of the self-correcting natural processes of the social system.

Francis Hutcheson, moral philosopher and Smith's teacher, believed there was a "moral sense" that existed as an innate sixth sense in each man. Smith rejected the idea of a "moral sense" as too individualistic. He argued that there is no need for a special faculty of moral intuition for perceiving the general principles of natural law. He believed that moral distinctions are founded on immediate sense and feeling, but that these feelings are latent within us and develop only as we come into contact with other human beings. Sympathetic interaction was Smith's term for this socialization process. What is moral is known through original experiences and the related feelings that a person has with respect to his own actions and feelings and to the actions and imagined feelings of others. Smithian man is a social creature who acquires a moral code via experience and induction. However, this code is founded upon the innate moral sentiments that nature has given to him. These innate moral sentiments include both selfish ones and sympathetic feelings for others.

Mutual Sympathy and the Acquisition of Moral Standards

According to Smith, people have an innate desire for mutual sympathy of sentiments and gain pleasure from seeing their own sentiments reflected in others. It follows that people desire mutual sympathy of sentiments with others. Smith explains that a man can engage feelings beyond himself and, through imagination, can identify with the feelings of others and can experience a fellow-feeling with them. Each person has the propensity to sympathize with others and secure by communication their predispositions and sentiments. For Smith, the basis for morality is sympathy—the ability to enter into the emotions of other people. By sympathy, Smith means harmony of any emotion ranging from compassion to pity to joy.

Smith explains that God has endowed man with principles of nature that interest him in the welfare of others and that make their happiness necessary to him. It follows that a Smithian man is a moral person who can achieve his true nature and potentialities only in society. He is a being who requires the praise and approval of others, in addition to his own approval of himself as a virtuous man, in order to be happy.

According to Smith, moral judgments arise only in the interaction of sympathetic actors in society. Sympathy between people is the operative faculty in determining moral propriety. People are pleased when they recognize that their sentiments correspond with those of other individuals. Each person's propensity for sympathetic interaction allows him to enter deeply into others' passions and sentiments, causing him to experience like passions and inclinations. We observe others and their actions and discover what they are feeling by placing ourselves in their position. We judge their sentiments compared to what our own would have been if we were in the same situations. When we judge the propriety of an action, we are judging the appropriateness of the motives of the action to the person's situation. We imagine ourselves in another's place and imagine our emotional reaction to such a situation. We then judge the propriety or impropriety of the feelings of other people by their correspondence or disagreement with our own. We approve of another's action if it is one in which we can sympathize with the feelings that motivated the act. If we cannot so sympathize, we do not approve of it.

Sympathy also helps people see themselves as others see them. Smith explains that we are naturally inclined to view ourselves according to how we appear to others and that we prefer an image of ourselves as just and virtuous. He states that the way in which we behave is related to how our actions and ourselves will be perceived by others. This is because people have an original desire to please others and a natural aversion to offending them. He goes on to explain that God has endowed man with the natural desire to be the proper object of love and the dread of being the deserved object of hatred. A man thus wants to be loved and worthy of love and to be praised and worthy of praise. He wants to be virtuous and not merely to be thought of as virtuous.

In addition to having the need to attain the approval of others who are judging us, Smith maintains that we have a non-selfish interest in the happiness and pleasure of others. We attempt to adjust our behavior so that others experience pleasure. To please others we must give them objects (i.e., ourselves) to observe that will promote pleasurable sentiments in them. It gives them pleasure when they can sympathize with our motives, where they can identify with the gratitude of the beneficiaries of our actions, when they can see the compatibility of our behavior with society's general rules, and when they can view our actions as a component of one grand system.

Over time, the shared process of searching for sympathy of sentiments leads to mutually acceptable standards. This reciprocal adjustment process of correction, revision, and fine-turning results in an unintended and, for the most part, unconscious system of standards. According to Smith, the process of sympathetic interaction results in the development of the higher virtues, moral norms, and moral order. The general rules comprising such a system of morality are the result of an induction process that each person performs based on his experiences. General rules are based upon individuals' attempts to sympathize with specific actions. It is found by induction that all actions of a certain type, or circumstanced in a particular way, gain approval or disapproval.

The Impartial Spectator Procedure

At this point, Smith observes a problem with his theory and adds the notion of an "impartial spectator" to deal with it. He notes that it is possible for an individual to be judged unfairly based on biased or incomplete information. The judgments of real persons as spectators are partial and biased as a result of limited knowledge of the observed person's situation or the lack of knowledge of the agent's true sentiments. Although the general rules of society that have developed serve as one corrective for partiality, Smith sees the need to introduce a further corrective in the form of the mental construct of the impartial spectator.

Smith explains that sympathy, being rooted in human nature, is an imperfect tool and is only approximate. A person's sympathy is limited because it is impossible to truly become another. A man can never fully duplicate the feelings that he imagines exist in the other person. Impartiality involves the absence of particular personal interests. Smith explains that a person's initial assessment has to be corrected by imagining how someone more impartial than he himself would react.

Smith states that a person sympathizes most with himself and with those who are close to him and least with those whom he never sees. There is a hierarchy of attachments that runs from the most immediate (i.e., self and family) to the most distant. Although a man has the capacity for sympathy with others' feelings, this capacity is only exercised in diminishing degrees as the connection to himself becomes more and more weakened. The familiarity principle states that there is an ascending level of benevolence and a descending order of self-interest as we go from strangers, to acquaintances, to friends, and to family.

According to Smith, people learn to adopt the viewpoint of an outside and impartial observer from which to judge their own conduct and the behavior of others. This impartial spectator, the ultimate arbiter of conduct, creates a totally unbiased perspective. Smith is thus assuming that a person is capable of stepping outside of himself in order to make an impartial assessment that considers all aspects of the situation. Smith says that a man can ask if this well-informed and unbiased spectator, with no particular relationship to any of the parties in the situation, could sympathize with the feelings motivating the various agents' actions. To decide if the impartial spectator would approve of a person's own actions, the person would have to imagine himself in the spectator's place and imagine the spectator imagining the agent's (i.e., his own) feelings, and then consider whether or not this imaginary person would sympathize with, and be able to enter into, those feelings. In other words, each person attempts to judge his own conduct by imagining how a fair and impartial spectator would judge it. We might say that a man's conscience is his personal internalized impartial spectator.

Smith's idea of an impartial spectator is ambiguous. It is unclear whether the impartial spectator epitomizes a perfect ideal or whether it symbolizes any well-informed, but impartial, observer who is not personally affected and who has the normal feelings of a typical human being. If the former is what he means, then we are dealing with a fictional selfless observer who judges from beyond the limitations of individuality, finite consciousness, and self-interest. This would be similar to Rousseau's general will or Kant's noumenal self (or will) or autonomous self-legislator. This would be problematic because the impartial observer would represent a person who judges from beyond reality.

Smith assumes that every person has the same natural sentiments implanted in them by God or nature that call for the same moral judgments by all once partiality has been eliminated. However, there are some people who cannot form or have not formed their consciences because they have no impartial spectator. It may be that some people have not had sufficient experiences or information to develop their sympathetic feelings. Others may just become rule-followers because they lack the necessary sensibilities to feel the emotions upon which society's rules are founded. It follows that the impartial spectator guides only those who have developed their consciences. Because justice is necessary for the preservation of society, God has designed nature as a system in which people pursuing their own interests in the economic realm, without thought to others or the whole, still act in ways that benefit society. According to Smith, the propensity to exchange and the desire to better one's condition are basic to human nature.

For Smith, the most virtuous of men govern themselves by self-command. A person can control and exercise his actions and emotions by self-command. At one level, self-command consists in a person adjusting his actions to what he imagines will enable others to sympathize with them. At a higher level, self-command means disciplining oneself to act in accordance with the virtuous dictates of the impartial spectator. Smith considers self-command to be a virtue. This is true only if a man has free will. If his idea of self-command is meant to imply free will, then, at best, it can only be an attenuated and limited form of free will because Smithian man, being a Humean slave of the passions, can only choose among the various sentiments he experiences.

Commercial Man and the Marketplace

Smith contends that many men never get beyond the level of the lower or commercial virtues. They are likely to wrongly believe that goods will make them happier and, therefore, seek them for that reason. Smith explains that men's selfish desires are there for a positive and useful purpose. When individuals pursue their own private interests in the economic sphere, society will be best served. From a person's desire to seek his own advantages and improve his conditions, wealth arises and an unintended or spontaneous order results. A free economy in which people seek their own private interests is said to be lead by an "invisible hand" in directions that benefit all.

Although Smith doubts that wealth can bring happiness, as an economist he teaches that capitalism can provide wealth. As a philosopher, however, he tells us that material possessions are not all that conducive to one's happiness. He says that men should realize that there is more to life than material well-being.

Smith views the world, including human nature, as a machine or system designed by God to maximize human happiness. Man is a natural component of a natural *telos*. Teleological design is fundamental to Smith's work in which he attributes the observed order in the world to a benevolent deity. Providence has constructed external nature and man's internal sentimental predispositions as to make the universe's processes favorable to man. In fact, deception by nature is essential to Smith's stoic system. Deception by nature leads individuals to attain what they believe are their own purposes, but which actually fulfill the purposes of the designer of the universe.

Men are led to imagine greater pleasure from wealth than there actually is. Although individuals are misled by the deceptive appearances of wealth, this delusion can be a desirable thing. People are deceived by nature so that the economy may thrive. Although wealth does not make a man happy, the pursuit of wealth benefits society. This is the essence of Smith's attempt to explain why God created human beings with the irregularity of sentiments that frequently makes intentions and outcomes disproportionate.

In Smith's system, the market is the aggregate of all the exchanges of the production from all the various industries and occupations. An unintended order is the outcome of all the transactions in an economy in which individuals are free to find the most profitable use of their labor or capital. Smith's conception of natural liberty is an application of natural law and natural justice doctrines to the phenomenon of exchange. Free trade requires reciprocal or commutative justice. He explains that the laws of the marketplace are the laws of an organized society. As a moralist, Smith maintains that an ethical economy is necessary to ensure the just treatment of all. A moral economic process is needed in order to develop human passions to reach a higher level of virtue and morality.

The lower virtue of prudence guides the virtuous man in the pursuit of his own well-being. The commercial man is part of virtuous man and performs his proper function when he attends to his own happiness by pursuing fundamental goods such as property, health, and reputation. In part, he desires wealth for the approval it will attain for him in the eyes of other men who gain pleasure when they see him as successful and productive. A prudent man demonstrates self-command when he denies himself present pleasure for future pleasures that he believes will be greater. A prudent man's habits of economy, industry, attention, discretion, frugality, and application of thought are self-interested and praise-worthy. A prudent man realizes that production is good, that labor is more pro-ductive when it is more specialized, and that the more people involved in mutual exchange, the more specialized each person can be.

Smith situated labor at the center of his economic value theory. For him, human labor was the ultimate source of value. His mistaken labor theory of value states that labor cost is a real, original, and elemental measure of value. Smith characterized labor as a good that has value for its own sake. He identi-fied the value of an exchange in terms of the labor embodied in the goods. His erroneous value theory thus shifted economics away from the ideas of scarcity, utility, and subjective preferences and toward the notion of "natural price" based on the expenditure of labor in the production of goods. For Smith, the value of a good is inherent in the good and its exchange value depends on how much it costs to produce a good.

Smith's View of Nature and Science

It is evident from a study of Smith's system that he was a deist who subscribed to a stoic worldview. As a deist, he views the creator as a benevolent but de-tached force in the world's order. He believed that providence had endowed men with the propensities and capacities to make such a rationally ordered system possible. Smith's world was one of undeniable natural laws through which God guided the world. He viewed the world as a great machine, the aim of which is the maximization of happiness. It follows that what is in man's nature was put there intentionally by God. As a natural religionist, Smith envisioned a system of nature designed by God in which individuals pursuing their own legitimate interests unknowingly benefit the good of all. Human strengths, weaknesses, and the system of human affections and dispositions are God-given for his own good reasons. Smith's project was to determine the natural principles which govern men's conduct. He attempted to elucidate the natural laws regulating the moral laws of men.

It is important for us to understand how Smith views the role of science, philosophy, and theory. This can be found in his *History of Astronomy*. Accord-ing to Smith, philosophy is a discipline that attempts to connect and regularize the data obtained from everyday experiences into a theoretical system. He says that scientists develop systems which are imaginary machines or explanations that soothe the imagination. Science is a process of finding connecting principles that satisfy our interior needs for comfort and stability. The imagination feels discomfort when it encounters disruptions in experience. Unexpected appear-ances and events, evidencing gaps in connections of thought, produce wonder and discomfort. Seeking to ease the disturbances caused in the imagination, thinkers develop a new theory or system that will incorporate the new appear-ance, returning people to a sense of tranquility in their interior mental states.

Smith's view of science is amazingly close to that of Thomas Kuhn, who said that revolutionary paradigm changes result from discoveries brought about by encountering anomalies.

Smith surmises that a new, more elegant system satisfies one's imagination more than the system that it replaces. He doubts that any system of thought will ever be final and incapable being improved upon. Apparently, Smith must have also viewed his own project in *TMS* and *WN* as a system that soothed the imagination with respect to economics better than other systems of thought available to individuals in his own time.

From Adam Smith to the Present

Adam Smith's system is certainly flawed in comparison to the systems of Carl Menger, Ludwig von Mises, Murray Rothbard, and Ayn Rand. However, their insights would have been much more difficult, or even impossible, to attain if there had been no Adam Smith. Smith's grasp of incomplete truths in misinterpreted ways helped lead to the Industrial Revolution and, without the Industrial Revolution, these thinkers would have a much tougher task to undertake. Smith identified a general body of truths that brought some conceptual clarity to the apparent chaos of the free market. He developed a set of principles that would profoundly affect the civilized world. His demonstration of the inherent stability and growth of the free-market system helped produce the Industrial Revolution which advanced people's material well-being and increased their life expectancy, which in turn, permitted individuals to establish long-range goals for their personal flourishing. Although Menger, Mises, and Rothbard made many advances in economic theory, it was left to Rand to formulate a more explicit and fundamentally moral, rather than economic, justification for capitalism. Her rationale was based on moral individualism, rational self-interest, rational epistemology, and reason as the paramount and fundamental means for people to associate and interact with one another.

Recommended Reading

Anderson, Gary M. "Adam Smith, Justice, and the System of Natural Liberty." *Journal of Libertarian Studies* 10, no 2 (1988).

Anspach, Ralph. "The Implications of the Theory of Moral Sentiments for Adam Smith's Ecomomic Thought." *History of Political Economy* 4 (1972): 176–206.

Berry, Christopher J. "Adam Smith's Considerations on Language." *Journal of the History of Ideas* 35 (1974): 130–38.

Booth, William J. "On the Idea of the Moral Economy." *American Political Science Review* 88, 3 (September 1994): 653–67.

Brown, Maurice. *Adam Smith's Economics: Its Place in the Development of Economic Thought*. London: Croom Helm, 1988.

Campbell, T. D. *Adam Smith's Science of Morals*. London: Allen and Unwin, 1971.

Coase, Ronald H. "Adam Smith's View of Man." *Journal of Law and Economics* 19 (1976): 538–39.

Cropsey, Joseph. *Polity and Economy: An Interpretation of the Principles of Adam Smith.* The Hague: Martinus Nijhoff, 1957.

Dankers, Clyde E. *Adam Smith: Man of Letters and Economics.* Hicksville, NY: Exposition Press, 1974.

Den Uyl, Douglas J., and Charles L. Griswold, Jr. "Adam Smith on Friendship and Love." *Review of Metaphysics* 49 (March 1996): 609–37.

Dickey, Laurence. "Historicizing the 'Adam Smith Problem': Conceptual, Historiographical, and Textual Issues." *Journal of Modern History* 58 (September 1986): 579–609.

Fitzgibbons, Athol. *Adam Smith's System of Liberty, Wealth, and Virtue: The Moral and Political Foundations of The Wealth of Nations.* Oxford: Oxford University Press.

Fleischacker, Samuel. *On Adam Smith's Wealth of Nations.* Princeton, NJ: Princeton University Press, 2004.

Fry, Michael, ed. *Adam Smith's Legacy.* London: Routledge, 1992.

Garrison, Roger W. "The Intertemporal Adam Smith." *Quarterly Journal of Austrian Economics* 1, no. 1 (1998).

Griswold, Charles L., Jr. *Adam Smith and the Virtues of Enlightenment.* Cambridge: Cambridge University Press, 1999.

Haggarty, John. *The Wisdom of Adam Smith.* Indianapolis, IN: Liberty Press, 1976.

Hirst, Francis W. *Adam Smith.* London: Macmillan & Co., 1904.

Hollander, Samuel. *The Economics of Adam Smith.* Toronto: University of Toronto, 1973.

Jenkins, Arthur H. *Adam Smith Today: The Wealth of Nations Simplified, Shortened, and Modified.* New York: Richard R. Smith, 1948.

Kleer, Richard A. "Final Causes in Adam Smith's *Theory of Moral Sentiments*." *Journal of the History of Philosophy* 33 (April 1995): 275–300.

Land, Stephen K. "Adam Smith's 'Considerations Concerning the First Formation of Languages.'" *Journal of the History of Ideas* 38 (1977): 677–90.

Lux, Kenneth. *Adam Smith's Mistake: How a Moral Philosopher Invented Economics and Ended Morality.* Boston: Shambhala, 1990.

Manley, Michael. "Adam Smith Was Right." *New Perspectives Quarterly* 9, 3 (Summer 1992): 46–51.

Martin, Marie A. "Utility and Morality: Adam Smith's Critique of Hume." *Hume Studies* 16, no. 2 (1990): 107–20.

Montgomery, George S. *The Return of Adam Smith.* Caldwell, ID: The Caxton Printers; New York: The Free Press, [1949] 1993.

Muller, Jerry Z. *Adam Smith in His Time and Ours: Designing the Decent Society.* New York: The Free Press, 1993.

Oncken, August. "The Consistency of Adam Smith." *Economic Journal of London* 7 (1897): 443–50.

Otteson, James R. "Adam Smith on the Emergence of Morals: A Reply to Eugene Heath." *British Journal for the History of Philosophy* 8, no. 3 (October 2000): 545–51.

———. *Adam Smith's Marketplace of Life.* Cambridge: Cambridge University Press, 2002.

Paul, Ellen Frankel. "Adam Smith: A Reappraisal." *Journal of Libertarian Studies* 1, no 4 (1977).

Rae, John. *Life of Adam Smith.* London: Macmillan, 1895.

Raphael, D. D. *Adam Smith*. Oxford: Oxford University Press, 1985.

Reisman, D. A. *Adam Smith's Sociological Economics*. London: Croom Helm, 1976.

Robertson, H. M. and W. L Taylor. "Adam Smith's Approach to the Theory of Value." *Economic Journal* 67, no. 266 (June 1957): 182–98.

Rosenberg, Nathan. "Adam Smith and the Stock of Moral Capital." *History of Political Eocnomy* 22, no. 1 (1990): 1–17.

Ross, I. S. *The Life of Adam Smith*. Oxford: Oxford University Press, 1995.

Rothschild, Emma. "Adam Smith and the Invisible Hand." *American Economic Review* 84, no. 2 (May 1994): 319–22.

Smith, Adam. *An Inquiry into the Nature and Causes of Wealth of Nations*. R. H. Campbell, A. S. Skinner, and W. B. Todd, eds. Oxford: Oxford University Press, (1776) 1976.

———. *Correspondence of Adam Smith*, edited by E. C. Mossner and I. S. Ross. Oxford: Oxford University Press, 1987.

———. *The Theory of Moral Sentiments*. Edited by D. D. Raphael and A. L. Macfie. Oxford: Oxford University Press, (1759)1976.

Steward, Duguld. "Account of the Life and Writing of Adam Smith." In *Stewart's Collected Works*, edited by Sir William Hamilton. Edinburgh: Thoemmes Continuum, 1858.

Viner, Jacob. "Adam Smith and Laissez Faire." In *Adam Smith, 1776–1926: Lectures to Commemorate the Sesquicentennial of the Publication of "The Wealth of Nations,"* edited by John M. Clark, et al. Chicago: University of Chicago Press, 1928.

———. *Guide to John Rae's Life of Adam Smith*. New York: Augustus M. Kelley, 1965.

West, E. G. *Adam Smith: Architect of Freedom*. New Rochelle, NY: Arlington House, 1969.

Winch, Donald. *Adam Smith's Politics*. Cambridge: Cambridge University Press, 1978.

PART III

THE LATE MODERN PERIOD

Chapter 10

Jean-Baptiste Say's Law of Markets: A Fundamental, Conceptual Integration

Political economy, in the same manner as the exact sciences, is composed of a few fundamental principles, and of a great number of corollaries or conclusions, drawn from these principles. It is essential, therefore, for the advancement of this science that these principles should be strictly deduced from observation; the number of conclusions drawn from them may afterwards be either multiplied or diminished at the discretion of the inquirer, according to the object he proposes.

—Jean-Baptiste Say

John-Baptiste Say (1767-1832) is one of the most important and insightful thinkers in the history of economic science. Say was a major proponent of Adam Smith's self-directing economic system of competition, natural liberty, and limited government. He frequently praised the Scotsman's work, publicized it, and described his own work as mainly an elaboration of Smith's *The Wealth of Nations*. In fact, however, the economic doctrines and analysis of this "French Adam Smith" went further than, and departed from, Smith's ideas on some important points. For example, he stated that Smith's *The Wealth of Nations* was without a method; was obtuse, unclear, and unconnected; and included far too many digressions and divergences.

An Overview

Say understood that natural law underpins economic behavior, making it orderly, predictable, and universal. He stressed reason's role in economic analysis, wealth creation, and the earning of profit. Viewing economics as a discipline capable of attaining universal truths, his economic method was that of an essentialist and a realist.

He disliked ivory tower theory but was also skeptical of blind empiricism and the accumulation of mathematical and statistical facts without relating them to theory. Say emphasized the observation of the facts of reality at the same time he dismissed rationalism. To do this he derived economic laws by induction. He believed that economics should begin with the reason and experience of the human person rather than with abstract mathematics and statistical analyses. After laws and theories were formulated, he believed in then testing them with observations and facts. Say presented his economic ideas using precise and simple language that was easily understood.

Say's farsighted analysis made him a precursor of the Austrian school of thought. He connected with the Austrians with respect to methodology, his emphasis on the importance of entrepreneurship, monetary theory, and value theory.

Say, the first professor of political economy in France, introduced free-market economics to Europe in general and to France in particular. This great hero in the history of economic thought presented the true laws of political economy in his 1803 masterpiece, *A Treatise on Political Economy*.

Say invented the term "entrepreneur" and emphasized the vital and creative roles of the entrepreneur in the economy as forecaster, project appraiser, and risk taker. He saw that effective entrepreneurs must possess the moral qualities of judgment and perseverance, and also have a knowledge of the world. Say realized that wealth is essentially and originally metaphysical and the result of creativity, ideas, imagination, and innovation. He thereby placed the role of the entrepreneur at the hub of economic theory. Say understood that economic advancement requires entrepreneurs and the accumulation of capital.

Rejecting the labor theory of value that was held by Adam Smith and other classical economists, Say states that the basis for value is utility—the capability of a good or service to meet some human desire. He maintained a subjective utility theory of value rather than a labor theory of value. Say understood that it was the way and the extent to which potential customers value a good or service that determine its value and whether or not it is produced. He recognized that the prices of goods and services reflect their utility to the buyer and that prices of factors of production are imputed from the prices of the goods produced. He differentiated between use value and exchange value, but like Aristotle wrongly concluded that all exchange transactions must involve the exchange of equal values. Say thus fell short of the economic thought of the Austrians, like Carl Menger, who recognized the necessity of positive-sum transactions through which both the buyer and the seller gain utility. In addition, Say came close to discerning, but fell a bit short of discovering, marginal utility theory.

Historical Context

Let's take a look at the historical context in which Say wrote. The prevailing doctrine at this time was mercantilism, which held that money (particularly gold and silver) creates wealth and stimulates economic growth. Mercantilists were worried that there are limits to growth, concerned about the likelihood of business cycles, and believed that at certain points there will not be sufficient purchasing power. They claimed that business slumps would occur when producers produced too much and that there would be waiting periods during which demand would catch up. This idea of excess supply is known as the "glut of commodities" doctrine. To remedy the existence of an excess supply of commodities some economists proposed the stimulation of extra demand through money creation. This proposed solutions was known as "consumptionism." The idea was that the goods are already here so that production must not be the problem. Instead, they saw the production of consumption as the problem. This led to the proposal that the government and the banking system should artificially activate the extra needed demand by bringing new credit and new money into existence. This pronouncement was termed "credit creationism." Worried about the scarcity of money during economic crises, economists saw the solution as "to find more money and spend it." They mistakenly thought that spending and consumption is the engine of economic growth.

Say attacked the scarcity of money doctrine at the turn of the eighteenth century by taking on the "glut of commodities" hypothesis and the "credit creationists." He contended that it is not money that creates demand but rather is the production of goods and services. According to Say, money is merely a medium or mechanism of exchange and the real cause of economic depression is the scarcity of other products and services. It follows that when the economy starts to recover it is because production has gone up, followed by consumption. Production leads to more consumption rather than the other way around. In order for consumers to exist, there must first be producers.

Say's Law of Markets

J. B. Say, the original supply-sider, seeing that production is the source or cause of consumption, placed supply over demand in the hierarchy of economics. A person's ability to demand goods and services from others proceeds from the income produced by his own acts of production. His level of production determines his ability to demand. Demanding products requires having money which, in turn, requires a prior act of supply. The production of goods causes income to be paid to those who produce. In other words, a person sells his labor services or assets for money which he then uses to demand products. In the end, when exchanges have been effected, it will be found that a person has paid for goods and services with other goods and services. The demand for any commodity is a function of the supply of other commodities. The need to offer a good to demand another good is obvious in a barter economy but also applies in a money or indirect exchange economy.

Wealth is created by production and not by consumption. Consumption actually uses up utility or wealth. Demand (i.e., consumption) follows from the production of wealth. People demand from the wealth their production created. What a person demands is predicated upon what he supplies. Say thus recognized that all men are both producers and consumers and that if a person wants to obtain a good he must provide something in return that is desirable to another. Money is the necessary means to acquire the goods that one desires. However, in order to procure money, a person must first produce a good or service that will exchange for money. No one can legitimately demand something before first supplying a product or service of value to others.

Say's Law of Markets, a key component of the classical school of economics, describes the process through which supplies in general are translated into demands in general. For Say, the balance between aggregate supply and aggregate demand is an *ex ante* identity. From this perspective, supply equals demand only because of, and to the amount of, people's demand for other goods. Demand is supply seen from another angle. Because supply is demand there cannot be an excess of supply over demand. The demand for products can be said to be rooted in the production of products.

Say never did write the phrase "supply creates its own demand." That phrase can be attributed to John Maynard Keynes, who misunderstood and misinterpreted Say's Law of Markets. Keynes thought that Say meant that the supply of a particular good is the demand for that good. What Say stated was that the supply of a good constitutes demand for everything that is not that good. Aggregate supply thus creates its own aggregate demand. Within the context of a free market system, the supply of each producer makes up his demand for the supplies of other producers. Therefore, in the aggregate, demand always equals supply and the general overproduction of goods is meaningless and impossible. There is a direct interconnection in the economy between the acts of producers (i.e., suppliers) and the presence of any aggregate equivalent demand for these products and services by the same producers who provided them.

According to Say, it was possible to have a surplus or a shortage of any specific commodity. Production can be misdirected and too much of some products can be produced for which there is insufficient demand. He said that gluts of production did not occur through general overproduction, but instead through overproduction of certain goods in proportion to others which were underproduced. Say thus admits that there can be short-term gluts of a particular commodity. The market, left to its own devices, permits such imbalances to be corrected through adjustments of prices and costs. Any disequilibrium in the economy exists only because the internal proportions of output differ from the proportions preferred by consumers, not because production is excessive in the aggregate. It follows that Say's Law in no way implies that all products will ultimately be demanded in the market. The supply of a good does not guarantee it will be an effective demand by the producer of that good for other goods. If inventory does not sell, prices will be cut until, and if, it does. It follows that lower prices of some goods means that people have more money to spend on other goods and services. Through the price system, supply and demand adjust and markets clear if the market system is left free to perform the balancing and proportioning functions. It is through the change of prices that today's supplies are rationed among today's demanders. Prices bring about proper proportions and price signals communicate information for future allocation and supply decisions.

Say understood human nature and the fact that people tend to be rational but are not omniscient. It follows that overproduction of particular commodities by individuals firms and producers is possible when mistakes have been made. The glut of a specific commodity can arise from its production in excessive abundance outrunning the total demand for it or from the shortfall in the production of other commodities. A glut can only take place temporarily when too many means of production are applied to one type of product and not enough to others. This type of disequilibrium is normally quickly remedied in a free market economy as market incentives and rational self-interest lead to adjustments in production, prices, marketing strategies, and so on. People have a rational self-interest in correcting their errors.

What about savings? People do not spend all of the wealth that their production created. The demand for current goods and services fails to match the value of what has been produced as people choose to hold some of it in monetary form. According to Say, savings is beneficial and better than consumption because it is used in the production of capital goods or in additional production. Contrariwise, consumption does not provide a stimulus to wealth. When production exceeds consumption, the difference is savings, which goes toward the production of investment goods, and investment is the basis for future growth. Such a reinvestment process is fueled by entrepreneurs. If money is stored in the form of bank-created money such as checking accounts, the held-back consumption power will be transferred to borrowers from the bank that created it. In other words, the power to consume is shifted to the borrower. There will be no deficiency in aggregate demand as long as the banking system is free to carry out the process of transforming depositors' savings into borrowers' spending. As long as savings are reinvested in productive uses in the aggregate there need be no decreases in income, production, or consumption. Say argued that savings searching for profits goes quickly into investments for production.

Higher rates of savings bring about higher rates of subsequent growth in aggregate output. This takes place because someone else borrows the money that will produce an even greater number of goods. It follows that people need incentives for working, saving, investing, and risk-taking. Say's insight was that incomes are always totally spent on commodities satisfying current wants (i.e., consumption) or on commodities satisfying future wants (i.e., savings accumulation) and that savings are essential if the economy is to grow. Demand thus comes from supply whenever you demand it. People save in order to expand their production or to live on their savings when and as they need them. Savings buy time for people to do more than just work. It could be said that consumption is the final cause of production and that saving is the efficient cause of production. Say taught that income not devoted to consumption will be spent on investment and that the market would automatically and fairly rapidly return toward equilibrium.

Say contended that money is a neutral mechanism through which aggregate supply is transformed into aggregate demand. He viewed money as an intermediate good or conduit that enables people to buy. Like Menger, Say described the spontaneous evolution of a commodity to become money. He favored commodity money and free banking. In Say's system, money serves chiefly as a medium of exchange and was not explicitly identified as a store of wealth. Say denounces state manipulation of money through debasement of the value of currency. He observes that such manipulation of monetary values confuses the pricing system. He viewed inflation as a monetary phenomenon rather than the result of excessive employment and economic growth.

Say viewed interest rates as the price of credit. He understood that market-determined interest rates perform the function of a market clearing price for money. However, he did not explicitly recognize or discuss the relationship between interest rates and time preferences as did the later Austrian thinkers.

Say on Government Interference

According to Say, the cause of, or reason for, an excess supply of goods is an excess demand for money of which there is shortage. In turn, an excess demand for, or general shortage of, goods can only come about if there is an excess supply of the commodity that goods trade against, which is money. It follows that both a deficiency and an overabundance of money undermine the process of converting the savings of depositors into the spending of borrowers. If a general glut of products were to exist it would not be the cause of recession, but rather the effect of a recession caused by conditions (e.g., the actions of central bankers) which have caused gross misallocations of productive resources, unemployment, and the accumulation of inventory. Consumers would thus have less purchasing power due to the reduced demand for those goods until inventories are used up and misallocated resources become redirected.

Say is highly critical of taxation and loans to the government because they reduce the wealth to be exchanged in the private sector. He says that taxation injures production because it thwarts the accumulation of productive capital and that loans to the government remove productive capital from society only to be carelessly spent by government. The reduced capital available means that fewer goods will be exchanged and means a subsequent decline in wealth. Say thus viewed taxation as slavery and condemned government spending. He also noted that as the size of government increases, the range of efforts to redistribute wealth expands.

Seeing taxation as confiscatory and involuntary, Say understood the coercive nature of taxation and that taxation is the enemy of economic affluence. Taxation decreases the capital available in an economy by redirecting private investment to expenditures by the state. He saw that taxation not only destroys capital, it also inhibits the functioning of a free market and lowers citizens' standards of living. Noting that taxation and its related expenditures do more harm than good, Say states that the proper tax is the lowest possible tax.

According to Say, the goal of good government is to stimulate production while the goal of bad government is to foster consumption. He observes that an economy that stresses demand over supply is on the road to relative decline and stagnation. He also maintains that if business cycles occur then they are due to government intervention that impedes market forces and market clearing. Production and freedom are the concerns of good government. Say's discourse on government intervention provides a clear demonstration of the ineffectiveness of fiscal policy as a wealth creator.

Keynes Denies but Does Not Refute Say's Law

John Maynard Keynes (1883-1946) thought that Say and the other classical economists were saying that market economies will never create general gluts or shortages and that every increase in production constitutes its own demand. According to the classicals, this would be true only if goods and services are assigned without misallocation among all types of produce in the proportion which private interests dictate. In that situation only, the income generated by sales would be sufficient to purchase the quantity of goods available to be bought. Keynes mischaracterized Say's Law of Markets as "supply creates its own demand" and said that the law states that there is no obstacle to full employment and that full employment is the rule. Observing that full employment does not exist, Keynes concluded that Say's Law does not hold. Keynes misunderstood and/or misrepresented Say's views by claiming that they denied the possibility of depressions and unemployment. Keynes had singled out Say making him the antithetical background for his own views on how markets behave and the role that the government should play in the economy.

Keynes, the underconsumptionist, unlike Say, thought that production and consumption are disconnected activities. In addition, in the Keynesian system, saving and investment are not two perspectives of the same phenomenon. Instead, he saw them as two separate, unequal, and often discoordinated activities. For Keynes, the decision to save is not automatically coordinated with the amount of investment needed and desired by businessmen. He says that whether or not entrepreneurs and businessmen invest depends upon a number of subjective and irrational psychological factors instead of simply depending on the availability of savings at a low interest rate. According to Keynes, too much savings in the economy is the cause of the unemployment of resources. He contended that the Saysian system was only true in the special case of when savings equals investment. He says that, because this is rarely the case, economists need a general theory to explain unemployment. Keynes believed that the breakdown of Say's Law came about because of a lack of aggregate demand which results from the disequilibrium of planned savings and planned investment. For Keynes, savings can be too high or too low. Either way, he considers savings to be dangerous, self-defeating, and the source of the problem. According to Keynes, savings is a destructive "leakage" from the economy. In the end, after a series of convoluted discourses, Keynes concludes that (1) when savings are less than investment, government action is necessary to stimulate investment, and (2) when savings are greater than investment, government action is needed to encourage consumption expenditures. In both cases, it is up to the government to step in.

Keynes's solution to unemployment is an increase in government spending. His theory thus shifts from the classical economists' concern with production to a concern with consumption. He said that when supply outstrips demand some goods will not be sold and, as a result, production and employment will be cut back. His proposed solution is to increase consumption through government spending. Keynes says that general overproduction is the problem and that men are unemployed because they have produced too much. His proposed solution is to stimulate consumption and beat down production. He says that "aggregate demand" can be too low relative to "aggregate supply" and that government spending is needed to fill the gap left by private-sector demand to ensure full employment. For Keynes, spendthrifts, rather than savers, are virtuous. He holds that both consumer spending and government spending are the means to economic growth. His spending theory has enjoyed great popularity with statists who equate government spending with economic stimulus.

Keynes's solution for stimulating the economy is to have the government spend money thus bridging the gap between savings and investment. He advocates government schemes to pump up consumption such as printing and spending new money (which debases the currency and results in inflation), deficit spending, public works projects, higher taxes on producers, and the punitive graduated income tax which puts more money in the hands of the poor, who are said to spend a greater portion of their income.

Keynes maintains that sometimes people want to hoard money instead of saving it. When this money is withheld from investment, the result is unemployment which, in turn, causes overproduction. Unemployed people are not able to buy the previous output of products and depression results. According to Keynes, there will be an absence of savings during a depression as people withdraw money to survive. He goes on to say that (1) without savings there will be no investment; (2) without investment there will be no employment; (3) without employment there will be no spending; and (4) without spending there will be unsold goods.

Keynes explains that savings can overshoot the demand for investment in capital equipment, resulting in excess savings and the withdrawal of funds from circulation and from the necessary sufficient demand for goods. Drawing money away from the purchase of finished commodities makes them less profitable at the very same time that firms are seeking to set up additional capital resources to produce finished commodities. Keynes maintains that a deficiency of purchasing power is inevitable, resulting in an increased supply of, and a diminished demand for, products. As a result, profitable production cannot be continued and crises and depression begin. Keynes's solution for preventing or alleviating depressions is to either reduce the amount of savings or to stimulate consumption through government spending and/or the issuance of new money.

Keynes says that in a free market interest rates fail to perform the function of a market clearing price and that wage rates do not adjust. The result is underconsumption and unemployment in an unregulated economy. As a cure to bolster consumption, he proposed state management of the money market to supplement fiscal policies with respect to taxation and government spending.

Although Keynes was the most significant and substantial critic of Say's Law, he never really does refute it. Reality cannot be denied. Of course, Keynes's belief that he had invalidated Say's Law remains his most enduring legacy—a legacy that has crippled economic theory to this day. Contrary to Keynes, overproduction is not the problem. Rather, the problem is government intervention that penalizes production causing both capital and producers to go on "strike." For example, the Great Depression was due to government policies including high income taxes, quotas and tariffs, abandonment of the gold standard (i.e., objective money), and various and numerous regulations and controls.

Government efforts to stimulate the economy via direct spending and efforts to stimulate consumer spending are counterproductive. When the government spends an investment it must expropriate money from businesses to do so, thus ensuring a misallocation of resources. Government should get out of the way by reducing taxation, spending, regulations, and government control of money and the interest rate.

Say's Law: A Powerful Economic Truth

Say's Law, a landmark achievement of integration in economic science, is an essential foundation for a reality-based macroeconomic theory. It reflects the interconnectedness, reality, and harmony of human economic behavior in a free market economy. To produce requires rationality and self-interest. It is irrational and contrary to man's nature not to produce or to produce less than one needs to produce. Production is both necessary and primary for man's existence. Say thus recognized the fact that it is production that opens the demand for products. He saw that money is not the cause of prosperity but rather is its effect. This fact is eloquently stated in Ayn Rand's novel *Atlas Shrugged* (1957, 387) through her character Francisco d'Anconia, who said: "Money is made possible only by the men who produce. . . . When you accept money in payment for your effort, you do so only on the conviction that you will exchange it for the product of the effort of others." Say's Law is implicit throughout all of Francisco's "money speech."

The full explanatory power of Say's Law of Markets is that, because of the integration of all individual markets into one functioning system, it has to be the reality that government does not have to be concerned with artificially stimulating demand. There is one harmonious self-correcting system. Markets clear if not interfered with. Such a system leads to stability, justice, peace, and prosperity. It is no wonder that many consider Say's Law to be the broadest, most powerful, and most fundamental conceptual integration in the discipline of economics.

Recommended Reading

Balassa, Bela A. "John Stuart Mill and the Law of Markets." *Quarterly Journal of Economics* 73 (1959): 263–74.

Baumol, William J. "Say's (at Least) Eight Laws, or What Say and James Mill May Really Have Meant." *Economica* 44 (1977): 145–62.

———. "J. B. Say on Unemployment and Public Works." *Eastern Economic Journal* 23 (1997): 219–30.

Blaug, Mark. "Say's Law of Markets: What Did It Mean and Why Should We Care?" *Eastern Economic Journal* 23 (1997): 231–35.

Clower, Robert and Axel Leijonhufvud. "Say's Principle, What It Means and Doesn't Mean." *Intermountain Economic Review* 4 (1973): 1–16.

Cowan, Tyler. "Say's Law and Keynesian Economics." Pp. 160–84 in *Supply-side Economics: A Critical Appraisal*, edited by Richard H. Fink. Frederick, MD: Aletheia Books, University Publications of America, 1982.

Hazlitt, Henry. *The Failure of the "New Economics."* Princeton, NJ: D. Van Nostrand, 1959.

Hutt, W. H. *A Rehabilitation of Say's Law*. Athens: Ohio University Press, 1974.

Jonsson, Petur O. "On the Economics of Say and Keynes' Interpretation of Say's Law." *Eastern Economic Journal* 21 (1995): 147–55.

———. "On Gluts, Effective Demand, and the True Meaning of Say's Law." *Eastern Economic Journal* 23 (1997): 203–18.

Kates, Steven. "Keynes, Say's Law and the Theory of the Business Cycle." *History of Economics Review* 25 (1996): 119–26.

———. "A Discussion of Say's Law: The Outcome of the Symposium." *Eastern Economic Journal* 23 (1997a): 237–39.

———. "On the True Meaning of Say's Law." *Eastern Economic Journal* 23 (1997b): 191–202.

Lange, Oskar. "Say's Law: A Restatement and Criticism." *Studies in Mathematical Economics and Econometrics: In Memory of Henry Schultz*. Chicago: University of Chicago Press, 1942.

Mises, Ludwig von. "Lord Keynes and Say's Law." *The Freeman* (October 30, 1950). Reprinted on pp. 64–71 in *Planning for Freedom*. 4th ed. South Holland, IL: Libertarian Press, 1980.

Palmer, R. R. *J. B. Say: An Economist in Troubled Times*. Princeton, NJ: Princeton University Press, 1997.

Patinkin, Don. "Relative Prices, Say's Law, and the Demand for Money." *Econometrica* 16 (1948): 135–54.

Salerno, Joseph T. "The Neglect of the French Liberal School in Anglo-American Economics: A Critique of Received Explanations." *Review of Austrian Economics* 2: 113–56.

Skinner, A. S. "Say's Law: Origins and Content." *Scottish Journal of Political Economy* 16 (1967): 177–95.

———. "Of Malthus, Lauderdale and Say's Law." *Scottish Journal of Political Economy* 16 (1969): 177–95.

Sowell, Thomas. *Say's Law: An Historical Analysis*. Princeton, NJ: Princeton University Press, 1972.

———. *Classical Economics Reconsidered*. Princeton, NJ: Princeton University Press, 1977.

Thweatt, William O. "Early Forumulators of Say's Law." *Quarterly Review of Economics and Business* 19 (1979): 79–96.

Thweatt, William O. "Baumol and James Mill on 'Say's Law of Markets.'" *Economica* 47 (1980): 467–69.

Weinburg, Mark. "The Social Analysis of Three Early 19th Century French Liberals: Say, Comte, and Dunoyer." *Journal of Liberatarian Studies* 2, no.1 (1978): 45–64.

Chapter 11

Herbert Spencer on Liberty
and Human Progress

Social life must be carried on by either voluntary cooperation or compulsory cooperation; or, to use Sir Henry Maine's words, the system must be that of contract or that of status; that in which the individual is left to do the best he can by his spontaneous efforts and get success or failure according to his efficiency, and that in which he has his appointed place, works under coercive rule, and has his apportioned share of food, clothing, and shelter.

—Herbert Spencer

Herbert Spencer (1820-1903), British philosopher and sociologist, was a prominent, late-nineteenth-century defender of individual freedom and critic of state violence and coercion. A Lamarckian, rather than a Darwinian, pioneer in evolutionary theory, Spencer believed in inevitable human progress that develops naturally when people are free. He contended that well-being flourishes in moral societies where equal freedom is the ultimate principle of justice. According to Spencer, moral rights to life and liberty are requirements to happiness. It follows that people in societies in which moral rights are protected are happier and more successful. He held that to flourish there must be as few unnatural restrictions on individuals as possible. Progress is attained only through the free use of human faculties. This implies that the only legitimate function of government is the policing and protection of individual rights. The sole purpose of the state is to protect its citizens against external and internal aggression. Spencer's ideas are developed in a number of works, including *Social Statics* (1851), *Principles of Psychology* (1855), *Principles of Biology* (1864), *The Study of Sociology* (1873), *The Man Versus the State* (1884), and *The Principles of Ethics* (1892).

Spencer explains that human nature, the sum of men's sentiments and instincts, adapts over time to the conditions of social existence. His idea of human nature involves the adaptation of men's faculties to their organic, social, and psychological needs. His progressive adaptation involves an increasing adjustment of inner subjective relations to outer objective relations.

Epistemology

According to Spencer, a person cannot know the nature of reality in itself—there is something essentially unknowable. He says that we can know that the real exists but that we cannot know its nature nor have definite knowledge of its attributes. Spencer does not make any metaphysical commitment regarding the nature of reality. His theory of "transfigured realism" merely holds an objective existence as separate from, and independent of, subjective (i.e., phenomenal) existence.

Despite the fact that Spencer states that men's knowledge is phenomenal and applies only to appearances, he does not maintain that such knowledge is unreliable. Explaining that appearance without reality is inconceivable, he states that phenomenal knowledge is produced by external forces and is not created by a person's mind. For Spencer, reality is evidenced via persistence in consciousness. If the relation between one's mental states and objective reality is consistent, persistent, and invariable, then a person has justified beliefs. For Spencer, "persistence in consciousness" is the judge by which a person differentiates between the real and the unreal. This is Spencer's theory of indirect correspondence.

It follows that Spencer does not, and cannot, hold a true doctrine of natural law although he says that society should be organized in accordance with the laws of nature, that individuals have rights based on a law of life, and that justice has its foundation in natural law. In fact, his ethics and political philosophy actually depend on a somewhat truncated theory of natural law. For example, Spencer believes that people have rights that are recognized by "a priori cognition" or "a priori intuition." His earlier writings positioned his defense of natural rights on a theological foundation. Later, he became a dissatisfied deterministic agnostic who defended his notion of natural rights and his normative conclusions on totally secular premises.

Spencer's Evolutionary Individualism

Spencer was a Lamarckian who believed that acquired characteristics are transmitted to later generations. This means that the adaptations of a generation that permitted it to survive are transmitted to the succeeding generation, thus equipping it with superior capabilities. Lamarck held that evolutionary change takes place through the transmission to offspring of all changes undergone by the parent generation. Spencer says that hereditary transmission pertains to psychical traits and characteristics as well as to physical ones.

Spencer maintained that intuitions are biologically inheritable and therefore intuitions increase in following generations. Adopting a Lamarckian-style evolutionary theory, Spencer contended that characteristics acquired by parents via education can be inherited by their children. He saw an inextricable linkage between biological theory, social theory, and political theory.

Spencer has been inaccurately described as a "Social Darwinist." He was strongly committed to Lamarckian evolutionary thought which rejects the notion of random variation that is critical to Darwinian theory. Spencer's biological and social evolutionary synthesis emphasized Lamarckian evolutionary principles. More specifically, Spencer explains that evolutionary change takes place through the shift from the homogenous to the heterogeneous, from the similar to the dissimilar, from the simple to the complex, and from the undifferentiated to the differentiated.

Spencer considers the "survival of the fittest" as a law of existence applied to life. Life is the continuous adjustment of internal relations to external relations. For Spencer, the phrase, "survival of the fittest," is descriptive rather than evaluative—it describes a value-free evolutionary process. To be fit is to be adapted to the conditions of survival in a given environment.

He explains that pleasure-producing activities create biologically inheritable associations between feelings and ideas. Spencer's theory of the association of ideas holds that ideas become pervasive and connected when people experience the causes producing them as repeatedly occurring together. The results of repeated occurrences accumulate in successions of individuals and are transmitted as modifications of the nervous system.

Reason (i.e., intelligence) is an adaptive mechanism—it is a means of promoting a person's life-sustaining activities. Spencer explains that persistent impressions change the nervous system underpinning intelligence. Those resulting modifications are passed from one generation to another. The characteristics of the real (i.e., noumenal) world establish corresponding relations in consciousness through alterations of the nervous system. External relations affect consciousness, thereby causing particular internal relations to develop into persistent features of thought. According to Spencer, multitudinous experiences of human beings have altered the structure of man's nervous system.

Habitually repeated, life-affirming actions generate feelings of pleasure and life-negating actions generate feelings of pain. Life-sustaining activities tend to be habitually repeated when pleasure becomes associated with them and life-negating actions tend to be avoided when pain is associated with them. Spencer explains that this pleasure-pain response is an element in life's adaptive mechanism. Pleasure makes life valuable and supplies the motivation to take part in life-advancing activities. Pleasure is the cause of action and is the motive for actions. Life-affirming activities must give pleasure in order to elicit more activities of the same type and life-negating activities of the same type must yield pain in order to discourage habits that lead to failure. He states that, wherever utility becomes intuitive, societies tend to be more vibrant and better able to thrive.

Happiness, the excess of pleasure over pain, is what an individual seeks. Spencer thought that a form of hedonism explains the behavior of human beings—pleasure itself is the value. It is the connection between pro-life activities and pleasure that makes life valuable. Habits are produced through the repeated association of actions and pleasure. According to Spencer, these habits become organic via hereditary transmission. He states that people become fit through the evolution of mainly intellectual and moral characteristics. It follows that human beings supply evolution with intellectual and ethical checks. Ultimately, people are able to consciously acknowledge and intentionally refine the utility of their inherited moral intuitions. Spencer's fusion of science and ethics led him to advocate egoism and rational, utilitarian, moral theory. He says that social improvement depends upon ethical improvement in individuals.

New emotions adapted to new environments evolve. Spencer teaches that the evolution of moral sentiments is an essential component of man's evolutionary development. Moral sentiments and social conditions are inextricably connected, constantly interact, and influence one another. For Spencer, men are primarily motivated by moral habits that largely stem from moral sentiments. It thus appears that reason is less important than emotions for Spencer's explanation of human action. In the end, it is pleasure that is the standard of moral phenomena. Pleasure and value are connected in a person's moral consciousness.

Life and happiness are a person's proper goals that can be attained solely by the use of a person's faculties. Happiness can be achieved only if an individual is permitted to express his right of freedom to do all that his faculties drive him to do. A man's freedom is restricted only by the equal freedom of others. Spencer says that persons must be free to adapt to changing circumstances. All humans have the moral right to exercise their faculties with the freedom of each individual bounded by the like freedom of others. Spencer's equal-freedom doctrine states that the freedom of each person is limited to the degree that the freedoms of others are not impinged upon.

The law of equal freedom states that every individual has the freedom to do as he wills as long as he does not infringe upon the equal freedom of any other person. If given adequate room for making decisions, individuals thus learn the value of equal freedom and equal rights. Specifically, the law of equal freedom leads to rights of speech, private property, press, religion, and so on.

Human progress develops naturally when people are free. Spencer contends that when individuals are free to adapt to changing conditions, progress becomes inevitable. He maintains that social evolutionary advancement requires the freedom of actions of autonomous individuals. The voluntary action of self-interested individuals provides force to positive social evolution. Progress derives from individual motivations, ingenuity, and efforts to adapt. It is apparent that Spencer's case for freedom rests on the grounds that evolutionary progress requires it. He says that, as society evolves, voluntary cooperation will become the dominant form of interaction. With the evolution of societies based on voluntary contract and division of labor, there will develop a harmony of individual interests. If voluntary cooperation is to evolve, persons must be free to experience the consequences of social cooperation.

Militant Society versus Industrial Society

Spencer explains that persistence of force is a principle of nature that cannot be produced artificially by the state. It follows that the best government is the one that interferes least in the lives of its citizens. Spencer disdains the state that decides who deserves what. State interference with the natural evolutionary processes is immoral and dangerous. In the natural evolutionary process the individual is integrated by adaptation in accordance with the functions he is required to execute. Government attempts to speed up the process will have the result of restricting individual freedom and dynamism. Voluntary cooperation is by its very nature more efficient and more just than state force.

According to Spencer, social order does not require deliberate design for its emergence. Order arises spontaneously through the workings of natural laws. Anticipating the writings of F. A. Hayek, Spencer explained that spontaneous market activity is responsible for men's achievements. Man, as a social being, can achieve individual happiness only within a social framework provided by competitive market forces and ethical principles. Spencer distrusted the use of government power to regulate market forces, thereby constraining the social and intellectual development of man. He was against the impersonal and dehumanized controlling state that wanted to direct individual interests according to government plan.

Spencer classified the two chief modes of social organization as militant and industrial. The militant way operates through compulsion and is oriented toward conflict and the industrial manner is characterized by voluntary cooperation and peaceful exchange. Spencer's goal is to replace the militant method of social organization with the industrial approach. He explains that it is natural for society to evolve from a militant to an industrial form of social organization. Voluntary contractual society evolves from a society of status. People will learn progressively and gradually the superiority of nonlegal social controls over state coercion and cooperation will replace exploitation. Spencer points out that industrial civilization emerged despite the existence of legal obstacles. He adds that coercive centralized approaches to social problems are counterproductive and are likely to be dispensed with by the spontaneous forces of social evolution. Whereas the militant social structure is a hierarchy in which each person obeys those above him, industrial society is regulated by competitive market forces and ethical principles.

Spencer's evolutionary synthesis explains the change from a homogenous social structure to a heterogeneous social structure. He explains that an enduring militant society would tend to hinder differentiation and social evolution. However, homogeneous structures are unstable and ultimately progress to more complex forms. As society evolves, persons become more individuated at the same time they become more voluntarily associated. In a free society, honest, innovative, and industrious people prosper and advance by providing others with desired goods and services. Spencer notes that an increasingly libertarian society becomes increasingly more industrial and less militant. The natural course of social evolution is one of increasing heterogeneity. Contributing to the evolutionary trend from homogeneity to heterogeneity is the multiplication of effects.

Spencer is against government interference in the lives of persons. His concern is that a political community could violate the law of equal freedom. Spencer explains that the state was founded to reduce disorder by defending individuals against one another and by protecting each society from attack by others. It is not within the jurisdiction of the state to administer education, charity, or religion. Critical of undue state authority, regulation, and interference, Spencer surmises that the collective wisdom of the state should not be trusted. He does not want political power available to certain people who would enrich themselves at the expense of others.

Opposed to coercive taxpayer-funded, state-enforced charity, Spencer favored charity that was voluntarily conferred. It is unjust for one to be forced to help others but ethically a person may be obligated to do so. He says that noninterference is the essence of justice but that ethics involves positive beneficence. Voluntary charitable assistance should have the goal of helping the recipient become productive and should not lead to dependency. According to Spencer, when the state takes from some to give to others, society is made weaker. He says that the state thereby supports the survival of the unfittest. Government interference with the adaptation of individuals serves as a regressive force. With lessening of the role of government, men will learn to govern themselves so that coercion can be decreased.

Spencer maintains that the state should not interfere with the relationship between causes and consequences of human action. A person should be free to experience the natural good or bad consequences of his own actions. By so doing, sentiments congruent with voluntary cooperation will evolve over time. If the causal relationship is dissociated, then moral sentiments unsuitable to progress will develop and the evolutionary process will be hindered. Spencer strongly emphasizes the importance of preserving the relationship between conduct and consequence. State co-optation of nature would produce more pain in the long run than would have occurred if well-intentioned state officials had restrained the desire to intervene with the competitive sector of human society.

Spencer proposed abolishing government welfare, all trade restrictions, government education, government church subsidies, medical licensing, the government postal monopoly, the central bank, legal tender laws, overseas colonies, and nondefensive wars. He also condemned imperialism, slavery, censorship, and sexual inequality. Generally against the majority imposing its will on the minority, Spencer said it was permissible only when matters fall under the state's proper jurisdiction which is the protection of individual rights.

Against the idea of "national interest" and aggressive warfare abroad, he explained that foreign expansion leads to domestic tyranny. The warring state stifles change from the similar to the dissimilar and paves the way for the government to dictate the interests of its citizens. War is a path of societal devolution. Furthermore, it is difficult, if not impossible, to respect the individuality and autonomy of people while proclaiming that they owe their lives to the state. Spencer dreaded expansion of the role of government at the demands of the military or others because it would hamper the achievement of Spencer's utopian society.

Egoistic Ethics

Spencer holds a fundamentally egoist ethics although he does argue that life with and among others is important. People have mutually compatible self-interested goals. Spencer's egoistic ethics increases the chances of the compatibility of interests among intelligent and virtuous people whose actions gain benefits when they are principled and rational. He says that by pursuing one's own ends, while adhering to the principle of justice, a person unintentionally benefits others. When properly understood, human interests are so interdependent that a person cannot truly pursue his own welfare without giving others their due.

Spencer's optimal development path is the one that progresses toward a world where people's conduct is regulated primarily by competitive market forces and by ethical principles. For Spencer, the evolutionary process is progressive in a moral sense. Of course, the progress of moral sentiments, like all progress, is conditional. Moral sentiments are subject to evolutionary progress if suitable conditions are sustained. As societies become more specialized and differentiated, voluntary cooperation and exchange become necessary for human survival and sentiments appropriate to such activities will also evolve.

In Spencer's ethical naturalism, ethical propositions are descriptive propositions with respect to causal relations. Spencer's "oughts" possess a suppositional or hypothetical character. He would say that, if a person values his life and believes that life results in greater pleasure than pain, then he should be concerned with rules of conduct by which life is maintained and advanced. Spencer's goal was to make ethics into a science and to be able to deduce moral rules from the causal laws of life.

He contends that there is an innate and evolving moral sense by which people access moral intuitions and from which laws of moral conduct can be deduced. The principles of human moral sense are the accumulated effects of inherited or instinctual experiences. The accumulated responses of past generations result in moral sentiments. His moral science doctrine provides an example of Spencer's notion of the persistence of force.

Spencer explains that sentiments develop that induce people to respect others' natural rights and, at the highest level of social evolution, to voluntarily advance the welfare of other individuals. He says the people demonstrate a natural concern and sympathy toward one another and that compassion and altruism, apart from the family, evolved only recently. Spencer recognized the importance of altruism in human evolution and politics and the interrelationship between social evolution and moral evolution. He maintains that people need to develop higher emotional sentiments such as positive beneficence and says that those sentiments will evolve if given the chance. Positive beneficence, an occurrence in the highest form of society, involves spontaneous efforts to advance the welfare of others.

Only when the individual is free to live under the law of equal freedom can social and moral evolution reach its highest level. Spencer explains a free individual society of mutual noninterference among its members is necessary in order to develop the moral sentiments including the sentiments of justice. The sentiments of justice include both egoistic and altruistic elements.

Spencer discussed both an absolute ethics and a relative ethics and stated that absolute ethics pertained only to a perfectly evolved peaceful society. The absolute ethical code thus only applied to man at his highest stage of evolution and not to imperfect man. In effect, then, he is saying that natural rights do not take full effect before the appearance of the total development of society and human nature. He says that, because of the highly developed sense of justice of perfected human beings, the state will ultimately not have many functions to perform. In his absolute ethics no coercion at all was allowed. Of course, the implication is that during transition from relative ethics to absolute ethics, some state coercion such as taxation and conscription may be permissible.

Unfortunately, Spencer's idea of universal causation prompts him to dismiss any theory of free will in human beings. He says that men have the illusion of free will because of the observable absence of consistency in human action. Because he rejects the notion of freedom of the human will, Spencer's theory of ethical egoism must be viewed as flawed. His determinism eliminates the possibility of true human choice.

Conclusion

Despite his errors, Spencer continues to be read today. He was a systematic thinker who had a utilitarian perspective on rights and who believed that utility and liberty were compossible. Spencer optimistically held that the long-run direction of social evolution is toward industrial civilization but was pessimistic regarding the near future as the world was moving toward militarism, centralization, and regulation. He witnessed public opinion increasingly in favor of government intervention during the late nineteenth century. Throughout his lifetime, Spencer saw society moving far away from his evolutionary synthesis as public opinion had accepted the view of positive freedom.

Recommended Reading

Andreski, S. *Herbert Spencer: Structure, Function and Evolution*. London: Joseph, 1972.

Compayre, G. *Herbert Spencer and Scientific Education*. Translated by M. E. F. Findlay. London: Harrap, 1908.

Dewey, J. "The Philosophical Work of Herbert Spencer." *Characters and Events*. New York: Holt, 1929.

Duncan, D. *The Life and Letters of Herbert Spencer*. London: Methuen, 1908.

Gray, Tim. *The Political Philosophy of Herbert Spencer*. Aldershot, UK: Ashgate Publishing, 1996.

Kennedy, James G. *Herbert Spencer*. Boston: Twayne Publishers, 1978.

Lauwerys, J. A. "Herbert Spencer and the Scientific Movement." In *Pioneers of English Education*, edited by A. V. Judges. London: Faber, 1952.

Low-Beer, A. *Spencer*. London: Collier-Macmillan, 1969.

Peel, J. D. Y. *Herbert Spencer: The Evolution of a Sociologist*. London: Heinemann, 1971.

Ritchie, David G. *The Principles of State Interference: Four Essays on the Political Philosophy of Mr. Herbert Spencer, J. S. Mill and T. H. Green*. London: Swan Sonnenschein, 1891.

Smith, George H. "Herbert Spencer's Theory of Causation." *The Journal of Libertarian Studies* 2 (Spring 1981).

Spencer, Herbert. *The Proper Sphere of Government*. London: W. Brittain, 1843.

———. *Social Statics*. London: Chapman, 1851.

———. "A Theory of Population Deduced from the General Law of Animal Fertility." *Westminster Review* (1852): 498–501.

———. *The Principles of Psychology*, London: Longmans, 1855. 2nd ed. 2 vols. London: Williams & Norgate, 1870–1872; 3rd ed. 2 vols. 1890. [*A System of Synthetic Philosophy* v. 4–5].

———. *First Principles*. London: Williams & Norgate, 1862; 6th ed., revised, 1904. [*A System of Synthetic Philosophy* v. 1].

———. *The Principles of Biology*. London: Williams & Norgate, 1864–186.; 2nd ed., 1898–1899. [*A System of Synthetic Philosophy* v. 2–3]

———. *Social Statics*. London: Williams & Norgate, 1868.

———. *The Study of Sociology*. London: Henry S. King and Co., 1872.

———. *The Principles of Sociology*. London: Williams & Norgate, 1876-1896.

———. *First Principles*. New York: A. L. Burt, [1862] 1880.

———. *Principles of Sociology*. London: Williams & Norgate, 1882.

———. *The Principles of Sociology*. 3 vols. London: Williams & Norgate, 1882–1898 [*A System of Synthetic Philosophy* v. 6–8]

———. *The Man versus the State*. London: Williams & Norgate, 1884.

———. *The Factors of Organic Evolution*. London: Williams & Norgate, 1887.

———. *Essays: Scientific, Political, and Speculative*. London: Williams & Norgate, 1891.

———. *The Principles of Ethics*. 2 vols. New York: Hurst, 1892–1893.

———. *The Principles of Biology*. London: Williams & Norgate, [1864] 1898.

———. *Principles of Ethics*. London: Williams & Norgate, 1900.

———. *Facts and Comments*. London: Williams & Norgate, 1902.

———. *An Autobiography*. 2 vols. New York: Appleton & Co., 1904.

————. *The Man Versus the State with Six Essays on Government, Society and Freedom.* Indianapolis, IN: Liberty Classics, 1981.

————. *The Man Versus the State.* Reprinted. Indianapolis, IN: Liberty Fund, Inc. 1982.

Stocking, George W., Jr. "Lamarckianism in American Social Science: 1890-1915." *Journal of the History of Ideas* 23:2 (1962): 239–56.

Taylor, M. W. *Men versus the State.* Caldwell, ID: Caxton, 1940.

Turner, Jonathan. *Herbert Spencer: A Renewed Appreciation.* Beverly Hills, CA: Sage Publications, 1985.

Wiltshire, David. *The Social and Political Thought of Herbert Spencer.* New York: Oxford, 1978.

Chapter 12

Carl Menger's
Economics of Well-Being

Value is therefore nothing inherent in goods, no property of them, but merely the importance that we first attribute to the satisfaction of our needs, that is, to our lives and well-being, and in consequence carry over to economic goods as the exclusive causes of the satisfaction of our needs.

—Carl Menger

Carl Menger (1840-1921) began the modern period of economic thought and provided the foundation for the Austrian school of economics. In his two books, *Principles of Economics* (1871) and *Investigations into the Method of the Social Science with Special Reference to Economics* (1883), Menger destroyed the existing structure of economic science, including both its theory and methodology, and put it on totally new foundations.

Marginal Utility Theory

Carl Menger is perhaps best known for his development of marginal utility theory. One of the three pioneers of marginal utility theory, Menger formulated and codiscovered marginal utility theory simultaneously with, and independently of, Jevons and three years ahead of Walras. Jevons and Walras concentrated on marginal utility as the mathematical concept of the first derivative of a total utility function. They were responsible for introducing the mathematization of subjective preferences in economic analysis.

Contrariwise, Menger's concept of marginal utility was an implied ordinal ranking of utility rather than the first derivative of some idea of total utility. Menger does not attempt to mathematically simplify by assuming continuity, divisibility, or a perfect market. Greater realism and generality can be attained when economic propositions are not confined by implicit assumptions of continuity and differentiability of functions. Menger emphasized variable elements such as needs and wants instead of more stable factors such as labor costs and production costs.

Menger stressed the role of subjective evaluation with respect to the principle of marginal utility. Whereas Jevons and Walras were concerned with equilibrium, Menger was interested in process. Menger extensively developed the subjectivist dimensions of the marginalist revolution. He did this by emphasizing an individual's subjective satisfaction, the subjectivity of decisions, the limitations of knowledge, the uncertainty of choices, and the possibility of error. He also employed the time dimension in connection to the study of economic quantities necessary for the satisfaction of wants. It was more important for Menger to comprehend the meaning of individual choices than to artificially calculate the intensity of their choices.

According to Menger, goods are valued because they help to appease some human need or want. A given unit, quantity, or amount of a particular good will satisfy a person's most intense need or desire. After each unit consumed or used, a man's need or desire may be less intense. Each increment of that specific good available to him will be less valuable in his eyes. The value of goods are mutually interdependent in a given location and the exchange value of a certain increment of each product or service will be determined by the relationships between the aggregate amount available and the intensity of the human need or desire that it meets. The economic value of goods hinges on their respective quantities in relation to the human needs and desires they are expected to meet.

Metaphysics and Epistemology

Menger sees the world, which includes both physical and mental aspects, as existing independently of our reasoning and thinking activities and as organized in an intelligible fashion. We can know what the world is like due to its conformity to laws that are accessible to reason. Menger is an immanent realist who says that we can know what the world is like both via common sense and through the scientific method. Menger's Austrian Aristotelianism is a doctrine of ontology that informs us what the world is like and what its objects, processes, and states are. His commonsense realism says that we have access to what is real through our everyday experiences. Menger argues that there is one reality knowable by rational means and that all things are subject to the laws of cause and effect. Laws of causality have an ontological or metaphysical reality—how a thing acts is determined by what a thing is. Entities in reality act according to their natures. An object necessarily tends to behave in a particular way by virtue of its real essence.

According to Menger, there are intelligible a priori essences or natures existing autonomously in reality. Because these essences and essential structures are knowable, corresponding laws of and connections between these structures are able to be comprehended. These essences and the laws governing them are manifested in the world and are strictly universal. These tell us what kinds of relations can exist between various components of reality. Menger sees intelligible, law-governed change in the particulars of the world. The essences or laws are precisely universal in that they do not change and in that they are capable of being instantiated in all cultures and at all times. For Menger, theory must relate to knowledge that must endure and extend in time beyond immediate and present knowledge. The essences relevant to the various different aspects or levels of reality make up a graphic representation of structural parts. Reasoning using essences or universals as simple conceptual elements will proceed according to the nature of objects and will deduce conceptual systems of causality consonant with the causality of the real world.

Menger's essentialism holds that general essences do not exist in isolation from what is individual. Universals are said to exist only as aspects of specific objects and phenomena that are not directly observable in pure form. Every experience of the world involves both an individual and a universal or general aspect. According to Menger, we can know what the world is like in both its individual and general features.

A realist about universals, Menger observes that they exist in reality and that they are attributes shared by many particular objects. The particulars are individual, whereas the universals are general. In order for the universals to be phenomena of conceptualization, they have to be abstracted from empirical reality. Essential or necessary characteristics of an object are those of its real essence. A depiction is concrete if it concerns particulars and is abstract if it is about universals. Only particulars have the capacity to act. Universals not only do not possess the power to act, they cannot exist without the particulars.

Menger believes in the knowability of general laws. However, he says that our knowledge of the general aspect of experience is in no way infallible. There may be difficulties in gaining knowledge of essential structures and converting such knowledge into the form of a strict theory. Despite the existence of problems and obstacles, he says it is possible for our knowledge of essential structures and laws to be exact and that our knowledge will in all probability exhibit a progressive improvement.

For Menger, these structures are a priori categories in reality that possess an intrinsic simplicity and intelligibility that makes them capable of being apprehended in a straightforward manner. The nature of objects in the world can be read off directly through both external observation and introspection. Menger acknowledges the existence of both intelligible (i.e., law-governed) structures and structures of accidental association that can be comprehended.

Menger follows Aristotle in saying that all knowledge about the world begins with induction. He reasons that we can actually detect essences in reality through repeated observations of phenomena, which reveal certain similarities according to which objects would be grouped into types or classes via a process of abstraction. Induction involves inference from experience and going from the particular to the general. It follows that even deductions are ontological since they are based on metaphysical reality. Deductions are made from inductively known facts and premises. They are based on reality and are not purely a priori mental categories. Introspection is an ingredient in Menger's epistemology. He says that introspection gives people access to some limited useful and reliable knowledge about other human persons and their experiences, such as the experience of making choices. Menger's epistemology makes use of the internal perspective on human action that people share because of their common humanity. He says that introspection should be included in a legitimate epistemology because we live in a world inhabited by other human minds as well as our own.

Menger's doctrine of ontological individualism states that there are no "social organisms" or "social wholes." Explanations of such social phenomena are traceable to the ideas and actions of individual persons. He explains that the individual precedes the state and other collective bodies both chronologically and metaphysically.

Menger's view is that man has no innate ideas but does have the ability to reason. Man begins uninformed and becomes ever more knowledgeable about the world. Although he espouses that man has free will, he displays what might be regarded as deterministic overtones in his belief in the existence in human nature of fundamental common influences of, or motives for, human behavior, including the economic, moral sentiments, altruism, and justice. Menger observes that the impulse for one's economic self-interest is man's primary and most common trait. He says that man is ingrained with a drive for self-interest in a healthy sense, rather than in a Hobbesian one. According to Menger, the individual, although desiring to satisfy his needs, is not directly driven or determined by them.

Menger's rational egoism recognizes that value is grounded in human needs and their satisfaction. Man's physical and intellectual needs derive from genuine needs of the species. Equating self-interested behavior with economic behavior, Menger says that men do, and should, rationally seek to attain economic advantages or gains for themselves. He is finding a basis for economics in biology. Man's metaphysical and biological needs are not arbitrary and must be met if he is to survive and prosper. Rational self-interested behavior is thus viewed as good behavior.

Rationality does not imply omniscience. Menger explains that men are born into ignorance and that their primary enterprise is to learn the causal connections between objects and the satisfaction of their needs in order to make rational decisions regarding their well-being. Economic life is constructed around the acquiring of knowledge. Menger portrays rational, economic man as an uncertain being who gradually gains the knowledge and resources necessary to attain his ends. He also explains that economic progress is caused by the growth in knowledge.

Economic Goods

Menger explains that all things are subject to the law of cause and effect and that if one passes from a state of need to a state in which the need is satisfied then sufficient causes for this change must exist. Accordingly, useful things are those that can be placed in a causal connection with the satisfaction of human needs. The satisfaction of human needs is the final cause in Menger's exact theory and the driving force of all economic activity. Human needs are the beginning and the end of human activity because nothing would take place without human needs and the requirements of satisfying them. By conceptualizing the law of cause and effect, man recognizes his dependence on the external world and transforms it into the means to attain his ends. Man thereby becomes the ultimate cause as well as the ultimate end in the process of want satisfaction.

After discussing the properties of a useful object, he proceeds to discuss those of a good, and then of an economic (or scarce) good. According to Menger, a thing becomes a good or acquires a goods-character if all four of the following conditions are simultaneously present: (1) a need on the part of some human being; (2) such properties that render the object capable of being brought into a causal connection with the satisfaction of this need; (3) knowledge of this causal connection on the part of the person involved; and (4) command of the thing sufficient to direct it to satisfaction of the need. Goods are those elements of the external world that are integral to the causal process of want satisfaction and upon which action operates. Goods exist only to serve human satisfactions. Goods can be divided into material goods and useful human actions (e.g., labor services).

Menger's explanation of goods relates them back to human needs and human nature. Linking the idea of utility to biology, Menger believes that human wants are to a great extent determined by physiological needs. He sees the biological foundations of human needs as the key to integrating economics with material reality. People can comprehend the goal of much activity in terms of its relation to an organism's biological needs. Through the study of biology and physiology, Menger formulates a theory of needs to complement his theory of value. A person's biological and intellectual needs have to be met and satisfied if he is to survive and prosper. Menger thus emphasizes the biological and the choices people make beyond the purely biological.

According to Menger, the combination of the views an individual holds about things as economic objects and the laws describing the categories to which economic objects are members is what makes an object economic. In order for something to be an economic good: (1) the judging subject must perceive an object as scarce; (2) the thing must be evaluated in relation to needs known to the self-interested judging subject as urgent; (3) the judging subject must perceive a causal connection between the object and the fulfillment of a mediate or immediate end; and (4) the subject must believe that he has a feasible command of the thing sufficient to be able to direct it to the satisfaction of an end.

For Menger, the nature of the world and the scarcity of its natural resources, combined with human nature and people's desires for greater satisfaction of their wants, circumscribe the fundamental nature of the economic world. Menger defines economics as the science which examines the laws of cause and effect that control the processes through which goods satisfy human needs. He meditates on the nature of human striving to satisfy wants and deduces its immediate implications. Through this process, Menger discovers that the laws of human needs are entirely sufficient to explain the basic facts regarding all the phenomena of the exchange economy. He envisions the economy as a system driven by the valuations and choices of consumers.

The idea of scarcity underpins Menger's analysis of economic goods and economic value. Every choice involves scarcity. Dealing with scarcity is an essential feature of the human condition that necessitates the allocation of means to attain ends. Economic judgments include evaluations aimed at choosing among known alternatives. Menger calls choosing "economizing."

Economic judgments that a person makes indicate the degree to which he believes an object may satisfy his needs. Menger's economic object is thus a subject-dependent entity in the sense that the manner of its existence depends upon its being perceived as economic by the agent. The economic character of a good cannot be determined in the absence of a mind judging or perceiving the significance of an object in relation to an end.

Whereas the judgment regarding an economic entity is subjective, its truth or untruth can be determined objectively via a realist economic ontological theory of truth involving the correspondence of facts about the object with the judgment that is made. What decides the truth in economic judgment is the correspondence between expectations and their instantiation in facts. The fulfillment of a person's expectations is based on the facts, of which some are intrinsic properties of the object. Although the truth or falsity of an economic judgment can be settled objectively based on facts in the world about the object in its role as an economic good and their correspondence to the agent's expectations, it is clear that no one except the acting subject could make the verdict.

Menger thus demonstrates that economic subjectivism can be compatible with philosophical realism. Economic judgments depend on men's minds for their existence but not for their truth. Menger reconciles the subject-dependent character of economic phenomena with objectivity of representations regarding the nature of these phenomena. An economic object is a subjective entity because its existence is contingent upon its being viewed as economic by a subject. However, its truth can be judged objectively by the correspondence of the judgment with the facts of reality.

Menger emphasizes and expresses the causal interplay between the subjective and objective aspects of action. In his theory of goods, or general theory of the good, there must be a belief or opinion by the agent that there is a causal connection between the object and the satisfaction of the human need under consideration. Menger thus even contends that imaginary goods may derive a goods-like character from attributes they are imagined to have or from needs merely fantasized by men.

What makes something an economic good is a combination of the views a person has about objects as economic goods and the exact laws governing the categories of economic objects. The term "economic goods" applies to both material objects and to intangible ends that almost always have tangible things as mediate ends.

Noneconomic goods are available in superabundance in that the quantity available exceeds the amount necessary to satisfy all human wants for them. On the other hand, economic goods are those available in a quantity insufficient to totally appease all human wants for them. Menger explains that there is an objective relationship between how much of a good could be used to satisfy all needs and how much of the good exists. An economic good exists when the total demand for it is greater than the amount in supply. The existence of an economic good leads to economizing or making the best use of available but scarce resources. The economic or noneconomic character of goods is not inherent in them or in any of their properties. Rather, a good achieves economic character when it enters into the quantitative relationship of scarcity and loses it when it is no longer scarce. Goods are thus able to change economic character.

According to Menger, all market transactions and every act of production are set in motion by consumer preferences. In fact, Menger attempts to construct economics using the human person as the creative actor and starting point of all social processes. Specifically, Menger sees the purpose of the study of economics as to understand the conditions under which men engage in activity directed to the satisfaction of their needs.

Menger perceives a causal connection between goods. He sees that goods of the lowest order, consumer goods, have a direct causal connection with the satisfaction of needs. Goods of higher order or factors of production have only an indirect causal connection with men's needs. People produce for the sake of goods that can be consumed.

Goods desired and available for consumption or direct use are termed goods of the first order. Goods of the second order consist of raw materials and other factors necessary to produce goods of the first order. In turn, factors required to produce goods of the second order are called goods of the third order, and so on. Goods of higher order do not possess intrinsic value but derive their goods-character from that of the corresponding goods of lower order which they cooperate in producing. Menger thus theorizes based on a process of action, including a series of intermediate steps beginning with the production of economic goods of a higher order and ending when the final consumer good is attained.

Menger stresses the importance and implications of time and uncertainty in the production process. Because production occurs in real time it is necessary to anticipate the future, which is uncertain. All economic activity implies risk because perfect knowledge does not exist. Menger sees risk and uncertainty in the time-consuming nature of economic processes. It takes time to produce and producers cannot know with certitude what market conditions will exist when the final product is ready for sale. The ideas of time and causality cannot be separated. A change process such as productive action takes time and is inherently uncertain.

Causal productive processes are planned and carried out by economizing individuals who in social situations become increasingly perceptive of, and attentive to, their economic interests. With respect to economic goods, people economize them in order to satisfy their wants for them as fully as possible. Economizing, the purposive behavior of action, involves evaluating and arraying wants for goods according to their greatest importance or urgency and then deciding to assign units of a good to those uses that meet the most important wants. Menger's economizing man allocates scarce means in order to achieve his most highly valued ends.

Menger explains that the entrepreneur is an economizing man who initiates and directs an uncertain causal process. The entrepreneur's activities include the set of functions essential for mobilizing the production process. His most important mission is to visualize and predict future wants, gauge their relative importance, and attain knowledge of potentially available means. Menger recognizes that knowledge is limited and that the acquisition of knowledge is the cause of wealth. He is especially concerned with improved resource use as a result of enhanced knowledge of production processes. Evidencing a belief that knowledge is power, Menger maintains that economic life is constructed around the gaining of knowledge with respect to the causal relationship between objects and satisfactions, the relationship between goods of a higher order and goods of the first order, economic opportunities and situations, and so on.

Mengerian economics is concerned with goods, expectations, knowledge, and property. The notion of property is inherent in the idea of economizing. In fact, Menger's vision assumes a given structure of property rights and property laws. Because various individuals will attain different degrees of success, it is necessary to protect individuals in the possession of goods against possible acts of force and fraud. The basis for protection of ownership lies in the fact that some men will have interests opposed to those of the current possessors of property.

Menger contends that markets will express consumer sovereignty in the absence of errors, aberrations, and departures from the carefully defined assumptions of his theoretical system. Of course, in the real world, consumers may be mistaken regarding what is actually in their own best interests. In addition, there may be complicating considerations regarding the protection of property rights and proper functions of the state.

Value Theory

Menger states that goods have no inherent or intrinsic value in themselves and that their value is not related to the amount of labor expended in producing them. He contends that the labor theory of value held by Adam Smith and other classical economists is wrong. Menger observes that the so-called objective approach of adding up various costs, the most important being labor, is vague and produces contradictions. The classical labor or cost-value theory is called "objective" because it is based on the costs that go into making the object. In fact, it is a theory of intrinsic or inherent value. A keen observer of reality, Menger, who worked as a commodities analyst and reporter, recognizes that prices often have no relation to the labor added to particular goods. He notes that the price of a finished product might bear no resemblance to the costs of production because the two represent market conditions at very different periods of time. He also sees that a price can be seen as objective only in the sense that it is an objective magnitude of a numerical value that can mutually be agreed upon.

Menger explains that value is a judgment made by economizing individuals regarding the importance of particular goods for maintaining their lives and well-being. A person assigns value to a good based on the end it enables him to achieve. Applying the concept of intentionality to economic value, Menger stresses that only individuals value and act. His value theory incorporates an analysis of natural human behavior. His theory focuses on individual action itself, rather than on the social phenomena that develop out of individual action. A value must require action in order to be reached. Value in every case is a function of valuing acts of an individual given his own particular context. Individual judgments are acts of preference or evaluation.

Menger seems to want to find a basis for economic value in biology. He explains that economic goods have value because of their ability to fulfill human needs and wants. Like Aristotle, he views goods as the means of life, well-being, and needs satisfaction. Self-interested behavior (i.e., attaining goods) is economic behavior and is good behavior. The value of a good is a necessary consequence of the knowledge that the maintenance of one's life and well-being depends upon the control and use of that particular good. Value derives only to the extent that a product satisfies a human need or want. Menger recognizes that value originates in a relationship between man and his survival requirements. Value arises out of a relationship between human beings and what they require for their survival and well-being. Human beings must value because they have needs as living, conditional entities.

Menger accounts for value in terms of the satisfaction of human needs and wants. Value is "subjective" in the sense that it stems from a personal estimation of products and attributes of products with respect to the satisfaction of a man's needs. These needs are not arbitrary. They are real needs, the satisfaction of which forms the basis of valuation.

The value of goods emerges from their relation to our needs and is not inherent in the goods themselves. Nor is value merely in a man's mind independent of reality. While most accounts reduce value to either some intrinsic property of things or to the mind, Menger demonstrates that value results from an interplay between a man's conceptual consciousness, human needs, and the physical ability of goods to meet those needs. Value is not in man alone nor inherent in the goods themselves. Value is a necessary consequence of economic activity. Goods are the objects of a person's economizing and valuation.

Value must be in a man's mind but also must be based in reality. While Menger recognizes that value does not exist outside the consciousness of a human being, he also does not disregard the realm of external reality. For value to exist, consciousness must recognize a connection between means and an end in reality. A value must be to a particular valuer in his unique and specific context for an end to which the value is a means. A person's life is seen by Menger as the ultimate end of valuation and action. Life requires action and is an end in itself—an end which is not a means to any further end. Men must act to reach values in order to survive.

What a man needs depends on the facts of his nature and on the facts of things in reality. Menger recognizes that there are facts of economic reality. Values are neither subjective, arbitrary, nor intrinsic but are objective when a person's wants correspond to the objective state of affairs. Menger understands that the process of want satisfaction is not entirely cognitive and internal to the human mind, but dependent on the external world and upon the law of cause and effect. For value to exist, there must be a connection in reality grasped by consciousness with respect to means and ends which support a particular man's life. Knowledge in the form of a means-end relationship grasped by reason is a precondition for value. The evaluation of facts is necessary for the creation of value. In this sense, values can be said to be "products" of the mind. In addition, values can only be said to be "subjective" from the perspective that the evaluation of a causal connection with the satisfaction of an end is performed by an individual subject's consciousness. Subjective conditions of satisfaction are elements in the very causal series that includes objective states of reality.

In a larger sense, values as depicted by Menger are not subjective (i.e., arbitrary) nor inherent but are objective. Unfortunately, because the label "objective value theory" had already been attached to the labor theory of value, Menger's new value theory was eventually accorded the mistaken label of subjective value theory. Menger's theory explains the inextricable ontological connection between the realm of cognition and the sphere of objective causal processes that results from valuation and economizing. Value is a judgment made by economizing individuals regarding the importance of things for maintaining their lives and advancing their well-being. A person's judgment of value can be said to have been objectively made when it derives from knowledge based on the facts of the reality and on reasoning in accordance with the laws of logic.

Menger equates self-interested or selfish behavior with economic behavior. He says that it is proper for an individual to attain economic advantages or gains for himself. The satisfaction of one's needs constitutes economic activity. It follows that to act uneconomically means acting against one's own self-interest.

He explains that a person values most highly what he needs most highly and that value is the importance a person assigns to objects of the external world with respect to his well-being. According to Menger, value is the importance that individual goods or quantities of goods have for us because we are conscious of our dependence on the command of them for the satisfaction of our needs. The value of all goods can be seen as the imputation of the importance of satisfying our needs to economic goods. In the end, it is man's life that is the standard of economic value.

Because of the scarcity of available means such as time, labor, and resource goods, individuals must choose which ends to try to satisfy. Menger demonstrates that it is the consumer evaluation of output that tends to be reflected in the prices of inputs. Both resource goods and producer goods are valued according to the value of the ends they seek, which are sequentially determined by the consumers. In other words, the value of goods at earlier stages in the production process is derived from the values to consumers of the product at later stages. Economic value thus derives from the valuing acts of ultimate consumers.

Consumer goods (i.e., goods of the first order) are valued only because people are aware of their dependence on particular quantities of these goods for the satisfaction of their specific needs and wants. The value of goods of higher order (e.g., capital goods) is derived from or determined by the prospective value of goods of lower order which they produce. The factors of production that cooperate in producing consumer goods have no immediate connection with the satisfaction of human needs and wants, but through the causal production process they do contribute to the process of need and want satisfaction. The value of higher order goods is thus dependent upon the expected value of goods of lower order that they produce. Valuations are communicated upward through the economic system to goods of higher order, determining how higher order goods are allocated among industries and products and how they are valued and compensated. Menger refutes the labor theory of value when he points out that costs of production are simply the aggregate of the prices paid for various types of higher order goods and that it is impossible for the prices of consumer goods to be determined by the costs of production, which themselves are ultimately determined by the prices of the consumer goods.

According to Menger, because of time lapses inherent in production, the value of goods of higher order is determined by the prospective value of the product. A change process, such as production, takes time and is inherently uncertain.

In addition, Menger preferred a time preference theory of interest as opposed to a productivity theory of interest. The rate of interest is simply the market's reflection of time preference. Menger presents interest as a phenomenon of exchange. It is the expression of individual preference for present goods as compared to future goods. Positive time preference is seen as a necessary and sufficient condition for the emergence of the phenomenon called interest. For a producer, Menger sees the ownership of capital goods as equal in present value to the holding of a supply of future consumption goods. The difference between the present value and future value represents interest. In other words, Menger explains that the total present value of all complementary goods of higher order required for the production of a good of lower order or first order is equal to the prospective value of the product. However, he goes on to more specifically say that it is necessary to include not only goods of higher order required for production but also the services of capital and the activity of the entrepreneur. It follows that the present value of the technical factors of production is not equal to the full prospective value of the product, but acts so that a margin for the value of the services of capital and entrepreneurial activity can result.

As observed earlier, Menger distinguishes between the value of a thing and the thing itself. He also points out that only concrete things are available to economizing individuals. The articles that exist objectively are, without exception, specific things or quantities of things and their value is invariably something fundamentally different from the objects themselves.

In reality, there are only concrete wants and concrete goods. It follows that only actual units of a good are relevant to human valuation and choice. Menger explains that the want for any good is really a succession of wants for a discrete unit of the good. Implied in the concept of human action is the personal ranking of different satisfactions expected to be obtained from a particular unit or a definite quantity of a good.

Menger's value theory depends upon both the objective and subjective elements influencing supply and demand. Objectively, there is an exact quantity of a particular good in existence. From a subjective standpoint, a good is demanded by individuals in society, with the first units being valued most highly and the last ones being valued least highly by each particular person. Regardless of which specific unit of a person's supply is removed, he will economize by deciding to reallocate the remaining units in order to satisfy his most important needs and wants and to do without the satisfaction of only the least important needs and wants of those formerly satisfied by the more plentiful supply.

Menger's theory views the value of all goods and services precisely in terms of how much satisfaction will be foregone without them. It is the least important satisfaction that is dependent on an item of the person's supply of a good. This is known as marginal utility. It is because of the reverse working of the idea of diminishing marginal reliability that as a shortage becomes larger the higher the value of the good in question rises. As unmet needs and wants increase, so does the per-unit value of the required goods.

Methodology

Menger began the bitter conflict known as the Methodenstreit with the 1883 publication of his *Investigations into the Method of the Social Sciences with Special Reference to Economics*. This was twelve years after he published his *Principles of Economics*, the book that made him famous and enabled him to attain a prestigious chair of economics at the University of Vienna. In *Investigations* Menger elaborated upon the methodology he had originally presented in *Principles of Economics*. In *Investigations* he offered a written argument against the German Historical school's idea of economics as a historically based discipline to be studied solely by the application of concrete-bound empiricism. In addition, he denied the existence of any essential differences between the natural and the social sciences. In contrast, the Historical school assumed that the natural sphere was governed by strictly universal laws, but that the search for such laws in the social realm would be futile. For the German historicist, economic theory did not possess the scientific nature of the natural sciences.

Menger sought to develop a categorical ontology of economic reality in an Aristotelian sense. His causal-genetic method was rooted in Aristotelian metaphysics and epistemology. Menger thereby destroyed the existing structures of economic thought and established economics' legitimacy as a theoretical science. Menger advanced an ontology of economic objects by providing a description of the exact laws of economic phenomena. In the absence of exact laws, there could not be a science of economics, and without empirical realism, economics could not be termed a social science.

Menger argues that exact theory, theory based on a few evident axioms, is possible in economics. He reasons that there are specific pure and simple categories which are universal, capable of being exemplified in principle in every economy, and able to be understood as universal by economic theorists. He goes on to say that exact laws are the propositions that express the relationships among these categories. These exact laws are not laws of mathematical precision, but instead are laws which follow inexorably from the essential nature of the elements involved. These laws are changeless and invariably true regardless of time and place. Exact laws are the propositions expressing universal connections among essences. Menger's exact method is limited to essences and to elementary and rationally intelligible essential connections only.

Unlike the historicists, Menger acknowledged the coexistence of different but complementary approaches to economics. Study for the sake of knowing the individual aspects of economic phenomena is the province of economic history and statistics. The goal of attaining knowledge of the general aspects of economic phenomena belongs to the field of theoretical economics. While he insisted on the need for theoretical reasoning, Menger also explained the need for and relationship between the realistic-empirical tendency and the exact tendency in economics and the other social sciences. He argued that the exact orientation in theoretical research has a proper place next to a realistic-empirical orientation to theoretical research. This is because experience of the world in each and every instance involves both a general and an individual aspect. Men understand a concrete phenomenon in a specifically historical way through the investigation of its individual processes of development. A concrete phenomenon is understood in a theoretical way when it is recognized to be a distinctive case of a particular regularity in the succession or in the coexistence of phenomena. It follows that theories, laws, and strictly universal statements are necessary for both historical and theoretical explanations. Economics as a theoretical science provides knowledge that transcends immediate particular and tangible experience. Menger thus maintained that both empirical and exact theories are descriptive of reality. Each method produces theories that differ in the degree of absoluteness or strictness from the other.

For the German historicists, only a historical approach would enable empirical regularities to be incorporated into theory. Menger clashes with this approach when he observes that there are no graspable laws of historical development. He says that no theories may be extracted directly from history, but contrariwise, theory is required in order to interpret history properly. Menger adamantly declares that the Historical school is mistaken when it claims that the historical method is able to produce universally valid laws and that the truth of empirical laws is more legitimate than the truth of exact or theoretical laws.

In his methodology, Menger stressed that economics is a science by demonstrating that there are economic regularities and that the phenomena of economic life are ordered strictly in accordance with definite laws. Insisting on the exactness of economic theory, he used the language of the pure logician when he analyzed relationships between variables. It is the knowledge of exact laws (i.e., those subject to no exceptions) which comprises scientific knowledge and scientific theory. Exact theory is developed by searching for the simplest, strictly typical elements of everything real.

Menger looked for the essence of economic relationships. He delved for those features which must be present by the nature of the relationship under study. He held that there are simple economic categories which are universal and capable of being understood as such. Exact laws are propositions expressing the relationships among such categories. There are certain elements, natures, or essences in the world, as well as connections, structures, and laws regulating them, all of which are precisely universal. Menger's term, exact laws, refers to propositions expressing universal connections among essences. A scientific theory consists of exact laws. For Menger, the goal of research in theoretical economics is the discovery of the essences and connections of economic phenomena. The aim of the theoretical economist is to recognize general recurring structures in reality. According to Menger, the universals of economic reality are not imposed or created, but rather are discovered through theoretical efforts. Economics, as an exact science, is the theoretical study of universals apprehended in an immanent realist manner. Theoretical economics understands economic universals as real objects that the mind has abstracted from particulars and isolated from other universals with which they coexist. If a person has an idea of the essence of something, he can explain its behavior as a manifestation of its essence. In other words, the manner in which objects act depends upon what those objects are. Menger's theoretical framework deals with the intensive study of individual economic units and the observation of how they behave.

Menger distinguishes between the realistic-empirical orientation to theory and the exact orientation to theory. Whereas the realistic-empirical branch of economics studies the regularities in the succession and coexistence of real phenomena, the exact orientation studies the laws governing ideal economic phenomena. He explains that realistic-empirical theory is concerned with regularities in the coexistence and succession of phenomena discovered by observing actual types and typical relationships of phenomena. Realistic-empirical theory is subject to exceptions and to change over time. Theoretical economics in its realistic orientation derives empirical laws that are valid only for the spatial and temporal relationships from which they are observed. Empirical laws can only be alleged to be true within a particular spatiotemporal domain. The realistic orientation can only lead to real types and to the particular. The study of individual or concrete phenomena in time and space is the realm of the historical sciences. According to Menger, it is the aim of the practical or historical sciences to discover the principles, policies, and procedures that are needed in order to shape the phenomena according to predetermined goals.

The aim of the exact orientation of research is the determination of strict laws of phenomena. Exact economic laws are established through a precise understanding of the way typical economizing individuals react to given situations. Menger insists on the precision and exactness of typical behavior. He maintains that once it is acknowledged that rational behavior is the typical behavior of economizing individuals, economists can logically derive theorems that will make up what Menger terms an exact and absolutely true theory. For Menger, theoretical research seeks to identify the simplest and strictly typical elements of everything real.

Menger's view implies that economic reality manifests certain simple and intelligible structures. Economic reality is constituted in intelligible ways out of structures depending upon human thought and action. The individual and his behavior are the most basic elements by means of which Menger explains economic phenomena and derives universal laws. Mengerian economics is built on the basis of the idea that there are, in the realm of economic phenomena, indispensable structures to every economic action that are manifested in every economy. Economic universals involve economizing action on the part of individuals. These universals of economic reality are discovered through theoretical efforts and are not arbitrary creations of the economist.

Menger's understanding of economic theory is essentialist and grounded in Aristotelian metaphysics. His causal-realistic economic method is a search for laws about actual, observable events. It follows that Menger's economics is actually a theory of reality. Menger is concerned with essences and laws manifested in this world. For Menger, as well as Aristotle, what is general does not exist in isolation from what is particular. Menger's theoretical economics studies the universal aspects of particular phenomena. These economic universals are said to exist only as instantiated in specific economic actions and institutions. For Menger, the goal of theoretical research is to discover the simplest elements of all things real which must be apprehended as strictly typical merely because they are the simplest. Of course, it is not an easy matter to discover those structures and to construct workable theories about them. There may be huge difficulties in gaining knowledge of essential structures and in converting such knowledge into the organized system of a strict theory.

Menger's theoretical economics is an exact science that investigates exact types and exact laws. Whereas exact types can be seen as first-order universals, exact laws may be viewed as second-order universals which are concerned with connections between and among exact types. These connections can be seen as involving real necessities. Because first-order universals (such as economizing action, value, money, division of labor, sales, rent, profit, etc.) are what they are, their interrelations inevitably are of certain types. Menger contends that economists must study the essences and relations or connections between such economic phenomena.

Menger denies that exact laws supply knowledge simply for its own sake. He contends that even exact laws assist people in controlling and predicting reality, thereby enabling them to live more successfully. According to Menger, even exact laws are practical in helping us to control and enjoy our existence. They are practical primarily because they are exact. Exact laws contribute to our understanding of the real world. In other words, both the realistic and exact orientations are means for understanding, predicting, and controlling economic phenomena. These two orientations allow people to understand the whole sphere of economic phenomena, each contributing in its own characteristic fashion.

Menger finds it necessary to justify inductively the basic causal categories that are arrived at by the analytic part of scientific method. The scientist needs to learn to recognize the general recurring structures in constantly changing reality. He says that theoretical knowledge is gained only by apprehending the phenomenon in question as a special case of a particular regularity in the succession or in the coexistence of phenomena. Economic reality manifests specific simple intelligible structures which the economic theorist is capable of grasping.

Menger endeavors to develop a categorical ontology of economic reality which he says cannot be attained through any mere inductive enumeration of cases. Exact laws are not simply derived from empirical inquiry. He states that they can be scientifically authenticated, but not through the tabulation of approximate statistical data based on a finite number of observation statements. Of course, Menger's exact theory is necessarily partially based on empirical inquiry that reveals what is typical about economic behavior. After what is typical is discovered, logically derived theories are thus developed from the typical elements to construct a strictly exact and true theory. These theories make up the form which expresses the essences of economic phenomena. Such theories are developed via a process of introspection or internal reflection as part of a logical process based on deductive reasoning from inductively derived concepts.

It is apparent that Menger recognizes the difference between empirical knowledge and strict empiricism as a method. Although empirical knowledge originates from the use of a person's senses, it also necessitates the use of one's reason to interpret and analyze the data supplied by the senses. All knowledge can be said to be empirical in the sense that it begins with observed experience of external reality. On the other hand, strict empiricism or positivism states that a person is incapable of knowing the essence of a class of entities and therefore can only know the particular concrete entities they study. It follows that the approach of the empiricist with respect to the verification of knowledge must be continual testing to find out if past relationships between entities still hold.

Menger says that we can find regularity all around us and that, through common sense and scientific reasoning, we can reduce complex abstractions down to their simplest elements, which are strictly typical, and from these we can build exact laws. He explains that the main goal of theoretical activity is to search for laws and to propose theories and strictly universal statements.

In explaining the transition from particulars (i.e., real types) to universals (i.e., exact types), Menger contends that it is acceptable to omit principles of individuation such as time and space. In order to derive exact laws it is first essential to identify the essential defining quality or essence in individual phenomena that underpins their recognition as representations of that type. Menger thus seeks the simplest elements of everything real (i.e., the typical phenomena) in solving the problem of universals or concepts. To find the simplest elements, a person must abstract from all particular spatiotemporal circumstances.

Experience, reason, and insight are critical and essential to have a science of economics. Exact laws involve introspection and an act of mental effort based on inductive and deductive processes of logic. However, these exact laws are not constructions of the mind but rational descriptions of eternal configurations and regularities in real economic life. Menger believes that general connections or typical relationships between economic phenomena can be apprehended in an exact sense as exact laws. He maintains that the regularities in the coexistence and succession of phenomena discerned through the exact approach allow for no exceptions because of the process of cognition through which they are discovered. In his search for economic laws, he aspires to isolate them and to utilize the simple elements so acquired to deduce more complicated phenomena from the simplest. The exact orientation reveals to us the simplest and strictly typical constitutive factors of phenomena. Exact laws, laws of complicated phenomena which are built up out of simple elements, result from the exact orientation. Exact laws are rarer than empirical laws, are laws without exceptions, and are exact for all times and places. They are validated in reality, but not with formal empirical testing. Strictly universal theories can only be constructed at the expense of empiricism. Menger says that it is a methodological absurdity to assume that an economist can test conclusions derived from exact laws by means of empirical evidence. Conclusions arrived at through the exact orientation cannot be corrected or altered by evidence produced through the empirical approach.

Menger states that the results of exact research are true only under certain assumptions which in reality may not always be present. His theoretical system applies only to problems stated under carefully defined presuppositions. In fact, an abstract statement or pure type of relationship found through the exact orientation may be considered realistic and representative of objectively existing facets of the economy even if the pure type does not have an exact ontological correlate. Because of disturbing factors in reality, there is no guarantee that a pure type can be studied in pure form in empirical reality. Menger's argument for an exact orientation of theoretical research is independent of empirical testing. However, his theoretical research does establish the existence of strictly typical elements by means of an only partially empirical-realistic analysis which does not then consider whether or not these elements are present in reality or independent phenomena. The empirical search is only a limited one because it is irrelevant to see if the considered elements are pure or if they are mixed with disturbing influences. Menger's exact theory applies only if the elements are pure because such flawlessness or completeness is presupposed by his approach.

It follows that a theoretical understanding of concrete phenomena cannot be achieved through mere inductive enumerations of cases that are subject to contaminating influences. Whereas exact economics makes us aware of the laws holding for an abstractly conceived economy, an empirical-realistic economy makes us aware of the regularities in the succession and coexistence of real but isolated economic phenomena in their full empirical reality, thus containing numerous elements not emergent from that abstraction.

According to Menger, theoretical sciences in their exact orientation abstract from disturbing factors such as error, ignorance, and external compulsion. Accordingly, Menger's exact laws rely on the following definite presuppositions, which in reality do not always apply: (1) people tend to be selfish, egoistic, or self-interested; (2) people tend to be rational; (3) people have full, complete, or perfect knowledge of the economic situation with which they are confronted; and (4) people are uninfluenced by error, ignorance, and external compulsion (i.e., they are free and uncoerced by government). There can be exact laws to the extent that individuals are rational, self-interested, informed, and free. For example, Menger would contend that an essential relationship necessarily exists between needs, values, and prices unless the relationship is hindered by disturbing factors, such as government interference through price controls. When Menger's four conditions exist, we can have exact laws and economic prices. In their absence, the best we can have are real prices. For a realist like Menger, the only way to arrive at essences from a succession of concretes is to conceive of an abstract world that holds to his four conditions. There are no guarantees that exact laws will correspond to empirical laws given the actual relationships which the world of phenomena offers to us. History occurs with theory and consists of the numerous empirical facts that form matter in an Aristotelian sense.

According to Menger, the variance or divergence between the theorems of exact theory and the results of empirical studies is not a distinguishing characteristic of economics and the other social sciences, but instead, also pertains to the natural sciences. In physics, the actual movements of bodies do not conform to the theories of pure physics just as in economics exact theory does not exactly correspond to the observed behavior of economic actors.

Menger's scientific realism involves the use of isolation and abstraction. During the process of isolation, the economist selects a limited set of elements from a total situation or task environment and excludes the other elements from mental analysis. Isolation, a subset of abstraction, involves the separation of a universal attribute of the object of study from its other characteristics. Exact theoretical sciences study solitary particular sides of phenomena and abstract from disturbing factors.

Menger identifies fundamental motives for human behavior, including economy, moral sentiments, altruism, and justice. He thus isolates or delineates the boundaries between corresponding scientific disciplines such as economics, ethics, social philosophy, and justice. Each of these disciplines would study the behavior of human beings from one of these viewpoints while excluding the others. In addition, within each discipline, the functioning of any one basic human drive or motive could be studied by abstracting it from disturbing factors which are present in the real world. Mere isolation does not guarantee that a factor can be studied in pure form. To study it in pure form, one must abstract from other factors which restrict the total operation of that single factor.

With respect to economics as an exact theoretical science, Menger abstracts from disturbing factors such as error, ignorance, the presence of external force, and the extent to which an individual is influenced by the various fundamental motives for human behavior. Economics as an empirical discipline would isolate economics from other fundamental motives but would not abstract from disturbing factors. However, economics as an exact theoretical discipline would isolate and abstract economics from other fundamental motives and from disturbing factors. The exact method is concerned with isolated aspects of ideal phenomena.

Note

This chapter is a shortened and edited version of chapter one of my *Philosophers of Capitalism* (Lexington Books, 2005).

Recommended Reading

Alter, Max. *Carl Menger and the Origins of Austrian Economics*. Boulder, CO: Westview Press, 1990.

Birner, Jack. "A Roundabout Solution to a Fundamental Problem in Menger's Methodology and Beyond." Pp. 241–61 in *Carl Menger and His Legacy in Economics*, edited by Bruce J. Caldwell. Durham, NC: Duke University Press, 1994.

Blaug, Mark, ed. *Carl Menger*. London: Edward Elgar, 1992.

Bloch, Henri-Simon. "Carl Menger: The Founder of the Austrian School." *Journal of Political Economy* 3 (1940): 428–33.

Bostaph, Samuel H. "The Methodological Debate between Carl Menger and the German Historicists." *Atlantic Economic Journal* 4 (1978): 11–15.

Caldwell, Bruce J., ed. *Carl Menger and His Legacy in Economics*. Durham, NC: Duke University Press, 1990.

Dolan, Edwin G., ed. *The Foundations of Modern Austrian Economics*. Kansas City, MO: Sheed & Ward, 1976.

Gloria-Palerno, Sandye. *The Evolution of Austrian Economics*. London: Routledge, 1999.

Grassl, Wolfgang, and Barry Smith, eds. *Austrian Economics: Historical and Philosophical Background*. London: Crook Helm, 1986.

Hayek, Fredrich, A. von. "Carl Menger." *Economia*. (November 1934): 393–420.

———. "The Austrian School." *International Encyclopedia of the Social Sciences* (1968).

———. "The Place of Menger's Grundsatze in the History of Economic Thought." In *Carl Menger and the Austrian School of Economics*, edited by J.R. Hicks and W. Weber. London: Oxford University Press, 1973.

Hicks, J. R., and W. Weber, eds. *Carl Menger and the Austrian School of Economics.* Oxford: Clarendon Press.

Howey, R. S. *The Rise of the Marginal Utility School: 1870–1889.* Lawrence: University of Kansas Press, 1960.

Hutchinson, T. W. *A Review of Economic Doctrines: 1870-1929.* Oxford: Clarendon Press, 1953.

Jaffé, William. "Menger, Jevons, and Walras Dehomogenized." *Economic Inquiry* 4 (1975): 511–21.

Kauder, Emil. "Intellectual and Political Roots of the Older Austrian School." *Zeitschrift für Nationalökonomie* 17 (1958).

Kirzner, Israel M. "The Entrepreneurial Role in Menger's System." *Atlantic Economic Journal* 3: (1978) 31–45.

Mäki, Uskali. "Mengerian Economics in Realist Perspective." In *Carl Menger and His Legacy in Economics,* edited by Bruce J. Caldwell. Durham, NC: Duke University Press, 1990.

Menger, Carl. *Principles of Economics.* New York: New York University Press, [1871] 1981

———. *Investigations into the Method of the Social Sciences with Special Reference to Economics.* New York: New York University Press, [1883] 1985.

Milford, Karl. "Menger's Methodology." In *Carl Menger and His Legacy in Economics,* edited by Bruce J. Caldwell. Durham, NC: Duke University Press, 1990.

Mises, Ludwig von. *The Historical Setting of the Austrian School of Economics.* New Rochelle, NY: Arlington House, 1969.

Moss, Lawrence S. "Carl Menger's Theory of Exchange." *Atlantic Economic Journal* 3 (1978).

Oakley, Allen. *The Foundations of Austrian Economics from Menger to Mises.* London: Edward Elgar, 1998.

Roll, Eric. *A History of Economic Thought.* 4th ed. Homewood, IL: Richard D. Irwin, 1974.

Seager, H. R. "Economics at Berlin and Vienna." *Journal of Political Economy* 1 (1893): 236–62.

Smith, Barry. "Aristotle, Menger, Mises: An Essay in the Metaphysics of Economics." Pp. 263–88 in *Carl Menger and His Legacy in Economics,* edited by Bruce J. Caldwell. Durham, NC: Duke University Press, 1990.

———. *Austrian Philosophy: The Legacy of Franz Brentano.* LaSalle, IL: Open Court, 1994.

Vaughn, Karen I. "The Reinterpretation of Carl Menger: Some Notes on Recent Scholarship." *Atlantic Economic Journal* 3 (1987): 60–64.

Wicksell, Knut. "The New Edition of Menger's Grundsütze." In *Selected Papers on Economic Theory,* edited by Erik Lindahl. London: Geo. Allan and Unwin, 1958.

Younkins, Edward W., ed. *Philosophers of Capitalism: Menger, Mises, Rand, and Beyond.* Lanham, MD: Lexington Books, 2005.

PART IV

THE CONTEMPORARY PERIOD

Chapter 13

Ludwig von Mises on Human Action

The scope of praxeology is the explication of the category of human action. All that is needed for the deduction of all praxeological theorems is knowledge of the essence of human action. . . . The only way to a cogitation of these theorems is logical analysis of our inherent knowledge of the category of action. . . . Like logic and mathematics, praxeological knowledge is in us; it does not come from without.

—Ludwig von Mises

Ludwig von Mises (1881-1973), the Austrian philosophical economist and social thinker, is one of our most passionate, consistent, and intransigent intellectual defenders of capitalism. This chapter provides a systematic survey and overview of Mises's ideas, which are most fully expressed in his 1949 magnum opus, *Human Action*, one of the most uncompromising and vigorously reasoned arguments for capitalism that has ever appeared.

From Historicist to Praxeologist

Mises began his career as an economic historian in the German Historical school. His enthusiasm for the historical approach waned when, at age twenty-two, he read Menger's great polemic against the German Historical school, *Principles of Economics*, and was convinced that although historical research was important and needed, there are factors which could not be grasped by the historicists' empirical field studies and archival research. He soon realized that economic history could not produce economic laws or principles and that historicism simply supplied pure propaganda for the welfare state.

Menger had contended that the purpose of economic theory is to elucidate causal-genetic explanations of market phenomena. Mises was dissatisfied with

Menger's Aristotelian methodology, which for Mises was too closely related to reality. Menger had based his method on realism and had explained in detail two orientations or ways to know reality—the realistic-empirical orientation and the exact orientation. Mises argued that concepts can never be found in reality. He wanted to study and develop pure theory and maintained that "theory alone" could provide firm guidance. Mises wanted to construct a purely deductive system and was searching for a foundation upon which to build it.

The Historical school could only offer limited help to Mises in his endeavor. The theory of understanding and the concept of ideal types developed by Max Weber, a prominent German historicist and sociologist, provided Mises with some useful instruction, but Mises found his method to be insufficiently idealistic. Although he generally admired Weber's work, Mises concluded that Weber's interpretation of economics as involving historical ideal types was not acceptable.

Mises was searching for a theoretical foundation that could not be questioned or doubted. He wanted to find knowledge of logical necessity. He also wanted to escape from the concrete-based empiricism of historicism. His mission became to look inward in order to deduce a system that was logically unobjectionable. He wanted to find laws that could only be verified or refuted by means of discursive reasoning.

Mises makes a distinction between understanding and conception. His description of understanding is based upon Henri Bergson's idea of intuition. The understanding that Mises discusses is essentially that of Weber and of members of the German Historical school. Whereas understanding is intuition, conception for Mises was ratiocination. The substance of an action is disclosed by the a posteriori insights of understanding and the form of action is revealed via the a priori logic of what Mises calls praxeology. Conception of a priori concepts of human action provides the framework for understanding specific actions. Conception involves knowledge understood prior to experience. To find such knowledge, Mises needed a Kantian base.

Mises's axiom of action, the universal introspectively known fact that men act, was the foundation upon which Mises built his deductive system. Action, for Mises, is the real thing. Mises says that action was a category of the mind, in a Kantian sense, that was required in order to experience phenomenal reality (i.e., reality as it appears to us). The unity found in Mises's theorems of economics is rooted in the concept of human action. Mises's economic science is deductive and based on laws of human action that he contends are as real as the laws of nature. His praxeological laws have no spatial, temporal, or cultural constraints. They are universal and pertain to people everywhere, at every time, and in all cultures.

Mises Reconstructs Menger's Value Theory

Mises was not only dissatisfied with Menger's Aristotelian methodology, he was also critical of Menger's value theory. He thought that Menger used unclear language to describe value theory and that Menger carried over ideas from classical liberalism's theory of objective value. According to Mises, Menger makes statements that are incompatible with the basic principles he advanced. He says that Menger was inconsistent in elaborating his ideas and contended that Menger did not pursue subjectivism consistently enough. Mises therefore set out to correct or rehabilitate Menger's theory of value.

Remember that Menger's value theory eventually was labeled subjective value theory because the description of objective value theory was already assigned to the classical liberals' labor theory of value. Mises was convinced that Menger actually meant Misesian subjectivism despite the fact that Menger described his "subjectivism" as more of an objective value approach. Menger understood that values can be subjective, but that men should rationally seek objective life-affirming values. He explained that real wants correspond with the objective state of affairs. Menger distinguished between real and imaginary wants depending upon whether or not a person correctly understands a good's objective ability to satisfy a want. Individuals can be wrong about their judgment of value. Menger's emphasis on objective values is consistent with philosophical realism and with a correspondence theory of truth.

Menger does trace market exchange back to a person's subjective valuations of various economic goods and observes that scales of value are subjective and variable from person to person and subject to change over time. There are certainly subjectivist features in Menger's economic analysis, which is founded on his methodological individualism. Methodological individualism implies that people differ and have a variety of goals, purposes, and tastes. Subjectivism is therefore inherent in a principled and consistent understanding of methodological individualism.

Menger explains that objective value originates in a relationship between a man's consciousness (i.e., reason) and his survival requirements. To have an objective value a man's mind must grasp the relationship between the facts of existence and his life. He points out very clearly that a person can be mistaken with respect to his judgments of economic value. Consciousness can be wrong regarding what a man's authentic needs really are, the actual relative importance of his needs, and the products or services that truly seem to meet his needs. Menger also states that it is only the evaluating subject who can make the determination that his judgment was wrong.

Some of Menger's propositions and concepts are incompatible with Mises's brand of subjectivism. Mises did not believe that Menger really meant what he asserted about objective wants corresponding to an objective state of affairs. In other words, Mises thought Menger actually meant values that are purely subjective. Mises is an absolute subjectivist who contends that all values emanate from the consciousness of the valuer.

Mises uses the term "value" in a completely nonnormative, nonphilosophical manner. He insists that economic theory does not incorporate any idea of a correct preferential ordering among goods and services. His subjectivism emphasizes the private personal character of preferences, costs, and benefits. Mises's praxeology does not pass judgment on action. It simply explains market phenomena on the basis of a given action and not on the basis of right action. For Mises, to state that an object has value is merely to state that it is the goal of a personally chosen course of action. The Misesian sense of value is purely formal and indicates nothing about whether or not an end (i.e., a value) is in fact valuable. Values are embedded deeply in personal, subjective acts of valuation and depend upon the personal assessment and reaction of an individual to the choices available.

For Mises, an economist deals with subjective factors in the form of the meanings of events and objects for individuals. Economic events are thus the outcomes of valuations. Misesian economic science is therefore free from the value judgments of an economist who must take the value judgments found in the marketplace as his given data. An economist, in his role as economist, does not approve of or denounce individuals' ends. He does nothing more than ask if the means chosen are appropriate for their purposes. Men act and choose according to their hierarchy of values. The foundation upon which the hierarchy is based is irrelevant to Misesian praxeological economics.

Mises's Neo- Kantianism

In order to understand Mises's economics, one needs to be familiar with his philosophical theory of knowledge (i.e., his epistemology). Epistemology is the study of (1) what man is capable of knowing; (2) how man can attain knowledge; and (3) the validity of his knowledge. The first 142 pages of Mises's 889-page magnum opus, *Human Action*, are concerned with epistemological issues.

Mises's epistemological ideas are influenced by Immanuel Kant (1724-1804) and by neo-Kantians Max Weber and Morris Cohen. Not a strict Kantian, Mises modifies and extends Kant's epistemology. However, he does make use of Kant's main terminological and conceptual distinctions and basic insights into the nature of human knowledge.

Like Kant, Mises believes that the human mind understands the world only through its own categories. However, Mises is not a pure Kantian. Unlike Kant, Mises does not attempt to make a transcendental argument to derive the categories. He merely says that there is a group of common categories lodged in men's minds through which they grasp that which exists. What Mises considers as critical in Kant is his conviction that reason can supply universal and necessary knowledge.

Mises also disagrees with Kant regarding freedom of the individual. Kant conceives of the noumenal or real self as possessing free will and of the phenomenal self as being determined by the rational desire for happiness. Mises views freedom as the use of reason to attain one's goals. Assuming as little as possible, Mises says that we should assume people to be free and rational actors in the world as we perceive it since we have no certain knowledge of any determinants of human action. Mises is a metaphysical and cosmological agnostic regarding materialist or spiritual explanations of mental events.

Mises extends Kant by adding an important insight. Kantianism has been viewed as a type of idealism due to its failure to connect the mind's categories to the world. Mises further develops Kantian epistemology when he explains that the laws of logic affect both thought and action. He says that we must acknowledge that the human mind is a mind of acting persons and that our mental categories have to be accepted as fundamentally grounded in the category of action. Mises states that when this is realized, the notion of the existence of true synthetic, a priori categories and propositions can be accepted as a realistic, rather than as an idealistic, philosophy of knowledge. The mind and physical reality make contact via action. Mises believes that this insight fills in the gap between the mental world and the outside physical world. Mises thus contends that epistemology depends on our reflective knowledge of action.

Mises considers the law of human action to be a law of thought and a categorical truth prior to all experience. Thinking is a mental action. For Mises, a priori means independent of any particular time or place. Denying the possibility of arriving at laws via induction, Mises argues that evidence for the a priori is based on reflective, universal inner experience.

Unlike Menger, the father of Austrian economics, Mises did not believe that the essential defining qualities or essences existed in individual phenomena that made possible their recognition as representatives of that type. If he had held to the notion that there are certain ontological, a priori, and intelligible structures in the world, then he may have considered the law of human action to be a law of reality rather than a law of thought. An a priori in reality would not be the result of any forming or shaping of reality on the part of the experiencing subject. Rather, essences or universals would then be said to be discerned through a person's theoretical efforts.

Natural Sciences versus Human Sciences

Despite the singularity of the logical structure of human thought, Mises explains that people have access to two separates spheres of scientific thought—the science of nature and the science of human action. Whereas the natural sciences are the experimental sciences, the science of human action includes praxeology and history. Humans experience both the external world of natural phenomena and the internal world of thought, values, and feelings. Mises observes that we approach the subject matter of the natural sciences from the outside and the subject matter of the human sciences from within. He says that we are unable to reduce conscious and intentional human action to the physicalist methods of the natural sciences. Whereas nature reacts, humans act. Mises thus declares the need for a methodological dualism—one methodology for the external world of chemical, physical, and physiological phenomena and another one for the internal world of purposeful action. The natural sciences are distinct and separate from the human sciences. Because in the natural order, objects do not choose their behavior, it follows that there exist causal regularities and constant relationships between them. In the human sciences, there is only the regularity of the logical structure of the human mind. There is a major difference between the laws of nature and of teleology (i.e., purposeful action). Study of the logic of human action is essentially different from the method used by scientists to gain knowledge about the physical world.

The inanimate matter of the external natural world can be measured, quantified, and systematized based on hypotheses, observations, and experiments. It follows that empiricism and pragmatism are correct approaches for the natural sciences. Experimental sciences are based on the assumption of constant relations (i.e., the same results occur when the same conditions exist). Mises finds strict regularity in natural phenomena. In the physical world, the objects of study consist of phenomena of constant relations. Mises concludes that positivism is the correct methodology for the natural sciences. In the natural sciences we can only hypothesize, test quantitatively, and draw tentative conclusions that may later be falsified. We do not know the consequences in the natural sciences until we attempt something and then observe what occurs. Even after observing specific outcomes over time, our predictions will continually and permanently be merely hypothetical. The best we can achieve is a never-ending trial-and-error process in which our knowledge can be progressively and incrementally improved. Within the natural realm, there are constant relations among magnitudes, which men are able to discern with a reasonable degree of precision.

Mises observes that social processes cannot be controlled and manipulated like inanimate material in laboratory experiments. Social processes have their basis in, and can be traced back to, the actions and reactions of individual persons. In the human sciences, people have the ability to understand the nature and causes of the social processes. The social scientist is a human being and thus can make use of a source of knowledge unavailable to the natural scientist. Through introspection, the social scientist can understand the meaning of human action. He can grasp the meaning that the actor has ascribed to his action.

Mises declares that the two main branches of the human sciences are praxeology and history. Praxeology is the study of what is universal about actions and history is the study of what is specific about them. Whereas praxeology studies the formal relationship of ends and means, history examines the content of means and ends. Mises separates the domain of knowledge into conception, the mental tool of praxeology, and understanding, the mental device of history. Like the natural sciences, history deals with the past. Praxeology deals with what is universal and necessary in the actions of individual men. Not a historical science, praxeology is a systematic and theoretical science, whose subject matter is the concept "human action" and its implications, whose methods are a priori and purely logical, and whose principles are eternally and apodictically certain and objective. History, on the other hand, deals with data that is unique and complex, uses methods that are partially a posteriori and partly a priori, and makes judgments that are approximate and tentative. Through the above distinctions, Mises has created a dualism between a priori praxeology and a posteriori history.

Misesian Praxeology

According to Mises, axioms are facts which all humans must presuppose are certain. He states that axioms do not arise from observations but emanate only from reflective understanding (i.e., introspection). A human being can look within himself and discern the logical and formal attributes of his own mental processes. By understanding the logic of his reasoning process, a man can comprehend the essentials of the reasoning process of all men. Mises thus contends that all men, regardless of their class or race, possess the same logical structure of thought and therefore can and do make the same logical inferences during the reasoning process. People share a common logical structure and thus can understand and communicate with one another. Mises contends that men's minds are equipped with the same set of tools for apprehending reality and that these tools are possessed prior to experience.

Mises states that his action axiom, the proposition that men act, meets the requirements for a true synthetic, a priori proposition. This proposition cannot be denied because the denial itself would necessarily be categorized as an action. Mises defines action as purposeful behavior. He explains that it cannot be denied that humans act in a purposeful manner because the denial itself would be a purposeful act. All conscious human action is directed toward goals because it is impossible to conceive of an individual consciously acting without having a goal. Reason and action are congeneric. For Mises, knowledge is a tool of action and action is reason applied to purpose. When people look within, they see that all conscious actions are purposeful and willful pursuits of selected ends or objectives. Reason enables people to choose.

Human actions are engaged in to achieve goals that are part of the external world; however, a person's understanding of the logical consequences of human action does not stem from the specific details of these goals or the means employed. Comprehension of these laws does not depend on a person's specific knowledge of those features of the external world that are relevant to the person's goals or to the methods used in his pursuit of these goals. Praxeology's cognition is totally general and formal, without reference to the material content and particular features of an actual case. Praxeological theorems are prior to empirical testing because they are logically deduced from the central axiom of action. By understanding the logic of the reasoning process, a person can comprehend the essentials of human actions. Mises states that the entirety of praxeology can be built on the basis of premises involving one single non-logical concept—the concept of human action. From this concept all of praxeology's propositions can be derived. Mises contends that the axiom of action is known by introspection to be true. In the tradition of Kant, Mises argues that the category of action is part of the structure of the human mind. It follows that the laws of action can be studied introspectively because of aprioristic intersubjectivity of human beings. Not derived from experience, the propositions of praxeology are not subject to falsification or verification on the basis of experience. Rather, these propositions are temporally and logically prior to any understanding of historical facts.

Praxeology studies only purposeful, chosen human actions without regard to the action's motives or causes, which are the objects of study of psychology. Mises's position is that we must treat human beings as free and rational actors because we do not know how or if action is determined. Mises says that although human thought and action are affected by a person's facticity (i.e., his physiological inheritances and past experiences), we do not know how or to what extent his thought and actions are influenced by these factors. He states that all human actions involve choice and that the principles of choice are valid for every human action without consideration of underlying goals, motives, or causes. Each human being has internal purposes, ends or goals that he attempts to attain and ideas about how to attain them. Valuation reflects the internal scale of preferences of the acting person. Separate individuals value the same things in different ways and valuations change for the same individual with changing conditions and over time. Every human activity is engaged in under the motivating power of human values.

Mises explains that every person is a constant valuer who attempts to improve his position, uses means in his attempts to attain his ends, estimates his costs, and chooses his course of action, which ultimately results in either a success or a failure. Every human action can therefore be viewed as a purposeful attempt to substitute a more satisfactory state for a less satisfactory one. The existence of an unsatisfactory state presupposes scarcity and the choice between different alternatives. The aim, goal, or end of any action is relief from a felt uneasiness. Put another way, humans act purposefully to increase their happiness. The sought-after end of every action is the exchange of a better state of affairs for the current state.

Action is purposeful behavior where a person with limited knowledge uses means to attain a desired end, and this relation is influenced by logical laws. Means are used as effectively as possible to attain an end. Acting persons understand that they are employing limited means to attain goals. Every action has a cost and a potential gain. Man, as conscious being, finds some aspects of his condition wanting, imagines ends that he would like to achieve, and perceives means and methods to attempt to attain them. Confronted with the necessity of selecting from among desired goals, he uses his means to pursue the goals to which he has assigned the greatest importance. Implicit in the necessity of choice is scarcity. All action entails choosing one thing instead of another. All means, including time, are scarce. Means have multiple uses, so decisions have to be made regarding the best way to use them. A person must also choose among the ends for which scarce means could be applied. Choosing reflects man's free will, reason, and subjective evaluations regarding the continual removal of felt uneasiness. Each person is a purposeful and rational subjective valuer whose ends, means, thoughts, and actions are integrated into cause-and-effect relationships.

All action requires giving up the most highly valued alternative that is not pursued. The alternative foregone represents the opportunity cost of the action. At the moment of action, a person is also choosing what his options are. He identifies for himself which alternatives are worth pursuing. Mises views action as the determination of both what the feasible alternatives are and the ranking of their relative desirability. His vision is of each individual arranging all of one's innumerable possible ends and means in a series and ranking them according to his own scale of preference. Choices do not simply reflect the subjective preferences of the agent among given alternatives. Rather, the choice manifests the actor's subjective judgment regarding the range of alternative courses of action available and with respect to the likelihood of the outcome of each alternative. Human action emphasizes purposefulness in an open-ended future world of uncertainty. It follows that decisions are made that will maximize the perceived probability of the achievement of one's purposes. Each person, therefore, attempts to influence the degree of uncertainty about what the future might hold for him. Mises thus includes an entrepreneurial element in human choice. He perceives individuals as purposeful agents who are alert to opportunities as well as to threats. Mises views human action as essentially entrepreneurial and sees each person, to some degree, as an entrepreneur. Acting includes the discovery of opportunities and the exploitation of those opportunities.

Mises explains that causality is a prerequisite of action and that the mind comprehends phenomena in a cause-and-effect manner. He states that there exist discoverable causal relationships in the world that can bring about desired effects if they are taken advantage of by human actors. To act means to intervene at some earlier point in order to effect some later outcome. Human action originates change and continuous alteration of the world.

Economics as Praxeology

For Mises, economic behavior is simply a special case of human action. He contends that it is through the analysis of the idea of action that the principles of economics can be deduced. Economic theorems are seen as connected to the foundation of real human purposes. Economics is based on true and evident axioms, arrived at by introspection, into the essence of human action. From these axioms, Mises derives logical implications or the truths of economics. Mises's methodology thus does not require controlled experiments because he treats economics as a science of human action. By their nature, economic acts are social acts. Economics is a formal science whose theorems have no formal content and whose propositions do not derive their validity from empirical observations. Economics is the branch of praxeology that studies market exchange and alternative systems of market exchange.

Mises insists that the core propositions of economics are based on methods distinct from those of the natural sciences, including the natural science of experimental economics. He says that "economists" who claim to do science based on the model of physics and chemistry disregard the distinctive nature of economics as a social science. Mises is opposed to the positivist method in which the role of economic theory is to observe quantitative statistical regularities of human economic behavior and then to conceive of laws which would then be used to make predictions and which would be tested based upon additional statistical evidence. Mises explains that statistical data does not provide any universal laws and is limited to indicating particular trends and thus can be used to predict the future only in a qualified and minimal way. He warns that the positivist method is congenial to the idea of economics as planned and governed by social engineers who would deal with human beings in the manner that technology and the physical sciences permit engineers to deal with physical objects and inanimate matter. By contrast, the laws of economics are logical, rather than empirical, relationships that are not open to quantitative prediction or verification. Unlike inanimate objects, men have free will, the ability to choose, and the capacity to imagine and pursue new possibilities.

Mises explains that in economics the unit of analysis is individual human action, which we can know from within. Mises's study of the human sciences is based on his methodological individualism. He argues that all theorems of economics must be properly predicated upon the supremacy of the reasoning individual. People choose how to act. Mises argues that it is only at the level of the individual that an observer can assign meaning to social action. He explains that it is only individuals and their actions that provide meaning to social arrangements. Only individuals have purposes and plans and act by organizing the means at their disposal to attempt to attain the desired goals. Methodological individualism is the best method to discover the principles on which a group of people interact. All social processes are derived from the choices and actions of individuals taking part in the social and market order. Individuals cooperate with other people because such cooperation enables them to attain their own desires better than solitary action would. Mises is not an atomistic individualist. In his system of thought he views man as a social being. Most of the time, human purposes can be fulfilled only by the concurrent fulfillment of the purposes of others. Mises's individualism is a philosophy of social cooperation.

Misesian economics recognizes that ends are subjective. Therefore, human action is the ultimate given and cannot be reduced to further causes. All action must be viewed as rational from the point of view of economics because it cannot be analyzed further. For Mises, to be rational is to engage in purposeful behavior. Mises explains that value is the perceived usefulness of a good or service for the attainment of an end. Economic values are subjective, existing within the minds of acting individuals. Values express a ranking or ordering of alternatives. These values cannot be measured or calculated, but each man has a scale of values through which he ranks every possible alternative ordinally.

Contending that determinism has no use in the study of economics or other praxeological sciences, Mises says that we must assume that the mind operates autonomously and that each individual possesses free will. He explains that we do not know how external events affect human thought and value judgment. Avoiding any propositions regarding metaphysical, cosmological, or religious constructs, he argues that any such theories that assign specific causes to thought and values must be dismissed. Mises is agnostic regarding the nature of human nature and the world. Rather than disdain spiritual goods, he is merely not sure about them. He says that metaphysical arguments cannot be used to dispute economics because human beings cannot know the ultimate truth.

Mises's use of apriorism in economic theory clearly differentiates him from mainstream economists. Through the use of abstract economic theorizing, Mises recognizes the nature and operation of human purposefulness and entrepreneurial resourcefulness and identifies the systematic tendencies which influence the market process. Mises's insight was that economic reasoning has its basis in the understanding of the action axiom as a true synthetic, a priori proposition. He says that sound deductions from a priori axioms are apodictically true and cannot be empirically tested. Mises developed through deductive reasoning the chains of economic theory, based on introspective understanding of what it means to be a rational, purposeful, and acting human being. The method of economics is deductive and its starting point is the concept of action.

According to Mises, all of the categories, theorems, or laws of economics are implied in the action axiom. These include, but are not limited to: subjective value, causality, ends, means, preference, cost, profit and loss, opportunities, scarcity, choice, marginal utility, marginal costs, opportunity cost, time preference, originary interest, association, and so on.

Mises maintains that all economic reasoning rests on (1) an understanding of the categories of human action and the meaning of a change taking place in phenomena such as knowledge, values, preferences, means, ends, costs, etcetera, and (2) the logical deduction of the consequences which would emerge from the accomplishment of some particular action or of the outcome which would arise from a specific action if the circumstances were altered in some specific way. Economics identifies consequences using its concepts of subjectively perceived values and costs.

Economics is the study of all men's aims and the means they use to try to attain their aims. Individuals have purposes and plans and act by arranging the means available to them to achieve the ends sought. These ends always involve the satisfaction of some subjective desires of men who are constantly choosing, rejecting, and acting. A means is what serves the attainment of an end. To act means to intervene at some earlier point in order to cause some later result. It follows that every actor presupposes and acknowledges the existence of causality.

Mises argued that all human action is motivated by personal desires and discomfort. There must be a felt uneasiness, an imagined preferable stage of affairs, and the belief or expectation regarding the availability of means and methods to bring the preferred state of affairs into existence. The function of man's reason is to acquire knowledge to enable him to proceed in his endeavors to remove uneasiness. Humans act because they believe their action will result in a state of affairs more desirable to them.

The aim, goal, or end of an action is the result sought by it. A means is what the acting individual uses in his attempts to achieve his end. A good is any means or ends—it is whatever an individual desires. Mises distinguishes between a consumer good which itself promotes satisfaction to the individual and a producer good which must be combined with other goods to produce a consumer good. Production is the use of human reason to direct resources for the achievement of human ends.

Acting is choosing. To select an end is to choose it from an array of alternatives. To attain an end one must use means appropriate to its accomplishment. Choosing involves making trade-offs and weighing costs and benefits. The price of any action is that which is given up. Mises says that the cost is the value of the price paid to the individual paying the price. People buy and sell only because they appraise what they are giving up as less than what they are receiving. The profit (gain), loss, or net yield of an action is the difference between the cost of an action and the value of the end attained by the acting person. Success or efficiency is subjective and must always be measured in relation to the individual's chosen end. Profits and losses inhere in all actions of all individuals and are purely subjective and ordinal.

Man decides on the basis of marginal utility. Most decisions are incremental, rather than categorical, and are made at the margin. An important implication of human action is the law of diminishing marginal utility that says that, as a person obtains successive units of a good, he assigns that good to a lower priority. Mises demonstrated that marginal utility is purely an ordinal ranking in which a person lists his values by preference without assigning any unit or quantity of utility.

The idea and reality of time cannot be separated from the human condition. Time is limited and must be economized and allocated like other scarce resources. All other things considered to be equal, the satisfaction of a want or need in the nearer future is preferable to its satisfaction in the more distant future. Time preference is an unqualified requisite of human action. The concepts of human action, change, and time are inextricably related. Unlike some other resources, time cannot be reversed. When time is used for one purpose it cannot be reallocated to another purpose.

The idea of time preferences manifests itself in Mises's notion of originary interest, which is the discounting of future goods against present goods. The originary (or neutral) rate of interest is the product of the higher valuation of current goods as compared with future goods. It is the ratio between prices of present goods and future goods. The originary rate of interest is independent of the money supply.

Mises's Utilitarianism as Social Cooperation

Mises's utilitarianism is a priori by nature. He deduces the idea that individuals cooperate because work performed under the division of labor is more productive than work done in isolation. Not only are men innately unequal in their ability to perform various types of labor, nonhuman factors of production (i.e., natural resources, raw materials, and climatic conditions) are unequally distributed around the world. Also, there are many endeavors which simply exceed the capacities of any one person. Mises proclaims that the discovery that higher productivity results from a division of labor is one of the greatest achievements of mankind. Cooperative action based on the division of labor recognizes and gains from the innate inequality of persons and increases the output per unit of labor expended.

In effect, Mises extended Ricardo's Law of Cooperative Advantage. Ricardo had illustrated the profitability of division of labor to all market participants, even in the case where one individual is more productive in every instance and respect. For Mises, the law of cooperative advantage becomes the law of human association, through which each person finds his most profitable niche in the collaborative activities of production and exchange. Mises argues that social cooperation under the division of labor is the fundamental source of man's success in the quest for survival and flourishing and in his efforts to improve his material conditions. Social cooperation is deemed to be essential to individuals' accomplishments of their own diverse and freely chosen pursuits. According to Mises, social cooperation is essential to the survival and prosperity of the human race.

Mises views society as the concerted action or cooperation of individuals that is a product of their conscious and purposeful behavior. A product of human reason and volition, society is the total complex of mutual relations created by collaborative action for the attainment of individual ends. Human society is a rational phenomenon because it is through reason that people are able to grasp the benefits of social cooperation, which results when people are free to know, choose, and act. Human society is an association of persons for cooperative action, resulting in greater productivity and mutual benefits. Mises contends that the recognition of the mutual benefits resulting from specialization was the origin of society and the beginning of the development of civilization. The gain which a society of social cooperation provides is the basis for its origin and persistence of existence.

Mises teaches that social cooperation is a more effective and efficient means to attain one's self-interest than is social conflict. Conflicts are naturally resolved through the division of labor and the substitution of economic competition for biological or Hobbesian competition. What makes friendly relations possible and preferable is the high productivity of the division of labor, which eliminates conflicts of interest. Mises wanted men to have the chance to pursue their happiness successfully. That chance presupposes social cooperation, meaning a peaceful and secure society in which individuals can interact to their mutual benefits while seeking their own diverse projects, specializations, and forms of flourishing.

Mises contends that prosperity is expressed by the fulfillment of diverse human purposes. His ultimate concern is the survival of the human race, which he views as prosperity in the broadest sense. Mises maintains that social cooperation is required for the achievement of human prosperity and happiness. Mises's utilitarian benchmark to be applied to social institutions, law, and moral codes is effectiveness with respect to human welfare. Mises's utilitarianism focuses on outcomes or consequences. It follows that political legislation and moral rules are to be judged based on their consequences or effects. Mises offers the proposition that one must judge legislation according to its logically deduced probable consequences. Rules, therefore, derive their value as preconditions to social cooperation.

According to Mises, social institutions, law, and normative rules of conduct are the outcomes of an evolutionary process and the product of efforts by individuals to purposively and rationally adapt their behavior to the demands of social cooperation under the division of labor. In Mises's view, the type of society we live in is a product of reason and choice. Through the deliberate use of reason people grasped the idea that the division of labor is the essence of society, and they consciously used that idea to improve their welfare. The idea of the division of labor has been progressively extended and intensified over time to include ever-greater numbers of individuals and groups and to achieve an ever-increasing variety of individual goals. Mutual prosperity is increased through the facilitation of social cooperation. By taking advantage of individual circumstances and talents through specialization, the total quantity and quality of the output of society can be increased.

Mises emphasizes that priorities are those of individuals. It is individual men who endeavor to advance their priorities and to attain prosperity. For individual persons, social cooperation is a means to attain all of their ends. Through specialization and division of labor the independent individual becomes a social being. Mises maintains that only a system based on freedom for every person elicits the greatest productivity of human labor, and is in the interest of all individuals. It follows that Mises assigns importance to social cooperation achieved impersonally through the free market process. Free markets promote prosperity by allowing individual purposes to be fulfilled. An act of exchange achieves prosperity by simultaneously fulfilling the purposes of both involved parties. Free markets permit and enable men to achieve their own goals through mutual cooperation and exchange. Mises's defense of individual freedom is on the consequentialist grounds that freedom leads to good results. Mises's kind of individualism is thus utilitarian individualism.

Mises distinguishes between social cooperation based on freely made contracts and social cooperation based on subordination. If social cooperation is voluntary, it is contractual, and if it is based on subordination and command, it is hegemonic. Mises favors contractual social cooperation because the maximization of individual free choice is a means to achieve greater prosperity for everyone in society. Any interference with the free market is interference with the freedom of human choice and action. Mises thus concludes that the free market and the social order based on it comprise the only viable system of social cooperation and division of labor. He argues that men's potential for cooperation depends upon freedom, peace, private property, individual rights, limited government, and inequalities of wealth, income, talents, and natural resources.

Utilitarianism is based on the notion that happiness (i.e., human flourishing) is good and that suffering is bad. Utilitarianism favors institutions, laws, rules, and traditions that underpin the types of society that permit people to make satisfactory lives for themselves. Such institutions and practices facilitate cooperation among persons as they pursue their diverse specific goals. Utilitarianism views social cooperation as valuable to human life.

Mises maintains that the survival of the human race hinges on the recognition and application of economic truth. He sees economic knowledge as a necessary condition for the continuing existence of human civilization. It follows that the goal of economic inquiry is the promotion of the survival of the civilized human race. For Mises, economic theorizing and evaluation are deductive, stable, definite, and totally unaided by experience. He insists upon the purely aprioristic and scientific character of economics.

Mises was a passionate advocate of the free market while at the same time insisting upon the value-neutrality of economics and the economist. He believed that it was possible and desirable to have a clear-cut boundary between an economic scholar's analysis and his personal and political value judgments. For Mises, economics is a neutral or value-free theoretical science. Such ethical neutrality means that economics is concerned with deductively tracing the consequences of market activities and economic policies. Economics, like any scientific project, must be conducted in a manner severed from the investigator's motivations, values, beliefs, and preferences. Mises was truly a philosopher of economics who wanted to systematize and make explicit the nature of economics.

Mises explains that economic theory examines the efficiency and effectiveness of the means selected to attain chosen ends. Since action pursues definite chosen ends, it follows that there can be no other standard for evaluating actions but the desirability or undesirability of their effects. The given purpose of economics is to preserve the order of social cooperation and social harmony. This is done by deducing the outcomes of purposive actions undertaken within the framework of the division of labor. Actions, institutions, laws, and so on are correct if they sustain social cooperation, which is a precondition of the happiness of individuals within society. In the other words, social cooperation facilitates and contributes to human flourishing and happiness.

Mises contends that economics is the foundation for politics, even though economics itself is value-free and apolitical. He explains that the political doctrine of classical liberalism is a direct application of the scientific findings of economics. Mises's case for classical liberalism is a utilitarian one because when an economist proclaims that a certain economic system or policy is bad he is saying that it is inappropriate to the desired goal. In assessing an economic doctrine, one only has to ask if it is logically coherent and if its practical application will enable people to attain their desired goals. Mises's concern is whether policies and institutions serve or undermine social cooperation and individuals' happiness. He thus sees classical liberalism, a political doctrine, as an application of theories developed by praxeology and based on rational economics. According to Mises, classical liberalism is a coherent theory of man, society, and the institutional arrangements required to provide social harmony and cooperation.

Mises maintains that sound, value-free economic reasoning leads a person to favor laissez-faire economic systems. He deduces the nature and outcomes of human cooperation in a market economy based on private property and the division of labor and compares these with the means employed and outcomes achieved under alternative systems such as socialism and interventionism. As an economist, he employs the logic of praxeology to work toward his goal of comparing systems with regard to their capacity to attain ends. He thus advocates the market economy because economic reasoning shows that it best enables people to achieve their chosen ends.

Mises explains that well-intentioned government interventions interfere with the tendency of the free market to respect the sovereignty of the individual. Interventionist policies will fail to attain their objectives, generate unintended and undesirable results, and lead to further government controls. Interventionism involves regulations and controls that divert production from the projects that would have been undertaken if people were free to follow their own judgments. These interventions reduce the standard of living by disturbing the division of labor.

Mises observes that it is impossible to have rational central planning under socialism. This is the basis of his epistemological case against socialism. Without market-based prices, decision-making by central planners would be irrational and arbitrary. Because of the elimination of market-based prices, a fully centralized planned economy would be unable to allocate resources rationally. Socialism, even more than interventionism, obstructs the operation of market processes, thereby decreasing the rationality in the social system.

According to Mises, socialism is inherently unworkable, destroys individual motivation, and suppresses the means of economic calculation. Economic calculation through the use of market prices is a logical precondition for the existence of society. Reason and society develop together and it is impossible to have a society without calculable action. The rational calculation of costs and benefits is the basis for economic efficiency. Socialism lacks this means to calculate and thus has to resort to irrationality.

Monetary calculation is a tool of action. Mises defines catallactics as the analysis of actions which are performed on the basis of monetary calculations and prices. It is prices, articulated through the common denominator of money, that makes economic calculation possible. The free market permits economic calculation—the mental tool that allows the development and evolution of the system of division of labor. It is through the system of division of labor that men are able to improve their earthly existence.

Socialism destroys the incentive of profits and losses, private ownership of property, and the benefits of competition. Mises explains that there is room for everyone in the market economy, even those with unexceptional abilities. He specifies that the function of competition is to designate to every member of a social system that position in which he can best serve. Competition is a method for choosing the most able men for each task. The competitive process is characterized by an absence of artificial barriers to entry (i.e., government-granted monopoly privileges). Competition requires freedom of entrepreneurial entry.

Mises insisted on the value freedom of the theoretical character of economics. He sees economics as a theoretical science that abstains from any judgment of value. For Mises, economics simply judges whether a specific policy will attain the ends that the proposer of the policy has in mind. Economics merely asks, given certain ends, how can those ends be best achieved? Mises sees no logical contradiction between himself (or any other economist) as an objective scientist and rational agnostic and, on the other hand, as an advocate of classical liberalism and denouncer of protectionism, antitrust policy, price-fixing, etc., based on the conclusions of economic science.

Mises explains that a policy is bad when it can be deduced to generate results which are inconsistent with the objectives intended for the policy by the policy-proposers themselves. He illustrates that statist interventions in the market bring about consequences which are worse than the state of affairs they were meant to improve. He demonstrates with deductive logic that every political intervention hurts some individuals and makes society less prosperous.

Mises contends that the reasoning of a value-free economics could be used to demonstrate that interventionist and socialist policies cannot attain a goal that their proponents are explicitly or implicitly attempting to accomplish—the goal of progress with respect to the material well-being of individuals in society. Realizing that social progress depends upon the construction and acceptance of a proper ideology of social life, Mises endeavors to formulate a theory of society that is as value-free and objective as possible. As a scientist and economist, Mises logically analyzes the ends of specific ideologies and the means available to attain these ends. The goal of his economics is to identify incorrect and correct views about how individuals in society can achieve their ends. His value-neutral economic science identifies free markets as best. Laissez-faire economics leads to progress and prosperity and lessens the incentive to go to war. Mises's evaluation of laissez-faire is an approval of the system of private property and voluntary social cooperation. It follows that, as a political ideology, classical liberalism is not neutral with respect to the values and ends sought by human actors.

According to Mises, government is a necessary prerequisite for a free market society. The free market requires an institutional framework that identifies and protects individual rights. This framework includes private property, freedom to contract, and government monopoly of coercion. As the monopoly of violence in society, government maintains peace and enforces rules so that individuals can cooperate and enjoy the benefits of that cooperation. Although Mises saw a role for government, he vehemently maintained that the exercise of state function conveys no innate dignity, virtue, or prestige.

Mises's utilitarianism starts with the goal of human flourishing and moves to social cooperation and the existence of individual rights. It does not explicitly include natural law, which Mises thinks is unnecessary and problematic and which he equates with intuitionism. Mises says that he is agnostic with respect to the nature of human nature. With regard to individual rights, he says that there exists a private domain in man which should not be regulated or violated. This realm constitutes what is deepest, highest, and most valuable in the individual human being.

Although he says he rejects natural law, Mises's approach to justifying the free society has a great deal in common with natural law constructs. The life-affirming rules for social cooperation and for interpersonal conduct that he deduces seem to be based on the essential nature of human life. For Mises, the reason or goal for this system of rules is to maintain and promote social harmony and human life. These rules for the protection of individual rights are essential for social cooperation on the part of rational human beings with free will. In the end, Mises's utilitarianism appears to be based, at least implicitly, on a principled, categorical, natural-law-like framework.

Note

This chapter is a shortened and edited version of chapter two of my *Philosophers of Capitalism* (Lexington Books, 2005).

Recommended Reading

Anderson, William P. "Mises versus Weber on Bureaucracy and Sociological Method." *Journal of Libertarian Studies* 18, no. 1 (2004).

Brätland, John. "Human Action and Socially-Optimal Conservation: A Misesian Inquiry into the Hotelling Principle." *Quarterly Journal of Austrian Economics* 3, no. 1 (2000).

Butler, Eamonn. *Ludwig von Mises: Fountainhead of the Modern Microeconomic Revolution.* New York: Universe Books, 1988.

Ebeling, Richard M., ed.. *Human Action: A Fifty-year Tribute.* Hillsdale, MI: Hillsdale City Press, 2000

Eshelman, Larry J. "Ludwig von Mises on Principle." *Review of Austrian Economics* 6, no. 2 (1993): 3–41.

Foss, Nicolai J. "Misesian Ownership and Coasian Authority in Heyekian Settings: The Case of Knowledge Economy." *Quarterly Journal of Austrian Economics* 4, no. 4 (2001).

Gallaway, Lowell, and Richard K. Vedder. "Wages, Prices, and Unemployment: Von

Mises and the Progressives." *Review of Austrian Economics* 1, no. 1 (1987).

Garrison, Roger W. "In Defense of the Misesian Theory of Interest." *Journal of Libertarian Studies* 3, no. 2 (1990): 141–50.

Gertchev, Nikolay. "Dehomogenizing Mises's Monetary Theory." *Journal of Libertarian Studies* 18, no. 3 (2004).

Gonce, R. A. "Natural Law and Ludwig von Mises's Praxeology and Economic Science." *Southern Economic Journal* 39 (April 1973): 490–507.

Gordon, David. "The Philosophical Contributions of Ludwig von Mises." *Review of Austrian Economics* 7, no. 1 (1994): 95–106.

———. "Justice and Redistributive Taxation: James Buchanan versus Ludwig von Mises." *Review of Austrian Economics* 8, no. 1 (1995).

Gunning, J. Patriack. "Interest: In Defense of Mises." *Quarterly Journal of Austrian Economics* 8, no. 3 (2005).

———. "Mises on the Evenly Rotating Economy." *Review of Austrian Economics* 7, no. 1 (1990).

Herbener, Jeffrey M. "Ludwig von Mises and the Austrian School of Economics." *Review of Austrian Economics* 3, no. 1 (1991).

———. *The Meaning of Ludwig von Mises: Contributions in Economics, Sociology, Epistemology, and Political Philosophy.* Dordrecht: Kluwer Academic Publishers, 1992.

Kirzner, Israel M. *Method, Process, and Austrian Economics: Essays in Honor of Ludwig von Mises.* Lanham, MD: Lexington Books, 1982.

———. "Reflections on the Misesian Legacy in Economics." *Review of Austrian Economics* 9, no. 2 (1996): 143–54.

———. *Ludwig von Mises.* Wilmington, DE: ISI Books, 2001.

Lavoie, Donald C. "From Hollis and Nell to Hollis and Mises." *Journal of Libertarian Studies* 1, no. 4 (1977).

Mises, Ludwig von. *The Theory of Money and Credit.* Translated by H. E. Batson. London: Jonathan Cape, [1912] 1934.

———. *Socialism: An Economic and Sociological Analysis.* Translated by J. Kahane. London: Jonathan Cape, [1922] 1936.

———. *Bureaucracy.* New Haven, CT: Yale University Press, 1944.

———. *Omnipotent Government: The Rise of the Total State and Total War.* New Haven, CT: Yale University Press, 1944.

———. *Planned Chaos.* Irvington-on-Hudson, NY: Foundation for Economic Education, 1947.

———. *Human Action: A Treatise on Economics.* New Haven, CT: Yale University Press, 1949.

———. *Planning for Freedom, and Other Essays and Addresses.* South Holland, IL: Libertarian Press, 1952.

———. *The Anti-Capitalist Mentality.* Princeton, NJ: Van Nostrand, 1956.

———. *Theory and History: An Interpretation of Social and Economic Evolution.* New Haven, CT: Yale University Press, 1957.

———. *Epistemological Problems of Economics.* Translated by George Reisman. Princeton, NJ: Van Nostrand, [1933] 1960.

———. *The Free and Prosperous Commonwealth: An Exposition of the Ideas of Classical Liberalism* Translated by Ralph Raico. Princeton, NJ: Van Nostrand, [1927]1962.

———. *The Ultimate Foundation of Economic Science: An Essay on Method.* Princeton, NJ: Van Nostrand, 1962.

———. *The Historical Setting of the Austrian School of Economics*. New Rochelle, NY: Arlington House, 1969.

———. "Comments About the Mathematical Treatment of Economic Problems." *Quarterly Journal of Libertarian Studies* 1, no. 2, (1977).

———. *A Critique of Interventionism*. Translated by Hans F. Sennholz. New Rochelle, NY: Arlington House, [1929] 1977.

———. *Nation, State, and Economy*. Translated by Leland B. Yeager. New York: New York University Press, [1919] 1983.

———. "The Equations of Mathematical Economics and the Problem of Economic Calculation in a Socialist State." *Journal of Austrian Economics* 3, no. 1 (2000).

Pongracic, Ivan. "How Different Were Röpke and Mises?" *Review of Austrian Economics* 10, no. 1 (1997).

Raico, Ralph. "Mises on Fascism, Democracy, and Other Questions." *Journal of Libertarian Studies* 12, no. 1 (Spring 1995): 1–27.

Reekie, W. Duncan. "Interpreting *Caritas*: Did Frank Knight and Ludwig von Mises Get it Wrong?" *Quarterly Journal of Austrian Economics* 7, no. 2 (2004).

Reisman, George. "Environmentalism in the Light of Menger and Mises." *Quarterly Journal of Austrian Economics* 5, no. 2 (2002).

Rothbard, Murray N. "Laissez-Faire Radical: A Quest for the Historical Mises." *Journal of Libertarian Studies* 5, no. 3 (Summer 1981): 237–53.

———."Ludwig Von Mises and Natural Law: A Comment on Professor Gonce." *Journal of Libertarian Studies* 4, no. 3 (1980): 289–97.

Salerno, Joseph T. "Ludwig von Mises as Social Rationalist." *Review of Austrian Economics* 4, no. 1 (Spring 1990) 26–54.

Stalebrink, Odd J. "The Hayek and Mises Controversy: Bridging Differences." *Quarterly Journal of Austrian Economics* 7, no. 1 (2004).

Tucker, Jeffrey A., and Llewellyn H. Rockwell, Jr. "Cultural Thought of Ludwig von Mises." *Journal of Libertarian Studies* 10, no. 1 (Fall 1991): 284–320.

Yeager, Leland B. "Mises and Hayek Dehomogenized." *Review of Austrian Economics* 6, no. 2 (1993): 113–48.

———. "Mises and Hayek on Calculation and Knowledge." *Journal of Libertarian Studies* 3, no. 2 (1994): 141–50.

Younkins, Edward W., ed. *Philosophers of Capitalism: Menger, Mises, Rand, and Beyond*. Lanham, MD: Lexington Books, 2005.

Chapter 14

Ayn Rand's Philosophy of Objectivism

Capitalism demands the best of every man—his rationality—and rewards him accordingly. It leaves every man free to choose the work he likes, to specialize in it, to trade his product for the products of others, and to go as far on the road of achievement as his ability and ambition will carry him. His success depends on the objective value of his work and on the rationality of those who recognize that value. When men are free to trade, with reason and reality as their only arbiter, when no man may use physical force to extort the consent of another, it is the best product and the best judgment that win in every field of human endeavor, and raise the standard of living—and thought—ever higher for all those who take part in mankind's productive activity.

—Ayn Rand

Ayn Rand (1905-1982), the best-selling novelist and world-famous philosopher, developed a unique philosophical system called Objectivism which has affected many lives over the last half century. This chapter represents an introduction to her systematic vision by presenting her essential ideas in a logical, accessible manner. This should contribute toward the appreciation of Rand's profoundly original philosophical system.

The specific purpose of this chapter is to introduce, summarize, logically rearrange, and clarify through rewording the ideas distributed throughout her books, essays, lectures, and novels (especially *Atlas Shrugged*), and as authoritatively described and systematically explained in Leonard Peikoff's monumental *Objectivism: The Philosophy of Ayn Rand*. Another fine but shorter source of much the same material as found in Peikoff's book is Allan Gotthelf's *On Ayn Rand*. Written from the viewpoint of a generalist in economics, philosophy, and the social sciences, this chapter is meant to provide a background for readers who wish to study specialized aspects of Rand's philosophy in greater detail.

Metaphysics is the subdivision of philosophy that studies the nature of the universe as a totality. Epistemology is concerned with the relationship between a man's mind (i.e., his consciousness) and reality (i.e., the nature of the universe) and with the operation of reason. In other words, epistemology investigates the fundamental nature of knowledge, including its sources and validation. One's theory of knowledge necessarily includes a theory of concepts and one's theory of concepts determines one's theory or concept of value (and ethics). The key to understanding ethics is in the concept of value and thus ultimately is located in epistemology and metaphysics. The purpose of this chapter is to delineate the inextricable and well-argued linkages between the various components of Ayn Rand's philosophy of Objectivism. Rand's philosophy is a systematic and integrated unity, with every part depending upon every other part.

The Essence of Objectivism

Hierarchically, philosophy, including its metaphysical, epistemological, and ethical dimensions, precedes and determines politics, which, in turn, precedes and determines economics. Rand bases her metaphysics on the idea that reality is objective and absolute. Epistemologically, the Objectivist view is that man's mind is competent to achieve objectively valid knowledge of that which exists. Rand's moral theory of self-interest is derived from man's nature as a rational being and end in himself, recognizes man's right to think and act according to his freely chosen principles, and reflects a man's potential to be the best person he can be in the context of his facticity. This leads to the notion of the complete separation of "political power" and "economic power"—the proper government should have no economic favors to convey. The role of the government is, thus, to "protect man's rights" through the use of force, but "only in retaliation and only against those who initiate its use." "Capitalism," the resulting economic system, "is based on the recognition of individual rights, including property rights, in which all property is privately owned." For Rand, capitalism, the system of laissez-faire, is the only moral system.

Metaphysics

Metaphysics is the first philosophical branch of knowledge. At the metaphysical level, Rand's Objectivism begins with "axioms"—fundamental truths or irreducible primaries that are self-evident by means of direct perception, the basis for all further knowledge, and undeniable without self-contradiction. Axioms cannot be reduced to other facts or broken down into component parts. They require no proofs or explanations. Objectivism's three basic philosophical axioms are "existence," "consciousness," and "identity"—presuppositions of every concept and every statement.

"Existence exists" and encompasses everything, including all states of consciousness. The world exists independently of the mind and is there to be discovered by the mind. In order to be conscious, we must be conscious of something. There can be no consciousness if nothing exists. Consciousness, "the faculty of perceiving that which exists," is the ability to discover, rather than to create, objects. Consciousness, a relational concept, presupposes the existence of something external to consciousness, something to be aware of. Initially, we become aware of something outside of our consciousness and then we become aware of our consciousness by contemplating on the process through which we became aware.

The axiom of identity says that to be is to be "something" in particular. Identity means that a thing is "this" rather than "that." What exists are "entities" and entities have identity. The identity of an entity is the total of its features, including its potentialities for change. To have identity is to have specific characteristics and to act in specific ways. What an entity can do depends on what it is. A thing must be something and only what it is. In order for knowledge to exist, there must be something to know (existence), someone to know it (consciousness), and something to know about it (identity). That existence exists implies that entities of certain types exist and that a person is capable of perceiving that entities of various types exist. "Existence is identity" and "consciousness is identification."

All actions are caused by "entities." Rand connects "causality" to the law of identity and finds necessity in the nature of the entity involved in the causal process. She explains that "the law of causality is the law of identity applied to action" and that "the nature of an action is caused and determined by the natures of the entities that act; a thing cannot act in contradiction to its nature."

The concept of entity is presupposed by all subsequent human thinking because entities comprise the content of the world men perceive. Rand contends that the universe is not caused, but simply is, and that "cause and effect . . . is a universal law of reality." Knowledge of causality involves apprehending the relationship between the nature of an entity and its method of action.

Rand explains that the "metaphysically given (i.e., any fact inherent in existence apart from the human action) is absolute" and simply is. The metaphysically given includes scientific laws and events taking place outside of the control of men. The metaphysically given must be accepted and cannot be changed.

She explains, however, that man has the ability to adapt nature to meet his requirements. Man can creatively rearrange the combination of nature's elements by enacting the required cause, the one necessitated by the immutable laws of existence. The "man-made" includes any object, institution, procedure, or rule of conduct created by man. Man-made facts are products of choice and can be evaluated and judged and then "accepted or rejected and changed when necessary."

Rand explains that the existence of consciousness is obvious and fundamental, that consciousness is a characteristic of particular living creatures, that consciousness has causal ability, and that there is a basic consonance between mind and body. To deny consciousness is self-refuting. That consciousness can direct action is evident through extrospection (i.e., observation) and introspection. A man's consciousness is integrated with his body and is subject to his free-will control. Rand contends that there is only one reality (not two opposing ones), that "consciousness is the faculty of awareness" (rather than of creation), and that the effects of consciousness are the caused outcomes of the interplay between a conscious person and the world.

Epistemology

Epistemology refers to the nature and starting point of knowledge, to the character and correct exercise of reason, to reason's connection to the senses and perception, to the possibility of other origins of knowledge, and to the constitution and attainability of certainty. Rand explains that reason is man's cognitive faculty for organizing perceptual data in conceptual terms through the use of the principles of logic. Knowledge exists when a person approaches the facts of reality through either perceptual observation or conceptualization.

Epistemology exists because man is a limited fallible being who learns in disjointed incremental steps and who therefore requires a proper procedure to acquire the knowledge necessary to act, survive, and flourish. A man does not have innate knowledge or instincts that will automatically and unerringly promote his well-being. He does not inevitably know what will help or hinder his life. He therefore needs to know how to acquire reliable and objective knowledge of reality. A man has to gain such knowledge in order to live. A person can only know from within the context of a human way of knowing. Because human beings are "neither infallible nor omniscient," all knowledge is contextual in nature.

"Sense perception" is man's initial and direct form of recognition of that which exists (i.e., of entities, including their characteristics, associations, and actions). Senses provide man with the start of the cognitive process. The senses neither err nor deceive a man. The senses do not judge, identify, or interpret, but simply respond to stimuli and report or present a "something" to one's consciousness. The evidence provided by the senses is an absolute, but a man must learn to use his mind to properly understand it. The task of identification belongs to reason operating with concepts. Man's senses only inform him that something is, but what it is must be learned by the mind which must discover the nature, the causes, the full context of his sensory material, and so on. It is only at the conceptual level, with respect to the "what," that the possibility of error occurs. On the conceptual level, awareness can lead to mistaken judgments about what we perceive. Conceptualization entails an interpretation that may differ from reality. However, man's reason can be used to correct wrong judgments and expand one's knowledge of the world.

A man's senses react to the "full context" of the facts. Sense perceptions are valid in that they are perceptions of entities which exist. Sensations are caused by objects in reality and by a person's organs of perception. It is the purpose of the mind to analyze the perceptual evidence and to identify the nature of what is and the causes in effect.

A difference in sensory form among various perceivers is merely a difference in the form of perceiving the same object in reality. As long as a person perceives the underlying objects and relationships in reality in some form, the rest is the mind's work, not the work of the senses.

Any perceptual mechanism is limited. It follows that the object as perceived is the result of an interaction between external entities and a person's limited perceptual apparatus. Forms of perceptions are circumscribed by a person's physical abilities to receive information interacting with external objects in connection with the laws of causality. In other words, perceptual awareness is the product of a causal interaction between sense organs and entities.

Perceptual awareness marks the beginning of human knowledge. In order to understand the world in a conceptual manner, man must integrate his percepts into concepts. A "concept" integrates and condenses a number of percepts into a single mental whole. Although based on sensory percepts, human knowledge, being conceptual in nature, can depart from reality. The mind is not infallible nor automatic and can distort and be mistaken. A man can only obtain knowledge if he adheres to certain methods of cognition. The validity of man's knowledge depends upon the validity of his concepts.

Whereas concepts are abstractions (i.e., universals), everything that man apprehends is specific and concrete. "Concept formation" is based on the recognition of "similarity" among the existents being conceptualized. Rand explains that an individual perceptually discriminates and distinguishes specific entities from their background and from one another. A person then groups objects according to their similarities, viewing each of them as a "unit." He then integrates a grouping of units into a distinct mental entity called a concept. "The ability to perceive entities or units is man's distinctive method of cognition" and the gateway to the conceptual level of man's consciousness. According to Rand, "a concept is a mental integration of two or more units which are isolated according to one or more characteristics and united by a specific definition." A definition is the condensation of a large body of observations.

Whereas a concept is assigned precise identity through the use of a definition, the integration (i.e., the concept) itself is kept in mind by referring to it by a perceptual concrete (i.e., a "word"). Words are concrete audiovisual representations of abstractions called concepts. "Words transfer concepts into (mental) entities" whenever definitions give them identity. Language makes this type of integration possible.

Concept formation is largely a mathematical process. There is a "connection between measurement and conceptualization." Similarity, an implicit form of measurement "is the relationship between two or more existents which possess the same characteristics but in different measure or degree." The mental process of concept formation consists in retaining the characteristics but omitting their measurements. The "relevant measurement" of a particular attribute "must exist in some quantity, but may exist in any quantity." The "measurements exist, but they are not specified." A concept is a mental integration of units possessing the same differentiating characteristics with their specific measurements omitted.

Rand explains that a "conceptual common denominator" is made up of the attributes reducible to a unit of measurement by which a person distinguishes two or more existents from other existents possessing the attributes. In other words, the comprehension of similarity and difference is necessary for conceptualization.

Perceptual data lead to "first level concepts." In turn, higher-level concepts are formed as "abstractions from abstractions" (i.e., from abstractions and subclassifications of previously formed concepts). Concepts differ from each other not only with regard to their referents but also in their distances from the perceptual level. Knowledge is hierarchical with respect to the order of concept formation. It consists of a set of concepts and conclusions ranked in order of logical dependence upon one another.

The last step in concept formation is "definition." A definition identifies a concept's units by particularizing their fundamental attributes. "A definition is a statement that identifies the nature of the units subsumed under a concept." A definition differentiates a given concept from all others and keeps its units distinguished in a person's mind from all other existents. The differentiation must be limited to the essential characteristics. Rand employs Aristotle's "rule of fundamentality" when she explains that the essential characteristic is the one that is responsible for, and therefore can explain, the greatest number of the unit's other distinguishing characteristics.

She explains that concepts are instruments to save space and time and to attain "unit-economy" through the condensation of data. Concepts have a metaphysical basis since consciousness is the ability of comprehending that which exists. Concepts result from a particular type of relationship between consciousness and existence.

Definitions are statements of factual data as compressed by a human consciousness. Definitions involve the condensation of a multitude of observations of similarity and difference relationships. They are also "contextual" because they partly rely upon the definer's context of knowledge. A new or revised definition does not invalidate the objective content of the old definition. It simply encompasses the requirements of an expanding cognitive context—the sum of cognitive elements conditioning an item to knowledge. Full context is the sum of available knowledge.

According to Rand, the essential characteristics of a concept are epistemological (i.e., contextual and relational) rather than metaphysical. Rand explains that concepts are neither intrinsic abstract entities existing independently of a person's mind nor are they nominal products of a person's consciousness, unrelated to reality. Concepts are epistemologically "objective" in that they are produced by man's consciousness in accordance with the facts of reality. Concepts are mental integrations of factual data. They are "the products of a cognitive method of classification whose processes must be performed by a human being, but whose content is dictated by reality." For Rand, essences are epistemological instead of metaphysical.

Rand contends that, although concepts and definitions are in one's mind, they are not arbitrary because they reflect reality, which is objective. Both consciousness in metaphysics and concepts in epistemology are real and part of ordinary existence—the mind is part of reality. She views concepts as "open-ended constructs" which subsume all information about their referents, including the information not yet discerned. New facts and discoveries expand or extend a person's concepts, but they do not overthrow or invalidate them. Concepts must conform to the facts of reality.

In order to be objective in one's conceptual endeavors, a human being must fully adhere to reality by applying certain methodological rules based on facts and proper for man's form of cognition. For man, a being with rational consciousness, the appropriate method for conforming to objective reality is "reason" and "logic." In order to survive, man needs knowledge, and reason is his tool of knowledge.

Rand observes that human knowledge is limited and that humans are beings of bounded knowledge. It is because of this constraint that it is imperative for a man to identify the cognitive context of his analysis and conclusions. She points out that contextualism does not mean relativism and that context is what makes a properly specified conclusion objective. Certainty is a contextual evaluation.

Where do emotions fit in the Objectivist world? According to Rand, an emotion is an "automatic response" to a situation based on a person's perception, identification, and evaluation of the situation. Emotions are states of consciousness with bodily accompaniments and intellectual causes. Different from sensations, emotions are caused by what a person thinks. Emotions are the result of a man's value premises which stem from his thinking about, and in reaction to, situations he has met in life. After a person has made a range of value judgments, he makes them automatic. Present in one's unconscious, value judgments affect man's evaluative and affective experiences. Emotions are reactions to a person's perceptions and are the automatic results of a mind's previous conclusions. "Emotions are not tools of cognition"—they are not a substitute for reason. Truth cannot be attained through one's feelings. However, emotions do play a key role in one's life. They do provide the means for enjoying life. A person could not achieve happiness without them.

Rand contends that people are born both conceptually (i.e., cognitively) and emotionally "tabula rasa." For her, emotions are dependent phenomena and are the automatic products of man's value judgments. Rand believes that reason must "program" emotions properly if a person is to achieve happiness. She sees man with no inborn instincts and views reason as a person's only guide to knowledge. According to Rand, people do not have inborn emotions, temperaments, desires, personality characteristics, or ingrained behavior of any kind. She says that men's brains are not hardwired and that all human behavior is learned behavior.

Ethics

Objectivism's ethical system rests upon the claim to have derived the "ought" from the "is." The defense of this claim starts by inquiring about the facts of existence and man's nature that result in value—"that which one acts to gain and/or keep." The concept of value "presupposes an entity capable of acting to attain a goal in the face of an alternative. Where no alternative exists, no goals and therefore no values are possible." The one "basic alternative" in the world is "existence vs. nonexistence." Since "the existence of inanimate matter is unconditional," "it is only a living organism that faces a constant alternative: the issue of life or death." Inanimate matter may change forms, but it cannot go out of existence. When a living organism dies, however, its basic physical elements remain, but its life ceases to exist. Life, "a process of self-sustaining and self-generated action," "makes the concept of 'Value' meaningful." "An organism's life is its standard of value." Whatever advances its life is good and that which endangers it is evil.

The nature of a living entity determines what it ought to do. All living entities, with the exception of man, are determined by their nature to undertake automatically the actions necessary to sustain their survival. Man, like an animal or a plant, must act in order to live and must gain the values that his life requires. Man's distinctive nature, however, is that he has no automatic means of survival. Man does not function by automatic sensory or chemical reactions. "Thinking," the process of abstraction and conceptualization, is necessary for man's survival. Thinking, man's basic virtue, is exercised "by choice"—"man is a being of volitional consciousness." Reason, "the faculty that perceives, identifies, and integrates the material provided by the senses," does not work automatically. Man is free to think or not to think. The tool of thought is logic—"the art of non-contradictory identification."

According to Rand, man has no innate knowledge and, therefore, must determine through thought the goals, actions, and values upon which his life depends. He must discover what will further his own unique and precious individual human life and what will harm it. Refusal to recognize and act according to the facts of reality will result in his destruction. The Objectivist view is that the senses enable man to perceive reality, that knowledge can only be gained through the senses, and that the senses are able to provide objectively valid knowledge of reality.

For man to survive, he must discern the "principles" of action necessary to direct him in his relationships with other men and with nature. Man's need for these principles is his need for a "code of morality." Men are essentially independent beings with free wills; therefore, it is up to each individual to choose his code of values using the standard that is required for the life of a human being. If "life as a man" is one's purpose, he has the right to live as a rational being. To live, man must think, act, and create the values his life requires.

Rand holds that morality (and ethics) depend upon a person's "pre-moral" choice to live. "To live is his basic act of choice. If he chooses to live, a rational ethics will tell him what principles of action are required to implement his choice."

Rand explains that moral values are neither subjective constructs nor intrinsic features of morality, but rather are objective. "The good is neither an attribute of things in themselves nor of a man's emotional state, but an evaluation made of the facts of reality by man's consciousness according to a rational standard of value." When one attributes moral value to something, he must address the questions of "to whom" and "for what." If something is a value, it must have a positive relationship to the end of a particular individual's life. Value is a function of the interaction between what is deemed valuable and the person to whom it is valuable. Value is neither totally internal nor completely external but is a function of a specific connection between external objects and an individual's ends.

Rand states that values reflect facts as evaluated by persons with respect to the goal of living. Whether or not a given object is a value depends upon its relationship to the end of a person's life. Life's "conditionality" is the basis of moral value. The thing in question must have certain attributes in order to further an individual's life, and the individual must seek his life, for that object to be valuable. The objectivity of value derives from the fact that particular kinds of action tend to promote human life. A specific object's value is a function of the factual relation between the object and a particular person's life. The valid attribution of value reflects a factual relationship. Rand's theory of objective value is both functional (i.e., directed toward certain ends) and naturalistic. It is naturalistic because values stem from certain facts about the nature of human life.

The requirements of a man's survival are determined by reality and the good is an aspect of reality that has a positive relationship to a man's life. An object's value thus depends on what the object is and on the way in which it affects a particular person. It follows that a variety of different things can be objectively valuable to different persons.

From an epistemological perspective, it is individuals who are objective (or are not objective) with respect to their judgments regarding value. A value's objectivity reflects the reality that values are the conclusions of a person's "volitional consciousness" and that individuals can be correct or can be mistaken in their judgments and choices. An authentic value must derive from a life-affirming relationship to a human being and must exist in a correct connection to his consciousness. A man's consciousness and elements of the external world must connect in order to properly judge particular things as objectively valuable.

For Rand, the designation objective refers to both the functioning of the cognitive process and to the output of that process when it is properly performed. A man's consciousness can acquire objective knowledge of reality by employing the proper means of reason in accordance with the rules of logic. When the mind conforms to mind-independent reality, the cognitive process being followed can be termed objective. In turn, when a correct cognitive process has been followed it can be said that the output (i.e., the conclusion reached) of that process is objective.

Rand explains that all abstractions stem from facts, including the abstraction "value." All ideas, including the idea of value, are features of reality as they pertain to individuals. Values are metaphysically objective when their propriety and attainment requires conformity to reality and are epistemologically objective when they are discovered via objective conceptual processes.

Rand asks what fact or facts of reality give rise to the concept of value. She reasons that there must be something in perceptual reality that results in the concept value. She argues that it is only from observing other living things (and one's self introspectively) in the pursuit of their own lives that a person can perceive the referents of the term "value." For example, people act to attain various material and other goods and determine their choices by reference to various goals, ends, standards, or principles.

For Rand, the concept of value depends upon and is derived from the antecedent concept of life. It is life that entails the possibility of something being good or bad for it. The normative aspect of reality arises with the appearance of life.

The fundamental fact of reality that gives rise to the concept of value is that living beings have to attain certain ends in order to sustain their lives. The facts regarding what enhances or hinders life are objective, founded on the facts of reality, and grounded in cognition. This should not be surprising because people do think, argue, and act as if normative issues can be decided by considering the facts of a situation.

Rand explains that the key to understanding ethics is found in the concept of value—it is thus located in epistemology. Her revolutionary theory of concepts is what directly leads her to innovations in the fields of value theory and ethics and moral philosophy.

Rand's theories of concepts, values, and ethics accurately reflect man's epistemic nature. Objectivism endorses a theory of objective value and an ethics that reflects the primacy of existence. Because Rand identifies and comprehends the epistemological nature of concepts and the nature of the concept of value itself, it is possible for us to understand them and to explain to others the logical steps that are included in their formulation.

Without self-value, no other values are possible. Self-value has to be earned by thinking. Morality, a practical, selfish necessity, requires the use of man's rational faculty and the freedom to act on his judgments. A code of values accepted by rational choice is a code of morality—choice is the foundation of virtue. "Happiness is the state of consciousness which proceeds from the achievement of one's values."

Because men are creatures who think and act according to principle, a doctrine of rights ensures that an individual's choice to live by those principles is not violated by other human beings. For Rand, all individuals possess the same rights to freely pursue their own goals. Since a free man chooses his own actions, he can be held responsible for them.

Ayn Rand defines value as "that which one acts to gain and/or keep." A value is an object of goal-directed action. In this sense we can say that everyone pursues values. The term "value" thus can refer in a descriptive sense to what is observable. We see people going after things. Initially, we do not consider whether or not people are choosing properly when they pursue their values. As children, we first get the idea of value implicitly from observation and introspection. We then move from an initial descriptive idea of value toward a normative idea of value that includes the notion that a real value serves one's life.

Each derivative value exists in a value chain or network in which every value (except for the ultimate value) leads to other values and thus serves both as an end and as a means to other values. A biological ends-means process leads to the ultimate end of the chain, which, for a living entity, is its life. For a human individual, the end is survival and happiness, and the means are values and virtues that serve that end. Values and virtues are common to, and necessary for, the flourishing of every human person. However, each individual will require them to a different degree. Each man employs his individual judgments to determine the amount of time and effort that should go into the pursuit of various values and virtues. Finding the proper combination and proportion is the task for each person in view of his own talents, potentialities, and circumstances. Values and virtues are necessary for a flourishing life and are objectively discernable, but the exact weighting of them for a specific person is highly individualized.

In order for a chain of values to make sense, there must be some "end in itself" and "ultimate value" for which all other values are means. "An infinite progression" or chain of ends and means "toward a nonexistent end is a metaphysical and epistemological impossibility." All must converge on an ultimate value.

Each component of action of one's life (i.e., one's work life, love life, home life, social life, and so on) is an end in itself and a means to the end of one's life in total. "Man's life is a continuous whole." One's life in total is an end in itself and an ultimate value. An ultimate value is required for a person to rationally decide how to act. Evaluation necessitates teleological measurement in order to make our potential values comparable. When different values come into conflict a person refers to a higher value in order to resolve the conflict.

An individual's task is to choose from among numerous values to find the most appropriate for himself. A person must make specific choices with respect to his career, his relationships, and so on. A "hierarchy of values" helps people make judgments regarding what to do or to pursue. To do this, an individual must assign a weight, either explicitly or implicitly, to his values. Values need to be weighted or ranked in terms of ordinal numbers. He must judge the ultimate contribution to the value of his life that exists at the apex of his hierarchy.

A value is an object of "goal-directed behavior." The fact that a person has values implies the existence of his goal-directed actions. Values are distinct from goals despite the fact that in general parlance goals and values are often used interchangeably. Actions are performed in response to one's values and are undertaken to achieve some goal or end.

To be a value means to be good for someone and for something. "Life" is one's "fundamental value" because life is conditional and requires a particular course of action to maintain it. Something can be good or bad only to a living organism, such as a human being, acting to survive. "Man's life" is the ultimate value and the "standard of value" for a human being.

A value exists in a chain of values and must have some ending point. There must be some "fundamental alternative" that marks the cessation of one's value chain. It is his life, "a process of self-sustaining and self-generated action," that is the fundamental alternative at the end of a person's value chain. One's life is the alternative that underpins all of his evaluative judgments.

Ethics, a code of values to rationally guide man's choices and actions, "is an objective, metaphysical necessity of man's survival." A proper ethics gives practical guidance to help people think and direct their lives. Ethics aids a man in defining and attaining his values, goals, and happiness. A man needs ethics because he requires values to survive. The *telos* of ethics is a person's own survival and happiness. The realm of ethics includes those matters that are potentially under a man's control. A man's uncoerced volition is necessary to have an objective theory of morality. He can discover values only through a volitional process of reason.

Rand's ethics identifies the good and bad according to the rational standard of value of "man's life qua man." Her Objectivist ethics focuses on what is, in reality, good or best for each unique individual human being. Such an ethics is rational, objective, and personal. Accordingly, a man's goal should be to become the best possible person in the context of who and what he is and of what is possible for him.

A person requires moral "knowledge" in the form of "abstractions" to guide his actions. Moral concepts necessarily come into play when one acts. A man needs an adequate set of general evaluative principles to provide basic guidance in living well. He must consciously identify the "principles" he wants to live by and must critically evaluate his values and principles.

Rational moral principles guide us toward values and are essential for achieving moral integrity, character, and happiness. When we habitually act on sound moral principles, we develop virtues and incorporate our moral orientation into our character. Rand connects virtues to the objective requirements of man's survival and flourishing. Moral principles are needed because the standard of survival and flourishing is too abstract. Acting on principles cultivates corresponding virtues which, in turn, leads to value attainment, flourishing, and happiness. According to Rand, "value is that which one acts to gain and/or keep—virtue is the act by which one gains and/or keeps it."

"Focus," a quality of alertness, involves a man's primary free will decision to activate his mind. It takes effort to stay in focus by using one's volition to activate his consciousness and mental resources. Although focus is not automatic and takes effort, it is rewarding and natural. Focus enters in the development of one's ideas, in the choice of his values, and in the selection of his moral principles. In addition, when one acts, he needs to focus in order to keep his ideas, values, and moral principles in his consciousness. A person must be alert for opportunities to form one's ideas, values, and principles and he must also use his free will to be in focus for his thinking to guide his actions. A person can be in focus, passively out of focus, or he can actively evade particular mental content. Rand says that "evasion is . . . the willful suspension of one's consciousness, the refusal to think . . . the refusal to know."

Moral principles are true or absolute in a given "context." A person needs to recognize the moral context of a situation. A man should not evade relevant knowledge nor drop context when he acts. Some cases will fall outside the context in which they are defined and applicable. Thinking is needed in order to understand the facts of a situation and to apply appropriate principles to the circumstances. For example, "honesty," as a principle, states that it is immoral to misrepresent the truth in a context in which a person's goal is to "attain values" from others. It follows that in a different context in which someone is attempting to use deceit or force in order to gain values from an individual, it is appropriate for the wronged individual to choose self-defense (e.g., dishonesty) as the applicable principle instead of honesty. The context is different from one calling for honesty on his part. In this case, the person who is properly lying is not trying to gain a value. Instead, he is rationally acting in his own interest to protect a value that is being threatened.

Honesty is an essential principle because the proper end of a man's actions is his own objective flourishing. The moral appropriateness of honesty is grounded in metaphysics. A person must focus on what reality requires if he is to attain his ends. A person should tell the relevant truth. What the relevant truth is depends on the type of relationship a person has with the individual with whom he is dealing.

In Rand's biocentric ethics, moral behavior is judged in relation to achieving specific ends, with the final end being an individual's life or flourishing. The act of deciding necessitates the investigation of how an action pertains to what is best for one's own life. This is not done in a duty-based ethic that is limited to precepts and rules that are placed between a person and reality. In a biocentric ethics what is moral is the understood and the chosen rather than the imposed and the obeyed. Principles are valuable ethical concepts that do not require imperatives or obligations as their justification.

Altruist moralities hold that morality is difficult and involves ideas such as self-abnegation and self-sacrifice. Contrariwise, an egoist morality, such as the one found in Objectivism, maintains that morality is natural and enjoyable. Of course, there is work involved in staying in focus, acquiring knowledge, formulating moral principles, and applying them in the appropriate contexts. Morality is demanding but it is also indispensable and rewarding.

Values and Virtues

Rand explains that to live, men must hold three ruling values—"reason, purpose, and self-esteem." These values imply all of the virtues required by a man's life. "Rationality," the primary virtue, is the recognition of objective reality, commitment to its perception, and the "acceptance of reason as one's source of knowledge, one's only judge of values, and one's only guide to action." "Independence," the acceptance of one's intellectual responsibility for one's own existence, requires that a man form his own judgments and that he support himself by the work of his own mind. "Honesty," the selfish refusal to seek values by faking reality, recognizes that the unreal can have no value. "Integrity," the refusal to permit a breach between thought and action, acknowledges the fact that man is an indivisible, integrated entity of mind and body. "Justice," a form of faithfulness to reality, is the virtue of granting to each man that which he objectively deserves. Justice is the expression of man's rationality in his dealings with other men and involves seeking and granting the earned. A trader, a man of justice, "earns what he gets and does not give or take the undeserved." Just as he does not work except in exchange for something of economic value, he also does not give his love, friendship, or esteem except in trade for the pleasure he receives from the virtues of individuals he respects. Love, friendship, and esteem, as moral tributes, are caused and must be earned. "Productiveness," the virtue of creating material values, is the art of translating one's thoughts and goals into reality. "Pride," the total of the preceding virtues, can be thought of as "moral ambitiousness."

Capitalism and Individual Rights

Rand's justification of capitalism is that it is a system based on the logically derived code of morality outlined above—a code of morality that recognizes man's metaphysical nature and the supremacy of reason, rationality, and individualism. The ruling principle of capitalism is justice. The overall social effect—the fact that individuals and groups who live under capitalism prosper—is simply a byproduct or secondary consequence. Political and economic systems and institutions which encourage and protect individual rights, freedom, and happiness are proper systems.

"A right is a moral principle defining and sanctioning a man's freedom of action in a social context." According to Rand, rights are innate and can be logically derived from man's nature and needs. The principle of man's rights, like every other Objectivist moral principle, is derived by way of ethical egoism. The state is not involved in the creation of rights and simply exists to protect an individual's natural rights. There are no group rights—only individual rights. Group rights are arbitrary and imply special interests.

Humans are material beings who require material goods to sustain their existence. If one's life is the standard, man has the right to live and pursue values as his survival requires. He has the right to work for and keep the fruits of his labor—the right of property. "Without property rights, no other rights are possible." A man who has no right to the product of his efforts is not free to pursue his happiness and has no means to sustain his life.

A violation of a man's property rights is an expression of force against the man himself. The purpose of government is to "protect man's rights" (including property rights) and enforce contractual agreements—a breach of contract is an indirect use of force. The state's function is thus restricted to the "retaliatory use of force."

Under Randian capitalism, which historically has never existed, there is a complete separation of state and economics. Men deal with each other voluntarily by individual choice and free trade to their mutual benefit. The "profit motive" is just and moral. "Profit" is made through moral virtue and measures the creation of wealth by the profit-earner. The "market price" is objectively determined in the free market and represents the lowest price a buyer can discover and the highest price a seller can obtain. Freedom guarantees that both parties will benefit—no one is willing to enter into a one-sided bargain to his detriment. A person's wealth under capitalism depends on his productive achievements and the choice of others to recognize them. Rewards are tied to production, ability, and merit. A producer can do with his wealth what he chooses. "Charity" is rational, objective, and genuine when, rather than being offered indiscriminately, it is offered only to those who deserve it. "Generosity" toward those who are innocent victims of injustice or who are fighting against adversity is proper. It is wrong to help persons with no virtue. By giving unconditionally you deceive the recipient into thinking that wealth and happiness are free. Charity must be voluntary. Forced redistribution will result in the curtailment of effort of the productive and a decrease in the amount of real wealth (i.e., real virtue) within society.

Conclusion

Despite inciting a number of vehement and critical commentaries, Rand's controversial, original, and systematic philosophical positions should be taken seriously and treated with respect. She persuasively expounds a fully integrated defense of capitalism and the component metaphysical, epistemological, psychological, ethical, social, political, cultural, and historical conditions necessary for its establishment and survival. Rand presents Objectivism as an integrated new system of thought with an organized, hierarchical structure. Whatever one's ultimate evaluation of her theories, Rand's unique vision should be considered worthy of comprehensive, scholarly examination.

Ayn Rand was a philosophical system-builder who consistently integrated the various aspects of her clearly written and compelling work. Rand's view of the world and of human possibility in the world is at the heart of her system. She sees a benevolent world that is open to man's achievement and success. Happiness and great accomplishment are possible in the world. To succeed, man must comprehend the nature of the world and of man and must define, choose, and passionately pursue rational values. Moral greatness is possible for each of us if we rationally strive to live up to our potential, whatever that potential may be. A person who selects rational values and who chooses ends and means consonant with the nature of reality and with the integrity of his own consciousness exemplifies a moral ideal and can certainly be viewed as heroic. As a rational goal, Rand's ideal of moral greatness is available to every human being.

Note

This chapter is a shortened and edited version of chapter three in my *Philosophers of Capitalism* (Lexington Books, 2005).

Recommended Reading

Badhwar, Neera K. *Is Virtue Only a Means to Happiness? An Analysis of Virtue and Happiness in Ayn Rand's Writings.* Poughkeepsie, NY: The Objectivist Center, 2001.

Baker, James T. *Ayn Rand.* Boston: Twayne, 1987.

Binswanger, Harry. *The Ayn Rand Lexicon: Objectivism from A to Z.* New York: New American Library, 1988.

Branden, Barbara. *The Passion of Ayn Rand.* New York: Doubleday, 1986.

Branden, Nathaniel. *Judgment Day: My Years with Ayn Rand.* Boston: Houghton Mifflin Company, 1989.

———. *My Years with Ayn Rand.* San Francisco, CA: Jossey-Bass Publishers, 1999.

Den Uyl, Douglas, and Douglas Rasmussen, eds. *The Philosophical Thought of Ayn Rand.* Chicago: University of Illinois Press, 1984.

Ellis, Albert. *Is Objectivism a Religion?* New York: Lyle Stuart, 1968.

Erickson, Peter. *The Stance of Atlas: An Examination of the Philosophy of Ayn Rand.* New York: Herakles Publishers, 1997.

Gladstein, Mimi. *The Ayn Rand Companion.* Westport, CT: Greenwood, 1984.

———. *The New Ayn Rand Companion, Revised and Expanded Edition.* Westport, CT: Greenwood Publishing Group, 1999.

Gotthelf, Allan. *On Ayn Rand.* Belmont, CA: Wadsworth, 2000.

Greiner, Donna, and Theodore B. Kinni. *Ayn Rand and Business.* New York: W.W. Norton & Company, 2001.

Hamil, Virginia L. L. *In Defense of Ayn Rand.* Brookline, MA: New Beacon, 1990.

Kelley, David. *The Contested Legacy of Ayn Rand.* Poughkeepsie, NY: The Objectivist Center, 2000.

Long, Roderick T. *Reason and Value: Aristotle versus Rand.* Poughkeepsie, NY: The Objectivist Center, 2000.

Machan, Tibor R. *Ayn Rand.* New York: Peter Lang, 1999.

Mayhew, Robert, ed. *Essays on Ayn Rand's "We the Living."* Lanham, MD: Rowman & Littlefield, 2004.

Merrill, Ronald E. *The Ideas of Ayn Rand.* Chicago: Open Court, 1991.

Nyquist, Greg S. *Ayn Rand Contra Human Nature.* Bloomington, IN: iUniverse, Inc., 2001.

O'Neill, William F. *With Charity Toward None.* New York: Philosophical Library, 1991.

Peikoff, Leonard. *Objectivism: The Philosophy of Ayn Rand*. New York: Dutton, 1991.

Porter, Tom. *Ayn Rand's Theory of Knowledge*. Reseda, CA: Tom Porter, 1999.

Rand, Ayn. *Atlas Shrugged*. New York: Random House, 1957.

———. *For the New Intellectual*. New York: Random House, 1961.

———. *The New Left*. New York: Signet, 1963.

———. *Capitalism: The Unknown Ideal*. New York: The New American Library, 1967.

———. *Introduction to Objectivist Epistemology*. New York: The Objectivist, 1967.

———. *The Romantic Manifesto*. New York: The New American Library, 1971.

———. *Philosophy: Who Needs It*. Edited by Leonard Peikoff. New York: Bobbs-Merrill, 1982.

———. *The Early Ayn Rand*. Edited and annotated by Leonard Peikoff. New York: New American Library, 1984.

———. *The Voice of Reason*. Edited by Leonard Peikoff. New York: Penguin Books, 1990.

———. *Ayn Rand's Marginalia: Her Critical Comments on the Writings of Over 20 Authors*. Edited by Robert Mayhew. New Milford, CT: Second Renaissance Books, 1995.

———. *Journals of Ayn Rand*. Edited by David Harriman. New York: Plume, 1997.

———. *Letters of Ayn Rand*. Edited by Michael S. Berliner, with an introduction by Leonard Peikoff. New York: Penguin, 1997.

———. *Without a Prayer: Ayn Rand and the Close of Her System*. Unicoi, TN: Trinity Foundation, 1997.

———. *Russian Writings on Hollywood*. Edited by Michael S. Berliner. Irvine, CA: Ayn Rand Institute Press, 1999.

Robbins, John W. *Answer to Ayn Rand*. Washington, DC: Mount Vernon Publishing, 1974.

Ryan, Scott. *Objectivism and the Corruption of Rationality: A Critique of Ayn Rand's Epistemology*. Lincoln, NB: Writers Club Press, 2003.

Sciabarra, Chris Matthew. *Ayn Rand: The Russian Radical*. University Park: Pennsylvania State University Press, 1995.

———. *Ayn Rand: Her Life and Thought*. Poughkeepsie, NY: The Objectivist Center, 1999.

Seddon, Fred. *Ayn Rand, Objectivists, and the History of Philosophy*. Lanham, MD: Rowman & Littlefield, 2003.

Smith, Tara. *Ayn Rand's Normative Ethics*. Cambridge: Cambridge University Press, 2006.

Valiant, James. *The Passion of Ayn Rand's Critics*. Dallas, TX: Durban House Publishing, 2001.

Walker, Jeff. *The Ayn Rand Cult*. Chicago: Open Court, 1999.

Yang, Michael B. *Reconsidering Ayn Rand*. Cincinnati, OH: Enclair Publishing, 2000.

Chapter 15

Murray Rothbard's Randian Austrianism

Thus, while praxeological economic theory is extremely useful for providing data and knowledge for framing economic policy, it cannot be sufficient by itself to enable the economist to make any value pronouncements or to advocate any public policy whatsoever. More specifically, Ludwig von Mises to the contrary notwithstanding, neither praxeological economics nor Mises's utilitarian liberalism is sufficient to make the case for laissez faire and the free-market economy. To make such a case, one must go beyond economics and utilitarianism to establish an objective ethics which affirms the overriding value of liberty, and morally condemns all forms of statism.

—Murray N. Rothbard

Murray N. Rothbard (1926-1995) was a grand system builder. In his monumental *Man, Economy, and State* (1962), Rothbard continued, embodied, and extended Ludwig von Mises's methodological approach of praxeology to economics. His magnum opus was modeled after Mises's *Human Action* and, for the most part, was a massive restatement, defense, and development of the Misesian praxeological tradition. Rothbard followed up and complemented *Man, Economy, and State* with his brilliant *The Ethics of Liberty* (1982) in which he provided the foundation for his metanormative ethical theory. Exhibiting an architectonic character, these two works form an integrated system of philosophy.

Praxeology

In a 1971 article in *Modern Age*, Murray Rothbard declared that Mises's work provides us with an economic paradigm grounded in the nature of man and in individual choice. Rothbard explains that Mises's paradigm furnishes economics in a systematic, integrated form that can serve as a correct alternative to the crisis situation that modern economics has engendered. According to Rothbard, it is time for us to adopt this paradigm in all of its facets.[1]

Like Mises, Rothbard begins with the axiom that human beings act and believes that all of economic theory can be logically deduced from this starting point. Committed to the praxeological method, Rothbard's writings are characterized by value-free deductive reasoning, abstract universal principles, and methodological individualism. He agrees with Mises that the basic test of economic theory is the truth of the premise and the logical chain of reasoning involved. By setting out from the undeniable fact that a person acts, Rothbard establishes economics as a logic of action.

Rothbard defends Mises's methodology but goes on to construct his own edifice of Austrian economic theory. Although he embraced nearly all of Mises's economics, Rothbard could not accept Mises's Kantian extreme aprioristic position in epistemology. Mises held that the axiom of human action was true a priori to human experience and was, in fact, a synthetic a priori category. Mises considered the action axiom to be a law of thought and thus a categorical truth prior to all human experience.

Murray Rothbard agreed that the action axiom is universally true and self-evident but argued that a person becomes aware of that axiom and its subsidiary axioms through experience in the world. A person begins with concrete human experience and then moves toward reflection. Once a person forms the basic axioms and concepts from his experiences with the world and from his reflections upon those experiences, he does not need to resort to external experience to validate an economic hypothesis. Instead, deductive reasoning from sound basics will validate it.

Rothbard, working within an Aristotelian, Thomistic, or Mengerian tradition, justified the praxeological action axiom as a law of reality that is empirical rather than a priori. Of course, this is not the empiricism embraced by positivists. This kind of empirical knowledge rests on universal inner or reflective experience in addition to external physical experience. This type of empirical knowledge consists of a general knowledge of human action that would be considered to be antecedent to the complex historical events that mainstream economists to try to explain. The action axiom is empirical in the sense that it is self-evidently true once stated. It is not empirically falsifiable in the positivist sense. It is empirical but it is not based on empiricism as practiced by today's economics profession. Praxeological statements cannot be subjected to any empirical assessment whether it is falsificationist or verificationist.

In a 1957 article in the *Southern Economic Journal,* Rothbard states that it is a waste of time to argue or try to determine how the truth of the action axiom is obtained. He explains that the all-important fact is that the axiom is self-evidently true for all people, at all places, at all times, and that it could not even conceivably be violated. Rothbard was not concerned with the controversy over the empirical status of the praxeological axiom. Whether it was a law of thought as Mises maintained or a law of reality as Rothbard himself contended, the axiom would be no less certain because the axiom need only to be stated to become at once self-evident. In Rothbard's words:

> Whether we consider the Axiom "a priori" or "empirical" depends on our ultimate philosophical position. Professor Mises, in the neo-Kantian tradition, considers this axiom a *law of thought* and therefore a categorical truth *a priori* to all experience. My own epistemological position rests on Aristotle and St. Thomas rather than Kant, and hence I would interpret the proposition differently. I would consider the axiom a *law of reality* rather than a law of thought, and hence "empirical" rather than "a priori." But it should be obvious that this type of "empiricism" is so out of step with modern empiricism that I may just as well continue to call it *a priori* for present purposes. For (1) it is a law of reality that is not conceivably falsifiable, and yet is empirically meaningful and true; (2) it rests on universal *inner* experience, and not simply on external experience, that is, its evidence is *reflective* rather than physical; and (3) it is clearly *a priori* to complex historical events.[2]

The Aristotelian, neo-Thomistic, and natural-law-oriented Rothbard refers to laws of reality that the mind apprehends by examining and adducing the facts of the real world. Conception is a way of comprehending real things. It follows that perception and experience are not the products of a synthetic a priori process but rather are apprehensions whose structured unity is due to the nature of reality itself. In opposition to Mises, Rothbard contends that the action axiom and its subsidiary axioms are derived from the experience of reality and are therefore radically empirical. These axioms are based on both external experience and universal inner experience. By 1978, Rothbard was stronger in voicing his opposition to Mises's Kantian epistemology:

> Without delving too deeply into the murky waters of epistemology, I would deny, as an Aristotelian and neo-Thomist, any such alleged "laws of logical structure" that the human mind necessarily imposes on the chaotic structure of reality. Instead, I would call all such laws "laws of reality," which the mind apprehends from investigating and collating the facts of the real world. My view is that the fundamental axiom and subsidiary axioms are derived from the experience of reality and are therefore in the broadest sense empirical. I would agree with the Aristotelian realist view that its doctrine is radically empirical, far more so than the post-Humean empiricism which is dominant in modern philosophy.[3]

Rothbard nevertheless continued to endorse Mises's monumental, integrated, and systematic treatise, *Human Action*, as a complete and true paradigm based on the nature of man and individual choice. Although he disagrees with Mises's epistemology, he does agree that Mises's praxeological economics appropriately begins with, and verbally deduces logical implications from, the fact that individuals act. Rothbard contends that it's time for Mises's paradigm to be embraced if we are to find our way out of the methodological and political problems of the modern world.

Anarcho-Capitalism

Rothbard was totally committed to the praxeological method. In fact, he thought that Mises was not sufficiently thoroughgoing or revolutionary enough with respect to his praxeological deductions. By consistently taking the praxeological path in economics, Rothbard arrives at the desirability of a pure anarcho-capitalist society. He convincingly argues that a stateless society is the only society totally consonant with natural rights to person and property. For Rothbard, freedom means private property, consent, and contract. It follows that the institutions and projects of a legitimate society stem from consensual agreements between property owners. Rothbard endorsed private property anarchism because he could not reconcile a coercive monopoly government with men's natural rights to liberty and legitimately acquired property.

For Rothbard, the state cannot be defended on praxeological or moral grounds. He systematizes a fully consistent argument against government intervention in human pursuits in any form or circumstances. Rothbard demonstrates that there exists no proper role for the State by explaining how market enterprises or associations can supply any good or service desired by individuals. Private companies and voluntary associations can do whatever needs to be accomplished. The market can produce all goods and services, including defense, security, and arbitration activities.

Ethics

Rothbard produced a system of political and social philosophy based on economics and ethics as its foundations. First, he presented an exhaustive case for a pure market economy resting on the observation that "men act" in *Man, Economy, and State*, and then in *The Ethics of Liberty* he explained the relationship between economics and ethics that is grounded in the concept of property. Rothbard teaches that economics can provide data and knowledge for a libertarian position, but that it cannot morally validate that political philosophy. Insisting that economics, as a science, is value-free, he contends that an ethical foundation must be established in order to make the case for individual freedom. According to Rothbard, economics and ethics are separate disciplines, complement one another, and are based on the nature of man and the world. He recognizes the need for an ethic to underpin, accompany, and enhance a value-free economics in order to solidify the argument for a free-market society. To make a case for laissez-faire, Rothbard goes beyond economics by formulating a metanormative objective ethics that affirms the essential value of liberty.

Separating praxeological economics from the science of ethics, Rothbard bases his ethical system upon the principles of self-ownership and first use–first own. Beginning with axiomatic principles about the nature of man and the world, Rothbard devises a radical dualistic dissociation between political ethics and personal morality. In essence, he is distinguishing between the metanormative sphere of politics and law and the normative domain which concerns moral or ethical principles for one's self-fulfillment and flourishing. Rothbard is differentiating between natural rights and the morality or immorality of the exercise of those rights. There is a critical distinction between the right to take a particular action and the morality of that action.

Rothbard's *The Ethics of Liberty* is not a prescription for personal morality. Instead, in it he concentrates on the political dimension of social relations by constructing a framework of political philosophy that only expresses what ought to be permitted and not what is desirable or proper. Rothbard's goal was to develop the branch of natural law that involves natural rights and that pertains to the political realm. He was concerned with building a system of rules consistent with social cooperation, interpersonal conduct, and the maintenance and facilitation of human life.

Rothbard's libertarian ethic considers nonaggression to be an absolute principle prior to any foundation for personal morality. In other words, he separates the form of human liberty from any specific noncoercive context in which a person's liberty is used. Rothbard is morally neutral with respect to the particular values and goals at which a person aims as long as the individual does not initiate the use of force or fraud against other people. Although Rothbard realized the importance of an individual's personal moral values, he viewed them as separate from, but dependent upon, the institution of a libertarian social order.

Rothbard deduces the entire body of a libertarian law code, including the laws of appropriation, contract, and punishment. This nonstatist code of nonaggression establishes the framework for a competitive method regarding the furnishing of legal, defense, and judicial services.

Comparing the Ideas of Rothbard and Rand

Both Murray Rothbard and Ayn Rand were concerned with the nature of man and the world, natural law, natural rights, and a rational ethics based on man's nature and discovered through reason. They also agreed that the purpose of political philosophy and ethics is the promotion of productive human life on earth. In addition, both adopted, to a great extent, Lockean natural rights perspectives and arguments that legitimize private property. Additionally, they both disagreed with Mises's epistemological foundations and on very similar grounds.

Both Rothbard and Rand endeavored to determine the proper rules for a rational society by using reason to examine the nature of human life and the world and by employing logical deductions to ascertain what these natures suggest. They agreed with respect to the volitional nature of rational human consciousness, a man's innate right of self-ownership, and the metanormative necessity of noncoercive mutual consent. Both thus subscribed to the nonaggression principle and to the right of self-defense.

Rothbard and Rand did not agree, however, on the nature of (or need for) government. They disagreed with respect to the practical applications of their similar philosophies. Rejecting Rand's idea of a constitutionally limited representative government, Rothbard believed that their shared doctrines entailed a zero-government or anarcho-capitalist framework based on voluntarism, free exchange, and peace.

Rothbard and Rand subscribed to different forms of metanormative libertarian politics—Rothbard to anarcho-capitalism and Rand to a minimal state. Unlike Rand, Rothbard ended his ethics at the metanormative level. Rand, on the other hand, advocated a minimal state form of libertarian politics based on the fuller foundation of Objectivism through which she attempted to supply an objective basis for values and virtues in human existence. Of course, Rothbard did discuss the separate importance of a rational personal morality, stated that he agreed essentially with most of Rand's philosophy, and suggested his inclination toward a Randian ethical framework. The writings of Murray Rothbard, much like those of Carl Menger, the founder of Austrian economics, have done a great deal toward building a bridge between Austrian economics and Objectivism.

Notes

1. Murray N. Rothbard, "Ludwig von Mises and the Paradigm for Our Age," *Modern Age* (Fall 1971): 370-79.

2. Rothbard, "In Defense of 'Extreme Apriorism," *Southern Economic Journal* (January 1957): 314-20.

3. Rothbard, "Praxeology: The Methodology of Austrian Economics," in Edwin Dolan (ed.), *The Foundations of Modern Austrian Economics*. Kansas City, MO: Sheed and Ward, 1976.

Recommended Reading

Block, Walter. "Austrian Law and Economics: The Contributions of Adolf Reinach and Murray Rothbard on Law, Economics, and Praxeology." *Quarterly Journal of Austrian Economics* 7, no. 4 (Winter 2004).

Boettke, Peter J., and Christopher J. Coyne. "The Forgotten Contribution: Murray Rothbard on Socialism in Theory and in Practice." *Quarterly Journal of Austrian Economics* 7, no. 2 (Summer 2004).

Maltsev, Yuri. "Murray N. Rothbard as a Critic of Socialism." *Journal of Libertarian Studies* 12, no. 1 (Spring 1996).

Raimondo, Justin. *An Enemy of the State*. Amherst, NY: Prometheus Books, 2000.

Rothbard, Murray N. "In Defense of Extreme Apriorism." *Southern Economic Journal* (January 1957): 314–20.

———. *Man, Economy, and State: A Treatise on Economic Principles*. 2 vols. Princeton, NJ: D. Van Nostrand Co., 1962.

————. *What Has Government Done to Our Money?* Colorado Springs, CO: Pine Tree Press, 1963.

————. *Economic Depressions: Causes and Cures.* Lansing, MI: Constitutional Alliance, Inc., 1969.

————. *Man, Economy, and State.* Los Angeles: Nash Publishing, 1970.

————."Ludwig von Mises and the Paradigm for Our Age." *Modern Age* (Fall 1971): 370–79.

————. *Education, Free and Compulsory: The Individual's Education.* Wichita, KS: Center for Independent Education, 1972.

————. "Value Implications of Economic Theory." *The American Economist* 17 (Spring, 1973): 35–39.

————. "Praxeology: The Methodology of Austrian Economics." In *The Foundations of Modern Austrian Economics*, edited by Edwin G. Dolan. Kansas City, MO: Sheed and Ward, 89–111, 1976.

————. "Praxeology, Value Judgments, and Public Policy." In *The Foundations of Modern Austrian Economics*, edited by Edwin G. Dolan. Kansas City, MO: Sheed and Ward, 89–111, 1976.

————. *Power and Market.* Kansas City, MO: Sheed, Andrews, and McMeel, [1970] 1977.

————. *For a New Liberty, the Libertarian Manifesto.* New York: Macmillan, 1973. Revised edition, New York: Collier Books, 1978.

————. *Individualism and the Philosophy of the Social Sciences.* Washington, DC: Cato Institute, 1979.

————. *The Ethics of Liberty.* Atlantic Highlands, NJ: Humanities Press, 1982.

————. "Concepts of the Role of Intellectuals in Social Change Toward Laissez Faire." *Journal of Libertarian Studies* 9, no. 2 (Fall 1990).

————. *The Case Against the Fed.* Auburn, AL: The Ludwig von Mises Institute, 1994.

————. *Making Economic Sense.* Auburn, AL: The Ludwig von Mises Institute, 1995.

————. *The Logic of Action One: Method, Money, and the Austrian School.* Glos, UK: Edward Elgar Publishing, Ltd., 1997.

————. *The Logic of Action Two: Applications and Criticism from the Austrian School.* Glos, UK: Edward Elgar Publishing, Ltd., 1997.

Sciabarra, Chris Matthew. "Rothbard's Libertarianism." *Liberty* 4, no. 2 (1991).

Chapter 16

The Road to Objective Economics:
Hayek Takes a Wrong Turn

It may indeed prove to be far the most difficult and not the least important task for human reason rationally to comprehend its own limitations. It is essential for the growth of reason that as individuals we should bow to forces and obey principles which we cannot hope fully to understand, yet on which the advance and even the preservation of civilization depend.

—Friedrich A. Hayek

Carl Menger (1840-1921) took the first steps on the road toward objective economics with his Aristotelian approach to metaphysics and epistemology and his relational theory of value. Ludwig von Mises (1881-1973) took a few more steps down that road but got off the path with his neo-Kantian aprioristic perspective on epistemology. Murray Rothbard (1926-1995) put economists back on track when he explained that a realist natural-law-oriented approach could provide a better underpinning for Misesian praxeology. Unfortunately, Friedrich A. Hayek (1899-1992), 1974 Nobel prize winner and the most well known of the Austrian economists, took a wrong turn by ignoring the foundations provided by natural law and the praxeological method and drifted further and further into error.

Critique of Human Reason

Hayek is primarily concerned with the nature, scope, limits, use, and abuse of reason in human life. For Hayek, a man's knowledge of the world and himself is at best limited, incomplete, and uncertain. Viewing the task of philosophy as the investigation of the limits of reason, he said that men needed to be aware of the limits of one's knowledge and that each of us should take our ignorance seriously. Analogously, the function of economics is to show men how little they know about what they presume that they design. He emphasized the extent of human ignorance with regard to the decisions of particular individuals. Hayek explained that the fatal conceit was man's undue faith in the power of reason. Speaking of man's inevitable ignorance, he says that a person should be cognitively humble and should not exhibit the pretense of knowledge. Hayek is particularly concerned with the hubris of reason that distinguishes constructivist rationalism. According to Hayek, if people are to understand how society works, they must try to define the nature and extent of their ignorance regarding it. It is important for social scientists to "know" that they are ignorant and that they can never know or act in total consideration of all the facts relevant to a particular situation. It follows that social order cannot be the product of a directing intelligence.

A critic of political utopianism, Hayek argues that there is no way for bureaucrats to make intelligent decisions to deliberately plan or design an economy because it is impossible for them to gain and possess sufficient knowledge. Individuals act on the basis of local knowledge and their dispositions and preferences that they cannot totally express to themselves, let alone communicate them to some central authority. In other words, social arrangements cannot be products of deliberate calculations by social engineers. He explains that it is man's fallibility together with the limits of reason that mitigate against a designed utopian order. Centrally directed economies are therefore bound to fail because they rely upon the limited knowledge of those who give the orders. Hayek explains that the proper role of the state is to create general rules which facilitate mutually beneficial interactions rather than to prescribe specific outcomes. It follows that by not interfering in the spontaneous social order, concrete practical knowledge can most effectively be employed.

Spontaneous Social Order

Hayek rejects central social planning as a solution to the problem of attaining social order. Instead, he emphasizes the importance of decentralized decision making in the achievement of spontaneous social order. Hayek described and expanded the idea of spontaneous order first articulated by Adam Ferguson and Adam Smith. His notion of spontaneous order refers to social institutions and practices that are the products of human action but not of human design. Hayek argues that many forms of social interaction are coordinated through institutions that are unplanned and part of a far-ranging spontaneous order. Spontaneous orders include language, markets, money, customs, traditions, and rules of conduct as exhibited in moral systems and systems of law. These have evolved without any conscious designer guiding them. The convergence of numerous rule-following people on one system of rules constructs social objects such as markets, money, language, law, and morality, which themselves are models of a spontaneous social order. Hayek maintains that institutions and values are determined as a part of a process of unconscious self-organization of a pattern or structure.

Hayek emphasizes the division of labor and its analogue, the division of knowledge. He explains that a spontaneous order can use fragmented knowledge that is dispersed among people. He says that each individual possesses specialized and local knowledge and that all the bits of specialized knowledge contribute to overall social order. Based on their local knowledge, people adapt to changing circumstances, pursue individual objectives, and engage in voluntary exchanges and cooperative relationships. It follows that civilization is founded on the use of much more knowledge than any one person is aware of or is capable of being aware of.

The division of knowledge increases the ignorance of any one person with respect to most of the knowledge. Hayek points out that the knowledge of which an individual is explicitly aware when engaged in some activity is only a small fraction of the knowledge necessary to successfully engage in that action. People cannot know nor articulate the full context of their decisions. Hayek contends that because it is undesigned, rather than being the product of rational thought, the spontaneous order of society can accommodate the ignorance we all share of the many bits of knowledge on which society depends. He says that the structure of human activities constantly adapts itself to a multitude of facts which in their entirety are not known to any one person.

Hayek explains that markets make use of knowledge that goes beyond what could be obtained by a central authority intent on instituting a consciously ordered pattern. The market via the competitive price system is able to coordinate the activities of the participants in the market. He goes on to say that the price system is undesigned and not intended to fulfill the various purposes that it actually serves.

According to Hayek, the rule of law underpins the idea of spontaneous order. As explained by Hayek, the rule of law requires law to be: (1) general and abstract, (2) known and certain, and (3) equally applicable to all people. The rule of law also necessitates independent judges unmotivated by political considerations and protection of a private domain of action and property. The rule of law is concerned with property, contracts, and torts and supplies a system of impartial rules that serve as a framework within which individuals and voluntary associations can seek their own diverse purposes and ends. When a free society is ordered through the rule of law it does not require a hierarchy of purposes or ends.

The rule of law is a metalegal principle. Similar to natural law theory, it provides a benchmark against which laws can be evaluated. From this perspective, law is about the discovery of the rules of just conduct. For example, the history of common law has been one of attempting to discover general rules that will foster a smoothly functioning social order. There is a large amount of natural law precedent embodied in the common law.

The rule of law ensures that judges decide disputes in terms of existing known and general rules and not according to the perceived desirability of particular outcomes. The purpose of the judge is to maintain an order, not to attain some specific result or direct society's resources to particular persons or uses. His function is to ascertain, articulate, and refine the rules of justice that will permit the preservation of the social order. A judge is not to issue edicts—he is only to rule when a dispute is brought to him. Once law has drawn the boundaries of individual discretion, courts should not second-guess individual use of that discretion. Judges should carry out the law—not change the law.

Distributive (i.e., social) justice is irreconcilable with the rule of law. The rule of law only establishes the rules for the social game. These rules of justice conduct are applicable to an as yet unknown and indeterminate number of persons, cases, and instances. These rules have no reference to particular persons, places, or objects. In short, such laws do not try to designate who will be winners or losers or what the society that emerges from these rules will look like.

Hayek has distinguished between two different kinds of laws. The first involves man's attempts to discover and express clearly what the general rules of justice really are. Here the law is essentially discovered, not made. These laws apply to all, including the leaders. Power should be divided, with laws made by one body and administered by another. Also, an independent judiciary is required to make certain that laws are administered fairly. Those who administer the law should have little or no discretion. The second type of law involves rules dealing with the internal operation of the organization. These administrative measures are devised to run the internal operations of the government. Essentially, these commands tell civil servants how to carry out their duties regarding the running of the bureaucratic public sector.

There has been a tendency for the law-finding function of the government to be confused with its administrative functions. A great deal of what we think of as law today is really administrative legislation meant to direct the internal operations of the government, rather than to preserve justice. In other words, the organizational rules of authorities are mistakenly given the same status as general rules of justice.

As the distinction between administrative commands and rules of justice became blurred, the restraints on government power have weakened. This led to the false impression that our elected officials possess and should possess as much power in deciding the rules of justice as it has in the formulation and execution of administrative proposals. It is no wonder that many of our elected officials think they are "running the country."

Hayek saw the problem as stemming from the fact that the power of conducting the government and the power of discovering the rules of just conduct are combined in the same representative bodies. As a result, over the years, legislation has increasingly included directives commanding people how to act, with the goal of attaining specific outcomes. During the last half of the century, the rule of law has been displaced with what has been termed *social justice*.

In addition, the rule of law is further weakened when legislative and judicial power is delegated to unelected government bureaucrats. Starting in the 1930s, Congress began passing general laws, leaving the details up to administrative agencies. These agencies enforce and interpret their own rules and regulations that, although they have the force of law, have not been ratified by the constitutional lawmaking authority.

Evolutionary Epistemology and Ethics

Knowledge, for Hayek, is a product of trial and error learning. It is an accumulation of functional and beneficial responses to the demands of man's survival. Hayek explains cultural evolution with his thesis of the natural selection of competitive traditions in which traditions and social systems compete to filter our errors. Knowledge and rules are tested out by people in both the physical and social environments and are selected via competition based on their value to human survival. It is through unplanned evolutionary progress with incremental alterations that human beings adapt themselves to life's contingencies. For Hayek, evolution simply means adaptation to changing environmental contexts. All rules governing social life are viewed as the products of evolutionary selection and modification. Social rules embody the knowledge of a given period. Hayek contends that systems of social rules providing successful behavior are adopted by others without conscious reflection.

Hayek's evolutionary perspective on human survival included an evolutionary theory of ethics. For Hayek, moral conventions are part of the evolving and spontaneous social order. He explains that values are relative to particular historical circumstances and that people accept the values for which critics cannot find a reason to reject them. These unplanned moral conventions are neither invariant nor immutable. They change in accordance with the circumstances and needs of people who sanction them. According to Hayek, evolved moral traditions surpass the capacities of reason. Like Hume, Hayek views morals as a presupposition of, rather than as a product of, reason.

For Hayek, moral principles are not objective and frequently are unable to be articulated. He rejects teleology and the possibility that a system of objective morality can be developed. According to his evolutionary and emotive theory of ethics, values are not absolute and are based on one's feelings and convictions. Values are ends that reason serve but which reason cannot determine.

Hayek as Communitarian

Hayek explains that social institutions and rules of conduct act as vehicles of knowledge regarding human beings and the world. Social norms, customs, mores, folkways, taboos, habits, and other rules build up over time and are learned through imitation. Rules are discovered when people interact through speech and example. These rules are accumulated, adapted, sometimes eliminated, and transmitted from person to person and from one generation to another. It is through emulation and mimetic contagion that rules conferring successful behavior replace rules that are misappropriate for the environment.

For Hayek, all knowledge is, at the core, tacit or practical knowledge that exists in the dispositions or habits of people to act in a rule-governed manner. This tacit knowledge is embedded in social rules internalized by one's personality. Know-how refers to one's capacity to act according to rules in concrete situations. He explains that doing something always involves a practical knowing-how that tends to be tacit or inarticulate and not susceptible to explicit formulation. Such knowledge is first embodied in practices and skills rather than in theories.

Hayek emphasized the socially constituted nature of man. He says that society defines the individual and that the self or human personality is made by social rules. Man's nature, character, and awareness of moral duty derive from man's social embeddedness. Hayek explains that inherited social rules of perception and action form a person's goals and construct his deliberative capacities. Social structure is a precondition of social agency, and shared values delineate the ends and set the bounds to such agency. According to Hayek, rules, traditions, folkways, customs, mores, and so on of a culture establish habits of thought and restrain people's actions.

According to Hayek, customs and conventions supply the template for the orderliness of the world, including our shared moral values. These rules help people to know what to do in various situations. Actions of others are predictable to the degree that a person shares with them a common framework of perception and action. It is because of the existence of such a framework, built up through trial and error, that an individual is not totally disoriented when he enters unfamiliar circumstances. Hayek is very interested in studying the patterns of communication through which a person understands others and anticipates their behavior.

Cultural and Biological Factors

Hayek maintains that a person obeys social norms because he feels that he must obey them. These norms, ingrained in biological and/or cultural structures, are transmitted through birth or education. Because they interact in complicated ways, Hayek says that we cannot precisely differentiate between instinct and habit as they affect norms. Such norms embody the experience gained through trial and error of many generations. Individuals pursuing their own goals learn to conform with shared norms and constraints so that their exchanges and interactions will be orderly and favorable.

Viewing man's reason as very limited, Hayek explains that a person develops "ideas" intuitively and passively. In fact, he says that a man's senses alone are able to discern recurring patterns or order in events without resorting to mental operations. According to Hayek, the capacity of a man's senses for spontaneous pattern recognition exceeds the ability of his mind to specify such patterns.

He contends that somehow a man's senses are able to theorize and to react to unconscious inferences in his perceptions. Hayek acknowledges the inability of the human mind to grasp the basic rules that govern its operations. He explains that conscious thought is governed by a supraconscious mechanism, which itself cannot be conscious, that operates on the contents of consciousness. This supraconscious or metaconscious mechanism is the sensory order.

Hayek's Philosophical Influences: Kant, Popper, and Wittgenstein

Hayek is a post-Kantian critical thinker. Like Kant, he disclaims a man's ability to know things as they are or the world as it is. For both Hayek and Kant, the world we see, the phenomenal world, is the product of the creative activity of our minds as they interact with the world. Any order a person finds in his experiences is the product of the organizing structure of his mind. In other words, man's mind is impotent to know true reality (i.e., the noumenal world). This led Hayek to proclaim that the concept of "things in themselves" served no purpose and thus could be omitted. Accordingly, he rejects the Aristotelian method of searching for the essences or natures of things. This leaves Hayek with the purely concrete-bound knowledge of the phenomenal world.

Hayek states that a person cannot step out of his human point of view so as to obtain a presuppositionless perspective on the world in its entirety and as it is in itself. As an element of the world, man does not have a privileged position that would permit him to stand outside and see objectively how reality and all of its laws go together. A person can never achieve a synoptic view of the world as a whole or of the workings of his own mind. Hayek says that it is impossible for a person's brain to produce a complete explanation of the specific ways which the brain itself classifies stimuli because any such device would necessarily have to possess a degree of complexity greater than that which is classifies. In other words, to fully explain a man's knowledge, he would have to know more than he actually knows or that he is able to know.

Unlike Kant, Hayek contends that the mind is subject to evolution and is constantly changing. Like Karl Popper, Hayek has championed an evolutionary epistemology which holds that the fundamental categories and structural principles of men's minds comprise evolutionary adaptations of human beings to the world. He explains that the mind categorizes phenomena which it uses to refine further its own categories. According to Hayek, because the mind's categories are changeable, logical reasoning may differ according to time, place, and person. Hayek's evolutionary epistemology, which includes the notion of the mind as consisting of matter and its relations, leads to the conclusion that there is no free will. He states that the controversy about free will is a "phantom problem" but he does accept that each person has a unique personal subjective will. By this vague statement he seems to mean that a person's "choices" are determined by the interaction of the material that makes up the specific person and the mate-

rial that constitutes the rest of the world. Hayek maintains that the causal determination of human action is compatible with assigning responsibility to human
agents for what they do.

Hayek, like Popper, views human beings as fallible and science as the product of a process of conjecture and refutation. Hayek adopted Popper's idea that it
is the falsifiability of a proposal, rather than its verifiability, that makes knowledge empirically testable. Both held a critical polemical approach to theory formulation contending that no knowledge can be verified. At best we can say that
it has not yet been falsified but that is falsifiable.

The writings of Ludwig Wittengstein, the philosopher and linguist, influenced Hayek's contention that the study of language is a necessary precondition
to the study of human thought. Wittengstein maintained that philosophy cannot
get beyond the limits of language. He inspired the logical positivists who explained that the purpose of philosophy is to analyze and clarify the meaning of
words. They also held that the only road to knowledge was through controlled
experiments employing quantitative and scientific methods. It was Wittengstein
primarily who prompted Hayek's interest in the way language influences a person's thoughts and creates his picture of the world. Hayek also followed Wittengstein with respect to his emphasis on the important role of social rules in the
transmission of tacit or practical knowledge.

For Hayek, as for the logical positivists, words, rather than reality, became
the starting point of analysis. Hayek engages in deconstruction by breaking
down words and language to find their meaning, which for him was determined
by agreement among minds. He was interested in studying the interaction between minds in which individuals' definitions and ideas are tested and corrected
by other people. Hayek saw linguistics as a coherent body of theory with which
to begin his study of the social world.

Getting Back on the Road to Objective Economics

Whereas Hayek exhibited breadth as an eclectic and intuitive scholar, he does
not present a logical and coherent philosophical system. Moreover, he saw himself as a dissector, analyzer, puzzler, and muddler and certainly not as a master
of his subject or as a systems-builder. His skeptical approach is grounded on a
view of the limits of human reason. Hayek is certainly correct in arguing for the
impossibility of using a particular understanding of reasoning (i.e., deliberative
reasoning) to engage in central social planning. Unfortunately, Hayek equates
individual human reasoning with the deliberative reasoning used by social de-
signers and engineers. An individual uses his practical reason to identify his
needs, wants, and constraints and to choose, create, and integrate all the values,
virtues, and goods that comprise his personal flourishing. By disparaging reason
in general, Hayek sanctions a type of spontaneous order that implies the unim-
portance and inadequacy of individual rationality. He would have been much

wiser to have rejected state planning on the moral grounds that such planning would frustrate individual sovereignty.

Although Ayn Rand (1905-1982) was not an economist, her rational epistemology and Objectivist ethics can not only bring us back on the road to objective economics traveled by Austrians such as Menger and Rothbard, her ideas can move us further down that road. Her epistemology transcends both Mises's rationalism and Hayek's empiricism. In addition, Objectivism's Aristotelian perspective on the nature of man and the world and on the need to exercise one's virtues can be viewed as compatible with Austrian economics. Ayn Rand's Objectivist worldview can provide a context to the economic insights of Menger, Mises, and Rothbard. Unfortunately, as detailed in this chapter, Friedrich Hayek is probably not even on the same road, but if he is on the same road he is traveling in the wrong direction.

Recommended Reading

Arnold, Roger A. "Hayek and Institutional Evolution." *Journal of Libertarian Studies* 4, no. 4 (Fall 1980).

Baumgarth, William P. "Hayek and Political Order: The Rule of Law." *Journal of Libertarian Studies* 2, no. 1 (1978).

Block, Walter. "Hayek's Road to Serfdom." *Journal of Libertarian Studies* 12, no. 2 (Fall 1996).

Buchanan, James. "Hayek and the Forces of History." *Humane Studies Review* 6 (1988-89): 3–4.

Burczak, Theodore. "The Postmodern Moments of F. A. Hayek's Economics." *Economics and Philosophy* 10 (April 1994): 31–58.

Butos, William. "Hayek and General Equilibrium Analysis." *Southern Economic Journal* 52, no. 2 (October 1985): 332–43.

Caldwell, Bruce. "Hayek's Transformation." *History of Political Economy* 20, no. 4 (Winter 1988): 513–41.

———."Hayek the Falsificationist? A Refutation." *Research in the History of Economic Thought and Methodology* 10 (1992): 1–15.

———."Hayek's Scientific Subjectivism." *Economics and Philosophy* 10, no. 2 (October 1994): 305–13.

———."Hayek and Socialism." *Journal of Economic Literature* 35 (December 1997): 1856–90.

———."Hayek and Cultural Evolution." Pp. 285–303 in *Fact and Fiction in Economics: Models, Realism, and Social Construction*, edited by Uskali Mäki. Cambridge: Cambridge University Press, 2002a.

———. "Popper and Hayek: Who Influenced Whom?" Paper presented at the Karl Popper 2002 Centenary Congress, Vienna, July, 2002b.

———. *Hayek's Challenge*. Chicago: University of Chicago Press, 2004.

Diamond, Arthur M., Jr. "F. A. Hayek on Constructivism and Ethics." *Journal of Libertarian Studies* 4, no. 4 (Fall 1980).

Dorn, James A. "Law and Liberty: A Comparison of Hayek and Bastiat." *Journal of Libertarian Studies* 5, no. 4 (Fall 1981).

Dostaler, Gilles. "The Debate Between Hayek and Keynes." Pp. 77–101 in *Themes in Keynesian Criticism and Supplementary Modern Topics*, edited by William J. Barber. Aldershot, UK: Elgar, 1991.

Ebenstein, Alan. *Friedrich Hayek: A Biography*. New York: Palgrave, 2001.

Feser, Edward, "Hayek on Tradition." *Journal of Libertarian Studies* 17, no. 1 (Winter 2003).

———, ed. *The Cambridge Companion to Hayek*. Cambridge: Cambridge University Press, 2006.

Fleetwood, Steve. *Hayek's Political Economy: The Socioeconomics of Order*. London: Routledge, 1995.

Gissurarson, Hannes. *Hayek's Conservative Liberalism*. London: Garland, 1987.

Gray, John N. "F. A. Hayek on Liberty and Tradition." *Journal of Libertarian Studies* 4, no. 2 (Spring 1980).

Hamowy, Ronald. "Law and the Liberal Society: F. A. Hayek's Constitution of Liberty." *Journal of Libertarian Studies* 2, no. 4 (1978).

———. "The Hayekian Model of Government in an Open Society." *Journal of Libertarian Studies* 6, no. 2 (Spring 1982).

Hayek, Friedrich A. *The Road to Serfdom*. Chicago: University of Chicago Press, 1944.

———. *Individualism and Economic Order*. Chicago: University of Chicago Press, 1948.

———. "The Use of Knowledge in Society." Pp. 77–91 in *Individualism and Economic Order*. Chicago: University of Chicago Press, [1945] 1948.

———, ed. *Capitalism and the Historians*. Chicago: University of Chicago Press, 1954.

———. *The Constitution of Liberty*. Chicago: University of Chicago Press, 1960.

———. *The Sensory Order: An Inquiry into the Foundations of Theoretical Psychology*. Reprint, Chicago: University of Chicago Press, [1952] 1967.

———. *Studies in Philosophy, Politics and Economics*. Chicago: University of Chicago Press, 1967.

———. "Rules and Order." *Law, Legislation and Liberty* 1. Chicago: University of Chicago Press, 1973.

———. "The Mirage of Social Justice." *Law, Legislation and Liberty* 2. Chicago: University of Chicago Press, 1976.

———. *New Studies in Philosophy, Politics, Economics, and the History of Ideas*. Chicago: University of Chicago Press, 1978.

———. *The Counter-Revolution of Science*. Indianapolis: Liberty Press, [1952] 1979.

———. "The Political Order of a Free People." *Law, Legislation and Liberty* 3. Chicago: University of Chicago Press, 1979.

———. "Toward a Free Market Monetary System." *Journal of Libertarian Studies* 3, no. 1 (1979).

———. *The Fatal Conceit: The Errors of Socialism*. Edited by W. W. Bartley III. Chicago: University of Chicago Press, 1988.

———. "Competition as a Discovery Procedure." *Quarterly Journal of Austrian Economics* 5, no. 3 (Fall 2002).

Howson, Susan. "Why Didn't Hayek Review Keynes' *General Theory*? A Partial Answer." *History of Political Economy* 33, no. 2 (Summer 2001): 369–74.

Kukathas, Chandran. *Hayek and Modern Liberalism*. Oxford: Clarendon, 1989.

Madison, G. B. "Hayek and the Interpretive Turn." *Critical Review* 3, no. 2 (Spring 1989): 169–85.

McCormick, B. J. *Hayek and the Keynesian Avalanche*. New York: Harvester Wheatsheaf, 1992.

Salerno, Joseph. "Learning from the Past: The Continuing Relevance of Hayek, Böhm-Bawerk, and Bastiat." *Quarterly Journal of Austrian Economics* 5, no. 3 (Fall 2002).

Shearmur, Jeremy. "From Hayek to Menger: Biology, Subjectivism, and Welfare." Pp. 189–212 in *Carl Menger and His Legacy in Economics*, edited by Bruce Caldwell,. Durham, NC: Duke University Press, 1990.

————. *Hayek and After: Hayekian Liberalism as a Research Programme*. London: Routledge, 1996.

Stalebrink, Odd J. "The Hayek and Mises Controversy: Bridging Differences." *Quarterly Journal of Austrian Economics* 7, no. 1 (Spring 2004).

Steele, David Ramsay. "Hayek's Theory of Cultural Group Selection." *Journal of Libertarian Studies* 8, no. 2 (Summer 1987).

Steele, G.R. "Hayek's Theory of Money and Cycles: Retrospective and Reappraisal." *Quarterly Journal of Austrian Economics* 8, no. 1 (Spring 2005).

Sugden, Robert. "Normative Judgments and Spontaneous Order: The Contractarian Element in Hayek's Thought." *Constitutional Political Economy* 4, no. 3 (1993): 393–424.

Vanberg, Viktor. "Hayek's Legacy and the Future of Liberal Thought: Rational Liberalism versus Evolutionally Agnosticism." Pp. 49-69 in *The Legacy of Friedrich von Hayek*, edited by Peter Boettke with assistance from Andrew Farrant, Greg Ransom, and Gilberto Salgado. Cheltenham, UK: Elgar, [1994] 1999.

Vaughn, Karen. "Hayek's Implicit Economics: Rules and the Problem of Order." *Review of Austrian Economics* 11, nos. 1-2 (1999a): 129–44.

Witt, Ulrich. "The Hayekian Puzzle: Spontaneous Order and the Business Cycle." *Scottish Journal of Political Economy* 44, no. 1 (February 1997): 44–58.

Chapter 17

Milton Friedman's Pragmatic and Incremental Libertarianism

It is worth discussing radical changes, not in the expectation that they will be adopted promptly but for two other reasons. One is to construct an ideal goal, so that incremental changes can be judged by whether they move the institutional structure toward or away from that ideal. The other reason is very different. It is so that if a crisis requiring or facilitating radical change does arise, alternatives will be available that have been carefully developed and fully explored.

—Milton Friedman

Milton Friedman (1912-2006) is a consequentialist libertarian and one of the most influential economists of the twentieth century. He has been able to create both academic and popular support for the idea of increasing individual freedom and reducing government controls. Friedman fervently believes in the power of a sort of secular religion of progress to move the world forward. His enthusiasm for the positive consequences for the world resulting from economic progress has been contagious.

Friedman achieved his influence as an economist and as a political commentator by first gaining impeccable credentials in technical economics. Once this highly respected student of the money supply had a firm standing in the academic world, he was thus free to look outward to the world of policy. He has had the courage and force of free will to take controversial positions in the face of widespread professional and public hostility. This leader of the Chicago School of monetary economics gained additional influence through his books and articles, op-ed pieces, lectures, *Newsweek* columns, testimony before Congress and his ten-part TV series, *Free to Choose*. As a result of his zeal, many of Friedman's economic ideas and public policy proposals have made the transition to conventional wisdom in a short amount of time.

Preferring not to be a theoretical system-builder, Friedman engages in rigorous, historical, empirical, quantitative, and equilibrating analysis and research to support his ideas and to empirically test his own ideas and those of the Keynesian model. He believes that positive economics can be value-free, scientific, and objective, and can provide a system of generalizations that can be employed to make correct predictions about the outcomes of changes in conditions. Holding that accurate predictions can be made from simplified assumptions, Friedman builds models involving uncomplicated suppositions to attain what he believes to be sound, powerful, predictable, and pragmatic conclusions. He maintains that, because the goals of value-free science are exclusively predictions, a theory that enables individuals to make reliable predictions is a good theory. Rejecting the idea held by Austrian economists that the natural and social sciences are separate realms requiring different methods of investigation, Friedman argues that an economic model should be judged only by its predictive power.

Friedman's highest ethical principle is the absence of coercion among individuals. He therefore advances a moral vision of a society where people are free to choose for themselves. Such a society requires individuals to be free to use their own resources in their own way. Friedman says that the essence of human freedom is the ability of people to make their own decisions as long as they do not prevent others from making their own decisions. He explains that economic freedom is a necessary, but not a sufficient, condition for political freedom. Recently, in addition to economic freedom and political freedom, Friedman has added the notion of social (or civil) freedom—the freedom to speak, to assemble, etc. He observes that human freedom is the only mechanism that allows a complex society to be organized from the bottom up. Because people generally know better than anyone else what they should do, they should be permitted to pursue their own interests. Friedman views social groups as contracts into which people have entered in order to further their purposes. The moral values of voluntary exchange and voluntary association provide the least coercive apparatus to organize social life. He says that the major aim of liberalism is to leave the ethical problem for the individual to wrestle with. The really important ethical problems concern what an individual should do with his freedom. Politics only provides the context for the exercise of this freedom.

According to Friedman, the goal of social policy is to permit as many individuals as possible to pursue their own interests as fully as possible. He says that he wants the smallest, least intrusive government compatible with the optimal freedom for each person to pursue his own projects and follow his own values as long as he does not interfere with any other person's like freedoms. Friedman explains that there is no basis upon which any one of us can judge the preferences of any other. It follows that the government should not attempt to substitute its own judgment for the judgment of free persons. He says that not only do such regulatory and welfare state attempts and measures unduly restrict freedom, they usually fail to accomplish what they were intended to do with disastrous results. Problems are either produced or aggravated by well-intentioned government efforts. Friedman also contends that there is no meaningful content to frequently espoused "ideas" of common good, public interest, or social justice.

Friedman states that the basic essential functions of government are: (1) to defend the nation from coercion from the outside and to defend individuals from coercion by others within the country; (2) to enable the free market by establishing rules for exchange and by providing the medium of exchange; and (3) to respond to neighborhood effects. He says that the government should do only what markets cannot do and should enforce the "rules of the game." Specifically, the government should maintain law, order, and policy to prevent coercion; preserve the peace and provide for national defense; adjudicate disputes and enforce contracts voluntarily entered into; define the meaning of property rights and provide the means for modifying them and the other "rules of the game"; provide a monetary framework; foster competitive markets and overcome technical monopolies; and address neighborhood effects which are actions affecting others (e.g., pollution) where it is not feasible to charge or reward them. Friedman explains that where the actions of one person affect another, and where the range and value of the effects can be controlled and determined, those involved should pay the price or receive the benefits or compensation for the actions.

Friedman is a scholar who was familiar with the Keynesian system and its policy implications and who used Keynes's own language and devices to prove him wrong. Friedman worked within the Keynesian system and used his statistical talents to examine the truthfulness of Keynesianism. He dismantled Keynesianism when he demonstrated that the Keynesian consumption function did not fit the historical data. Friedman's goal was to overthrow Keynesianism and replace it with his monetarist model.

Monetary Theory

Friedman used empirical evidence to attack the consumption functions, the spending multiplier, the importance of monetary policy, the Phillips curve, and more. He demonstrated that the Keynesian idea of household behavior was mistaken and that any advantage attained by government expenditures via the multiplier process was much smaller than had been claimed. Friedman's insight, the permanent income hypothesis, stated that households adjust their expenditures only to recognized changes in their long-term expectations with respect to their permanent income. In other words, he showed that transitory or temporary changes in income have little effect on consumption spending. Friedman also supplied evidence that what happens to the quantity of money is far more important than fiscal policy and that the Phillips Curve hypothesis was wrong in suggesting that there was a stable and enduring functional and inverse relationship between the rate of price inflation and the level of unemployment. He explained that, in the long run, unemployment returns to its normal rate regardless of the rate of inflation. In the short run, there is an inverse relationship between inflation and unemployment but in the long run the relationship disappears. Let's now consider the specifics of Friedman's positions.

In *A Monetary History of the U.S. 1867-1960*, co-written by Anna J. Schwartz, Friedman attacked Keynesian monetary theory and validated an updated version of the classical quantity theory of money. He demonstrated that monetary policy could be effective during both expansions and contractions. Friedman deepened people's understanding of the crucial role of money in determining the course of events and provided compelling evidence that federal government deficits do not have a stimulative effect. He recommended eliminating or playing down the role of fiscal policy and did not promote budget deficits to stimulate economic growth. On the other hand, he illustrated how changes in the money supply can cause ripple effects throughout the economy. Friedman's monetarism held that money supply and interest rates can do much more than fiscal policy to control business cycles. He also showed that, if misused, monetary policy could be devastating in its effects.

According to Friedman, the stock market collapse of 1929 was not the fault of the Federal Reserve but that subsequent mistakes by the government caused the resulting depression to worsen into the Great Depression. He maintained that what converted it into a major depression was bad monetary policy. In the late 1920s, there existed a bubble with respect to levels of stock market prices that were not justified by the real earnings of the companies whose stocks were being valued. In 1929, the bubble burst and equity markets in the United States fell eighty per cent over the next three years.

Friedman explains that by early 1930 the market had nearly recovered from its collapse the previous October, and that, if the Federal Reserve had followed a correct easy money policy, the bottom of the market would have taken place in 1930 or in 1931 rather than in 1933. He is convinced that the Great Depression resulted from deflation—a too-sharp reduction of money in circulation. In addition to blaming the Fed for permitting the Great Contraction of the money supply, he was also critical of it for raising interest rates in 1931 and for failing to bail out commercial banks and letting them fail.

In fact, it was in 1928 that the Fed began tightening monetary policy to curb speculation because of its concern with the stock market boom. This helped to lead to an economic slowdown and prompted people to realize that the economy was approaching a slump. However, at the time of the market crash in October 1929, there was no bank panic and the ratio of bank deposits to currency in circulation remained relatively high for months thereafter. Unfortunately, the Federal Reserve proceeded to follow mistaken policies which led to a decline in the quantity of money by one-third between 1929 and 1933, resulting in the collapse of the banking system and the destruction of people's savings. Between 1929 and 1933 about 10,000 banks failed, contributing to the huge drop in money supply and to widespread bankruptcies. Exploding unemployment, falling prices, and negative economic growth, therefore, characterized those years.

Friedman explained that the Fed converted an economic contraction into the Great Depression by letting the money supply decline and by failing to provide banks with liquidity during banking crises. If the Fed had done its job the result would have been a normal business slump. The money supply had declined sharply at a time when the Federal Reserve should have been pumping additional funds into the system to bring a stop to the deflation and to save the banks. Prosperity would have returned if the money supply had been expanded during the early 1930s.

In mid-December 1930, the Bank of the U.S. in New York failed, resulting in a run on banks. In anticipation of panic withdrawals of deposits, banks reduced their lending, further contracting the money supply. In addition, falling agricultural prices and farm bankruptcies helped to lead to bank failures. As a result, people stampeded out of bank deposits and into cash holdings. Government mismanagement had turned a recession into the worst depression of the century. The Federal Reserve could have prevented the decline of the stock of money during the depression and could have produced a necessary increase in the money supply.

Friedman explains that business cycles are government-induced and that monetary stability is a prerequisite for economic soundness. He demonstrated that there has been a systematic pattern of the effects of monetary policy on economic activity in the United States Monetary policy influences economic activity far more than does fiscal policy. In fact, his work casts strong doubts regarding the effectiveness of fiscal policy in combating recessions or inflation. He observes that the Fed places too much power in the hands of too few people. Friedman warns that an activist monetary policy is a source of instability. He therefore recommends that the monetary framework should operate under the rule of law rather than through the discretionary authority of government administrators. Friedman has said that he would like to abolish the Fed, but has also written on how the Fed should operate, if it exists.

Friedman proclaims that inflation is always and everywhere a monetary phenomenon and explains that stability in the growth of the money supply is critical for controlling inflation and recessions. The quantity of money is controlled by monetary policy. He therefore wants to sharply curtail the power of the Fed to create or to destroy money. The Fed should devote its attention solely to keeping a relatively stable price level of goods and services. Friedman desires a relatively automatic monetary system that will produce slow and steady monetary growth, bring inflation under control, and lead to sustainable economic growth. The government should be restricted to ensuring a constant rate of monetary growth. Friedman says that the Federal Reserve can be replaced by a computer that would implement his Monetarist Rule which automatically increases the money supply at a steady rate equal to the long-term average annual growth rate in the nation—most likely between 3 to 5 percent per year. The money supply could go up regularly, day by day, week by week, month by month. Friedman desires to curb inflation through carefully calibrated increases in the money supply at a fixed annual rate.

Friedman points out that the business of the Federal Reserve system is to keep general prices stable. It is not the Fed's business to attempt to control stock market prices. The Fed has never had control of the stock market but it has some control over the economy as a whole through the monetary growth within the economy. According to Friedman, the Fed should not let its monetary policy be determined by the stock market. He adds that central banks do not need to be worried about interest rates. In addition, he supports a 100 percent reserve rule with respect to demand deposits. Finally, he prefers a well-administered fiat money system over a commodity standard such as gold, which he says is uncertain and costly. He says that gold rushes may occur and that it would be a waste of resources to store gold in vaults and to watch over it. Of course, he did praise the classic international gold standard which was in effect during the early 1900s and said that the Great Depression could have been avoided if the classic gold standard had been in place at that time.

Economic Policy

Friedman has made two especially important and basic contributions to economic policy debates. They are his work on the Quantity Theory of Money and on the Phillips Curve. His relentless empiricism in these areas has been of enormous strategic importance in policy arguments with interventionists and collectivists.

The classical Quantity Theory of Money was based upon Irving Fisher's Equation of Exchange which stated that:

$MV = PT$
where:
M is the amount of money in circulation
V is the velocity of circulation of that money
P is the average price level and
T is the number of transactions taking place

Classical economists argued that the income velocity of the circulation of money (V) was a constant, that real income was unaffected by changes in the quantity of money (M), and that, therefore, changes in the supply of money (M) would directly affect the price level (P). These classical theorists suggested that V would be relatively stable and that T would always tend toward full employment.

Keynesians believed and argued that V was not a constant, but instead was highly variable and acted to suppress any change in the money supply from having an impact on either real output or the price level. Friedman responded by further developing and rehabilitating the quantity theory, and found that V could no longer be assumed to be a constant, bur rather was a stable function of several variables. Friedman explained that V responds to monetary expansion in the short run by reinforcing, instead of cushioning, the impact of a monetary expansion on the right hand side of the equation. He concluded that V and T were both independently determined in the long run and that, therefore, a change in the money supply would lead to a change in the price level. If the money supply grew faster than the growth rate of output there would be inflation.

The Phillips Curve is a graph portraying the relationship between the inflation rate on the vertical axis and the unemployment rate on the horizontal axis. A. W. H. Phillips in 1958 had discovered that there was a consistent negative, or inverse, relationship between the rate of inflation and the rate of unemployment in the United Kingdom between 1861 and 1957. The implication is that there is a tradeoff between the inflation rate and the unemployment rate. However, a problem emerged with the Phillips Curve in the 1970s when unemployment and inflation were found to rise together (i.e., stagflation).

Friedman had been arguing that inflation and unemployment tend in the same direction in the long run. In his view, government could not make a permanent trade-off between inflation rates and unemployment rates. This is because rational and well-informed workers and employers would pay attention only to real wages (i.e., the inflation-adjusted purchasing power of money wages). Friedman explains that only for a short time will people suffer from what economists call "money illusion," where people see that their nominal wages are rising but do not yet perceive that the general price level is rising throughout the economy. For a while, they are willing to supply more labor and the unemployment rate falls. Over time, they come to realize the truth and adjust their expectations and, as a result, real spending and labor supply return to their original levels, leaving only a higher inflation rate as the consequence. The real wage returns to its old level and the unemployment rate is restored to the natural rate. Unfortunately, inflation, brought on by the expansionary policies, will continue at new, higher rates. Friedman thus developed the idea of an "expectations-augmented" Phillips Curve that assumes that people suffer from no "money illusion" and will anticipate and expect higher prices and wages. He thus argued for a series of Phillips Curves—one for each level of expected inflation.

When the government decides that it wants to lower the unemployment rate it will take steps to boost demand through its expansionary fiscal or monetary policies. The increase in demand for goods and services will disappear as people realize that there has not been a real increase in demand. Firms will lay people off and unemployment will move back to where it began. The next time the government attempts to stimulate the economy, people will anticipate the inflation. Friedman notes that the imagined trade-off between inflation and unemployment is a trap, with joblessness declining only briefly before returning to the previous level.

Increased inflation reduces unemployment, but only in the short run. Friedman explains that unemployment below the natural rate can be maintained only by increasing rates of inflation. In 1967 Friedman introduced the natural rate of unemployment concept. This natural rate of unemployment is not constant but changes according to an economy's structural parameters. It is the rate prevailing in a perfectly competitive labor market. It is the rate of unemployment in an economy in which economic agents have full information about pricing activity and could anticipate the rate of inflation. He says that only one level of unemployment, the natural rate, is consistent with stable inflation. Friedman demonstrated that the Phillips Curve was unstable unless the economy operated at the natural rate of unemployment. Given the customs, institutions, and civil laws of an economy, beyond a particular point any increase in the rate of unemployment will result in deflation and a recession will take place until wages fall to a level that will encourage businessmen to begin hiring. Also, any decrease in unemployment below a certain point will result in inflation and a recession that will continue until employment returns to its natural rate.

According to Friedman, any rate of unemployment below the natural rate leads to inflation. When workers expect high inflation, they will demand more generous wages. The real wage remains unchanged when any increase in anticipated inflation is matched by wage inflation. With the real wage rate unchanged, the unemployment rate will remain constant. Friedman thus concludes that it is only unanticipated inflation that can lead to temporary reductions in unemployment below the natural rate. It follows that, in the long run, inflation is totally anticipated and there is no trade-off between inflation and unemployment.

The long-run Phillips Curve is a vertical line at the natural rate of unemployment. Once unemployment falls to its natural rate, expansionary policies will not take it any lower except for brief periods of time. If the government attempted to increase employment beyond that natural rate by injecting more money, the short-term trade-off between inflation and unemployment would be repeated at ever increasing levels of inflation and unemployment. In addition, the more quickly expectations of inflation adapt, the more quickly unemployment will return to the natural rate, and the less successful the government will be in reducing unemployment through its fiscal and monetary policies. Friedman determined that the impact of a fiscal deficit on nominal income is short-lived and that, after a lag, the increased rate of growth in the money supply has long-term effects on the rate of inflation. He demonstrated that, in the long run, additional monetary growth affects only the inflation rate and has essentially no effect on the level or rate of growth of real production.

Corporate Social Responsibility

Milton Friedman wrote "The Social Responsibility of Business is to Increase Profits" in the September 13, 1970, issue of the *New York Times Magazine*. This seminal article, along with several more to follow, contained Friedman's thoughts regarding the nature of corporations and the responsibilities of the parties involved with them.

Friedman explains that corporations do not exist in physical reality, that only people can have responsibilities, and that businesses have no responsibilities as such. He maintains that there is one and only one social responsibility of business—to use its resources and engage in activities designed to increase its profits so long as it stays within the rules of the game. To earn profit is the purpose of the corporation which should engage in open and free competition without deception or fraud. Friedman also contends that corporations do not and cannot have any objectionable degree of power except for that power that is received through government intervention. He says that there is a need to curb government power that contending interest groups attempt to use for their own advantages. He does not blame businessmen for going to Washington to attempt to get special privileges (within the rules of the game) but rather blames all of the citizens for adopting rules of the game that permit that to occur.

He says that the corporate executive is an employee of the owners of a firm and that the relationship between shareholders and the manager is an employee-owner or principal-agent one. His direct responsibility to his employers is to conduct the business in accordance with their desires. By implicit legal contract, salaried executives of a corporation have a fiduciary responsibility to the shareholders of the firm who assign them the right and duty to use corporate resources to increase the wealth of those shareholders by pursuing profits. Under this contract, they do not have the right to act on their own preferences by making discretionary decisions to spend the firm's resources to attain social goals that cannot be demonstrated to be directly related to gaining profits and to their fiduciary responsibility. Managers should use available assets to make investments to maximize the shareholders' wealth. They have no right to dispose of the shareholders' profits in any manner that does not directly benefit the corporation. The critical question is whether or not some action or project is enough in the interest of the corporation to justify the expenditures.

According to Friedman, if a corporation makes a donation to charity, it is actually the managers who are making donations of assets that belong to the shareholders. They would be spending others' money unless those shareholders express their desire to make such a donation. He explains that managers should not substitute their judgment for the judgment of the shareholders. Friedman maintains that another reason against a manager spending funds for social causes is that insofar as those actions increase consumer prices, he is effectively spending customers' money. Similarly, when such actions lower the wages of employees, he is disbursing their money.

Corporate executives, when acting in their official capacity and not as private persons, are agents of the corporation's shareholders. Friedman explains that the corporate executive is also a person in his own right and as a private person may voluntarily assume responsibilities and spend his money, time, and energy on them. Many supposed corporate socially responsible actions are actually a disguised form of the managers' own self-interest where they donate corporate funds to their own favored schools, hospitals, community organizations, or cultural associations. Friedman maintains that by maximizing corporate profits, executives contribute much more to "social welfare" than they would by spending shareholders' money on what they as individuals view as meritorious projects. He also says that the tax laws should not permit corporate contributions to be deducted and should abolish the capital gains tax (or at the very least index the basis for capital gains).

Friedman explains that it is better to return money to shareholders in the form of dividends (or as capital gains when they sell their stock) thus permitting them to decide which charities to support. He has argued for the abolition of all corporate taxes and for returning all corporate profits to the stockholders who can then decide as individuals how they will use their money. Individuals could be directly taxed on both their distributed and undistributed earnings and could then decide whether or not to reinvest their profits in that company depending upon their prospective returns from their alternative investment possibilities.

According to Friedman, businessmen undermine the basis of a free society when they espouse corporate social responsibility. He explains that many executives embrace and advance their social goals in order to please individuals and groups who believe that corporations have social responsibilities and thus should set social goals. Friedman says that the only legitimate way of enlisting the help of business in solving social problems is to frame laws that enable businesses to profit by providing for social needs.

Friedman's fundamentalist theory of social responsibility states that corporations have nothing more than obligations to make a profit within the framework of the legal system. He sees corporate social responsibility as a subversive doctrine and as a pernicious idea that shows a fundamental misconception of the character and nature of a free society and that undermines its foundations.

Friedman's view on corporate social responsibility could certainly have been strengthened if he had a theory of individual rights. He could have said that the social responsibility of the corporation, through its directors, managers, and other employers, is simply to respect the natural rights of individuals. Individuals in a corporation have the legally enforceable responsibility or duty to respect the moral agency, space, or autonomy of persons. This involves the basic principle of the noninitiation of physical force and includes: the obligation to honor a corporation's contracts with its managers, employees, customers, suppliers, and so on; duties not to engage in deception, fraud, force, threats, theft, or coercion against others; and the responsibility to honor representations made to the local community. Beyond the above, a corporation and its managers are not ethically required to be socially responsible. If managers, as agents of the stockholders, were to breach an agreement with the shareholders to maximize profits in order to give one or more groups more benefits than they freely agreed upon, they would be violating the rights of the owners. Managers should not divert corporate funds for other purposes. Of course, the idea that a corporation should respect rights leads to the same conclusions as Friedman reaches.

Public Policy

For the most part, Friedman rejects programs based on paternalism because they force taxpayers to provide assistance and limit the freedom of the recipients of the aid to act as they choose. He speaks of distortions in the marketplace that accompany government programs and proclaims that the only case for government occurs when it is not feasible for market arrangements to make individuals pay. Friedman declares that the market should be the main instrument for organizing economic activity but also acknowledges that there are areas that cannot be handled through the market or that can be privately conducted, but at so great a cost that political approaches may be preferable. He prefers to allow everyone the opportunity to use his own resources as effectively as he can to promote his own values as long as he does not interfere with anyone else. In addition, he naturally wants to leave problems of an ethical nature to the individual to deal with. Many of Friedman's policy prescriptions would reduce the centers of decision making by abolishing bureaucratic or political agencies.

Friedman has offered an astounding range of public policy ideas across a number of areas, including but not limited to: social welfare programs; taxation (including the negative income tax); education; social security; the Food Drug Administration (FDA); narcotics laws; trade restrictions; deregulation and privatization; discrimination; occupational and medical licensure; monopolies and antitrust; wage and price controls; fixed exchange rates; unions; labeling; environmental pollution; the all volunteer army; and the black market. We will now take a detailed look at his positions in several of these areas.

Friedman is in favor of a flat-rate income tax perhaps above a certain exemption but with no additional exemptions, deductions, or loopholes. With such a system he believes that there would be less interference with private incentives and that such a system would be more efficient and more equitable. It is interesting to note that Friedman was an employee of the Treasury Department between 1941 and 1943 and was involved in the development of the withholding tax—a government scheme that contributed to the growth of big government. Of course, he now says that he wishes there was some way to abolish it.

According to Friedman, the tax code can be used to get people off of conventional welfare in order to live on earned income while at the same time eliminating welfare bureaucracies. He was the first person to suggest that poverty could be abolished through a negative income tax involving the transfer of money directly to the poor by a much simpler formula and with fewer adverse effects on work incentives. Friedman sees the negative income tax as an expedient alternative to the present welfare system. His proposal would substitute a minimum income for the variety of welfare, disability, and unemployment programs that have multiplied ,each with its own inefficient and expensive administrative organization. There would be a floor below which no person's net income could fall—a guaranteed income. This "public charity" would be granted on the basis of income, up to a predetermined maximum, would eliminate bureaucratic determination, could be withdrawn by majority vote, and would be in cash so that recipients could spend it as they choose. People who work would lose only a fraction of a grant dollar for every dollar they earn thus providing them with an incentive to work. Under the negative income tax, the poor would fill out income tax forms and if a family's income falls below some predetermined level, the U.S. Treasury would write a check to bring the income up to a minimum amount. A version of Friedman's idea came into law with the tax credit for low-income taxpayers in the Tax Reduction Act of 1975. His negative income tax is still embodied in today's earned-income tax credit.

Friedman views public education at the elementary and secondary school levels as a large socialist enterprise that teaches socialist values. He wants to end compulsory education so that parents can decide if they want their children to attend school and when and where they should go to school. Friedman sees no valid reason for nationalized schools which limit parents' freedom to spend their own money on their own schooling choices. Public education is a monopoly insulated from the challenges of efficiency and excellence that stem from free competition. He states that competition would improve all schools and would provide variety and flexibility. He would like to see teachers' salaries to be able to respond to market forces. Friedman cautions businesses not to support government schools because businesses have been adversely affected by the low quality of the public school system. Instead, they should support private schools and the private school system.

Friedman laments the fact that a parent who decides to send his child to a private school is required to pay twice—once in the form of taxes and again in the form of tuition. He suggests providing parents with educational vouchers that they can spend at any school rather than solely through a monopolistic public school system. Friedman is a tireless advocate of free choice as a means of empowering parents and improving the performance of students and schools. A voucher system could be used to provide parents of school-age children with redeemable tuition certificates worth a certain number of dollars per child to spend on the schools of their choice as long as these meet certain educational standards. He is confident that parents would generally select a good education for their children. Friedman sees the voucher system as an incremental step in moving toward a private educational system. He maintains that vouchers are a good, partial, and attainable solution in moving away from a government system. Friedman would like to see the government entirely out of the education business but sees vouchers as a step in the right direction. Today's charter schools represent an adaptation of Friedman's voucher idea.

Against mandatory participation in the Social Security program, Friedman calls for separation of retirement funding from the state and wants people to be able to buy their annuities from private concerns. He is concerned about the redistribution of money from the young to the old and that poor people pay a larger percentage of their income into the system than do the wealthy. He criticizes the pay-as-you-go Social Security system for restricting the ability of persons to decide how much, and in what form, to save for retirement. Friedman explains that the fraction of an individual's income that it is appropriate for him to set aside for retirement depends upon that person's values and circumstances. Each person can best judge for himself how to use his resources.

Friedman wants to abolish the FDA. He says that it is in the self-interest of pharmaceutical firms to produce safe drugs and that tort law can handle any problems. Friedman points out that people never see the lives that are lost due to the slowness of the FDA in approving a drug that eventually turns out to be beneficial. He observes that the FDA has an interest in being late in approving drugs. If the FDA approves a drug that turns out to be bad, then it is in trouble. On the other hand, if it disapproves a drug that later turns out to be valuable, then it is only the drug companies that criticize the FDA. Friedman says that there is evidence that the FDA causes more deaths because of delayed approval than it has saved by early approval of drugs.

Friedman wants to legalize drugs. He says that the fight against narcotics is an immoral war that has destroyed the lives of people at home and abroad. The prohibition of drugs destroys civil rights at home and has wrecked nations. Victims of the "war on drugs" include many minority members who have been jailed for low-level drug offenses. Friedman contends that the United States has become a police state that arrests around one and a half million people annually who are suspected of drug offenses. He deplores the social tragedy that has resulted from the effort to keep people from ingesting an arbitrary list of substances depicted as "illegal drugs."

According to Friedman, the real cost of the war on drugs is what is done to our civil rights and judicial system, and to other countries. He observes that we have destroyed Colombia because we cannot enforce our own laws prohibiting the consumption of certain substances. Friedman argues that under prohibition law enforcement can temporarily reduce the supply of drugs, causing drug prices to rise. Higher prices, in turn, attract new sources of supply and newer drugs to the market, resulting in a greater supply. The government then reacts with tougher law enforcement and legislation.

He explains that individuals do not have great incentives to report drug crimes, which tend to be victimless crimes, much unlike assault, murder, and theft. When a willing buyer and seller transfer a drug, there is no real incentive to report what the government has declared to be a crime. Instead, evidence must be obtained through informants, searches, and seizures of property often without due process. Friedman contends that drug prohibition is unethical and that teenagers are primarily attracted to drugs because they are illegal. He says that the people who would benefit the most from legalization are addicts who would have an assurance of quality and who would not have to become "criminals" in order to support their habit. Friedman does not want people in prisons because of the mistaken attempt to control what people put into their bodies.

According to Friedman, the government should step aside from its efforts in a number of unjustifiable areas. He says that tariffs and other trade restrictions hurt us and that the United States should move unilaterally to free trade even if trading partners do not. This would be easier with floating exchange rates because they are prompt, automatic, and effective and do not require government involvement. International government should cease attempting to maintain fixed exchange rates and instead allow the market to determine the price of foreign currency.

In a private market, one person benefits only as long as the other person does also. On the other hand, in a government market a person can only satisfy his needs at the expense of someone else. It follows that Friedman is in favor of deregulation in areas such as airlines, trucking, railroads, utilities, interest rates, broker rates, the petroleum industry, and so on. He also wants to remove government support for the many medical, legal, and professional restrictions with respect to competition. According to Friedman, occupational and medical licensure and certification interfere with the rights of individuals to enter voluntarily into professions and to pursue activities of their own choosing. In the medical field, the restriction of new doctors forces people to pay more for less satisfactory medical services. Less expensive medical service would result if there were no monopoly. He says that, because only "first-rate" physicians are permitted, some people receive no medical care at all. Friedman adds that private markets, rather than the government, can take care of any needs for professional certifications. He is also in favor of private labeling because, if customers really want to know about a product's ingredients, it would be in the self-interest of the company producing it to list them on the package. He does not know why so-called experts in Washington know more about what customers want to be disclosed on packages. Although some reforms would be gradual and others immediate and radical, deregulation would result in enhanced and widespread competition and in reduced prices.

Friedman observes that many public enterprises should be privatized. This involves the transfer, divestiture, or contracting out of assets or services from the tax-supported public sector to the competitive markets of the private sector. In many cases, market arrangements are far more effective than command and control arrangements. He says that private monopoly is generally superior to public monopoly or regulation. He opposes government ownership or regulation of industries except where monopolies or other imperfections exist which result in divergences between social and private costs. Of course, even in these cases, he contends that government intervention is seldom justified. If a private venture fails, it shuts down, but if a government venture fails, it is expanded.

Friedman explains that public-sector spending would be severely reduced because private enterprises would do much of what government currently does. He notes the problem of overcoming vested interests and thwarting rent-seeking with respect to changing the status quo regarding government policies and programs. Privatization can be undertaken all levels of the government. At the national level, there are Social Security, national parks, the air traffic control system, AMTRAK, surplus military bases, public hospitals, the United States Post Office, turnpikes, and so on. At the state level, prison management and utilities are good examples. There are also numerous candidates at the local level including garbage collection, waste treatment, street cleaning, fire and police protection, parking structures, jails, snow removal, etc. It is obvious that Friedman's ideas for privatization and other steps toward smaller government have had a great influence in the United States and around the world.

Rather than direct regulation, Friedman has advocated graduated charges for pollution, thus creating a market incentive to clean up the air and water. He has talked about selling the right to emit a certain amount of pollutants into the air, thereby establishing a market in effluent rights.

Friedman is opposed to wage and price controls, price supports for agriculture, rent controls, government control of output, legal minimum wages or maximum prices, control of radio and TV by the FCC, and laws that favor unions which hold wage rates up artificially. He says he is more cautious regarding antitrust enforcement because the actual extent of market competition is a subtle matter that requires the analysis of empirical evidence in the form of concentration ratios, market share analyses, consumer surplus analyses, and so on. Friedman views the black market as a positive way of getting around government controls thus enabling the free market to work via mutually beneficial exchanges. He also defends the market as a destroyer of discrimination. Finally, Friedman is also famous for being the intellectual godfather of our all-volunteer army.

Methodology

Friedman says that economists form and use theories to help anticipate and control future events and that a theory is useful if it can predict and control such events. He says that the primary objective of positive economics is the making of ever more accurate predictions. His methodological position is based on the philosophy of science known as instrumentalism. If a theory predicts accurately, then it is a good theory. Predictive power is thus the hallmark of a good theory. Friedman requires that theories be simple yet have the ability to predict future events. He says that accurate predictions can be made from simplified assumptions, that truly important and significant hypotheses will be found to have assumptions that are wildly inaccurate descriptive representations of reality, and that, in general, the more significant the theory, the more unrealistic the assumptions.

Friedman says that predictions must be based on theories, in the sense of explanatory hypotheses, that must constantly be tested empirically. He focused on the problem of deciding whether or not a suggested hypotheses or theory should be tentatively accepted as part of a body of systematized economic knowledge. For Friedman, assumptions are useful as economical means of expressing and determining the status of the premises of a theory in order to provide an empirical basis for predictions. Assumptions specify the conditions under which the theory is expected to apply.

Friedman endeavors to demonstrate that economics meets positivist standards. He maintains that there is no test of a theory in terms of whether or not its assumptions are realistic and explains that the falsity of assumptions is unimportant unless such falsity detracts from the theory's ability to predict the phenomenon in question. His thesis is that the truth of assumptions is irrelevant to the acceptance of a theory, provided that its predictions succeed. Friedman also points to cases where changing premises to make them more realistic has resulted in the reduced usefulness (i.e., ability to predict) of the theories.

Relying on Popper's falsification criterion (and rejection of induction), Friedman maintains that confirming a proposition does not add to the probability that it is true. He says that we do not have an inductive logic and offers the alternative of accepting a hypothesis as a matter of methodological judgment as a positive statement to be tentatively accepted on the basis of empirical evidence. Friedman contends that we can never prove a theory—the most we can do is fail to disprove it. The process is to promulgate new theories and test them to see if they do in fact predict. An empirical process is used to eliminate those theories that do not predict the future and those that predict less reliably than others.

Friedman denounces the theorist whose goal is a set of assumptions that are more realistic. He rejects introspection and the realism or plausibility of assumptions of ways of assessing a theory. He asserts that assumptions for theorizing should be derived from observation rather than from introspection. Friedman explains that, with regard to introspection, realistic assumptions are needed to deduce acceptable economic theory, and that such assumptions cannot be made a priori in the absence of a true inductive process.

According to Friedman, efforts to eliminate unrealism deteriorate into pure tautology which avoids dealing with reality and makes impossible the refutable hypothesis, the primary research instrument. He also warns that economic theorists who value the realism of assumptions have to in some way take each new event and assimilate it into the theory. The theory thus becomes a description of what has occurred rather than a theory with predictive power.

It is interesting to note that in practice Friedman argues based on the realism or reasonableness of assumptions. He accumulates facts, forms a hypothesis to explain them, makes predictions, compares the predictions with facts, reviews his assumptions and hypothesis in response to the outcomes of his empirical testing, and continues in an iterative process. Although he says we do not need to test the truth of assumptions, he also acts to change an assumption that is false whenever he comes across a particular conclusion that is false.

Whereas absurd premises can yield correct conclusions, there can be no confidence that they will do so. Confidence in economics is based on direct and causal confirmation of realistic assumptions. Friedman's espoused approach can lead economists to give advice based on ridiculous theoretical constructs. It follows that he should stress understanding, as well as prediction, as the test of scientific validity.

Friedman's models are simplified representations of the entire economy and his economic concepts are aggregations and averages. His economic approach is to engage in a process of pattern prediction to see overall effects and order. We should not forget that these aggregates are the result of a multitude of individual human actions.

Conclusion

Milton Friedman has made significant contributions in macroeconomics, methodology, economic history, and in a variety of public policy areas. No one has done more to dismantle Keynesian economics and the welfare state. Friedman did this by using Keynes's own language and apparatus to prove him wrong. The paradox is that this libertarian economist, who shares the scientific paradigm of neoclassical social engineers, tries to defend incrementally more libertarian policies that are sometimes in contradiction with the principle of freedom. He has been known to use his talents to help the state to do more efficiently tasks that it should not be undertaking.

Friedman knows what the libertarian ideal is but is willing to entertain less than ideal changes as long as they point in the right direction. He draws a distinction between his ultimate goals and interventionist reforms that he believes will get us on the right path.

He maintains on empirical evidence that only competitive markets can coordinate the diverse elements of a complex society. Friedman constructs his liberalism around empiricism in attempting to refute the claims of interventionists. Unfortunately, empirical testing can only demonstrate that interventionist policies have contingently failed. This means that the failure of particular interventionist measures does not necessarily preclude the demand for more and different interventionist measures. Friedman's positivism and pragmatism have led to a number of incremental successes in the battle for a free society but more philosophical and moral approaches are required to win the war.

Recommended Reading

Burton, John. "Positively Milton Friedman." In *Twelve Contemporary Economists*, edited by J. R. Shackleton and Gareth Locksley. London: Macmillan, 1981.

Enlow, Robert. *Liberty and Learning: Milton Friedman's Voucher Idea at Fifty*. Washington, DC: Cato Institute, 2006.

Friedman, Milton. *Essays in Positive Economics*. Chicago: University of Chicago Press, 1953.

———, ed. *Studies in the Quantity Theory of Money*. Chicago: University of Chicago Press, 1956.

———. *A Theory of the Consumption Function*. Princeton: Princeton University Press, National Bureau of Economic Research, General Series Number 63, 1957.

———. "The Demand for Money: Some Theoretical and Empirical Results." *Journal of Political Economy* 67 (August 1959): 377–51.

———. *A Program for Monetary Stability*. New York: Fordham University Press, 1959.

———. "The Lag in Effect of Monetary Policy." *Journal of Political Economy* 69 (October 1961): 447–66.

———. "Interest Rates and the Demand for Money." *Journal of Law and Economics* 9 (October 1966): 71–85.

———. "Value Judgments in Economics." Pp. 85–93 in *Human Values and Economic Policy.* Edited by Sidney Hook. New York: New York University Press, 1967.

———. *Dollars and Deficits: Inflation, Monetary Policy and the Balance of Payments.* Englewood Cliffs, NJ: Prentice Hall, 1968.

———."The Role of Monetary Policy." *American Economic Review* 58 (March 1968): 1–17.

———. "Money: Quantity Theory." Pp. 423–47 in *International Encyclopedia of the Social Sciences.* New York: Macmillan and Free Press, 1968.

———. *The Counter-Revolution in Monetary Theory.* London: Institute of Economic Affairs, 1970.

———. "Have Monetary Policies Failed?" *American Economic Review, Papers and Proceedings* 62 (May 1972): 11–18.

———. *Milton Friedman's Monetary Framework: A Debate with his Critics.* Edited by Robert J. Gordon. Chicago: University of Chicago Press, 1974.

———. *Unemployment Versus Inflation?* London: Institute of Economic Affairs, 1975.

———. *Inflation and Unemployment.* London: Institute of Economic Affairs, 1977.

———. *Tax Limitation, Inflation, and the Role of Government.* Dallas, TX: The Fisher Institute, 1978.

———. *Focus on Milton Friedman.* Vancouver, BC: The Fraser Institute, 1982.

———. *Money Mischief: Episodes in Monetary History.* New York: Harvest/HBJ, 1994.

———. *Capitalism and Freedom: Fortieth Anniversary Edition.* Chicago: University of Chicago Press, 2002.

———. *The Essence of Friedman.* Edited by Kurt R. Leube. Stanford, CA: Hoover Institution Press, 1987.

Friedman, Milton, with Rose Friedman. *Tyranny of the Status Quo.* New York: Harcourt Brace Jovanovich; London: Secker & Warburg, 1984.

Friedman, Milton, and Walter W. Heller. *Monetary Versus Fiscal Policy.* New York: W. W. Norton & Co., 1969.

Friedman, Milton, and David Meiselman. 1963. "The Relative Stability of Monetary Velocity and the Investment Multiplier in the United States, 1897-1958." *Stabilization Policies,* a series of studies prepared for the Commission on Money and Credit. Englewood Cliffs, NJ: Prentice-Hall.

Friedman, Milton, and Anna J. Schwartz. *A Monetary History of the United States, 1867-1960.* Princeton, NJ: Princeton University Press, National Bureau of Economic Research Studies in Business Cycles 12, 1963.

Friedman, Milton, and Anna Schwartz. "Money and Business Cycles." *Review of Economics and Statistics* 45, pt. 2, supplement (February 1963): 32–64.

Friedman, Milton, and Anna J. Schwartz. *Monetary Statistics of the United States.* New York: Columbia University Press, National Bureau of Economic Research Studies in Business Cycles, 20, 1970.

Friedman, Milton, and Anna J. Schwartz. *Monetary Trends in the United States and the United Kingdom.* Kingdom. Chicago: University of Chicago Press, National Bureau of Economic Research Monograph, 1982.

Friedman, Milton, with Arnold S. Trebach and Kevin B. Zeese. *Friedman and Szasz on Liberty and Drugs: Essays on the Free Market and Prohibition.* Washington, DC: Drug Policy Foundation Press, 1992.

Hammond, J. Daniel. *The Legacy of Milton Friedman as Teacher (Intellectual Legacies in Modern Economics Series, No2).* Aldershot, UK: Edward Elgar Publishers, 1999.

————, and Craufurd D. Goodwin. *Theory and Measurement: Causality Issues in Milton Friedman's Monetary Economics (Historical Perspectives on Modern Economics).* Cambridge: Cambridge University Press, 2005.

Hirsch, Abraham and Neil de Marchi. *Milton Friedman: Economics in Theory and Practice.* Ann Arbor: University of Michigan Press, 1990.

Patinkin, Don. "The Chicago Tradition, the Quantity Theory, and Friedman." *Journal of Money, Credit, and Banking* 1, no. 1 (February 1969): 46–70.

Thygesen, Niels. "The Scientific Contributions of Milton Friedman." *Scandinavian Journal of Economics* 79), no. 1 (1977): 56–98.

Wood, John. *Milton Friedman (Critical Assessments).* London: Routledge Press, 1990.

Chapter 18

Mises, Friedman, and Rand:
A Methodological Comparison

The two methods which were contrasted were not mutually exclusive and had indeed been used together by the greatest of the classics. There is clearly room for serious disagreement about the choice of premises; but it is generally admitted that premises which stand at the beginning of the deductive process are themselves empirical in origin. Induction and deduction are interdependent.

—Eric Roll

Three of the most respected and influential free-market thinkers of the twentieth century are Ludwig von Mises (1881-1973), Milton Friedman (1912-2006), and Ayn Rand (1905-1982). The purpose of this chapter is to compare and evaluate the respective methodological approaches of each of these theorists who have influenced the course of history with their ideas. We will see how and why Rand's realist approach is superior to both Mises's rationalism and Friedman's empiricism.

Mises's Praxeology

Mises argued that concepts can never be found in reality, wanted to construct a purely deductive system, and was searching for a foundation upon which to build it. He was seeking a theoretical foundation that could not be questioned or doubted. He wanted to find knowledge of logical necessity and desired to escape the concrete-based empiricism of historicism. His mission became to look inward in order to deduce a system that was logically unobjectionable. Mises aspired to find laws that could only be verified or refuted by means of discursive reasoning.

Mises's action axiom, the universal, introspectively known fact that men act, was the foundation upon which he built his deductive system. Action, for Mises, is the real thing. Mises said that action was a category of the mind, in a Kantian sense, that was required in order to experience phenomenal reality (i.e., reality as it appears to us). The unity found in Mises's theorems of economics is rooted in the concept of human action. Mises's economic science is deductive and based on laws of human action that he contends are as real as the laws of nature. His praxeological laws have no spatial, temporal, or cultural constraints. They are universal and pertain to people everywhere, at every time, and in all cultures.

Human actions are engaged in to achieve goals that are part of the external world. However, a person's understanding of the logical consequences of human action does not stem from the specific details of these goals or the means employed. Comprehension of these laws does not depend on a person's specific knowledge of those features of the external world that are relevant to the person's goals or to the methods used in his pursuit of these goals. Praxeology's cognition is totally general and formal without reference to the material content and particular features of an actual case. Praxeological theorems are prior to empirical testing because they are logically deduced from the central axiom of action. By understanding the logic of the reasoning process, a person can comprehend the essentials of human actions. Mises states that the entirety of praxeology can be built on the basis of premises involving one single non-logical concept—the concept of human action. From this concept all of praxeology's propositions can be derived.

Mises contends that the axiom of action is known by introspection to be true. In the tradition of Kant, Mises argues that the category of action is part of the structure of the human mind. It follows that the laws of action can be studied introspectively because of the aprioristic intersubjectivity of human beings. Not derived from experience, the propositions of praxeology are not subject to falsification or verification on the basis of experience. Rather, these propositions are temporally and logically prior to any understanding of historical facts.

For Mises, economic behavior is simply a special case of human action. He contends that it is through the analysis of the idea of action that the principles of economics can be deduced. Economic theorems are seen as connected to the foundation of real human purposes. Economics is based on true and evident axioms, arrived at by introspection, into the essence of human action. From these axioms, Mises derives logical implications or the truths of economics. Mises's methodology thus does not require controlled experiments because he treats economics as a science of human action. By their nature, economic acts are social acts. Economics is a formal science whose theorems and propositions do not derive their validity from empirical observations. Economics is the branch of praxeology that studies market exchange and alternative systems of market exchange.

Friedman's Predictive Approach

Milton Friedman dismisses Mises's apriorism and aprioristic reasoning as a subjective method of considering the introspections of a person's own mind. Seeking objectivity and verifiability, Friedman prefers the empirical method, which uses publicly and socially available data. As an empiricist, he considers a theory to be useful if the theory permits individuals to predict occurrences of the phenomenon. This is in opposition to Mises and many other Austrian thinkers who regard the explanation of economic phenomena as making the world understandable in terms of human action in the pursuit of values and goals.

In his 1953 article, "The Methodology of Positive Economics," Friedman maintained that the realism or unrealism of the assumptions of economic theory is no guide to its usefulness. He rejected both introspection and the plausibility or realism of assumptions as a way of evaluating a theory. He asserted that these had no bearing on the predictive power of a theory or hypothesis with respect to its further applications. What matters to Friedman is whether or not the predictions of a theory correspond to empirical evidence. For Friedman, an instrumentalist, hypotheses are tentatively chosen because they have been successful in yielding true predictions.

Friedman contends that a hypothesis can be tested only by the conformity of its predictions or implications with observable phenomena and not by comparing its assumptions with reality. He applied the ideas developed by Karl Popper for use in the natural sciences in the realm of economics. Friedman argues that, as in the natural sciences, theories should be accepted provisionally or rejected only on the basis of the degree of correspondence of the predictions of a theory with the factual evidence obtained. Friedman asserted that a single empirical counter-example to a theory's predictions will falsify the theory. His idea of the role of testing thus involves induction via elimination or rejection. Friedman's approach is similar to the pragmatism of John Dewey.

For Friedman, the significance of a theory is not considered to be a direct result of the descriptive realism of the theory's assumptions. In fact, he extols the virtues of descriptively false assumptions. According to Friedman, "Truly important and significant hypotheses have assumptions that are wildly inaccurate descriptive representations of reality, and in general the more significant the theory, the more unrealistic the assumptions." Friedman explains that a person cannot say that a theory's assumptions are true because any of its conclusions are true but that a person could say that there must be at least one assumption that is false whenever some specific conclusion is false.

Friedman states that for a theory to be useful it must be an oversimplification of reality and therefore a false picture of reality. He goes on to say that, depending upon the theory and its uses, some of these false pictures, along with their assumptions, may be more appropriate (i.e., more predictively accurate) than others. For Friedman, abstraction involves a theory in which many actual characteristics of reality are designated as absent from the theory. Given this perspective, every advance in knowledge, new discovery, or inclusion of additional attributes would defeat, invalidate, and falsify the previous theory. Friedman views any theory as deficient and descriptively false when it fails to specify all of the characteristics of reality including all extraneous, nonexplanatory, and irrelevant characteristics. It follows that, for Friedman, all models or theories are imperfect or incomplete because they do not take into account all aspects of the economy. It is no wonder that he turned his attention to prediction rather than to explanation.

It is difficult to reconcile Friedman's practice with his methodological principles. In practice, he frequently argues on the basis of the plausibility or realism of a model's assumptions. After comparing predictions with outcomes he revises hypotheses and assumptions with the intention of making them more realistic. In the light of test results, economists (including Friedman) modify their hypotheses and assumptions in an ongoing and iterative process of observation and theory. Of course, Friedman should be concerned with the realism of assumptions. How else would he know what to attempt next when his predictions fail to square with the facts? If an economist does not assess the realism of his assumptions, the process of theory modification would be inefficient, futile, and based on speculative guesswork. It is apparent that Friedman is not a great theoretical system builder and is even inconsistent with respect to conforming his theory with his practice.

Rand's Objectivism

Ayn Rand's theory of concept formation transcends both Mises's apriorism and Friedman's empiricism. Rand explains that the acquisition of knowledge requires both induction and deduction. What is known is distinct from, and independent of, the knower. Knowledge is therefore gained via various processes of differentiation and integration from perceptual data. Empirical knowledge is acquired through observational experience of external reality. For example, people observe goal-directed actions from the outside and attain an understanding of causality and other categories of action by observing the actions of others to reach goals. Individuals also learn about causality by means of their own acting and their observation of the outcomes. Introspection is a reliable but ancillary source of evidence and knowledge with respect to what it means to be a rational, purposeful, volitional, and acting human being.

For Rand, the essential characteristics of a concept are epistemological rather than metaphysical. Concepts are epistemologically objective in that they are produced by a man's consciousness in accordance with the facts of reality. Concepts are mental integrations of factual data. Rand explains that concept formation involves the process of measurement omission. A concept is a mental integration of units possessing the same differentiating characteristics with their particular measurements omitted.

Mises explained that a man's introspective knowledge that he is conscious and acts is a fact of reality and is independent of external experience. Mises deduced the principles of economics and the complete structure of economic theory entirely through the analysis of the introspectively derived a priori idea of human action. While it is certainly important to understand and acknowledge the useful role of introspection in one's life, it is also necessary to realize that its role is limited, secondary, and adjunct to the empirical observation and logical analysis of empirical reality. It would have been better if Mises had said that external observation and introspection combine to reveal that people act and employ means to achieve ends. Introspection aids or supplements external observation and induction in disclosing to a man the fundamental purposefulness of human action.

Randian epistemology recognizes that Mises's action axiom could be inductively derived from perceptual data. Human actions would then be viewed as performed by entities who act in accord with their natural attributes of rationality and free will. All the essential principles and laws of economics could then be deduced from the action axiom.

The Randian or Objectivist view is that the best way for judging a model or a theory is to examine the plausibility of its assumptions. As Ayn Rand herself would put it, "Check your premises." Things which the assumptions abstract from should pertain importantly to the problem under examination. A hypothesis, complete with its assumptions, is both explanatory and predictive if it abstracts the crucial and common elements from the mass of detailed and complex conditions surrounding the phenomenon to be explained and furthers valid predictions of that phenomenon. The Objectivist view is that economic and other theories need to omit a lot of details. Roderick Long has observed that Randian realism does not require that all nonexplanatory extraneous particulars be specified.

The Randian conception of abstraction is to attend to some aspects or attributes of a phenomenon and to exclude others. From this perspective, certain actual characteristics are simply absent from specification or measurement. This is far different from and superior to Friedman's view that some actual characteristics are specified as nonexistent or lacking. From a Randian perspective, new knowledge may expand or refine a theory, concept, or model but it does not necessarily contradict or invalidate it. In other words and contrary to Friedman's view, the theory does not have to be descriptively false.

Ayn Rand's methodological approach overcomes the false alternatives of rationalism and empiricism by explaining how abstract knowledge of reality can be soundly derived from valid perceptual experience. Her method for overcoming these dichotomies includes a number of processes such as differentiation, induction, integration, deduction, reduction, measurement omission, and so on.

Recommended Reading

Backhouse, R. *Truth and Progress in Economic Knowledge.* Cheltenham, UK: Edward Elgar, 1997.

Blaug, M. *The Methodology of Economics*. Cambridge: Cambridge University Press, 1992.

Block, Walter. "On Robert Nozick's 'On Austrian Methodology.'" *Inquiry* 23, no. 4 (Fall 1980): 397–444.

———. "Realism: Austrian vs. Neoclassical Economics, Reply to Caplan." *Quarterly Journal of Austrian Economics* 6, no. 3 (Fall 2003): 63–76.

Boettke, P. "Ludwig von Mises." In *The Handbook of Economic Methodology*, edited by John Davis, D. Wade Hands, and U. Maki. Cheltenham, UK: Edward Elgar Publishing, 1998.

Boettke, P., and Peter Leeson. "The Austrian School of Economics, 1950-2000." In *The Blackwell Companion to the History of Economic Thought*, edited by Warren Samuels and Jeff Biddle. Oxford: Basil Blackwell Publishers, 2003.

Boland, L. "A Critique of Friedman's Critics." *Journal of Economic Lierature.* 17 (1979): 503–22.

———. *The Foundations of Economic Method*. London: Allen & Unwin, 1980.

———. *The Foundations of Economic Method*. London: Allen & Unwin, 1982.

Buechner, M. Northrup. "Ayn Rand and Economics." *The Objectivist Forum* (August 1982): 3–9.

Caldwell, B. *Beyond Positivism: Economic Methodology in the Twentieth Century*. London: Allen & Unwin, 1982.

Caplan, Bryan. "The Austrian Search for Realistic Foundations." *Southern Economic Journal* 65, no. 4 (April 1999): 823–38.

Egger, John B. "The Austrian Method." Pp. 19–39 in *New Directions in Austrian Economics*, edited by Louis M. Spadaro. Kansas City: Sheed Andrews and McMeel, Inc., 1978.

Fox, Glenn. "Economics as Prediction." Pp. 73–85 in Chapter 5 of *Reason and Reality in the Methodologies of Economics: An Introduction*. Cheltenham, UK: Edward Elgar, 1997.

Friedman, Milton. *Essays in Positive Economics*. Chicago: University of Chicago Press, 1953.

———. "The Methodology of Positive Economics." Pp. 3–43 in *Essays in Positive Economics*. Chicago: University of Chicago Press, 1953.

Hausman, D. *The Inexact and Separate Science of Economics*. Cambridge: Cambridge University Press, 1992.

Huerta de Soto, Jesus. "The Ongoing Methodensteit of the Austrian School." *Journal des Economistes et des Etudes Humaines* 8:1 (March 1998): 75–113.

Lawson, T. *Economics and Reality*. London: Routledge, 1997.

Long, Roderick T. "Realism and Abstraction in Economics: Aristotle and Mises versus Friedman." Austrian Scholars Conference 10, Ludwig von Mises Institute 19 March 2004.

Mäki, U., B. Gustafsson, C. Knudsen, eds. *Rationality, Institutions and Economic Methodology*. London: Routledge, 1993.

Mayer, Thomas. "Boettke's Austrian Critique of Mainstream Economics: An Empiricist's Response." *Critical Review* 12, nos. 1-2 (Winter-Spring 1998).

Melitz, Jack. "Friedman and Machlup on the Significance of Testing Economic Assumptions." *Journal of Political Economy* 73 (February 1965): 37–60.

Mises, Ludwig von. *The Ultimate Foundation of Economic Science*. Princeton, NJ: Van Nostrand Press, 1962.

———. *Human Action: A Treatise on Economics*. New Haven, CT: Yale University Press, 1963.

————. *Human Action.* 3rd rev. ed. Chicago: Henry Regnery Company, [1949] 1966.

————. *Epistemological Problems of Economics.* New York: New York University Press, 1978.

————. *The Ultimate Foundation of Economic Science.* Kansas City, MO: Sheed, Andrews, and McMeel, 1979.

————. *Theory and History.* Auburn, AL: Ludwig von Mises Institute, 1984.

————. *Human Action.* Auburn, AL: Ludwig von Mises Institute, [1966] 1999.

————. *Epistemological Problems of Economics.* Translated by George Reisman. Auburn, AL: Ludwig von Mises Institute, 2003.

Nozick, Robert. "On Austrian Methodology." *Synthese* 36 (1977): 353–92.

O'Driscoll, G., and Mario Rizzo. *The Economics of Time and Ignorance.* New York: Basil Blackwell Publishers, 1985.

Paqué, Karl-Heinz. "How Far Is Vienna from Chicago? An Essay on the Methodology of Two Schools of Dogmatic Liberalism." *Kyklos* 38 (1985): 412–34.

Peikoff, Leonard. *Objective: The Philosophy of Ayn Rand.* New York: Dutton, 1991.

Rand, Ayn. *Introduction to Objectivist Epistemology.* 2nd expanded ed. Edited by Harry Binswanger and Leonard Peikoff. New York: Meridian, [1966-1967] 1990.

Rosen, Sherwin. "Austrian and Neoclassical Economics: Any Gains from Trade?" *Journal of Economic Perspectives* 11 (Fall 1997): 139–52.

Rothbard, M. "Praxeology: The Method of Austrian Economics." In *Foundations of Modern Economics,* edited by Edwin Dolan. Kansas City, MO: Sheed and Ward, 1976.

Skousen, Mark. *Vienna and Chicago: Friends or Foes.* Lanham, MD: Capital Press, 2005.

Viner, Jacob. "Some Problems of Logical Method in Political Economy." *Journal of Political Economy* 25, no. 3 (March 1917): 236–60.

Chapter 19

James M. Buchanan: Constitutional and Post-Constitutional Political Economy

I resist, and resist strongly, any and all efforts to pull me toward positions of advising on this or that policy or cause. I sign no petitions, join no political organizations, advise no party, serve no lobbying effort. Yet the public's image of me, and especially as developed through the media after the Nobel Prize in 1986, is that of a right-wing libertarian zealot who is antidemocratic, antiegalitarian, and antiscientific. I am, of course, none of these and am, indeed, the opposites. Properly understood, my position is both democratic and egalitarian, I am passionately individualistic, and my emphasis on individual liberty does set me apart from many of my academic colleagues whose mind-sets are mildly elitist and, hence collectivist.

—James M. Buchanan

In 1986, James M. Buchanan (1919-) was awarded the Nobel Prize for economics for his efforts to study the public sector within the same microeconomic analytical framework that is used to study private economy. Buchanan applies economics to understanding how individuals interact in the public square to formulate collective decisions. His Public Choice research program offers a foundation for understanding and analyzing the behavior of persons in public choice, whether they are voters, politicians, bureaucrats, diplomats, or other public servants. Buchanan's contributions to this field can be found primarily in his *The Calculus of Consent* (1962) with Gordon Tullock, *The Limits of Liberty* (1975), and *The Reason of Rules* (1985) with Geoffrey Brennan.

Early Influences

Buchanan recognizes Chicago economist Frank Knight and Swedish economist Knut Wicksell as the two major influences on his economic thinking. Knight was Buchanan's early intellectual role model. Knight understood and taught that, although economics is a science, it is not a science in the traditional meaning of the physical sciences—economics is about individual human choice, exchange, and processes of adjustment. Buchanan's views on methodology and subjectivism were inherited from Knight, who also endorsed introspection as a valid and valuable tool of economic analysis. Knight explained human action within a subjectively perceived means-ends framework. In addition, he denounced positivism and maintained that economic prediction is limited to pattern prediction.

The strongest influence on Buchanan's views about the analysis of the public sector was the writings of Knut Wicksell. Wicksell contended that only taxes and government spending, that are unanimously approved of, could be justified. This is his principle or rule of just taxation. According to Wicksell, politics should be understood as an exchange framework with efficiency in the public sector assured only under a rule of unanimity for collective choice.

Wicksell was concerned about the injustice and inefficiencies that can result from majority rule. Based on his analysis of the relationship between public expenditures and taxes, Wicksell doubted the efficiency and justness of majority rules and proposed that voting rules be modified in the direction of unanimity. He had perceived that majorities were inclined to pass legislation aimed at benefiting their own members at the expense of others. Wicksell stated that if we wanted reform in economic policy, then we should change the rules under which political agents or their representatives act—majority rule should be modified in the direction of unanimity.

In his writings, Buchanan adopts, modifies, and transfers Wicksell's 1896 principle of unanimity to the constitutional stage of collective choice. Buchanan's "contract theory of the state" shifts Wicksell's analysis of taxation into the sphere of constitutional choice. Throughout his career, Buchanan has aspired to the Madisonian goal of first empowering and then constraining government.

Like Wicksell, Buchanan understood that institutions emerge through efforts by individuals or groups of individuals to achieve certain goals. He explains that his analysis of collective choice is based on methodological individualism and that the only way to understand the operations of any collective organization is to study the plans, choices, and actions of the individual members of the collective. Buchanan views government as an endogenous segment of the economic institutional arrangements through which individuals attempt to satisfy their individual wants. In turn, institutional arrangements provide opportunities for the imposition of constraints on individuals.

Methodology

Buchanan bases his analysis on methodological individualism, rational choice, individual utility maximization, and politics-as-exchange. All people in both the governmental and market sectors try to do the best they can for themselves, as they personally view their situation, within the set of constraints they face. Individuals thus attempt to pursue their broadly conceived and subjective self-interest. Each individual rational contractor will therefore ask to minimize his costs and to maximize his benefits. Buchanan even suggests substituting the word "catallactics" for the word "economics" in order to stress that the appropriate objects of study are individuals acting to advance their broadly defined interests through mutually beneficial transactions with other persons.

Economics is concerned with individual actors rather than with collective entities. Buchanan accepts individual economic man within politics as a modeling strategy for the design of a constitution. In his theory of public choice, Buchanan adopted an economist's interest in exchanges. In other words, he extends the assumptions of the economist to the behavior of individuals as they participate in the political process.

Buchanan employs conjectural history as an analytical tool to determine how a constitutional order could have emerged. He explains that a constitution is a voluntary agreement to which all citizens give their consent. In Buchanan's thought, the concept of agreement or consent serves as at type of an ethical surrogate in place of natural law. As an avowed Hobbesian and a contractarian procedural liberal philosopher, he attempts to demonstrate how men could agree upon a constitutional order which does not allow any one assortment of values to be adopted over all others. Buchanan contends that we must proceed on the presumption that no man's values are better than any other man's values.

Buchanan appeals to a hypothetical natural state with conditions not unlike Hobbes's state of nature—a natural state of anarchy and lawlessness. As a neo-Hobbesian social contractarian, Buchanan explains individuals agreeing to a social contract because of their desire to survive. In his later writings, Buchanan moves a bit away from his Hobbesian position and closer to John Rawls's emphasis on uncertainty and prudence and his veil of ignorance. As a contractualist, Buchanan views individual rights as a set of rights that have been agreed to, not as natural rights that can be justified by referring to human nature. Before the existence of a social contract, Buchanan envisions an anarchist equilibrium of production, predation, and self-protection. After a social contract is made, a government is needed to enforce it.

People make constitutional decisions under a veil of ignorance or uncertainty regarding their own future positions. There is a veil of uncertainty as to each person's particular interest and to future applications of the constitutional rules. Buchanan states that each individual has an incentive to create a state in order to decrease expenditures on his personal defense and to make the cost of unilateral withdrawal from the contract exorbitantly high. He says that another reason why people will agree to constitutional rules is to impose limits on the potential exercise of political authority.

According to Buchanan, the manner and limits of government authority are to be determined by asking what people would agree to in advance of entering civil society. He says that people make constitutional decisions with respect to drawing the boundary between private actions and collective actions. He explains that people will realize that some mutually beneficial exchanges cannot take place if all action is limited to strictly private transactions. It follows that a constitution is agreed to in order to have collectively furnished goods. Buchanan maintains that in collective decisions the correlative to mutual consent in market exchange is unanimity.

The State's Hobbesian Origins

In the beginning, there are no government bureaucracies or political agents—there are only the demands of individual persons pursuing each one's broadly conceived self-interest. By framing constitutional choice in the context of a Hobbesian state of nature with all self-interested citizens making decisions under a veil of uncertainty, Buchanan shows that unanimity is both conceivable and likely. He says that a political rule will attain the optimality criterion if it can gain unanimous consent or some kind of modified "workable unanimity."

According to Buchanan, under Hobbesian anarchy, individuals apportion their time between productive, protective, and predatory activities. He observes that self-interested behavior on the part of each person will lead to a stalemate situation with each individual dividing his time between productive private activities and military-type combat. It follows that rational people will agree to reduce their defensive and predatory actions so that more resources could be employed in the production of private goods. Buchanan explains that an original distribution of property rights must be negotiated and agreed upon along with rules standardizing their legitimate transfer throughout time.

Constitutional-level law can be seen as an array of restrictions on economic freedom that paradoxically allows individuals to prosper economically. It follows that a coercive agency, the protective state, originates by necessity to enforce this accord—its purpose is to define and protect property rights and their legitimate transfer over time.

Two Levels of Public Choice

Buchanan distinguishes between two levels of public choice—the initial or first level sets the rules of the game through the choice of a constitution and the second or post-constitutional level involves playing the game within the rules. Different rules have different distributional consequences and the rules chosen are applicable into the future. Constitutional politics thus places boundaries over what ordinary politics is permitted to do. Ordinary political decisions are made often based on majority voting. One of Buchanan's major contributions is bringing attention to the two-level structure of collective decision making.

Two types of analysis fall under the taxonomy of public choice: constitutional economics and operational public choice analysis. The purpose of constitutional economics is to legitimize the existence of a constitutionally circumscribed state and to discuss what type of constitutional rules could reasonably reach unanimous consent at the stage of constitutional choice. Buchanan's primary interest lies in constitutional choice and constitutional reform. Operational public choice analysis deals with political processes within existing constitutional structures. Operational public choice analysis involves the study of a nexus of evolving exchanges, bargains, trades, agreements, contracts, and side payments.

Buchanan explains that the unanimity principle does not have to apply to the stage of post-constitutional operations of the government established by the constitution. The level of routine government operations takes place under the constitutional process rules that are meant to apply to every individual situation. Buchanan says that rational contractors will unanimously agree to less than unanimity rules, which reduce decision making costs with respect to routine collective decisions. Obtaining unanimous consent is too costly so the framers set up a legislative process by which the original distribution of property rights could be changed in order to create otherwise unattainable public goods.

Majority Voting

According to Buchanan, people have agreed to majority voting because they expect to be more often in a winning coalition than in a losing coalition. Individuals within the political sector base their choices and coalition memberships on their personal evaluation of costs and benefits. He notes that majority coalitions tend to be unstable, temporary, and ever-changing. Majority rule is apt to lead to inefficient outcomes such as the overprovision of collectively supplied goods and services and majority cost-shifting of some of the costs onto the minority. These are the allocative effects of majority rule. Buchanan observes that when redistribution occurs individuals are no longer functioning under a veil of ignorance.

Majority-voting rules permit a multitude of separate potential coalitions to put forth taxing and spending proposals. At the post-constitutional stage a losing minority cannot legitimately claim that it was forced by the majority. Buchanan explains that government compulsion with respect to the supply of public goods is legitimate if the original contract (i.e., the constitution) is the product of an effective unanimity rule. Decisions regarding the financing of collective projects are regarded as the outcome of voluntary agreements among citizens. Political voting mechanisms thus serve as substitutes for decentralized private decisions where opportunities (for public goods) exist that cannot be easily embodied in private contracts.

Post-Constitutional Analysis

Politics consists mainly of individual and group attempts to obtain the most benefits from government and to pay the least amount of taxes. According to Buchanan, post-constitutional analysis involves the examination of strategies that players adopt within defined constitutional rules and principles. During the post-constitutional stage players treat the rules of the game as constraints and devise strategies to deal with them. Today, most government taxation and spending policy is dictated by pressure groups acting in their own perceived special interests and not by politicians acting in the public interest.

Buchanan distinguishes between the protective state and the productive state, which has "evolved" into the redistributive state. He says that what we generally consider to be a "limited" state actually includes more than merely the protective and judicial services associated with the "night watchman" state—it also includes the productive state, which furnishes public goods such as roads and schools. The protective state enforces agreed-to rights and the productive state produces collective goods. The protective state enforces neutral, unanimously agreed upon law. In turn, the productive state may operate through rules of less than unanimity given that at the constitutional stage those rules find unanimous agreement. Whereas the protective state functions in an objective fashion to determine rule infractions, the actions of the productive state are subject to choice. Buchanan's economic theory of the origins of law is consistent with the state provision of public goods. When the protective state was set up, the consenting persons discerned that public goods in the future may be wanted and that without a productive state many public goods would be unobtainable. The framers realized that there would be difficulties financing projects because anyone can use such services without contributing financially.

The modern state is transforming into the illiberal and redistributionist state as the productive state does not simply provide public goods but also intervenes in the private economy by promoting the same ends pursued in the private sector. The government has taken over many functions previously left to markets. With no meaningful distinction between public and private interests, people dissatisfied with their results in the private sector will increasingly turn to the public sector. Coalitions of voters seek special advantages from the state to obtain legislation favorable to them. Buchanan explains that looking to the government to remedy things can lead to more harm than good.

Much of today's politics can be viewed as rent-seeking activity (e.g., pork barrel politics). A rent-seeking society leads to the redistributive state that transfers wealth from one party to another through collective action. If there is value to be gained through the political process, people will invest time and resources in their attempts to capture this value for themselves. The emergence of the welfare state and the growth of government have increased opportunities for, and rewards of, redistributive activities. Interest groups in a rent-seeking society will make efforts to gain their own benefits at the expense of others through the use of government. More and more, individuals are investing in rent-seeking and rent protection.

The Public Choice application of the logic of microeconomics to politics has revealed the prevalence of rent-seeking and free-riding on the part of voters, politicians, bureaucrats, and the recipients of public monies. With costs spread over the taxpayers at large, individuals with concentrated interests in increased government expenditures (as benefits) take a free ride on people with diffuse interests in lower taxes. This reflects the logic of concentrated benefits and dispersed costs. Politics produces a policy mix which affords short term and easily identified benefits at the expense of largely hidden and long term costs. The resulting cost shifting leads to the overprovision of government goods and services as majority voting rules allow for many separate coalitions. When factions dominate the voting process, projects tend to be funded that cannot be justified on an aggregate cost-benefit basis. Value taken in the form of such transfers makes the investment wasteful in an overall sense.

Politicians and Public Servants

What about the behavior of politicians, legislators, and bureaucrats? Buchanan explains that problems are exacerbated by the rational, self-interested behavior of such individuals. He contends that when people enter government they act on the same motives as when they are agents in the private sector. It follows that bureaucrats want to maximize their budgets, thereby obtaining greater power, larger salaries, and so on. Government officials make choices based on their self-interest, thereby generating pressure for higher taxes, bigger budgets, more regulations, and more power. Politicians act, at least to a certain extent, out of self-interest and will attempt to gain as many votes as possible to reach positions of power and to receive larger budget allocations.

Public Choice studies the behavior of politicians and bureaucrats in a representative democracy like we have in the United States. Before Public Choice, economists assumed an objective welfare function that government officials sought to maximize and thought that political agents were inspired to pursue that objective welfare function. The assumption was that nobody in government maximized for himself—there was only the public good. Buchanan understood that political decision makers are not necessarily seekers of the public good but instead they are interested players who trade to their own advantages such as increased power and reelection. He says that people do not change when they take an oath of office or when they join a government agency.

Politicians, bureaucrats, and other public servants may say that they are devoted to the public interest, common good, general welfare, or social justice, or that they act from some altruistic motivation, but Buchanan maintains that public officials are not motivated by disinterested service to the public and that they, like everyone else, endeavor to maximize their own utilities. It is in the interest of political representatives to spend and say to their constituents that they voted for the benefit of their community. The result is competition between politicians for constituency support through the use of promises of discriminatory transfers of wealth. Bureaucracies tend to grow because of rent seeking, pork-barrel politics, deficit spending, and a tax system with loopholes, exemptions, credits, and so on. A massive expansion of the power to tax has enabled public officials to promote even more alleged social ends.

The rules of decision making regarding public spending are outlined in the constitution and create in the representatives a tendency to spend more than the revenue collected. Democratic governments have a significant tendency toward deficit spending unless they are constrained by some fundamental constitutional principle like that of the classical balanced budget. In addition, there was once the pre-Keynesian principle that public expenditures were to be funded by taxation and private spending was to be financed with people's income. Both citizens and politicians abandon their fiscal discipline when they resort to a debt-financed government. When the proper scope of the government is extended, it is difficult to limit its expansion. When budgets are maximized and deficits are incurred, the results include higher government spending, inefficient allocation among government agencies, and inefficient production within them.

Keynesians have failed to consider the implications of the intergenerational transfer of the debt burden. The burden of debt is passed on to future generations rather than paid for currently with the consumption of real resources. The phenomenon of stealing through the majoritarian processes of government is exacerbated through fiscal deficits that produce intertemporal wealth transfers.

Constitutional Reform

Buchanan claims that we need fundamental constitutional change if special interest legislation and factional rent-seeking or transfer-seeking activity is to be minimized. He says that we should be concerned with processes or procedures (i.e., rules and principles) through which interacting individuals create certain states of affairs. Men need to rethink and redesign their institutional structures in order to revive the classical political economy of the eighteenth century. He says that lasting reform results from adopting a constitutional perspective with respect to systemic change in the rules of government.

Buchanan employs primarily an "economic man" assumption and sees government officials as revenue maximizing rather than as wealth maximizing. He therefore wants rules that constrain the revenue-raising ability of government and the government freedom to select the spending mix. Buchanan advocates constitutional revisions in order to provide safeguards and to avoid a slippery slope. He says that taxes should be earmarked for particular services so that each type of government activity is financed by a tax on a base that is logically related to that activity. Buchanan explains that a system of multiple excise taxes, rather than a small number of broad-based taxes, would enable taxpayers to better control government by allowing them to avoid some taxation by decreasing their purchases of high-taxed items. In addition, he advocates constitutional rules requiring balanced budgets. Under a balanced budget requirement, money would be so limited compared to demand for it that near unanimity would be required before financing for a project would be approved.

Buchanan says that his contractarian approach and unanimity principle provide a way of normatively evaluating existing constitutional provisions and proposed constitutional changes. Unanimity thus becomes the benchmark for efficiency. He predicts that something like a two-thirds super-majority rule for the operations of the productive state should be, and would be, agreed upon at the constitutional stage. Buchanan says that people would want rules that are not so permissive that they permit the demise of individual property rights.

Contractual Rights Versus Natural Rights

Buchanan states that each person has an ethical obligation to join an ongoing constitutional dialogue but he fails to adequately describe the source of this ethical obligation. Remember that he has dismissed the possibility of any absolute moral values. He is a social contractarian who does not subscribe to the notions of natural law, natural rights, or natural objective moral value. Contractarian individual rights for Buchanan come from having reached an agreement. They are not something that is established by reference to human nature. Buchanan's subjective, nominalist, and deterministic philosophy would be much stronger if he had acknowledged that natural rights are an objective characteristic of the human social realm. If he had, then he may have realized that the "rules of the game" are metanormative in nature and that only the protective state can be justified. Such a state would be concerned solely with protecting the self-directedness of individuals thus ensuring the freedom through which individuals can pursue their flourishing and happiness. There would be no justification for the productive state or the redistributive state.

Recommended Reading

Atkinson, Anthony. "James M. Buchanan's Contributions to Economics." *Scandanavian Journal of Economics* 89, no. 1 (1987).

Boettke, Peter. *Virginia Political Economy: A View from Vienna.* Reprinted in *The Market Process: Essays in Contemporary Austrian Economics*, edited by Peter J. Boettke and David L. Prychitko. Indershot, UK: Edward Elgar Publishing, 1994.

Brennan, Geoffrey, and James M. Buchanan. *The Power to Tax.* New York: Cambridge University Press, 1980.

————. *The Reason of Rules*. New York: Cambridge University Press, 1980.

————. "Is Public Choice Immoral? The Case for the 'Nobel' Lie." *Virginia Law Review* 74 (March 1998): 179–89.

Buchanan, James M. "The Pure Theory of Government Finance: A Suggested Approach." *Journal of Political Economy* 57 (December 1949): 496–505.

————. "Individual Choice in Voting and the Market." *Journal of Political Economy* 62 (August 1954): 334–43.

————. "Social Choice, Democracy, and Free Markets." *Journal of Political Economy* 62 (April 1954): 114–23.

————. *Public Principles of Public Debt*. Homewood, IL: Richard D. Irwin, 1958.

————. *Fiscal Theory and Political Economy*. Chapel Hill: University of North Carolina Press, 1960.

————. *Cost and Choice*. Chicago: University of Chicago Press, 1969.

————. *The Limits of Liberty*. Chicago: University of Chicago Press, 1975.

————. *Freedom in Constitutional Contract*. College Station: Texas A&M University Press, 1977.

————. "Politics Without Romance: A Sketch of Positive Public Choice Theory and its Normative Implications." Inaugural lecture, Institute for Advanced Studies, Vienna, Austria. IHS Journal, Zeitschrift des Institus für Höhere Studien 3: B1-B11, 1979.

————. *The Economics and Ethics of Constitutional Order*. Ann Arbor: University of Michigan Press, 1991.

Buchanan, James M., and G. F. Thirlby, eds. *L.S.E. Essays on Cost*. London: London School of Economics, 1973.

Buchanan, James M., Robert D. Tollison, and Gordon Tullock, eds. *Towards a Theory of the Rent-Seeking Society*. College Station: Texas A&M University Press, 1980.

Buchanan, James M., and Gordon Tullock. *The Calculus of Consent*. Ann Arbor: University of Michigan Press, 1962.

Kelman, Steven. "Public Choice and Public Spirit." *Public Interest* 87 (1987): 93–94.

Krueger, Anne. "The Political Economy of the Rent-Seeking Society." *American Economic Review* 64 (June 1974): 291–303.

Mueller, Dennis. *Public Choice II*. Cambridge: Cambridge University Press, 1989.

Riker, William. *The Theory of Political Coalitions*. New Haven, CT: Yale University Press, 1962.

Romer, Thomas. "On James Buchanan's Contributions to Public Economics." *Journal of Economic Perspectives* 2, no. 1 (Fall 1988).

Sandmo, Agnar. "Buchanan on Political Economy: A Review Article." *Journal of Economic Literature*, 28, No. 1 (March 1990).

Tullock, Gordon. "Problems of Majority Voting." *Journal of Political Economy* 67 (December 1959) 571–79.

Vanbert, Viktor. "J. M. Buchanan and F. A. Hayek: The Thought of Two Nobel Larureates." Reprinted in *The Market Process: Essays in Contemporary Austrian Economics*, edited by Peter J. Boettke and David L. Prychitko. Aldershot, UK: Edward Elgar Publishing, 1994.

Chapter 20

Robert Nozick's Libertarian Framework for Utopias

Moral philosophy sets the background for, and the boundaries of, political philosophy. What persons may or may not do to one another limits what they may do through the apparatus of a state, or do to establish such an apparatus. The moral prohibitions it is permissible to enforce are the source of whatever legitimacy the state's fundamental coercive power has.

—Robert Nozick

Harvard professor Robert Nozick (1938-2002) was a staunch critic of his colleague John Rawls's egalitarian political philosophy, which held that it was proper for the state to redistribute wealth to help the disadvantaged and the poor. Nozick's premises, thesis, and conclusion in his 1974 book, *Anarchy, State, and Utopia* are very different from those reached by Rawls in his 1971 work, *Theory of Justice.* Nozick concludes that the welfare state was a type of theft and that taxation was equivalent to forced labor. Part one of *Anarchy, State, and Utopia* was dedicated to Nozick's attempt to justify the state and to devalue anarchy. In part two he demonstrates how nothing more extensive than a minimal state can arise without the violation of individual rights. Then in part three he explains how the minimal state can provide a meta-utopian framework for voluntary associations, communities, and utopian experiments.

Nozick's Argument for the Minimal State

Nozick gravitated toward the use of reason and rational analysis in the formulation of his social conclusions. His arguments are not influenced by customs, traditions, and historical accounts of social evolution. Nozick's rationalistic deductions lead to the notion of the spontaneous origin of the state. Although he did not maintain that the state literally came about spontaneously, he argues that it could have emerged inevitably.

Nozick vaguely uses state of nature theory as his point of departure. He explains that in a state of nature a person may enforce his own rights, defend himself, exact retribution, and punish. He sees these rights as boundaries that circumscribe an area of moral space around an individual. His argumentation is limited, however, due to his failure to precisely explain from where rights originate. Nozick's rights-based approach rests on Kantian intuitions and the Kantian categorical imperative regarding the treatment of persons as ends and not merely as means. He is a Kantian intuitionist with no grounded theory of rights. For Nozick, rights are emotionally intuited with no basis in natural law.

Nozick wants to demonstrate how a state would arise from anarchy through a process involving no morally impermissible actions. He wants to judge the possibility of evolving a state or "state-like entity" without violating individual rights. He asks if, and how, the voluntary assent of rational individuals can lead to an entity resembling the state.

In Nozick's hypothetical anarcho-capitalist society, individuals could subscribe to private protection agencies which could provide protective services in the market. He endeavors to demonstrate that a minimal state could develop from an open market where the existence of a large group of private defense agencies could lead to a monopoly provider whose sole legitimate function would be the protection of individual rights. The only morally defensible state would be one restricted to the functions of adjudication and defense against force and fraud.

Assuming that people have the right to liberty, Nozick deduced the type of society that he thought would emerge. All individuals have the right to self-defense and to property defense. These rights are included in the idea of individual rights itself. Individuals have a right to protect themselves and may also delegate this right to others. Within the state of nature, people could solve their self-defense problem through voluntary arrangements and agreements. For example, by banding together in a mutual protection association, individuals could combine their power and agree to help fellow members defend against and punish rights violators. Members of a protective agency would agree to protect one another from aggressors. Protection could become a commodity sold by competing associations or firms. People could join and pay dues or fees to private protection associations. They would find it efficient to pay agents to protect them. A protective association specializing in the defense of its clients would possess the sum of the rights delegated to it by those customers.

Protective services are unique due to the fact that they use coercion. Nozick assumes that each protective agency would require each of its customers to abdicate the right of private retribution against aggressors.

Nozick goes on to discuss what would occur when there is a conflict between customers of different agencies which have arrived at incompatible decisions. Protective agencies could be in discord in defending their respective clients. One possible result is war between the protective agencies. Disputes between customers of different agencies could involve physical battle between the providers. On the other hand, the agencies could agree in advance on a private appeals court or arbitration process to settle disputes.

Some of the competing protective agencies would be better or stronger than others. In time, one dominant protective agency would eliminate or incorporate its competition and emerge as the single protective agency in given geographical region. There would be a sole protection agency or a group of associations bound together in a federation. This dominant group or federation would be a self-defense league that has a monopoly on the use of violence in a specific territory. This monopoly (or near monopoly) could result through the defeat of rivals or through agreements to resolve cases when the agencies reach different decisions. Although different agencies may exist there would be one unique federal judicial system in which they are all members.

Nozick claims that there will emerge one dominant protective agency in each territory in which "almost all" the individuals in that area are included. At this point there may still be more independents who have chosen to enforce their own rights rather than to purchase the protective services of the dominant agency. Here Nozick says that we have an "ultraminimal state" that provides enforcement and protection service only to those who buy its service. Individuals will still be free to enforce private justice in an ultraminimal state.

The State as the Dominant Protective Agency

So far, Nozick has not yet derived the "minimal state" since there may be some individuals (i.e., independents) who are not protected by it. In order to arrive at the minimal state the independents must be absorbed into the dominant protective agency. Nozick contends that the ultraminimal state is unjust because it does not protect everyone's rights. His problem is to transform the ultraminimal state into the minimal state without violating anyone's rights, including those of the proprietors of the agencies eliminated from the market and those of their customers. Nozick's attempt to justify how an ultraminimal state developed within the natural social order can be transformed into a minimal state without violating individual rights has been viewed by some critics as flawed, unconvincing, and unsuccessful.

Nozick begins his explanation of how the ultraminimal state can be converted into the minimal state by observing that each person has a right to be judged according to the procedures which minimize the chance of his property rights being infringed. He goes on to say that each individual has the procedural right to have his guilt ascertained by the least dangerous of the known procedures for determining guilt. Such a procedure would be the one with the lowest probability of finding an innocent man guilty. Nozick contends that customers will not settle for less than the most reliable procedures pertaining to the apprehension, trial, and punishment of criminals.

According to Nozick, the dominant association would have the right to prohibit its competition and noncustomers from using risky and unreliable procedures. In other words, Nozick claims that the dominant agency has the right to prohibit risky procedures against its client. The near-monopoly agency's right to forbid these risky procedures is said to derive directly from a person's prelegal, procedural rights which Nozick assumes to exist in very much the same manner as property rights exist.

Nozick contends that rights enforcement by independents yields a dangerous risk of unjust punishment of the dominant association's patrons because of the independents' lack of impartial and reliable judicial procedures for determining guilt and appropriate punishment. Therefore, to protect its customers, the dominant protective agency may prohibit the independents from self-help enforcement or from hiring their own protective service.

Nozick argues that the independents must be compensated for having specific risky procedures and activities prohibited to them. His "principle of compensation" states that the risky procedures may be banned given that those who are forbidden to perform those actions are justly compensated for the forceful deprivation of their rights to engage in these activities.

The dominant protective agency deprives noncustomers of their rights to enforce justice themselves when they believe their rights have been violated. It follows that the customers of the dominant agency must compensate the independents for forcibly denying them their natural rights to punish violators of those rights. According to Nozick, if in defense of his procedural rights, a person deprives another of the means of protecting his natural rights, he must compensate that individual adequately to allow him to re-acquire those means. In other words, the dominant protective agency is viewed by Nozick as acting morally and properly as long as it compensates the independents sufficiently to buy protection from it without incurring extra costs. What Nozick is saying is that an agency may violate individual rights and in so doing creates a state if it compensates the person whose rights are violated for their losses.

To compensate for the infringement of the right of self-protection, the monopoly agency will extend their protective coverage to those who are not its customers. Nozick sees this as the most practical way of compensating the independents who have been prohibited from defending themselves. He contends that, in so doing, the dominant agency provides a service to all because it reduces the risk of dealing with other less able agencies. The dominant agency provides the independents and customers of other agencies with protection services which are more efficiently and effectively produced. Nozick states that the ultraminimal state is morally obligated to extend protection to those in its realm of dominance who have not chosen to be members of the ultraminimal state.

Nozick believes that his argument justifies the minimal state and that anything beyond the minimal state violates natural rights. He has argued that a minimal state could arise without violating anyone's rights. Any more extensive state could employ force to finance and promote services that some people will not want.

Many individuals who have read Nozick's work are bewildered by his claim that his minimal state could arise without any rights violation. They observe that the property rights of the customers of the competitors of the dominant agency are violated by being prohibited from using their resources in order to buy protection from the agency of their own choosing. They contend that free exchange has been stifled, that the right to contract has been restricted, that the independents' right to self-defense has been violated, and that the independents have not been treated as ends. Nozick is not convincing in his attempts to explain why it is permissible for a protection agency, in its efforts to achieve procedural fairness for its clients, to use force to keep others from engaging in risky activities so long as it provides compensation to those whose rights have been violated. Nozick's critics view his minimal state as merely a protection racket that has forced protection on its customers.

Nozick goes on to provide a persuasive and comprehensive case against Rawlsian justice by arguing for a theory based on the principle that all human beings have absolute rights to their person and to the fruits of their labor. Nozick compares and contrasts two systems of justice: (1) his own entitlement theory which is based on the historical process of acquiring and transferring resources and, (2) end-state or time-slice theory which is based on the current distribution of resources. Rawls's difference principle is of the latter type.

John Rawls's Theory of Blind "Justice"

In the Constitution, equality was not equated with justice. The framers believed that justice exists when all interactions among people are based on voluntary exchange. To them, it was the process of interactions, not the outcomes, which mattered. Today, however, a new idea of justice (often called social justice) equates justice with equality. This view is used to call for a process of enforced equalization and to make envy an acceptable emotion. Under this new concept of justice, an individual is free to exercise his rights as long as such exercise does not violate state-created superior or equal rights of others or the common good as defined by the state. The demand for equality, if fully recognized and implemented, would mean the end of a free society and would result in treating people unequally because the state would have to treat individuals differently in order to make up for their excess or deficiency of ability, motivation, and other attributes. The notion of social justice is used to foster social reform through state intervention and economic planning, devices which require the sacrifice of the moral ideas of individual freedom, individual responsibility, and voluntary cooperation.

The most widely discussed theory of distributive justice, during the past three decades, has been proposed by Harvard professor John Rawls. In lieu of the concept of the state of nature, Rawls introduced the methodological concept of an "original position," a hypothetical and counterfactual condition which requires us to visualize the negotiators of the basic terms of political association conducting their negotiations behind a "veil of ignorance" while having no knowledge of their individual life conditions, including their talents, intelligence, sex, race, class, religion, wealth, conception of the good, etc. Rawls's veil of ignorance blinds those in the original position to all the specific natural contingencies and social accidents that make up their particular identities except to the contingency that they are all beings with specific worldly identities who have particular, but unknown, traits and goals to which freedom, opportunity, and income are means. According to Rawls, to be fair in selecting the principles of justice, the possibility of bias must be removed. Fairness in Rawls's theory requires the more favored to agree to the type of distributive rule they would prefer if they were not more favored.

Rawls thus argues that the principles that should govern the basic structure of a just or well-ordered society are principles that would be selected by rational individuals in specially constructed, imaginary circumstances called the original position. For Rawls, a society is well ordered when (1) its members know and agree to the same principles of social justice, and (2) the basic institutions of society generally satisfy and are widely known to satisfy these principles. Rawls argues that if we are to justify the use of the coercive power of the state over individuals, it ought to be in terms of reasons that all can accept or should accept.

Rawls proposes that benighted persons in an original position will or should agree that all social primary goods (e.g., basic liberties such as political freedom and freedom of choice in occupations, opportunity, income, wealth, and the bases of self-respect) are to be distributed equally unless an unequal distribution of any or all of these goods is to the advantage of the least favored. Rawls thus depicts justice as an issue of fairness, focusing on the distribution of resources, and permitting an unequal distribution only to the extent that the weakest members of society benefit from that inequality. To Rawls, this justifies the coercive limitation of unjust resources and therefore redistribution where it would improve the situation of the disadvantaged. For Rawls, even if an inequality does not harm the least well off, it is unjust if it leaves them no better off than before. This emphasizes a redistributionist type of justice and a defeasible presumption in favor of equality in the distribution of primary goods such as wealth and income. Rawls's assumption that equality is desirable puts the burden of justification on those who support some type of inequality.

According to Rawls's difference principle, an inequality can be advantageous to the person who gets the smaller share because inequalities can constitute incentives which increase the size of the pie to be shared, so that the smaller piece may be larger in absolute terms than an equal share of the smaller pie that would have existed in the absence of such incentives. The difference principle collapses to strict equality under conditions where differences in income and other rewards have no effect on the incentives of individuals. However, in the real world currently and in the foreseeable future, greater rewards bring forth greater productive effort, thus increasing the total wealth of the economy and, under the difference principle, the wealth of the least advantaged.

A practical implication of the difference principle is that society must redistribute income up to the point where the wealth of the representative poorest individual (an abstraction) is maximized. In other words, "society" should tax and redistribute the wealth of the more advantaged up to the point where their incentives to produce more disappear.

Rawls recognizes that by allowing at least some greater level of rewards to accrue to the skilled and motivated, the poor will be better off than they would have been with a totally equal distribution of income. He also realizes that redistribution cannot go as far as his ethical preference for equality would recommend without making everyone (including the poor) worse off. At some point, impairing individuals' economic incentives would reduce the total wealth in society.

Rawls argues for inheritance taxes on the basis that an unregulated transfer of wealth from people to their children would result in the entrenchment of wealth in particular segments of society. According to Rawls, individuals who are not fortunate enough to have wealthy parents do not merit worse starting points and, consequently, worse life prospects than those who were so fortunate. Ignoring the right that people have to bequeath wealth to whomever they want, Rawls contends that society should equalize the prospects of the least well off by taxing the undeserved inherited gain of children of rich persons, and using the tax proceeds to aid the least well off.

Rawls describes his theory as political rather than metaphysical—it is political in the sense that it does not depend on any of the metaphysical assumptions that are disputed among reasonable citizens in a pluralistic society. Rawls argues that democracy is required by justice, because as a procedure it complies with the tenets of justice in that it assigns everyone equal and extensive rights and liberties and because of its propensity to produce just results. For Rawls, the function of justice is to ensure that disagreements are resolved on the basis of prior agreement instead of through force. Thus, even if there are disagreements about the justice of particular laws and policies, there should minimally be agreement with respect to the procedures used to resolve these conflicts. Rawls renounces what he refers to as liberal equality (i.e., political equality and a market economy tempered by interventionist government efforts aimed at furthering equality of opportunity). He finds liberal equality insufficient because it seeks to ameliorate only those inequalities stemming from differences in social and historical circumstances, thereby permitting real differences in individual ability and effort to emerge as the causes of economic success. Rawls believes there is no more good reason to allow the distribution of wealth and income to be determined by the possession of natural endowments than by social and historical factors. Rawls contends that individuals do not deserve the genetic assets they are born with. He explains that, from a moral perspective, the level of effort people are willing to put forth is, to a great extent, influenced by their natural endowments. Consequently, those who are more productive due to their greater natural abilities have no moral right to greater rewards, because the abilities and motivation that make up their work cannot be morally considered to be their own. In effect, Rawls's difference principle is an agreement to consider the distribution of natural talents as a common asset and to share in the fruits of this distribution, no matter what it ends up being. In this view an individual's natural endowments are not considered to be his own property, but rather the property of society.

Rawls contends that underserved inequalities call for redress in order to produce genuine (i.e., fair) equality of opportunity instead of procedural (i.e., formal) equality of opportunity. Rather than having all play by the same rules or being judged by the same standards, Rawls wants to provide everyone with equal prospects of success from equal individual efforts. Rawls's idea of fairness requires that the state have the power to control outcomes and to supercede the preferences of individual citizens.

What makes Rawls's idea of justice so important is that he systematically expresses a vision that had already underpinned a great deal of social policy, legal theory, and even international relations. The goal of Rawls's conception of justice is to put certain segments of society in the position that they would have been in except for some undeserved and unfortunate circumstances.

Rawls focuses on how goods are distributed among persons "representative" of various positions in society, but ignores which individuals have which goods and how they gained possession of them. Critics of Rawls argue that people hold an entitlement to what they produce or have legitimately acquired and therefore should be protected from Rawls's proposed redistributionist policies. They hold that the difference principle involves unacceptable infringements on liberty in that redistributive taxation to the poor requires the immoral takings of just holdings. Rawls's opponents contend that whether a given income or wealth distribution is just or unjust depends solely on the manner in which that distribution came about, not on the pattern of the distribution itself.

Another criticism is that fairness is not the proper standard of justice—the world is inherently unfair and thus "unjust." Nature does not produce a state of equality. No two people possess the same mental or physical attributes—some are smarter, more talented, better looking, etc. People have the free will to either use or not use the talents that nature has endowed them with. It follows that economic equality is a goal that is incompatible with nature. True justice is attained when people's lives and property are secure and they are free to own property, order its direction, determine the purpose to which their bodies are put, engage in consensual transactions and relationships with others, and freely pursue their conception of happiness.

Rawls also fails to recognize that talents are not a common pool. The aptitudes that one person enjoys in no way lessens the number and magnitude of abilities that are available to another. My talent is not acquired at your expense. Rawls is rebelling against reality, nature, and the existence of human talent. A natural fact, such as the existence of one's talents, is neither just nor unjust—it just is. So why should those "favored by nature" be made to pay for what is not a moral problem or an injustice and is not of his or her own making?

Finally, Rawls's theory can be challenged on the grounds that he is confusing justice with prudence—the virtue of advancing one's own well-being. To be prudent is to apply intelligence to changing circumstances. Rawls's maxi-min strategy appears to be a rational construction of prudence rather than of justice. A prudent man in the "original position" might choose a social structure under which he would be "least worse off" if things went badly for him. Such a choice could be called prudent, but certainly not just.

Nozick's Entitlement Theory of Justice

Nozick's entitlement theory holds that a distribution is just if it results through just acquisition from the state of nature or through voluntary transfer via trade, gift, or bequest from a prior just distribution. Nozick proposes that: (1) a person who acquires a holding in accordance with the principle of justice in acquisition is entitled to that holding; (2) a person who acquires a holding in accordance with the principle of justice in transfer, from someone else entitled to the holding, is entitled to the holding; and (3) no one is entitled to a holding except by (repeated) application of 1 and 2.

The principle of justice in acquisition states that an acquisition is just if the item is previously unowned and the acquisition leaves enough to meet the needs of others. The principle of justice in transfer is meant to protect voluntary contracts while ruling out theft, fraud, and so on. In other words, a holding is just if it has been acquired through a legitimate transfer from someone who acquired it through a legitimate transfer or through original acquisition. Nozick also proposed the principle of rectification of injustice in holdings. Although difficult to accomplish in some cases, an honest effort must be made to identify the origins of illegitimate holdings and to remedy the situation by compensating the victims of theft, fraud, and intimidation.

Nozick takes his lead from the Lockean notion that each person owns himself and that by mixing one's labor with the material world, one can establish ownership of a portion of the material world. Nozick explains that what is significant about mixing one's labor with the material world is that in so doing a person tends to increase the value of a portion of the external world. He reasons that in such instances, self-ownership can bring about ownership of a part of the physical world. According to Nozick, the Lockean Proviso means: (1) that previously unowned property becomes owned by anyone who improves it; (2) that an acquisition is just if and only if the position of others after the acquisition is no worse than their position was when the acquisition was unowned or owned in common.

For Nozick, the right not to have others interfere in one's life is fundamental—any coercion is illegitimate. Persons are viewed as having natural rights which are prior to society and which must be respected if we are to treat individuals as ends in themselves and not merely means in the endeavors of others. Kant's categorical imperative provides a foundation for Nozick's principle of transfer. Individuals should be treated as ends and never simply as means. A person's autonomy should always be respected. Only the individual person can legitimately decide what to do with his talents, abilities, and the products of his talents and abilities.

Nozick's idea of process equality means equal treatment before the law. The U.S. Constitution reflects this view in its due process and equal protection clauses. According to this perspective, all individuals should be identically subject to universal rules of just conduct and the state should not grant special privileges or impose special burdens upon any individual or group of individuals.

Nozick refers to the contrary view of equality as end-state equality. From this perspective equality among people is increased when the differences between their incomes, level of wealth, or standards of living are decreased. The second idea of equality is incompatible with the first. When the state interferes with the process of voluntary exchange to bring about more equality in the end-state sense, the state must treat individuals with unequal voluntary exchange outcomes unequally. In other words, the state would discriminate against those with better voluntary exchange outcomes in favor of those with worse voluntary exchange outcomes.

The process and end-state (i.e., distributive) theories of justice are irreconcilable. Since people have unequal endowments, the free market will inevitably lead to unjust, in the second sense, results. This injustice can only be remedied by coercive transfers which are unjust in the first sense.

Nozick advocates a system in which the role of the government is limited to the protection of property rights. This view rules out taxation for purposes other than raising the money needed to protect property rights. Nozick explains that any taxation of the income from selling the products of exercising one's talents involves the forced partial ownership by others of people and their actions and work.

Nozick argues that if we can determine that a specific person is entitled to a specific piece of property, then it is apparent that people with such claims can justly transfer property to whomever they see fit, such as their spouses, children, favored charitable organizations, etc. As long as the transfer is voluntary, Nozick contends that there is no need for "society" to worry about how the representative least well off person is affected. It follows that inheritance taxes are not legitimate according to Nozick's theory.

Nozick's Framework for Utopias

Nozick's minimal state provides society with a utopian foundation—one that permits as many persons as possible to live as closely as possible to the ways in which they want to live. There is room for a pluralist utopia within the minimal state. Nozick's utopia is actually a meta-utopia in which people are free to voluntarily join together to pursue and try to actualize their own view of the good life. His ideal society contains a diverse and wide range of communities which people can freely belong to if they are voluntarily admitted by others. Within

Nozick's framework for utopia, it is possible to design and create your own utopia if you can convince a sufficient number of people to join you. Of course, in Nozick's minimal state no one can impose his own utopian views upon other people.

Nozick foresees that numerous and varied types of voluntary associations, utopian experiments, and life styles will concurrently flourish within his framework for utopia. Within these voluntary communities, people may make commitments to each other which exceed those that they have within the minimal state which itself could go no further than enforcing the most basic level of ethics required for peaceful cooperation. Voluntary associations may implement rules and regulations that the state would be unable to enforce. Participation in specific communities may be conditional upon designated requirements.

Nozick's *Anarchy, State, and Utopia* made libertarianism's views on the nature and legitimacy of the minimal state respectable in academic circles. Nozick revived the classical liberal tradition with his abstract, clever, and often obscure explanation of how a minimal state might arise legitimately in the form of an all-inclusive, rights-respecting protection agency. He was instrumental in creating the intellectual and philosophical foundation that has allowed the creation and flourishing of today's numerous libertarian organizations. Nozick did this by persuasively arguing that government should do not more than protect citizens from violence, theft, and breach of contract. He maintained that individuals blessed with talent, money, motivation, or other social advantages were morally entitled to enjoy them and to benefit from them.

Nozick was a reluctant philosopher of freedom who perhaps did not want to see his theory applied in the real world. He wrote very little on political philosophy since writing *Anarchy, State, and Utopia* and subsequently confessed that he saw his own libertarian theory as inadequate. Nevertheless, he did make an important and enduring contribution to the libertarian movement.

Recommended Reading

Barnett, Randy E. "Whither Anarchy? Has Robert Nozick Justified the State?" *Journal of Libertarian Studies* (Winter 1977).

Brueckner, Anthony. "Unfair to Nozick." *Analysis* 51 (1991): 61–64.

Capaldi, Nicholas. "Exploring the Limits of Analytic Philosophy: A Critique of Nozick's Philosophical Explanations." *Interpretation* 12 (1984): 107–25.

Childs, Roy "The Invisible Hand Strikes Back." *Journal of Libertarian Studies* (Winter 1977).

Cohen, G. A. "Robert Nozick and Wilt Chamberlain: How Patterns Preserve Liberty." In *Justice and Economic Distribution*, edited by J. Arthur and W.A. Shaw. Englewood Cliffs, NJ: Prentice Hall, 1978.

Coleman, James S. "Individual Rights and the State: A Review Essay." *American Journal of Sociology* (September 1976).

Corlett, J. A., ed. *Equality and Liberty: Analyzing Rawls and Nozick.* New York: McMillan, 1991.

Davidson, Dale. "Note on Anarchy, State and Utopia." *Journal of Libertarian Studies* (Fall 1977).

Den Uyl, Douglas, and Douglas B. Rasmussen. "Nozick on the Randian Argument." *The Personalist* 59 (1978): 184–205.

Exdell, J. "Distributive Justice: Nozick on Property Rights." *Ethics* 88 (1977).

Lacey, A. R. *Robert Nozick.* Princeton, NJ: Princeton University Press, 2001.

Lipson, Morris. "Nozick and the Skeptic." *Australasian Journal of Philosophy* 65 (1987): 327–34.

Luper-Foy, Steven, ed. *The Possibility of Knowledge: Nozick and His Critics.* Totowa, NJ: Rowman & Littlefield, 1987.

Machan, Tibor. "Nozick and Rand on Property Rights." *The Personalist* 58 (1977): 192–95.

Mack, Eric. "Nozick's Anarchism." Pp. 43–62 in *Anarchism*, edited by J. R. Pennock and J. W. Chapman. New York: New York University Press, 1978.

———. "The Self-Ownership Proviso: A New and Improved Lockean Proviso." *Social Philosophy and Policy* 12 (1995): 186–218.

Megone, Christoper. "Reasoning about Rationality: Robert Nozick, The Nature of Rationality." *Utilias* 11 (1999): 359–74.

Nozick, Robert. *Anarchy, State, and Utopia.* New York: Basic Books, 1974.

———. *Philosophical Explanations.* Cambridge, MA.: Belknap Press, 1981.

———. *The Examined Life: Philosophical Meditations.* Simon and Schuster, 1989.

———. *The Nature of Rationality.* Princeton, NJ: Princeton University Press, 1993.

———. *Socratic Puzzles.* Cambridge, MA: Harvard University Press, 1997.

———. *Invariances.* Cambridge, MA: Harvard University Press, 2001.

Paul, Jeffrey. "Nozick, Anarchism and Procedural Rights." *Journal of Libertarian Studies* (Fall 1977).

———, ed. *Reading Nozick: Essays on Anarchy, State and Utopia.* Totowa, NJ: Rowman & Littlefield, 1981.

———. "Property, Entitlement, and Remedy." *Monist* 73 (1990): 564–77.

Rothbard, Murray, N. "Robert Nozick and the Immaculate Conception of the State." *Journal of Libertarian Studies* (Fall 1977).

Sanders, John T. "The Free Market Model Versus Government: A Reply to Nozick." *Journal of Libertarian Studies* (Winter 1977).

Schmidtz, David, ed. *Robert Nozick.* Cambridge, MA: Cambridge University Press, 2002.

Wolff, Jonathan. *"Robert Nozick: Property, Justice and the Minimal State."* Oxford: Basil Blackwell, 1991.

Young, Fredric C. "Nozick and the Individualist Anarchist" *Journal of Libertarian Studies* (Winter 1986).

Chapter 21

Reality Is Not Optional: Thomas Sowell's Vision of Man and Society

The principles applied in economic processes are general social principles.

—Thomas Sowell

In his various writings, Thomas Sowell (1930-) has presented a unified theoretical perspective and potent intellectual framework for analyzing the social order. Sowell's systematic and systemic approach derives mainly from free-market economics, is methodological rather than philosophical or political, and is consistent with the views of intellectuals such as Adam Smith, Thomas Hobbes, Alexander Hamilton, Edmund Burke, Oliver Wendell Holmes, Friedrich Hayek, and Milton Friedman.

Sowell's tragic (or constrained) vision of man and society is based on the acceptance of the realities of the human condition—we are all limited by independent realities which we ignore to our own detriment. According to Sowell's vision: (1) Human nature is essentially unchanging and unchangeable—there have been no great changes in the fundamental intellectual and moral capacities of human beings; (2) Human capabilities are severely and inherently bounded for all—man is sharply restricted in his capacity for improvement and has only a very limited ability to affect his surroundings; (3) Life is inherently harsh and difficult—suffering and evil are inherent in the innate deficiencies of human beings; (4) Man is basically self-centered; however, things can be improved within that constraint by primarily relying on incentives (rewards and punishments) rather than on dispositions; (5) Resources are always inadequate to fulfill all of the desires of all of the people; (6) Social outcomes are a function of incentives presented to individuals and the conditions under which they interact in response to those incentives; (7) Given the moral limitations of man and his egocentricity, the fundamental moral challenge is to make the best of the possibilities within the constraints of man's nature; (8) There are no solutions, only trade-offs that leave many desires unfulfilled and much unhappiness in the world; (9) It is imperative to have the right processes for making trade-offs and correcting inevitable errors; and (10) It is better to cope incrementally with tragic dilemmas than to proceed categorically with moral imperatives—for amelioration of evils and for progress it is generally preferable to rely on systemic characteristics of social processes (such as moral traditions, the marketplace, the law, or families) rather than solutions proposed by government officials.

Knowledge and Decision Making

Sowell portrays society as a collection of interconnected and overlapping decision-makers who operate under the inherent constraint of scarcity and consequently face the necessity of dealing with trade-offs—some desirable options must be foregone in order to pursue others. The goal of decision-making processes is to optimize well-being subject to constraints of time, wisdom, and resources. No social value is categorically a good thing to have more of without limits—all are subject to diminishing returns and ultimately negative returns. A person needs to accept somewhat less of one thing in order to get somewhat more of another.

Information means specific things that a man needs to know in order to make decisions affecting his own well-being. The relevant question is which among a number of options will optimize the satisfaction of the decision-maker. A continuing flow of information about the relative costs and benefits of doing or choosing one thing or another is needed to answer this question. Such knowledge can be extremely costly and is often widely scattered in uneven fragments—the communication and coordination of these scattered fragments is one of the basic problems of society.

According to Sowell, the crucial systemic process is the market, with its continuing flow of signals which allows decision-makers to review a constantly changing mix of options and resulting trade-offs and respond in a fine-tuned fashion by making a series of incremental adjustments based on the information attained. If decisions are to be incremental and flexible, they are best made by economic institutions rather than by political, administrative, or judicial ones.

Any individual's personal knowledge is quite small compared to the organized systematic knowledge through which society functions. Sowell argues that only by viewing the economic, social, and political orders as systems can we understand the real role of knowledge in society. In order to cope with the constraint of inadequate personal knowledge, a variety of social institutions and processes coordinate innumerable scattered fragments of knowledge, enabling a complex society to function. These social arrangements can largely be understood as mechanisms for economizing on knowledge.

Decisions are best made through systemic processes that encourage each of us to act upon the limited information we possess while permitting others to respond freely to our initiatives just as we react to theirs. Social causation thus operates in systemic ways, with innumerable interactions producing results controlled by no one but falling into a pattern determined by the incentives and constraints inherent in the logic of the specific circumstances. Since no individual has complete information, knowledge in the entire system is sorted and coordinated in fragments by the simple process of each transactor seeking the best deal from his own perspective. As a result, multiple individual choices, determined by immediate and narrow considerations, produce unintended consequences that are socially beneficial in the aggregate.

Sowell explains that better decisions are made through the market process as opposed to the political process because markets economize on the knowledge needed by any one person to make good decisions and because they convey a sharper sense of constraints, trade-offs, and incentives (rewards and penalties). In addition, people can generally make a better choice out of numerous options than by following a single prescribed process. Another virtue of the market is the promptness and effectiveness with which it transmits feedback, thus enabling decision-makers to correct errors and adapt to changing conditions. Feedback mechanisms (including incentives to act on that information) are critical in a world in which no decision-maker is likely to have enough knowledge to be consistently right the first time in his decisions. There is an independent reality which each person sees only imperfectly, but which can be understood more fully with feedback that can validate or change what was previously believed. Effective feedback is the implicit transmission of others' knowledge in the explicit form of effective incentives to the recipient.

Nobody needs to have complete information in order for the economy to convey relevant information through prices and achieve the same adjustments as if everyone had such knowledge. Prices are a mechanism for carrying out the rationing function and are a fast and effective conveyor of information through a society in which fragmented knowledge must be coordinated. Accurate prices resulting from voluntary exchanges allow the economy to achieve optimal performance in terms of satisfying each person as much as he can be satisfied by his own standards without sacrificing others' rights to act according to their own respective standards. Prices maintained by force convey misinformation. Regulatory measures such a price-fixing obscure the true cost of a course of action compared to its alternatives, inhibit the feedback that permits transactors to communicate, and create distortions that harm rather than help consumers.

The Superiority of Systemic Rationality

According to Sowell, knowledge consists largely of the unarticulated experiences and rationality of the many as embedded in customs, traditions, and systemic processes such as the market, family, language, and law. Knowledge is a multiplicity of social experiences distilled over generations in cultural processes.

Sowell argues that systemic rationality is superior to individual intentional rationality. Even the most outstanding individuals are very limited—man lacks the moral and intellectual prerequisites for deliberate comprehensive planning. The inherent constraints of human beings are sufficiently severe to preclude dependence on individual articulated rationality. Sowell is highly skeptical about the capacity of elites to master complexity and to choose on behalf of others. Not only are the elite and the ordinary person close in capability and morality, there are no uniquely correct answers that would justify transferring decision-making authority to elite surrogate decision makers. There are no solutions only trade-offs, with respect to problems such as crime, poverty, and irresponsibility. As a result, the preferred decision-making mechanism is systemic processes that convey the experiences and revealed preferences of the many. The historic systemic wisdom expressed inarticulately in the culture of the many is more likely to be correct than the special insight of the few. The degree of social rationality does not depend on the degree of individual rationality. The relevant comparison is between that total direct knowledge brought to bear through social processes versus the secondhand knowledge of generalities possessed by a smaller elite group.

Sowell puts his hopes for social order in sturdy institutions—he does not look for unsupported benevolence for society to progress or for solutions to social problems. To the extent that he envisions social changes, he thinks in terms of trade-offs rather than solutions. Trade-offs must be incremental rather than categorical if limited resources are to produce optimal results in any social system as a whole. Results depend on the kinds of social processes at work and the incentives, constraints, and modes of interaction generated by such processes. Incentives may be positive or negative (rewards or penalties) and may be structured so there are gradations corresponding to different kinds of results.

Systemic causation in the form of legal traditions, family ties, social customs, price changes, etc., creates an unintended order which arises as a consequence of individual interactions directed toward various and conflicting ends. These social processes are to be judged by their ability to extract the most social benefit from man's limited potentialities at the lowest cost. The world is a system of innumerable and reciprocal interactions constrained within the confines of natural and human limitations—individual problems cannot be solved one by one without creating or adding to problems in other areas.

Sowell takes evils for granted as inherent in human nature and seeks to discover contrivances by which they can be contained. He seeks the special causes of peace, wealth, and a law-abiding order rather than the causes of war, poverty, and crime. Since war is a rational activity engaged in by most nations whenever they have a prospect of gaining anything by it, the goal should be to raise the costs of war to potential aggressors through the threat of force (i.e., by military preparedness and military alliances). Since war originates in human nature, peace (not war) requires explanation and specific provisions to produce it. In addition, with respect to Third World countries, we need to explain the causes of prosperity and development (not the causes of the natural condition of poverty) through responsiveness to systemic economic incentives. Likewise, counterincentives such as moral training, social pressure, and punishment must be created and maintained in order to prevent or deter crime since incentives to commit crimes are commonplace.

A man has insufficient personal knowledge to rely on reason alone when making decisions. Rational decision-making has costs in terms of time and other resources—the cost of a decision is the cost of the process of deciding. Sowell explains that rational principles themselves suggest a limit to how much rational calculation to engage in. Trade-offs apply to the decision-making mechanism itself. For example, the sorting and labeling of people, activities, and things involves a trade-off of costs and benefits—the more finely tuned the sorting, the greater the benefits and the costs. Beyond some point, finer categories would not be worth the additional cost for the particular decision-making purpose. Also, culture offers a way of economizing on deliberate decision-making by providing a wide range of beliefs, attitudes, values, preferences, traditions, and customs (whose authentication has been historical and consensual) as low-cost inputs into the decision-making process as long as there is freedom for the individual to choose whether prospective incremental improvements in the particular decision are worth the additional cost of more rational calculation. These and other social arrangements such as firms, legal traditions, family ties, churches, politics, ideology, voluntary associations, the expert, etc., can be viewed as devices for economizing on knowledge.

Informal relationships such as personal ties within families and communities are able to acquire much knowledge at lower cost than formal organizations, generally able to apply it in more individualized fashion, and are less likely to adopt previously made decisions as precedents. Informal social processes can adjust the time, scope, and specialness of treatment of the pertinent characteristics of each individual and each episode. Social processes which rely on emotional ties and social penalties such as guilt, fear, shame, or stigma facilitate mutual accommodation without the use of force and avoid the inefficiencies of force as a social mechanism. Sowell explains that informal relationships or decision-making processes are generally preferable but are not categorically superior to more formal relationships or processes. There must be some discernible benefits peculiar to particular more structured relationships and precedental decisions that can be shown to be greater than the benefits of the corresponding informal decision processes. The apportionment of decision-making between informal and formal processes involves a trade-off of flexibility for security.

Freedom and Other Process Characteristics

One of the most important trade-offs is between the amount of freedom and the amount of other characteristics desired in a society such as material goods, scientific progress, or military power. For Sowell, freedom is a process characteristic referring to a social relationship among people—exemption from the arbitrary power of others but not release from the restrictions of circumstances.

Power is exerted to the extent that someone's pre-existing set of options is reduced—it is not an exercise of power to offer a quid pro quo that adds to his existing options. Sowell explains that using political power to deal with economic processes reduces freedom. He argues that efforts to produce social benefits must focus on general processes and on power restrictions, meaning restricting the ability of some to reduce the options of others. The most that man can do for freedom through social processes is to establish widely known rules which limit how much power is granted to one person over another and limit the specific conditions under which the power holder is authorized to exercise it.

According to Sowell, rights are rigidities and boundaries that limit the exercise of government power and carve out areas within which individual discretion is free to shape decisions without being second-guessed by political or legal authorities. Rights involve the legal ability of people to carry out certain processes without regard to the desirability of the particular results, as judged by others. Although rights belong to individuals, they originate, take their meaning, and find their limits in the needs of social processes. Political and legal institutions protect the rigidities people want in some areas of their life such as exemption from force or fraud as exemplified in laws on murder, kidnapping, property ownership, etc. The social benefits of property rights are that they present an economic process with greater efficiency, a social process with less strife, and a political process with more diffused power and influence. When general rights (such as those listed above) involve virtually universal desires, incorporating them into law eliminates the transaction cost of pointlessly litigating anew. In addition, peace of mind and a sense of independence and dignity are benefits from operating under known rules applicable to all, rather than being personally assessed and controlled by other individuals. Political and legal systems should be limited to areas in which they have a relative advantage in decision-making processes (such as reliability).

According to Sowell, rights can also mean legal entitlements regardless of their moral merits. In this sense, rights are simply factual claims about the availability of state power to back up individual claims. Social trade-offs are involved in the creation of rights, which includes a loss of flexibility—something that is incrementally preferable at a given point becomes categorically imposed at all points by the force at the disposal of the state.

For Sowell, equality is a process characteristic—a social process which ensures equal treatment represents equality whether or not the actual results are equal. Equality is the equalization of processes. As long as the process itself judges everyone by the same criteria, there is equality of opportunity. There would be a major conflict between allowing freedom of individual action and prescribing equality of social results.

The argument is not that it is literally impossible to reduce or eliminate specific instances of inequality, but that the very processes created to do so generate other inequalities, including inequalities of power caused by expanding the role of the state. Equal results may be attainable only by causing processes to operate very unequally toward different individuals or groups. Attempts to equalize economic power lead to greater and more dangerous inequality in political power. Social results such as differences in income are not deemed sufficiently important to override the process goals of freedom of civil and economic action.

Justice means adherence to agreed upon rules, the violation of which deranges the expectations of others and adversely changes their future conduct as they lose confidence in the general reliability of existing and future rules and agreements. Justice derives its importance from the need to preserve society through the provision of general principles. Sowell explains that men will suffer more by a breakdown of order than by some injustices. What is involved is a trade-off between individual justice and the social benefits of certainty. Judicial activism would derange the whole process. A better verdict may be reached in a specific case but at the cost of damaging the consistency and predictability of the law. There cannot be a law-abiding society if no one knows in advance what laws they are to obey but must wait for judges to create ex post facto legal rulings based on evolving standards rather than known rules. The losses of poorer judicial decisions are offset against the prospective guidance of known rules leading to fewer criminal law violations or needs for civil litigation. General stability of expectations and standards are more important than the particular benefits of wisdom and virtue. A judge should therefore apply the rules even if in the specific instance the known consequences will appear to be undesirable.

Law exists to preserve society. It follows that criminal justice is concerned with deterring crime, not with finely adjusting punishments to the individual. Sowell explains that law represents the evolved and codified experience of all men who have ever lived—it is the experience of the many, rather than the wisdom of the few.

Sowell contends that the best processes should be used and protected because the attempt to produce the best results directly is beyond human capacity. It is our bounded rationality that makes general rules of social processes necessary. However, adopting a systemic view does not entirely exclude the individual factor.

For Sowell, individualism means leaving the individual free to choose among systemically generated opportunities, rewards, and penalties. Each individual's best contribution to society is to adhere to the special duties of his institutional role. What is morally central is fidelity to duty in one's role in life. In carrying out defined roles the individual is relying on the experiential capital and unarticulated historical experience of the ages. For example, a businessman should promote stockholders' interest rather than attempt to improve society and a judge should carry out the law, not try to change it. Specialization is highly desirable. There is a superiority of experts within a narrow slice of understanding. Practically every individual has some advantage over all others because he possesses unique talents, resources, and information. What is denied is that expertise confers a general superiority which should supersede more widely dispersed types of knowledge.

Recommended Reading

Sowell, Thomas. "Karl Marx and the Freedom of the Individual." *Ethics* (January 1963): 119–26.

———. "Marxian Value Reconsidered." *Economica* (August 1963): 297–308.

———. *Say's Law: A Historical Analysis.* Princeton, NJ: Princeton University Press, 1972.

———. "Economics and Economic Man." In *The Americans: 1976* II: 191–209, edited by Irving Kristol and Paul H. Weaver. Lanham, MD: Lexington Books, 1976.

———. *Classical Economics Revisited.* Princeton, NJ: Princeton University Press, 1977.

———. "Adam Smith in Theory and Practice." Pp. 3–18 in *Adam Smith and Modern Political Economy*, edited by G. P. O'Driscoll, 1979.

———. *Knowledge and Decisions.* New York: Basic Books, 1980.

———. *Ethnic America: A History.* New York: Basic Books, 1981.

———. *The Economics and Politics of Race: An International Perspective.* New York: William Morrow Press, 1983.

———. "The Economics of the Bishops' Letter." *St. Louis University Public Law Review* (1986): 297–308.

———. *Marxism: Philosophy and Economics.* Acton, MA: Quill Press, 1986.

———. *A Conflict of Visions.* New York: William Morrow Press, 1987.

———. "Jean-Baptiste Say." In *The New Palgrave: A Dictionary of Economics* 4, no. 249, edited by John Eatwell et al. New York: Palgrave Macmillan, 1987.

———. "Democracy and the Market." *The World & I* (February 1988): 667–74.

———. *Is Reality Optional?* Stanford, CA: Hoover Institution Press, 1993.

———. "A Student's Eye View of George Stigler." *Journal of Political Economy* (October 1993): 784–92.

———. "Culture, Economics, and Politics." In *The Cultural Context of Economics and Politics*, edited by T. W. Boxx and G. M. Quinlivan. Lanham, MD: University Press of America, 1994.

———. *Race and Culture: A World View.* New York: Basic Books, 1994.

———. *The Vision of the Anointed.* New York: Basic Books, 1995.

———. *Migrations and Cultures: A World View.* New York: Basic Books, 1996.

———. *Conquests and Cultures.* New York: Basic Books, 1998.

———. *Barbarians Inside the Gates.* Stanford, CA: Hoover Institution Press, 1999.

———. *The Quest for Cosmic Justice.* New York: Free Press, 1999.

———. *Applied Economics: Thinking Beyond Stage One.* New York: Basic Books, 2003.

———. *Basic Economics: A Citizen's Guide to the Economy.* Revised and expanded. New York: Basic Books, 2004.

———. *On Classical Economics.* New Haven, CT: Yale University Press, 2006.

Chapter 22

Michael Novak's
Vision of Democratic Capitalism

Democratic capitalism is not just a system but a way of life. Its ethos includes a special evolution of pluralism; respect for contingency and unintended consequences; a sense of sin; and a new and distinctive conception of community, the individual, and the family.

—Michael Novak

Michael Novak (1933-), the preeminent Roman Catholic social theorist of our time, is the prolific author of numerous monographs, articles, and reviews, and has written over thirty influential books in philosophy, theology, political economy, and culture. He holds the George Frederick Jewett Chair in Religion, Philosophy, and Public Policy at the American Enterprise Institute in Washington, D.C., where he also serves as Director of Social and Political Studies.

Novak's achievement lies in his construction of a theory of democratic capitalism based on clear thinking about the world. He has identified and analyzed the underlying ideas that make our system of democratic capitalism meaningful. Although virtually all of his writings contribute to the portrait he has painted of democratic capitalism, four books in particular have made his case especially well. These are *The Spirit of Democratic Capitalism, Free Persons and the Common Good, This Hemisphere of Liberty*, and *The Catholic Ethic and the Spirit of Capitalism*.

The Spirit of Democratic Capitalism

This well-documented, thoughtful, and scholarly work is a classic in the field of political and economic philosophy. Novak's purposes in writing this book were:

(1) to defend democratic capitalism from the utopian challenge of socialism; (2) to demonstrate that democratic capitalism's principles are not only practical, but that, even in the abstract, they are superior to the socialist vision; (3) to provide a theoretical framework for democratic capitalism; (4) to persuade theologians and others that the values of democratic capitalism are not only consistent with, but supportive of, those of Christianity; and (5) to begin the construction of a theology of capitalism.

Novak envisions democratic capitalism as a trinity of systems in one—an economy based predominantly on markets and incentives, a democratic polity, and a moral-cultural system that is pluralistic and liberal. The free-market system fosters economic growth, social mobility, and self-reliance. Political liberty introduces pluralism, democracy, and the idea of a constitutional government. The moral-cultural system is buttressed by the mediating structures of family, church, and other voluntary associations. Novak's method is to move through a set of themes (pluralism, emergent probability, providence and practical wisdom, community, the communitarian individual, the family, and continuous revolution) in order to paint a picture of democratic capitalism.

The key component of democratic capitalism is freedom. No other system has produced an equivalent system of liberties, loosened the bonds of station and immobility, and so valued the individual. Democratic capitalism is a system of natural liberty that forms the basis of genuine community. People are free to associate (i.e., to form innumerable voluntary associations). Democratic capitalism destroys old static patterns of community but creates instead a more fluid form of communitarian free association. For example, the corporation (a voluntary association) unites people in a common goal and gives them a sense of meaning and purpose. The cooperative institution of the corporation illustrates that the spirit of democratic capitalism is far from the anarchic individualism that critics have claimed it to be. In fact, the system's antidote for social uprootedness is the corporation, in which populations of mobile workers are organized into teams of task-oriented colleagues.

Democratic capitalism assumes pluralism, recognizes that individuals have differing opinions and interests, and allows them to associate in order to further those interests. Pluralism assumes the reality of sin. Pluralism's multiple groups provide a balance of power. The chief purpose of pluralism is to fragment and check power—not to repress sin.

Democratic capitalism taps individual creativity and initiative and relies on self-interest, not in the sense of individual greed but to benefit others, the principal other being the family. Such a system produces not only wealth but also virtuous people whose worldly enterprise complements the work of the Creator. Democratic capitalism offers an outlet for greed and reinforces habits of prudence, thrift, industry, tolerance, and restraint in everyday life. These virtues are consistent with the Judeo-Christian tradition and are reflective of the Protestant work ethic. Novak goes on to discuss Ben Franklin's idea of time as "spendable grace" and democratic capitalism's fostering of bourgeois values and the bourgeois family with its habit of measuring children's worth by their achievements.

According to Novak, socialism is based on a number of assumptions similar to those underlying traditional society, which helps to explain its appeal in Third World countries. Both socialism and traditional society have "zero-sum" concepts of man, nature, and wealth. This view implies that no gain can be realized without cost. (As an example, no one can earn money without it being taken from someone else.) It follows that without strong control by government, religion, and tradition there would be a war of all against all. Control is thus needed to prevent excessive individualism. Both traditionalism and socialism represent rigid, closed societies that stifle individuality and creativity. Under the socialist view, (1) capitalists become wealthy by exploiting workers, (2) capitalist nations exploit Third World nations, and (3) the elimination of private property will end such exploitation.

Socialism is especially appealing to three groups. Political elites in socialist countries have a vested interest in maintaining a system that secures their influence. In addition, socialism offers political elites in Third World countries a chance to consolidate great power. Finally, socialism appeals to many intellectuals–especially Roman Catholic theologians. Many intellectuals have traditionally associated capitalism with the Protestant Reformation and have believed it to be excessively materialistic, individualistic, and destructive of community. They have been more attracted to socialism, which they believe is more consistent with religious doctrine that was formed before capitalism came into being. Socialism also offers intellectuals a way of participating in power and imposing their ideas on society.

Much of the evidence for Novak's position is based upon a comparison of North America and Latin America. He points out that their economic positions were roughly similar during the late eighteenth and early nineteenth centuries. The conventional explanation today for the fact that North America is rich and Latin America is poor is that North America exploited Latin America. However, Novak points out that United States investment in Latin America is actually relatively small and that its poverty existed well before there was any United States investment there at all.

Novak then explains the real reasons for poverty in Latin America: It did not adopt an economic system that would allow for development. Spain held a narrowly mercantilist economic theory, which emigrated to Latin America and provided a very weak foundation for economic development. Spain's mercantilism contrasts with the individualism of North America. The nineteenth-century Roman Catholic Church, by opposing capitalism at the time, is another cause of poverty in Latin America. Liberation theologians, opposed to the traditional Church hierarchy in virtually all other areas, agree with it in despising capitalism. Novak maintains that Southern European Catholicism shaped the development of Latin America with unfortunate consequences that liberation theologians now mistakenly attribute to Anglo-American capitalism. Most important, there is a philosophical gulf between Latin America and North America. Latin Americans and North Americans do not value the same moral qualities. Latin Americans feel inferior in practical matters and superior in spiritual ones. In

Latin America, powerful personages control nearly everything. The Catholic aristocratic ethic of Latin America places emphasis on luck, heroism, and status while the Protestant ethic of North America values diligent work, steadfast regularity, responsibility, and accountability. In Latin America, wealth is rather static and appears to justify the "zero sum" philosophy. Socialism feeds the strong, traditional, social sense of Latin America by meeting the need for a unitary order, sharply focused on feelings of resentment and economic inferiority and providing a simple scheme of good and bad. The involvement of Latin American clergy with liberation theology brings about the possibility of a church-state alliance. This blend of Christianity and Marxism offers a road to power and influence that Christianity alone can no longer provide. Liberation theologians claim that Christianity is the religion of which socialism is the practice.

Novak observes that the socialist speaks of possibilities while the capitalist speaks of realities. Socialism thus has appeal only in the abstract, as an ideal. However, Novak wants capitalism and socialism to be judged on their performance in the real world. Current arguments often have us contrasting capitalism's realities with socialism's ideals. Socialism is nearly always justified in terms of its vision. Novak's method is to apply practical wisdom to examine what really happens in this world. Novak gives socialists credit for pure idealism—however unworkable their theory becomes in practice. Socialists receive rhetorical points by comparing their utopian vision with the flawed realities of existing capitalist societies; however, when each system is measured by its real-world performance, capitalism proves to be more productive of goods, services, and personal liberation. An ideal that cannot be put into practice is false and morally unacceptable.

As history demonstrates, Marxist practice consistently fails. Novak argues that in Poland, four decades after the liberation of workers from capitalist oppression, workers are worse off than their counterparts in even the least developed capitalist states. The success stories of the Third World are countries that have supported capitalism (e.g., Taiwan and Singapore), while the failures are countries committed to socialism (e.g., Algeria).

Capitalism succeeds because it is an economic theory designed for sinners, of whom there are many, just as socialism fails because it is a theory designed for saints, of whom there are few. Capitalism is able to convert individuals' private ambitions into the creation and distribution of wealth so that everyone has a solid material base. Unintended consequences make moral systems out of a variety of motives (e.g., when individual self-interest leads to a system that produces economic abundance, political liberty, and a free pluralistic culture) and makes immoral systems out of moral motives (e.g., tyrannies that have emerged from modern experiments in collectivism). Capitalism demands freedom in order to function and thus liberates those who live under it; socialism ostensibly supports such liberation but, in fact, requires sharp restrictions of freedom in order to function.

Novak explains that many Catholic social teachings were formed in the precapitalist static world of medieval society, which prized stability in economics, politics, and religion. Papal teachings were thus more concerned with the just distribution of available goods than with the morality of systems that produce new wealth and sustain economic growth. The New Testament favors the poor. The spirit of socialism (including self-denial, cooperation, and human solidarity) thus initially appears to many as being closer to the Gospel vision of a redemptive community than the competitive spirit of capitalism. Catholicism has emphasized community and tradition while capitalism has emphasized individualism and innovation. As a result, North American theologians have generally been critical of the nation's economic system.

Free Persons and the Common Good

This book was written in commemoration of the fortieth anniversary of the publication of Jacques Maritain's *The Person and the Common Good*. In this work, Novak interweaves the traditions of Catholic social thought with classical liberal social theory. More specifically, he attempts to reconcile the social idea of the common good with the liberal emphasis upon the free person. Novak maintains that not only can a free society have a common good, but these two ideas naturally fit together. He argues that the liberal tradition of personal liberty has its own implicit doctrine of the common good. To advance his position, he analyzes a variety of ancient and modern teachings, both religious and secular, and discusses several theoretical arguments. Contributions to the discussion come from Aristotle, Aquinas, Tocqueville, Acton, Maritain, Locke, Madison, Jefferson, Simon, Bellah, Hobhouse, and the debates concerning the United States Catholic Bishops' pastoral letter on the economy.

Novak begins by explaining that the concept of the common good is of premodern origin. For Aristotle, the good is what all things aim at, and thus has primacy over persons. Novak rejects this idea and claims that persons should have primacy. In undifferentiated premodern societies, care for the common good was vested in the paternalistic authorities of church and state; however, in today's free and differentiated societies, individuals tend to have different aims. Although free persons do have some common purposes, they are almost always held for different reasons. Persons differ in their understandings of the good—both of the common good and of their own personal good. If free persons do have primacy, then the common good can be something that emerges from acts taken as free persons.

Novak relies on Aquinas, as interpreted by Maritain, to distinguish between the "person" and the "individual." Whereas an individual is merely a member of a species, a person is an individual with a capacity for insight and choice and, therefore, is both free and responsible. The purpose of every human person is to be with God in an eternal communion of insight and love—an end far beyond the power of earthly states and associations. In the Christian tradition, God is thought to more perfectly embody insight and choice than anything else known to humans. It follows that communion in perfect insight and love with God is both the common good of humankind and the personal good of each individual person. For God, an absolute person, there is an absolute coincidence of common and personal good. Analogously, to the degree that a created person acts with reflection and choice (i.e., as a person), the greater the tendency for the personal good and the common good to coincide. Certainly, human insight and love are deficient when compared to God's love. Yet, it follows that on earth the common good of persons is to live in as close an approximation of unity in insight and love as humans might attain. To learn and achieve the common good, free but flawed persons need institutions suitable to the task.

American liberalism makes the protection of individual rights central to the idea of the common good and allows for the development of institutions that nourish practical cooperation without requiring prior agreement with respect to final ends or personal motivations. The common good consists in treating each person as an end—never solely as a means to an end. In order to achieve both personal rights and the public good, the framers of the Constitution chose not to impose a moral-cultural system. Rather, they left the construction of such a system to institutions distinct from government (e.g., churches, the press, universities, and other voluntary associations). The Founders' idea of a limited state, whose power is restricted by a written constitution, is based on the idea of the inviolability of personal rights. The result is the separation of the powers of the state from the powers of society.

The common good is neither attained solely, nor primarily by the government but by a vast range of social institutions beyond the scope of the state—families, churches, schools, private enterprises, workers' associations, and so forth. The purpose of government is to provide opportunities for individuals to exercise their own freedoms. What makes a person free is the ability to form his own life purposes, aims, and intentions. The common good consists of mutual cooperation many times apart from common intentions, aims, and purposes. Things can be done publicly without being done governmentally. The common good is far greater than the political good. Economic and moral-cultural institutions play large roles in achieving the common good.

According to Novak, the main instrument of attaining the common good is not the state but society at large in its full range of social institutions, and not the atomistic individual but the communitarian individual—the person in his various freely-chosen associations. The communitarian individual may freely organize with others into a faction—a group moved by some common impulse, passion, or interest. Novak discusses Madison's views in *The Federalist Papers* to illustrate how self-interest and factions are able to serve the public good. Madison argues for the diversification and multiplication of factions. The multiplication of interests through factions is likely to prevent both majoritarian tyranny and the narrow-minded self-enclosure of minorities.

Novak then discusses Tocqueville's phrase "self-interest rightly understood"—the idea that man serves himself when he serves his fellow human beings. Persons' enlightened regard for themselves prompts them to help one another and to sacrifice voluntarily some of their time and property to the general welfare. Commercial activities are pursued with a view toward gain—gain that can be achieved on a long-term basis only if the needs of purchasers are served reliably and efficiently. Buyers and sellers seek their own self-interest while at the same time behaving so as to please the other. One must seek one's interest while also being other-regarding (i.e., attempting to satisfy market demands). The common good is therefore served, though neither buyer nor seller planned or intended it. The notion of self-interest rightly understood expresses the social nature of the human person whose interest it is to exercise his liberty in free, kind, and open cooperation with others.

According to Novak, the common good is actually many goods that are often in direct conflict. Free persons typically have diverse visions of the common good. Each person in a free society is responsible under the "veil of ignorance" for a concept of both his own good and the common good. The common good of pluralistic modern societies is thus something unplanned, unenforced, and unintended but achieved through the participation of all citizens. It follows that the kind of common good that can be achieved is the common good of a particular community at a particular moment—not *the* common good for all places and for all times. Today, the common good means: (1) a liberating framework of institutions designed to liberate free persons, (2) a concrete social achievement, and (3) a benchmark that reminds us that no level of common good as concrete social achievement has as yet met the full measure of legitimate expectation.

The main thesis of *Free Persons and the Common Good* is that if free persons do have primacy, then the common good can only be something that emerges from acts of free persons, and that individuals' freedom must be protected by economic and moral-cultural institutions that limit state power. Since free persons are ordered to the common good, citizenship requires attention to the institutions that secure personal freedoms. Common institutions (both voluntary associations and the government), in turn, are ordered to the development of free persons. It follows that the free person is ordered to the achievement of the common good by creating, nourishing, and developing communities, associations, and institutions worthy of free persons. The common good is ordered to the fulfillment of the free person through the development of his full human possibilities.

This Hemisphere of Liberty

In earlier works, Novak offered Latin Americans a philosophically, politically, and economically sound alternative to liberation theology. This current work reflects refinements to Novak's earlier views, offers an excellent and accurate analysis of the Latin American spirit, explains the philosophical link between North and South America, and discusses ways to build institutions of liberty— liberty from poverty, from tyranny, and from oppression of conscience. In this book, Novak uses an explicitly Catholic language in his efforts to integrate the communitarianism of the Catholic tradition with the dynamism and creativity inherent in economic liberalism.

The key idea of this work is the Catholic Whig tradition—a philosophical view that has roots in the thought of Thomas Aquinas. Catholic Whigs believe in the dignity of the human person, in liberty, in creativity, in humility, in productivity, and in steady, gradual institutional reform and progress. In addition, they have great respect for tradition, custom, habit, language, law, and liturgy. The Catholic Whig tradition is based on the four basic concepts of ordered liberty, the person, the community, and creativity.

Ordered liberty is not the power to do whatever we like but rather the freedom to do what we ought. Only when men are free can they be moral. Choice based upon reflection and deliberation maintains a sense of responsibility. Liberty has three parts—political, economic, and moral-cultural. Political liberty requires economic liberty, and both of these require moral-cultural liberty. Of the three, moral-cultural liberty has primacy. Freedom of the moral-cultural system refers to the free exercise of conscience, the free flow of information and ideas, and freedom for the basic institutions of the moral-cultural sector—churches, families, universities, the press, and so forth.

As previously discussed in *Free Persons and the Common Good,* the concept of person is richer than the concept of individual—the human person is a foundational source of insight and love. Each person is free to be a political agent, an economic agent, and a seeker of truth, justice, and love. Novak extends this idea in *This Hemisphere of Liberty* by co-defining community and person. A true community respects free persons. A fully developed person is capable of knowing and loving—two human capacities that are oriented toward community. To be a free person is to know and love others in community. A community is true when its institutions and practices enable persons to multiply the frequency of their acts of knowing and loving. The purpose of a true community is to nourish the full development of each person among its members. It is also in the nature of each person to be in communion with others. The inherent end of personhood is communion and the inherent end of a true community is full respect for the personhood of each of its members.

Democratic capitalism is a system of natural liberty that forms the basis for genuine community. People are free to form innumerable voluntary associations. Men are necessarily related to others; however, they can determine to a large extent the persons they will be related to and the ways in which they will be related. Men are responsible for creating and entering relationships that will enable them to flourish. Communities arise when persons unite together to search for and realize their essential being.

Inherent in respect for the human person is respect for the reflectively chosen forms of association that persons create to pursue their common interests. These freely chosen associations are not only philosophically and practically prior to the state but are also defenses against the state.

Another fundamental principle of the Catholic Whig tradition is the moral virtue of creativity, also known as enterprise—the capacity for insight, discerning new possibilities, and realizing one's creative insights. Rights inhere in persons because they were conferred on each by the Creator, who made all persons in His image. Man is a material and a spiritual creature capable of reason, insight, choice, and creativity—capacities shared with God. Humans are free and responsible before God and have inalienable rights to life, liberty, and enterprise. Enterprise, an intellectual virtue, is a central capacity of personhood. To exercise it is not only a right but a duty. Personal economic enterprise advances the common good—it is relational and usually fosters human interdependence. To exercise the human right of personal economic initiative is to fulfill the image of God inherent in every man and woman.

Novak argues that the virtue of enterprise can be taught and that a social system can be constructed to enable human beings to create wealth in a sustained and systematic way. The best way to help the poor is through a system that creates economic growth from the bottom up—a system that creates jobs for the poor. To help the poor is to help each poor person exercise his God-given right to personal economic initiative (i.e., to be creative). Novak contends that the wealth generated by a capitalistic model can best actualize the promise of self-betterment and freedom for the poor in Latin America and elsewhere. What is distinctive about the capitalist system is its discovery that the primary cause of economic development and the wealth of nations is wit, invention, discovery, and enterprise. Each nation's greatest resource is the creativity endowed in every single person by the Creator. God has given each the capacity to create more in a lifetime than he or she consumes. This is the very principle of human economic progress. One should leave the world better off than he or she found it. Democratic capitalism is the system that best allows one to create more than is consumed, and is the social system that best nurtures our capacities for liberty, responsibility, and growth in the political, economic, and moral-cultural spheres.

According to Novak, the basic reason that Latin America is poor is that it offers insufficient economic opportunity for the people. Latin America offers few cultural or legal supports for the operation of a capitalist economy. Latin America must address the question of the proper and just arrangement of social institutions that are oriented toward the multiplication of acts of reflective choice and the maximization of personal economic creativity for the sake of the common economic whole. Those who wish to liberate human beings from poverty should concentrate on their nation's primary resource—the minds and spirits of the citizens at the bottom of society.

The Catholic Ethic and the Spirit of Capitalism

Novak's earlier works, especially *The Spirit of Democratic Capitalism,* had a major influence on Pope John Paul II, who at one time had advocated a modified form of socialism and who now has endorsed the market economy. Novak's goal in writing *The Spirit of Democratic Capitalism* was to show that capitalism is compatible with Catholicism. This earlier work, however, failed to explain the relationship between capitalism and creativity, a key aspect of what he now calls the Catholic ethic, and devoted very little attention to analyzing papal social thought. In addition to echoing his previous arguments, this book advances the thesis that a hundred-year debate within the church has led to a fuller, more satisfying, and more humane vision of capitalism than that described in Max Weber's 1904 classic, *The Protestant Ethic and the Spirit of Capitalism*. Through a critical historical analysis of the major works of modern papal thought, Novak explains how the Catholic tradition has evolved to reflect this richer interpretation of capitalism.

He begins by arguing that the German sociologist Max Weber missed the mark by defining the spirit of capitalism too narrowly and attributing it to Calvinistic attitudes rather than to a range of values that were actually more generally shared by many types of Christians and Jews. Novak contends that Weber was wrong to believe that all versions of capitalism depend on the ascetic Protestant spirit for moral legitimation. Novak's insight is that the European continental version of capitalism should be distinguished from capitalism as it developed in England and the United States. According to Novak, the former version is in accord with the Weberian vision of a selfish, miserly, greedy, grasping, coldly calculating capitalism dedicated solely to wealth accumulation. He observes that a similar view was popularized by the Italian Christian Democrat Amintore Fanfani, whose 1935 book, *Catholicism, Protestantism, and Capitalism,* was revered by social democrats. Fanfani states that Catholicism is incompatible with capitalism, which he saw as petty, mean, materialistic, self-regarding, and ruthless.

For Weber, the spirit of capitalism involved a sense of duty to the discipline of work, the idea of work as a calling or God-given vocation, and an otherworldly austerity that, in turn, led to the acquisition of wealth, investment, and systematic saving. Through work, man served God. Planning, self-control, austerity, individualism, and devotion to occupations thereby pervaded the economic world. The Protestant ethic stressed the sacred nature of property, the virtue of hard work, and the importance of independence, thrift, and accumulation.

Novak acknowledges that the strength of Weber's position was that he associated capitalism with certain moral habits and with the human spirit. The weakness of Weber's view was that he limited the association to Calvinism and wrote only about one narrow and limited type of capitalist spirit. To replace the Protestant ethic with a view that is applicable to American and British capitalism, Novak espouses a Catholic (and catholic) ethic that appreciates the social dimensions of capitalism and that stresses the inventiveness, creativity, liberty, and responsibility of the individual.

Novak argues that capitalism depends on a culture characterized by creativity, inventiveness, discovery, cooperative effort, social initiative, openness to change, adaptability, generosity, experimentation, and voluntary participation. This is the type of capitalism advocated by Adam Smith and the Founding Fathers. This kind of capitalism is inherently social and brings companies and other voluntary associations into existence in order to create goods, services, and profits. In this way capitalism fosters the development of a variety of voluntary associations, nourishes virtues such as honesty, hard work, productivity, and thrift, and enriches the social and moral lives of the participants.

A major contribution made by Novak in this work is to redefine social justice as a personal virtue. The old vision of social justice is as a guiding rule asserted by a supreme authority in society (i.e., the state). Social justice, so defined, is realized through public institutions and authorities. This type of social justice is not a virtue. It gives the state, through its laws, constitutions, and institutions, the authority and power to determine the structural shape and form of society, that is, it brings about a legal and social order. It is no wonder that "social justice" has become the chief battle cry of those who would expand the role of the government, especially with respect to redistribution. This is the understanding of social justice that Hayek attacks as an arid, abstract ideal enforced by an all-powerful state that encourages dependency and submissiveness.

Novak contends that this is not the concept of social justice that Pius XI made canonical in 1931 in the encyclical *Quadragesimo Anno*. What Pius intended was not the corporatist state, ruled from the top down, but the revitalization of civil society by the "principle of association." Novak amplifies this view by reinterpreting social justice as a distinctive virtue of free persons associating themselves together, cooperatively, within a free society. The practice of social justice means activism, organizing, and trying to make the system better. Social justice is a specific modern form of the ancient virtue of justice that is exercised as a social habit when men and women join with others to change the institutions of society. It does not mean enlarging the state; rather, it means enlarging civil society. The concept of social justice defended by Novak links it to the concrete intelligence of individuals in their free associations, rather than to the state.

Social justice involves the readiness to use one's imagination and creativity to help others. For example, personal work among the needy should not be substituted for the bureaucratic welfare state. Novak explains that the habit of social justice has as its aim the improvement of some feature of the common good— possibly of the social system in whole or in part (e.g., the welfare system) but possibly as well of some nonofficial feature. Works of social justice might include diverse acts such as tutoring a disadvantaged person from the inner city, building a factory in a poor area, or organizing a drama club in a college. According to Novak, in a pluralistic society different grasps of current realities and different visions of the right ordering of the just society may lead people to opposite courses of action. This leads to the need for rigorous public debate and moral analysis. Novak goes on to explain that the concept of social justice has greater explanatory power when it is related to the concepts of civil society enlivened by the principle of subsidiarity, the tripartite nature of liberty, spontaneous order, common good (as detailed in *Free Persons and the Common Good*), and change as creative destruction.

Novak goes on to distinguish between two concepts of liberty. On the one hand, license involves the liberty to do whatever one wishes—it means freedom from the law to do whatever is not forbidden. On the other hand, ordered liberty is not the freedom to do whatever we like, but, rather, the freedom to choose to do what we ought to do. Ordered freedom, freedom under the law, derives the intelligibility of the free act from reason, law, duty, responsibility, reflection, and a rightly ordered conscience. John Paul II, a philosopher of liberty himself, believes in the second understanding of liberty—not an end in itself; freedom is for something and must be ordered by something.

Not only is John Paul II a philosopher of liberty, he is also a philosopher of creativity who has used the creation story to reconcile religion and economics. In his first social encyclical, *Laborem Exercens* (1981), he appealed to the anthropology implied in the Genesis account of creation—the underlying principle is the "creative subjectivity" of the human person. Then in *Sollicitudo Rei Socialis* (1987) he moved from "creative subjectivity" to "the fundamental human right of personal economic initiative," second only to the right of religious liberty and rooted in the image of the Creator endowed in every human being. Men and women are called to be co-creators in the economic realm. By the time of the appearance of *Centesimus Annus* (1991), he had shifted to a theory of the institutions necessary for the flowering of enterprise as a vocation, a virtue, and a right.

Novak calls *Centesimus Annus* a classic restatement of Christian anthropology in which John Paul II has rooted his social proposals in his anthropology of "the acting person" and "creative subjectivity." In this document the Pope emphasizes ordered liberty and calls for a tripartite social structure made up of a free political system, a free economy, and a free moral-cultural system. According to Novak, the Pope's fundamental insight in this encyclical is that every person has been created in the image of the Creator in order to help co-create the future of the world.

In the concluding section of *The Catholic Ethic and the Spirit of Capitalism,* Novak switches from an examination of the Catholic encyclicals and offers his own attempt to apply the Catholic ethic to poverty, race, ethnicity, and other social perplexities. He states that his recommendations, like all others, should be submitted for rigorous public criticism.

Novak observes that for any republic to survive, envy must be defeated, and the best systematic way to defeat this vice is through economic growth and open access. A system of open opportunity takes allocation, favoritism, and preferences out of politics. True social justice begins by removing systems of political allocation and group favoritism, so that the rule of law may be equally applicable to every individual. Multiculturalism is currently being used to single out certain cultures for special status, favors, and discriminatory treatment.

Novak emphasizes the primacy of morals—if our moral and cultural institutions fail, all the rest of ordered liberty is lost. He goes on to say that if the primary flaw lies not in the political system or the economic system but in our moral-cultural system, then the prognosis is hopeful. If the fatal flaw lies in our ideals and morals (i.e., in ourselves) then we have a chance to mend our ways. According to Novak, the hardest part of the moral task we now face is the power of the adversary culture, with its emphasis on equality of results and moral relativism. Philosophers such as Richard Rorty reject both metaphysics and the search for foundations. Representatives of this counter-culture repudiate the possibility of any objective, eternal, absolute, moral standard by which human deeds should be measured. For example, the idea of inalienable rights on which the American experiment rests is understandable only in terms of truth, nature, and God. To exist is to stand out from nothingness, to say yes to life and the will of God who gave us a vocation to wonder at His creation and to bring it to its latent perfection, to the best of our abilities.

Conclusion

In the four books discussed above, Novak thoughtfully makes the case, using a broad range of moral and theological arguments, that capitalism rightly understood is not only compatible with Catholic social teaching but is also the strongest force for liberation the world has ever known. These outstanding works mark an advance in political, economic, and religious thought regarding the right ordering of our lives. Novak's well-documented books offer an original and interesting explanation of the moral structure of the market economy and are indispensible reading for anyone concerned with morality in contemporary society. Novak's revolutionary insight is his explanation of the moral-cultural foundations of political and economic systems that give order, coherence, and moral direction to society. Novak reasons that moral and religious principles not only support democratic capitalism, but that the market, in turn, reinforces virtues such as honesty, hard work, humility, and charity.

Note

This chapter is a shortened and edited version of my article, "Michael Novak's Portrait of Democratic Capitalism." *Journal of Markets and Morality* 2, no. 1 (1999.)

Recommended Reading

Novak, Michael. "An Underpraised and Undervalued System." *Worldview* (July/August 1977).
———. "A Challenge to Business." *Dravo Review* (Spring 1979).
———. "Making the Case for Capitalism." *Commonweal* 106 (June 22, 1979): 366–69.
———. "Productivity and Social Justice." In *Will Capitalism Survive? A Challenge by Paul Johnson with Twelve Responses.* Washington, DC: Ethics and Public Policy Center, 1979.

————. "God and Man in the Corporation." *Policy Review* (Summer 1980).

————. "The Economic System: The Evangelical Basis of a Social Market Economy." *The Review of Politics* (July 1981): 355.

————. "The Moral-Religious Basis of Democratic Capitalism." In *Christianity and Politics, Catholic and Protestant Perspectives*, edited by Carol Griffith. Washington, DC: Ethics and Public Policy Center, 1981.

————. "The Vision of Democratic Capitalism." *Public Opinion* (April/May 1981).

————. "The Cultural and Moral Roots of Democratic Capitalism." In *Freedom, Order, and the University*, edited by James R. Wilburn. Malibu, CA: Pepperdine University Press, 1982.

————. "Capitalist and Proud of It." *Imprimis* (October 1983).

————. "The Judeo-Christian Values Which Characterize Economic Freedoms." In *The Economic System of Free Enterprise: Its Judeo-Christian Values and Philosophical Concepts*, edited by Paul C. Goelz. San Antonio, TX: St. Mary's University Press, 1983.

————. "Theologians and Economists: The Next Twenty Years." *This World* (Winter 1984).

————. "Corporation Support for Democratic Capitalism." *St. Croix Review* (December 1985).

————. "Economic Rights: The Servile State." *Crisis* (October 1985).

————. "Free Persons and the Common Good." *Crisis* (October 1986).

————. "Political Economy and Christian Conscience." *Journal of Ecumenical Studies* (Summer 1987).

————. "Economics and the Public Interest or Liberty, Equality and Democratic Capitalism." In *The Promise of American Politics*, edited by Robert L. Utley, Jr. Lanham, MD: University Press of America, 1989.

————. "Wealth and Virtue: The Development of Christian Economic Teaching." Pp. 51–80 in *The Capitalist Spirit: Toward a Religious Ethic of Wealth Creation*, edited by Peter L. Berger. San Francisco: ICS Press, 1990.

————. "Capitalism Rightly Understood: The View of Christian Humanism." *Faith and Reason* 17, no. 4 (Winter 1991): 317–52.

————. "Countering the Adversary Culture." Pp. 99–120 in *The Making of an Economic Vision*, edited by Oliver F. Williams and John Houck. Lanham, MD: University Press of America, 1991.

————. "Democratic Capitalism: Moral or Not at All." *Freedom Review* (May–June 1991): 12–14.

————. "Free Persons and the Common Good." In *Liberty/Liberati: The American and French Experiences*, edited by Joseph Klaits and Michael H. Haltzel. Washington, DC: Modern Writers Center Press, 1991.

————. "The Great Convergence: A New Consensus in Favor of Economic and Religious Liberty." *Crisis* 9 (December 1991): 28–33.

————. "Wealth and Virtue: The Moral Case for Capitalism." *Word and World* (Fall 1992).

————. "Two Moral Ideals for Business." *Economic Affairs* (Sept/Oct. 1993).

————. "Seven Plus Seven—The Responsibilities of Business Corporation." *Crisis* (July–August 1994).

————. "How Christianity Changed Political Economy." *Crisis* (February 1995).

————. "Is Business a Calling?" *Across the Board* (July/August 1996).

————. "The Future of Civil Society." *Crisis* (October 1996).

————. "Economics as Humanism." *First Things* (October 1997).

————. "Executives Must Be Allowed to Execute." *Directors and Boards* (Fall 1997).

————. "The International Vocation of American Business." Lecture given November 12, 1998, at the University of Notre Dame.

————. "The Judeo-Christian Foundation of Human Dignity, Personal Morality, and the Concept of the Person." *The Journal of Markets and Morality* (October 1998).

————. "Hayek: Practitioner of Social Justice." In *Social Justice Properly Understood*. Celebration of Friedrich Hayek's 100th Birthday. October 28, 1999.

————. "The Silent Artillery of Communism." In *The Collapse of Communism*, edited by Lee Edwards. Stanford, CA: Hoover University Press, 1999.

————. *Capitalism and Socialism: A Theological Inquiry*. Washington, DC: AEI, 1979.

————. *The Denigration of Capitalism: Six Points of View*. Edited by Michael Novak. Washington, DC: AEI, 1979.

————. *Freedom with Justice: Catholic Social Thought and Liberal Institutions*. New York: Harper & Row, 1984. 2nd ed. retitled *Catholic Social Thought and Liberal Institutions*. New Brunswick, NJ: Transaction, 1989.

————. *Free Persons and the Common Good*. Lanham, MD: Madison Books, 1989.

————. *This Hemisphere of Liberty: A Philosophy of the Americas*. Washington, DC: AIE, 1991.

————. *Will It Liberate? Questions about Liberation Theology*. Mahwah, NJ: Paulist Press, 1991. Lanham, MD: Madison Books, 1991.

————. *The Catholic Ethic and the Spirit of Capitalism*. 1993.

————. *Awakening from Nihilism: In Preparation for the Twenty-First Century—Four Lessons from the Twentieth*. Washington, DC: Crisis Books, 1995.

————. *Business as a Calling: Work and the Examined Life*. New York: Free Press, 1996.

————. *The Fire of Invention: Civil Society and the Future of the Corporation*. Lanham, MD: Rowman & Littlefield, 1997.

————. *On Cultivating Liberty: Reflections on Moral Ecology*. Edited by Brian Anderson. Lanham, MD: Rowman & Littlefield, 1999.

————. *In Praise of Free Economy: Essays by Michael Novak*. Edited by Samuel Gregg. Sydney: Centre for Independent Studies, 1999.

————. "On the Governability of Democracies: The Economic System." In *Three in One: Essays on Democratic Capitalism 1976-2000*, edited by Edward. W. Younkins. Lanham, MD: Rowman & Littlefield, 2001.

————. *Three in One: Essays on Democratic Capitalism 1976-2000*. Edited by Edward W. Younkins. Lanham, MD: Rowman & Littlefield, 2001.

————. *On Two Wings*. Lanham, MD: Encounter Books, 2001.

————. *The Universal Hunger for Liberty*. New York: Basic Books, 2003.

PART V

THE PHILOSOPHY OF FREEDOM:
IN RETROSPECT AND PROSPECT

Chapter 23

Revisiting the Intellectual Heritage
of a Free Society

*The ideas of economists and political philosophers, both when they are right
and when they are wrong, are more powerful than is commonly understood.
Indeed the world is ruled by little else. Practical men, who believe themselves
to be quite exempt from any intellectual influence, are usually the slaves of
some defunct economist.*

—John Maynard Keynes

This chapter surveys and revisits the intellectual heritage of a free society. The
origins of theoretical arguments for a free society make up a long and distinguished tradition which stretches back at least to the sixth century B.C. and
spans writers until the present day. Elements of the liberal outlook have been
discovered in the ancient world. Many individuals have attempted to find the
best case for a classical political liberal order and their philosophies have been
varied and numerous. The study of the classical liberal heritage is instructive for
its philosophical insights—much can be learned by studying the efforts of others. This survey of the ideas of major liberal philosophers and economists in
recorded thought will demonstrate that, to a great extent, modern thinkers restate
and build up on the ideas of the great thinkers of the past. What are seen as
"new" theories are oftentimes the result of a mixture of past theories. It has
taken a great deal of time and thought to reach the current stage in the development of the philosophy of freedom, as numerous individuals have contributed to
its development.

Ancient and Medieval Periods

Taoist philosopher Lao Tzu (604-531 B.C.) described general laws of nature that cannot be changed, but that could be employed to achieve one's goals. His naturalistic ethics promoted a doctrine of the liberation of the individual through withdrawal into the wisdom and values of the inner self. Desiring to permit each person as much freedom as possible, Lao Tzu said that inaction was the proper function of the government—the state should control through noninterference. Opposing a multitude of regulations, he taught that codified laws and rules are harmful. He cautioned rulers not to use coercion nor to permit others to use force against peaceful individuals. He said that, without law or compulsion, men would live in harmony.

Aristotle (384-322 B.C.) influenced so many thinkers, from Aquinas to Locke to the Founding Fathers, to Menger, Rand, Rothbard, and beyond. The roots of freedom and individualism can be traced back to Aristotle, who acknowledged their moral significance and the value of each individual's life and happiness. He taught that a person gains happiness through the exercise of his realized capacities and that the purpose of life is earthly happiness that can be attained via reason and the acquisition of virtue. In his ethics, Aristotle teaches that a human being uses his rational mind and free will to pursue his well-being and personal happiness (i.e., *eudaimonia*). *Eudaimonia* is a state of individual well-being brought about by rationality and characterized by self-actualization and maturation. He sees happiness as the product of a life well lived and explains that a person's own behavior is the largest single factor determining one's happiness. Aristotle recognizes that moral virtue is inextricably connected to an individual's capacity for initiative-taking, for choice, and for voluntary conduct. For Aristotle, human nature is teleological and that *telos* is self-perfection. An Aristotelian ethics of naturalism states that morally good conduct is that which enables an individual agent to make the best possible progress toward achieving his self-perfection and happiness. Aristotle did not think that ethics was an exact science. This may be due to his lack of the notion of objective concepts (including concepts such as value or good). He saw essences as metaphysical with universals existing within particulars and he seems, to many philosophers, to have relied on intuitive induction. Other thinkers interpret Aristotle as advocating mental effort in order to discern distinguishing features.

Aristotle, like other Greek thinkers, used reason to think systematically about the world. Failing to clearly distinguish between society and the state, Aristotle said that the purpose of the state was to advance the well-being and happiness of the members of political society. For Aristotle and for many other ancient philosophers, political associations exist for the sake of good actions—the state is to promote virtue. The promotion of the good or of virtue is the central goal of the *polis*—the *polis* exists for the sake of the good life. After emphasizing that the proper end of government is the promotion in its citizens' happiness, Aristotle goes on to advocate a "mixed regime." This was the beginning of the idea of constitutionalism, including the separation of powers and checks and balances.

Aristotle also developed the first components of a systematic economic theory. For Aristotle, economics is embedded in politics. The economic component in Greek philosophy, including that of Aristotle, was subordinated to the political and ethical dimensions. He explained that labor has value but that it does not give value. Aristotle also noted that value is assigned by man and is not inherent in goods. In addition, he anticipated the idea of diminishing marginal utility and commented favorably on the merits of private property.

For Epicurus (341-270 B.C.), the individual person is the domain of moral endeavor. All values must transpire during a person's life according to Epicurus's atomistic and materialistic theory of nature. He explains that the only intrinsic good is an individual's own pleasure or happiness, which consists of the absence of both physical pain and mental disturbances. He says that the pursuit of pleasure should be guided by reason and recommends a rather ascetic life as the most fitting way to attain pleasure. Epicurus identified both kinetic and static pleasures and said that men should aim for a state of contentment or tranquility of mind. He held that free-will liberty exists because some random elements exist in the world. Epicurus said that each person should be as free as possible to plan and live his own life and warned people not to get involved in politics because of the problems and worry that accompany it. Epicurus held a contractarian theory of justice and viewed friendships as a means of gaining pleasure.

Stoicism was an important philosophical movement from approximately the third century B.C. to the fourth century A.D. The essential idea of the natural law, a law by which even rulers could be judged, was developed in the Roman world by the Stoic philosophers. The Stoic philosophers were the first thinkers to develop and systematize, particularly in the legal realm, the concept and philosophy of natural law. Throughout history, liberal, moral, and political assertions have been grounded in theories of natural law and the later-developed but related concept of natural rights.

Thomas Aquinas (1225-1274) combined the philosophy of Aristotle with Christianity. It is sometimes said that Aquinas is Aristotle plus Augustine. Viewing philosophy and theology as complementary, Aquinas taught that natural law could be discerned by unaided reason and that positive laws should be derived from natural law. He said that there were two authorities, one spiritual and the other temporal. According to Aquinas, men need a civil authority such as the state and the state was a natural institution. He said that the state had limits, being bound by the laws of God's creation. Aquinas thus favored a mixed regime in politics. Aquinas added a supernatural end to Aristotle's naturalistic morality. Like Aristotle, he noted the inexact nature of ethics. Aquinas, the Christian Aristotelian, emphasized the role of virtue as man's *telos*. He saw virtue in the cultivation and enjoyment of one's earthly life. Perfect happiness may occur later, but in the meantime, a person can experience imperfect happiness on earth in the form of his personal human flourishing. Later, the sixteenth-century Spanish Scholastic thinkers (sometimes referred to as the School of Salamanca) further developed the work of Aquinas to explain theology, natural law, and economics. In doing so, they anticipated theories developed in the future by Adam Smith, the Austrian economists, and others.

Early Modern and Renaissance Periods

Thomas Hobbes (1588-1679) was not a liberal himself, but he did provide the philosophical foundations for a materialistic and reductionistic liberalism and for an economic approach to human social life. His radical individualism held that persons seek their own self-satisfaction and are instinctually disposed toward self-preservation. For Hobbes, the original state of nature is a state of atomistic isolation in which every man is against every other man. He observes that people are equal in their unending desires and limitless claims. The state of nature is thus insecure. Hobbes defends liberty against anarchy rather than liberty against oppression—his goal is peace. He explains that when people formed civil society the necessity for developing a legal system came about. Laws had to emerge in order to coordinate behavior. He saw the protection of laws as making self-satisfaction possible and thought that a strong state would best assure peace. It follows that Hobbes was an absolute monarchist in his politics. According to Hobbes, when the social contract was entered into each person forfeited his rights to a monarch or to a civil government so as to improve his self-interest in making progress in his life. Hobbes argued that individuals had "rights" in the state of nature in the sense that they are expected to act because they are determined to behave in a certain way—they are driven by the motive of self-preservation. It follows that Hobbesian rights lack a moral dimension. According to his psychological egoism, everyone pursues his self-interest in the form of some subjectively perceived good. An individual gives up or transfers his power and is obligated to obey the commands of the sovereign. By delegating all of one's authority, protection is made more efficient. Hobbes had no theory of the abuse of power by the absolute state.

Spinoza's (1632-1677) monist, deductive, and rationalist philosophy had no ontological hierarchy. He said that individuals are bound by natural laws and exist in order to assert themselves in the world in their unique singularity. Although he envisioned a deterministic universe, Spinoza held that an entity is free that exists by the necessity of its own nature and that is determined in its own actions by itself alone. Like Aristotle, Spinoza values something to the degree to which it realizes its nature. He sees freedom as meaning a person endeavoring to persist in his own being. To be free is to be guided by the law of one's own nature. Spinoza also observes that freedom means that options exist and that people have the ability to make value judgments and decisions. For Spinoza, the heart of virtue is the attempt a person makes to preserve his own being. To act with virtue is to pursue one's being in accordance with reason on the basis of what is of interest and useful to one's self. He cautions people not to be controlled by external forces or by their emotions. According to Spinoza, the free person is not afraid of eternal punishment nor does he expect any rewards in an afterlife.

Spinoza makes it clear that the individual maintains his natural rights when he enters civil society. He explains that the purpose of the state is freedom, that the state has no moral foundation, and that the state is without moral principles—morality is excluded from Spinoza's political theory. Politics is not suited for the production of virtue. A good government will provide as much freedom as possible, particularly the freedom to express one's views—people need freedom to philosophize and to hold religious beliefs. Spinoza did not want religion to be an interfering factor in politics. He therefore proposed the subordination of religion to politics in order to protect the state from the diverse proclamations and judgments of those with incommensurable religious beliefs. Spinoza recommended that the state have power over outward observances of devotion and external religious rites but not to inward worship of God. People's freedom of religious diversity would be restricted to private belief and worship.

John Locke (1632-1704) was an empiricist who taught that ideas begin with sense experience. Although he said that nature inclines man toward seeking happiness, he is able, with some difficulty, to defend free will in the sense that a person's mind has the power to suspend the execution of satisfactions and desires and is free to consider, examine, and weigh them—men can control their thinking. Locke's key concepts include the state of nature, natural law, natural rights, social contract, consent of the governed, and the right of property ownership.

Locke's state of nature includes moral elements. He saw a divinely orchestrated universe into which people are born free, independent, and equal. Locke espoused a natural law ethics which governs the state of nature and which guides a person's conduct prior to the construction of civil law. The state of nature is not a state of license. He said that natural rights exist in the state of nature before the introduction of civil government and that men in the state of nature know the moral law through reason. Locke recognized that the natural right to liberty is necessary for the possibility of moral action. He said that it is a law of nature that each person "owns himself," by which he means that the individual has the final authority for guiding and living his own life. Locke's doctrine of natural rights laid the foundation for the moral space of each person.

When men live in accordance with reason in the state of nature and abide by the laws of nature, then peace and goodwill will prevail. According to Locke, God wanted happiness and pleasure for his creatures and ordained that there was virtue in pleasure and pleasure in virtue—earthly happiness was seen as an end in itself. God made each person *tabula rasa* starting from the same initial position. Human nature implies natural rights so that each person shall be treated in a certain way and be permitted to govern his own life. The law of nature implies negative freedom including the right to private property. Locke explains that God gave property to all men in common, but that people can mix their labor with previously unowned property, thereby making it their private property. He says that civil power is derived from the individual right of each person to protect himself and his property. Private property is justified because the survival of each individual requires that he be able to use material objects to sustain his life. Locke's theory of first possession is his fundamental principle of property rights. This is also known as the labor-entitlement theory of property or as the homestead principle of the acquisition of previously unowned property. Locke emphasizes that, when property becomes private, processes emerge that increase and improve that which is left for others.

Society and government are founded when a social contract is entered into. Locke distinguishes between society and the state and explains that government is established to protect individual rights. That is the point of government. He states that consent is the source of a just government authority and of its citizens' obligations. Individuals' natural inalienable rights limit the proper sphere of government to the preservation of people's lives, liberties, and estates. If government exceeds that sphere then people can justifiably revolt. Locke thus focuses on the notion of freedom versus oppression when he speaks of the limited and revocable power of government to protect and preserve what the law of nature implies. He wants the power of a representative government to be separated. Consent of the governed is required to legitimize government and to limit its power.

A skeptic in his analysis of causation, the empiricist David Hume (1711-1776) did not believe that a person could really know human nature. The human mind could only know of sensory experience. He said that a person can only know his experiences and that the future can differ from the past. Therefore, a stable nature can only be suggested by experience. Aiming his radical empiricism at epistemological rationalists, he denied the possibility of moral, as well as scientific, knowledge. Hume rejects the possibility that a person could ever know what is morally right or wrong. He taught that a man should yield to the sentiments rather than to the judgment of reason. As a determinist, he denied free choice, agent causality, self-initiation, and self-governance. Espousing that no objective ethical standards exist (the is-ought gap), Hume explained that morality is subjective, intuitive, spontaneously evolved, and conventional. The skeptic and anti-rationalist Hume led to contemporary consequentialism and utilitarian liberalism. Assigning reason a subordinate role, Hume limited reason to the function of evaluating means to subjectively determined ends. He maintains that a person is free only to the degree that his will chooses from alternatives open to him.

The empirically and scientifically oriented Hume does affirm civil, political, and economic freedom. He contended that noninterference with market processes had instrumental value with respect to the facilitation of progress. Hume accepted the distinction between society and the state and maintained, as a utilitarian, that actions are good if they result in public benefits. He understood the productivity and benevolence of unhampered markets and argued for private property, voluntary contracts, free banking, and the spontaneous order of an open society.

Political economy began to become a more distinct area of study with the French physiocrats and Scottish philosophers. The physiocrats embodied economics in a system of political and social philosophy. The Enlightenment-era physiocrats showed an early theoretical awareness of the important function of natural law in economics. The physiocrats assigned priority to agriculture over the mercantile and industrial sectors of the economy. They did not equate wealth with money and explained that nature in its economic manifestation is the source of value. Land, as the ultimate producer of the necessities for human existence, is what should bear the tax burden. The physiocrats wanted to reduce taxes, have a more equitable distribution of the tax burden, and eliminate mercantilist and other trade restrictions. The physiocrats also espoused the idea of a spontaneously self-equilibrating economic system that was later made part of the classical tradition by Adam Smith.

An associate of the physiocrats, A. R. J. Turgot (1727-1781) viewed human progress as based on human capacities, free will, and natural law. He said that progress was both the inexorable result of historical development and the product of human will and rationality. This progress depended upon the ongoing accretion, inheritance, and communication of the inventory of knowledge. Like the physiocrats, Turgot advocated free trade and a single tax on the net product of land. He explained the mutual benefits of free exchange and that value was subjective (i.e., personal) and could only be measured ordinally. Turgot also held an early idea of diminishing marginal productivity and saw the relationship between saving and capital accumulation. Viewing money as a commodity, he explained interest in terms of time preference.

For Adam Smith (1723-1790), political economy grew out of moral philosophy. A deist who subscribed to the Stoic worldview, Smith said that the world is designed by God so as to maximize human happiness. The universe was seen by Smith as a rationally ordered system in which God had endowed men with capacities and propensities. The world was one of natural law and teleological design in which men were endowed with principles of their nature. Smith endeavored to outline a complete social philosophy in his *Theory of Moral Sentiments* and *The Wealth of Nations* that were meant to be compatible with one another. These works explain what Smith calls the system of natural liberty.

Smith viewed philosophy as the science of the connecting principles of nature. In ethics he said that sympathy was the connecting principle and that it was self-interest (or commercial ambition) in economics. He saw two types of appropriate human behavior—beneficence and self-interest. Smith envisioned an invisible hand inclining human action toward the public good. He spoke of God's liberal plan of equality, liberty, and justice. Smith went on to describe two levels of virtue—the primary (nobler) ones and the commercial ones.

According to Smith, man is a social being who acquires a moral code through experience—there is an evolutionary process by which moral sentiments and virtues develop. He says that each person has an innate desire for mutual sympathy—sympathy arises because of one's natural feeling for others' well-being. Smith explains that the process is aided by the use of what he calls

the impartial spectator procedure. He states that the motive for one's virtuous-
ness is the love of what is noble and honorable and of the dignity and superiority
of one's own character.

Smith holds that each person is naturally disposed to serve his own well-
being. Commercial man pursues his own well-being and performs his proper
role when he seeks fundamental goods. Commercial ambition aimed at one's
private interests secures public benefits in Smith's system of natural liberty. He
says that deception by nature leads men to think they will gain great happiness
when they seek their own self-interest. When each person is able to strive for his
own good, such efforts would best secure public wealth. He explains that the
less government there is the better the system works for prosperity.

Smith's *The Wealth of Nations* laid the foundation for the modern science
of economics. Although he does not emphasize individual rights, Smith acknowledges that such a system would underpin his system of free enterprise. He
also explains that governments are valued only to the extent to which they promote the happiness of the citizens living under them. Smith also developed the
idea that order in human affairs arises spontaneously.

Unfortunately Smith developed at best only a constricted and weak form of
free will in his writings. For Smith, man is merely a Humean slave of the passions who can only select from among the various sentiments he experiences.
Smith explains that a man can control and exercise his emotions and actions
through what he calls self-command.

The Late Modern Period

For John-Baptiste Say (1767-1832), natural law underlies economic behavior,
making it universal, orderly, and predictable. He emphasized the role of reason,
noting that people tend to be rational, but also that they are not omniscient. Say
rejected the labor theory of value and stressed that production is the cause or
source of consumption. Production is primary and necessary for a person's existence and metaphysically precedes consumption. He explained that wealth is
created by production (not by consumption) and that a man's production determines his ability to demand. Say maintained that there could be no long run glut
of commodities supplied because prices in a free market will adjust to bring
about proper proportions. He also championed savings, noting that they cause
subsequent growth in capital and in aggregate output. Furthermore, Say was
against taxation and loans to the government because they reduced the wealth
that would be exchanged in the private sector.

British defender of individual freedom and critic of state coercion, Herbert
Spencer (1820-1903), believed that inexorable human progress develops naturally when people are free and their moral rights are protected. His law or doctrine of equal freedom declares that a person's freedom is restricted only by the
equal freedom of others. When equal freedom is the ultimate principle of justice,
individuals are happier and more flourishing. Spencer states that happiness can

only be attained if a person is allowed to express his right of freedom to do all that his faculties induce him to do.

Spencer's case was deterministic and based on Lamarckian evolutionary theory. His notion of universal causation leads him to deny any theory of free will. Spencer maintains that human nature adapts over time to the conditions of social existence and that acquired characteristics are imparted to later generations. He explains that reason is an adaptive mechanism and an apparatus to promote an individual's life-sustaining actions. Spencer says that habitually repeated life-affirming actions lead to pleasure and become intuitive and that new emotions adapt to new conditions.

Spencer explains that social order does not require deliberate design and that evolution leads to differentiation. Spencer thought that individuation was a value generated by the evolutionary process. He envisions change from a homogenous social structure to a heterogeneous one, with the highest stage of community life being one of laissez-faire capitalism. Distinguishing between a militant society in which war prevails and the government controls the lives of the citizens, and industrial society where people produce and trade peacefully, Spencer observes that the state interferes with natural evolutionary processes. He anticipates the development toward a society where conduct is regulated by moral principles and competitive markets.

In ethics, Spencer argued for a type of rational egoism. He explains that the evolutionary process is progressive in a moral sense given the appropriate conditions of a free society. Spencer contends there is an innate and evolving moral sense through which men access moral intuitions and from which moral conduct can be derived. This moral sense represents the accumulated efforts of inherited and instinctual experiences.

Carl Menger (1840-1921) developed a number of fundamental Austrian doctrines including the causal-genetic approach, methodological individualism, the connection between time and error, and more. Menger incorporated purposeful action, uncertainty, the occurrence of errors, the information acquisition process, learning, and time into his economic analysis. He was an immanent realist who considered a priori essences as existing in reality. As an Aristotelian essentialist, he wanted to investigate the essences of economic phenomena. His goal was to discover invariant principles or laws governing economic phenomena and to elaborate exact universal laws. Menger acknowledged the co-existence of different but complementary approaches to economics—the realistic-empirical and the exact. To find strictly ordered exact laws he said we had to omit principles of individuation such as time and space. This entails isolation of the economic aspect of phenomena and abstraction from disturbing factors such as error, ignorance, and external compulsion.

Menger taught that there are objective laws of nature and that goods have objective properties that make them capable of fulfilling men's needs. He states that goods have no intrinsic or inherent value and that value is a judgment made by economizing individuals regarding the importance of particular goals for maintaining their lives and well-being. People have needs as living, conditional entities. The value of goods is contextual and emerges from their relationship to our needs. Subjective value (i.e., based on one's personal estimation) can be viewed as individual, agent-relative, and objective. According to Menger, judgments are subjective but the truth or untruth of them can be determined objectively. The truth requires correspondence of facts with the judgment that is made. Menger thus contends that economic subjectivism is compatible with philosophical realism.

The Contemporary Period

Building upon the work of Menger, Ludwig von Mises (1881-1973) reconstructed economics upon the foundation of a general theory of human action. His goal was to develop an edifice of irrefutable, coherent, universally applicable, formal economic theory using logical deduction and the sole axiom of human action without employing any other empirical or analytical assumptions. He says that it is possible to deduce the entirety of the logic of economic behavior from the fundamental undeniable axiom that men act. Mises contends that the concept of human action is universal, intuitive, a priori, and automatically built into each person's mental structure. His action axiom is the introspectively known fact that men act. As a neo-Kantian, Mises sees the category of action as part of the human mind. He contends that all of the categories, theories, or laws of economics are implied by the action axiom.

Not only was Mises dissatisfied with Menger's Aristotelian methodology, he was also critical of Menger's value theory. He said Menger's value theory was not consistent enough and that it retained elements of the objective value theory of the classical economists. Mises' sense of value is formal and indicates nothing about whether an end is, in fact, valuable. He speaks of nonnormative, personal, and subjective acts of valuation. His subjective view of value takes human ends as the ultimate given. All action is therefore viewed as rational. For Mises, economics is a value-free science of means rather than ends.

Mises's utilitarianism proceeds from the method of axiomatic reasoning from true premises—his utilitarianism is a priori. He deduces that division of labor and social cooperation are more effective and more efficient than social conflict as a means of attaining one's self-interest. Social cooperation is voluntary, contractual, maximizes individual free choice, and results in greater prosperity in society. Mises views social cooperation and coordination as a proxy for happiness which is similar to the Aristotelian notion of human flourishing. He says that although economics is value-free and apolitical, it is still the foundation for a free polity. Mises explains that value-free economics leads a person to form a free society because the achievement of one's goal is far more likely when people are left free than when they are not. He maintains that it is by means of its subjectivity that praxeological economics develops into objective science. Mises, the praxeologist, takes individual values as given and assumes that individuals have different motivations and prefer different things.

The philosophy of Ayn Rand (1905-1982) is a systematic and integrated unity that is founded on the axioms of existence, identity, and consciousness. Rand explains that knowledge is based on the observation of reality and that to attain knowledge a person employs the processes of induction, deduction, and synthesis. Her epistemology transcends both apriorism and empiricism. She contends that it is possible to obtain objective knowledge of both facts and values. Rand says that the essential characteristics of a concept are epistemological (she really means contextual and relational) rather than metaphysical.

Rand maintains that values are epistemologically objective when they are discovered through objective conceptual processes and that they are metaphysically objective when their achievement requires conforming to reality. She argues that man's life is the ultimate value and the standard of value for a human being—a creature possessing volitional consciousness. Her naturalistic value theory states that it is the concept of life that makes the concept of value possible and that reason is a man's only judge of value. Rand states that it is possible for a person to pursue objective values that are consonant with his own rational self-interest. According to Rand, ethics is rational, objective, and personal. Her rational egoism is based on the Aristotelian idea that the objective and rational end of a human being is his flourishing and happiness—egoism is a virtue because nature requires it. A person has the natural right to initiate his own conduct in line with his own judgment. She views rights as the link between a person's moral code and society's legal code.

Murray Rothbard (1926-1995) did not accept Mises's neo-Kantianism, but still argued that the action axiom is true—he says that a person becomes aware of action through experience in this world. Rothbard, working within an Aristotelian or Thomistic tradition, maintains that the action axiom is a law of reality that is empirical rather than a priori.

Rothbard contends that economics as a science is value-free and that economics and ethics are separate disciplines. He does go beyond economics to formulate a metanormative objective ethics that affirms the essential value of liberty. Rothbard explains that liberty deals with matters of private property, consent, and contract. He maintains that liberty supplies a universal ethic for human conduct and provides a moral axiom—the nonagression axiom which holds for all persons no matter their location in time or space.

Rothbard derives a radical dualistic separation between political ethics and personal ethics. He distinguishes between the metanormative sphere of politics and the normative domain concerned with moral or ethical principles of one's flourishing—there is a huge difference between having natural rights and the morality or immorality of the exercise of those rights. He considers nonaggression to be an absolute principle prior to any foundation for personal morality. An individual's personal moral values are separate from, but dependent upon, the existence of a liberal social order. Being morally neutral regarding various individuals' values and goals, Rothbard ended his ethics at the metanormative level. Considering the state to be a totally evil coercive institution, he was an anarcho-capitalist who advocated natural order with competing security, defense, conflict resolution, and insurance suppliers.

Friedrich A. Hayek (1899-1992) was concerned with the nature, scope, limits, use, and abuse of reason and formulated a largely antirationalist theory of a free society based on the inevitable ignorance and fatal conceit of intellectuals who think that they can design an economy better than what would result from the voluntary interactions of individuals. Developing an elaborate attack on constructivist rationalism, Hayek explains how little men know about what they design. He says that bureaucrats, whose fatal conceit is their undue faith in reason, have no way to make intelligent decisions with respect to deliberately designing or planning an economy. Hayek observes that centralized policy leads to the suppression of creativity, growth, and progress. He argues that relevant knowledge cannot be centralized in the hands of a person or a group who make such policy. Seeing a very limited role for reason, Hayek says that any person's knowledge is limited, incomplete, and uncertain. He, therefore, favors concrete practical knowledge and institutions and social order that are the product of human actions but not of human design.

Emphasizing the importance of decentralized decision making, Hayek explains that markets employ knowledge beyond what could be acquired by a central authority. He says that knowledge is a product of trial, error, and adaptation resulting in unplanned evolutionary progress. For Hayek, all knowledge is essentially tacit, existing in the habits or dispositions of people to act in a rule-governed manner. He views social institutions and rules of conduct as vehicles of knowledge.

According to Hayek, moral conventions are not objective, invariant, or immutable and they are a part of the evolving and spontaneous social order. He states that moral conventions frequently are unable to be articulated. His evolutionary epistemology and ethics emphasize the socially constructed nature of man—norms are ingrained in the biological and social structure of men and their markets. Hayek contends that people develop ideas passively and intuitively. Hayek does not defend free will—he says that free will is a phantom problem. As a post-Kantian, he believes that the categories of men's minds evolve. Hayek has a mechanistic and evolutionary concept of science and does not acknowledge natural laws or natural rights.

He does say that society requires rules of conduct that are minimal and spontaneously generated. Hayek distinguishes between two types of law— general rules of justice (i.e., general principles of conduct) and rules concerning the internal operations of government. Despite this, he ultimately accepts some form of welfare safety net. In the end, Hayek was not a consistent thinker and he failed to complete a systematic political and economic philosophy.

The neo-classical Chicago School economist Milton Friedman (1912-2006) did not provide a philosophical case for a free society. Instead, he relied on skepticism, ethical subjectivism, the notion of the greatest happiness for the greatest number of people, and the results of detailed empirical studies of government intervention. Friedman explains the errors of statism, skillfully refutes interventionist arguments, and applauds the coordinating mechanism of the free market, but has little to say about the nature of man or the ethical basis of capitalism. His highest ethical principle is the absence of coercion—he explained that political freedom could not be attained without economic freedom, including private property. Friedman attempts to demonstrate the superiority of a free society on purely empirical grounds.

Friedman's major achievements occur in the fields of monetary history, monetary theory, and consumption analysis. His economics is actually somewhat Keynesian in that it is macro-economic and demand-focused. Friedman's positive economics says that a theory is useful if the theory allows individuals to predict occurrences of some phenomenon. He desires accurate predictions and simplified assumptions. Friedman rejected introspection and the realism of assumptions. He even applauds the virtues of descriptively false assumptions and has said that wildly inaccurate representations of reality in assumptions are acceptable if accurate predictions occur. Friedman is a falsificationist who states that confirming a proposition does not add to the probability that a theory is true. For him, abstraction involves a theory in which many actual characteristics are disregarded as absent in the theory. Friedman views any theory as deficient and false when it does not specify all of the characteristics of reality, including all irrelevant, nonexplanatory, and extraneous ones.

Public Choice economist James M. Buchanan (1919-) has analyzed the nature, workings, and failings of governmental, political, and bureaucratic processes. Expanding economic analysis to politics, he built upon contractual and constitutional foundations in his theory of political and economic decision making. Buchanan's methodology includes rational choice, individual utility maximization, contractarian rights, and politics as exchange.

Buchanan employs deductive logic and conjectural history to discover how a constitutional order could have come about. He states that a legitimate social structure must ultimately stem from individual choice. His proceduralist contractarianism uses the Hobbesian model when he deduces contractarian consent for limited government as an alternative to anarchy and lawlessness. Buchanan's social contractarian approach repudiates the possibility of natural law, natural rights, and objective moral values. Although Buchanan's hypothetical state of nature is somewhat Hobbesian, he also believes that man has Lockean characteristics—Buchanan is not as pessimistic as Hobbes.

Buchanan's contract theory of the state explains that people agree to a social contract because of their desire to survive. He observes that men make constitutional decisions under a veil of ignorance or uncertainty and that under this veil, unanimity is both conceivable and likely. He argues strongly for the principle of unanimity at the constitutional stage of collective choice. Buchanan states that constitutional-level law places restrictions on individual freedom that permit people to progress. It follows that a coercive agency, the state, originates by necessity to enforce the social contract.

Buchanan discusses two levels of public choice—the first or constitutional level establishes the rules of the game and the second or post-constitutional level deals with playing the game within the rules. Constitutional politics sets boundaries for what ordinary politics is allowed to do. According to Buchanan, ordinary political decisions are often made by majority voting—the unanimity principle is not feasible at this stage. Buchanan wants a new constitution that requires much higher than majority agreement at the post-constitutional level in order to make it more difficult to fund government activities.

Harvard philosopher Robert Nozick (1938-2002) tried to justify the state and to dismiss anarchy. Nozick begins by merely assuming the existence of Lockean individual rights—he makes no attempt to derive them from a philosophical examination of human nature. He sees natural rights as limits to action or as boundaries that circumscribe the "moral space" around an individual. Unfortunately, his moral space doctrine and Lockean natural rights are not underpinned by a convincing moral theory. Nozick's sole reason for his theory of rights is a deontological appeal based on intuition. As a Kantian deontologist, he has also said that there exists no unambiguous concept of human nature that always defends individualism. As many have observed, there is an incoherence, inconsistency, and incompleteness in Nozick's body of thought.

Nozick says that in the state of nature, a man may enforce his own rights by defending himself. He contends that it is from this state of nature that rational and rights-respecting behavior will lead to a limited government form of political order. He attempts to show how a state would arise from anarchy through a process involving no morally impermissible actions. Nozick explains the emergence of the state, as dominant protection agency, through self-interested choices of people in the state of nature. He says that a monopolistic defense agency will arise and agree to supply protection to all those who have contracted with smaller protection agencies that it drives out of business. Many critics have commented that, if force had been used to establish the state's monopoly, then the state may have come about immorally. Nozick's entitlement theory of justice emphasizes just acquisition of property and is based on Lockean ideas. He explains the role of the government is to protect natural rights, including property rights. Nozick also defends the idea of process equality, which means equal treatment before the law.

Nozick wants people to be free to voluntarily join together in the pursuit of a good life. He has said that the minimal state should go no further than enforcing the most basic level of ethics required for peaceful cooperation—a state limited to protection against force, fraud, and theft and concerned with enforcing contracts is justified. According to Nozick, only negative rights (i.e., the ethics of respect) should be coercively enforced by the state. The ethics of respect requires voluntary cooperation to mutual benefit and its principles mandate the respect of another's life and autonomy. He says that the ethics of respect is the foundation that should be compulsory across all societies—all other ethical levels are optional and concerns of personal choice. Nozick emphasizes that there is a duty not to interfere with another individual's domain of choice.

Thomas Sowell (1930-) draws from Hobbes, Smith, Hayek, and Friedman in developing his constrained or tragic vision of man and society. Accepting the realities of the human condition, Sowell sees trade-offs but no solutions. He explains that a man's personal knowledge is far less than organized systemic knowledge and that markets economize on the knowledge needed by any one individual—no one has to possess complete information in order for the economy to convey relevant information through prices. Championing the supremacy of systemic rationality, Sowell states that knowledge consists largely of the unarticulated experiences and rationality embedded in traditions, customs, and systemic processes such as markets, families, and languages. He maintains that individuals lack the intellectual and moral ability for deliberate comprehensive planning based on intentional rationality. Sowell views freedom as a process characteristic and rights as boundaries or rigidities that limit the exercise of government power and establish areas for individual discretion.

A leading Catholic social theorist, Michael Novak (1933-), relies on the work of Aristotle, Aquinas and the Scholastics, Tocqueville, Maritain, Locke, Smith, and the Austrians to develop his concept of democratic capitalism, which consists of a market economy, a limited democratic government, and a pluralistic moral-cultural system. Novak particularly heralds the Austrian School of Economics for its contributions to the restoration of economics as a field worthy of study by moral philosophers. He views personalism as described in Catholic papal encyclicals, especially Pope John Paul II's view of the human person as subject, to be consonant with Austrian economic theory. Novak is thus concerned with "the acting person."

Novak explains that the human person is free, self-responsible, and accountable before God. He says that the right of personal economic initiative fulfills the image of God inherent in every person because each one of us is capable of insight and love. Concerned with the moral virtue of creativity, Novak maintains that people need a social system to enable them to create wealth in a systematic and sustained manner. Explaining that the human mind is the cause of wealth, he describes human economic progress as the capacity to create more in a lifetime than one consumes. Novak sees the free market and private ownership leading to positive-sum transactions in which each party benefits.

Skeptical of state power, Novak sees the limited state and the rule of law as man-made means of securing liberty and justice for all men. He espouses the principle of subsidiary, freedom of association, and the importance of mediating institutions. Novak has done much to improve upon and update the teachings of Aquinas and to bring the Catholic Church ever closer to embracing capitalism.

Lessons Learned

This brief review has shown that throughout history thinkers have held a range of perspectives with respect to the theoretical defense of a free society. We can learn a great deal from a survey of political and economic thinkers. We can draw from and integrate the teachings of many of them in our efforts to construct a conceptual foundation and edifice for a free society. The next chapter will see what we can use to elucidate a theory of the best possible political regime on the basis of proper conception of the nature of man, his actions, and society. Such a paradigm for a free society will address a range of issues in metaphysics, epistemology, value theory, economics, ethics, and so on in a systematic fashion. We will find that many of the ideas employed have had origins deep in the history of political and economic thought. There are a number of contemporary thinkers whose writings, I believe, agree with most of what I will present in the next chapter. Among the most prominent are Tibor R. Machan, Douglas B. Rasmussen, and Douglas J. Den Uyl.

Recommended Reading

Backhouse, R. E. *Economists and the Economy: The Evolution of Economic Ideas*. 2nd ed. New Brunswick, NJ: Transaction Press, 1994.

Barry, Norman. *On Classical Liberalism and Libertarianism*. New York: Palgrave Macmillan, 1987.

Blaug, Mark. *Economic Theory in Retrospect*. Cambridge: Cambridge University Press, [1985] 1992.

———. *Economic Theory*. 5th ed. Cambridge: Cambridge University Press, 1997.

Boorstin, Daniel J. *The Seekers*. New York: Random House, 1998.

Brue, Stanley L. *The Evolution of Economic Thought*. Mason, OH: Thomson Learning, 2000.

Buchholz, Todd. *New Ideas from Dead Economists*. New York: A Plume Book, 1990.

Canterbury, Ray. *The Literate Economist: A Brief History of Economics*. New York: Harper Collins, 1995.

Copleston, Frederick. *A History of Philosophy*. New York: Doubleday, 1985.

Doherty, Brian. *Radicals for Capitalism*. New York: New York Public Affairs, 2007.

Ebenstein, William, and Alan O. Ebenstein. *Great Political Thinkers: Plato to the Present*. Belmont, CA: Wadsworth Publishing, 1999.

Gordon, B. *Economic Analysis Before Adam Smith: Hesiod to Lessisu*. London: Macmillan, 1975.

Gordon, Scott. *The History and Philosophy of Social Science*. London: Routledge, 1991.

Hoffding, Harold. *History of Modern Philosophy*. New York: Dover Publications, 1924.

Hutchison, T. W. *A Review of Economic Doctrines, 1870–1929*. Oxford: Oxford University Press, 1953.

Jones, W. T. *A History of Western Philosophy*. New York: Harcourt, Brace, & World, 1962.

Kenny, Anthony. *A Brief History of Western Philosophy*. Oxford: Blackwell, 1998.

Langholm, O. *The Legacy of Scholasticism in Economic Thought: Antecedents of Choice and Power*. Cambridge: Cambridge University Press, 1998.

Lowry, S. T. *The Archaeology of Economic Ideas: The Classical Greek Tradition*. Durham, NC: Duke University Press, 1987.

Lowry, S. T., and B. Gordon, eds. *Ancient and Medieval Economic Ideas and Concepts of Social Justice*. Leiden, Neth.: E.J. Brill, 1998.

Meek, R. L., ed. *Precursors of Adam Smith, 1750–1775*. London: Dent, 1973.

Monroe, A. E. *Early Economic Thought: Selections from Economic Literature Prior to Adam Smith*. Cambridge, MA: Harvard University Press, 1965.

Newman, Stephen L. *Liberalism at Wits' End.* Ithaca, NY: Cornell University Press, 1984.

O'Brien, D. P. *The Classical Economists.* Oxford: Clarendon Press, 1975.

Price, B. B., ed *Ancient Economic Thought.* London: Routledge, 1997.

Robbins, L., S. G. Medema, and W. J. Samuels, eds. *A History of Economic Thought: The LSE Lectures.* Princeton, NJ: Princeton University Press, 1998.

Roncaglia, Allesandro. *The Wealth of Ideas: A History of Economic Thought.* Cambridge: Cambridge University Press, 2005.

Rosen, Stanley, ed. *The Examined Life: Readings in Western Philosophy from Plato to Kant.* New York: Random House, 2000.

Rutherford, M. *The Economic Mind in America: Essays in the History of American Economics.* London: Routledge, 1998.

Sabine, George H. *A History of Political Theory.* New York: Holt, Rinehart & Winston, 1961.

Schumpeter, J. A. *History of Economic Analysis.* London: Allen & Unwin; Routledge, [1954] 1986.

Spiegel, Henry William. *The Growth of Economic Thought.* Upper Saddle River, NJ: Prentice Hall, 1971.

———. *The Growth of Economic Thought.* 3rd ed. Durham, NC: Duke University Press, 1991.

Staley, Charles. *A History of Economic Thought: From Aristotle to Arrow.* Boston: Blackwell, [1989] 1992.

Strauss, Leo, and Joseph Cropsey, eds. *History of Political Philosophy.* Chicago: University of Chicago Press, 1987.

Stumpf, Samuel. *Socrates to Sartre.* New York: McGraw-Hill, 1993.

Vaughn, K. *Austrian Economics in America: The Migration of a Tradition.* Cambridge: Cambridge University Press, 1994.

Windelband, Wilhelm. *History of Philosophy.* New York: Harper and Row, 1958.

Chapter 24

Developing a Paradigm for a Free Society

It is only with abstract principles that a social system may properly be concerned. A social system cannot force a particular good on a man nor can it force him to seek the good: it can only maintain conditions of existence which leave him free to seek it. A government cannot live a man's life, it can only protect his freedom. It cannot prescribe concretes, it cannot tell a man how to work, what to produce, what to buy, what to say, what to write, what values to seek, what form of happiness to pursue—it can only uphold the principle of his right to make such choices. . . . It is in this sense that "the common good" . . . lies not in what men do when they are free but in the fact that they are free.

—Ayn Rand

Ideas rule the world. Especially important are the philosophical ideas that determine conceptions of the human person in relation to the world in which he lives. Throughout history, the philosophy of individual freedom has played a critical role in man's progress. Each individual is a discrete being with a unique mind and a distinctive set of abilities, desires, and motivations. Each person is a self-responsible causal agent who has the capacity to pursue his well-being through his intellectual and physical actions. By nature, each person has the right to have the opportunity to develop his potential as a free, individual human being. People are happier when their lives are lived in freedom. When people exercise their freedom they enter the arena of morality as responsible free agents.

The power of ideas is great. If we are to educate, persuade, and convert others to free-market thinking, we need to articulate, in structured form, the conceptual and moral foundations of a free society. We are obliged to expound a coherent and consistent body of principles that are in accord with reality and that properly reflect and explain capitalism. In other words, we must approach the idea of a free society from a philosophical point of view. The survival of free enterprise may be in jeopardy unless people understand its conceptual and moral foundations.

What is required is a rational doctrine based on a clear understanding of man and society in which economics, politics, and morality (all parts of one inseparable truth) are found to be in harmony with one another. What is needed is a systematic theory consistent with the nature of man and world.

A proper system of political economy would be connected with a realistic view regarding human life and its position in the ultimate order of things. Constructing a conceptual framework for such a system involves an interdisciplinary approach and philosophical perspective driven by the demands of truth. It is both necessary and profitable to mine ideas and theories of past thinkers, especially the great systematic holistic thinkers. Ideas of political economy were present even in antiquity and many of these ideas are still relevant to us today—ancient ideas are more important than their remoteness in time may seem to suggest. Much of what is good in the ancients can be found in the thought of modern and contemporary thinkers. Throughout time we have witnessed both the filtration and filiation of political and economic ideas. Many of the insights and arguments of the ancients remain unsurpassed in contemporary thought.

Mining the past offers concepts that point the way for more productive paradigm construction today. Once incorporated, these concepts may aid in improving our understanding and help us in addressing today's social problems. In developing a conceptual framework, it is necessary to learn from, and borrow from, the masters who laid the necessary groundwork. We can gain inspiration from past figures who have analyzed the political and economic world and who have shown us the potential for systems-building. Studying systems of thought can make valuable contributions in developing our own approaches to political and economic thought. We may find that it is possible to integrate components from divergent schools of thought into a cohesive and coherent worldview.

A Reality-Based Paradigm

A paradigm is a model, symbolic representation, or fundamental image of the subject matter of reality or some aspect of reality. It is a tool of the intellect that enables people to survive and prosper. A paradigm that parallels and reflects reality helps a person to understand and function in the world. Of course, reality is senior to any paradigm. A paradigm can only approximate reality and needs to be checked against reality. It is impossible to legislate reality.

A paradigm for a free society addresses a broad range of issues in metaphysics, epistemology, value theory, ethics, and so on, in a systematic fashion. Such a paradigm requires a sound theory of mind, reason, and free will, and logically grounded doctrines of natural rights and morality. Its derivation of natural rights would be grounded in its view of nature, knowledge, and values.

A conceptual and moral defense of a political and economic system must be grounded on the best reality-based ethical system that a reasoning individual can discover. A true paradigm or body of theoretical knowledge about reality must address a wide range of issues in metaphysics, epistemology, value theory, ethics, and so on in a well-ordered manner. The concern of the system-builder is with truth as an integrated whole. Such a body of knowledge is circumscribed by the nature of facts in reality, including their relationships and implications. When constructing a paradigm, it is legitimate to take a selective approach with respect to existing philosophical positions, because a paradigm's consistency with reality is all that really matters. It is thus appropriate for us to extract what is true and good from the writings of others and use those components as a basis for a better integration that allows for a deeper understanding of what would constitute a morally right socioeconomic system. By integrating and synthesizing essential elements of the ideas of the masters we can come closer to a comprehensive, logically consistent view of the world and a foundation and justification for laissez-faire capitalism.

The Aristotelian perspective is that reality is objective. There is a world of objective reality that exists independent of the consciousness of human beings and that has a determinate nature that is knowable. It follows that natural law is objective because it is inherent in the nature of the entity to which it relates. The content of natural law which derives from the nature of man and the world is accessible to human reason. Principles that supply a systematic level of understanding must be based on the facts of reality. In other words, the principles of a true conceptual framework must connect with reality. The only way to successfully defend principles and propositions is to show that they have a firm base or foundation.

We need to formulate principles explicitly and relate them logically to other principles and to the facts of reality. A systematic, logical understanding is required for cognitive certainty and is valuable in communicating ideas, and the reasoning underlying them, clearly and precisely.

This chapter presents a skeleton of a potential philosophical foundation and edifice for a free society. See the enclosed exhibit for an example model or diagram of what such a paradigm might look like. It is an attempt to forge an understanding from seemingly disparate philosophies and to integrate them into a clear, consistent, coherent, and systematic whole. A paradigm should conform with reality and focus on pertinent factors and relationships. It consists of a framework of essential principles that define the system. Understanding the world in terms of general principles permits us to integrate a large volume of information in a condensed form.

The main aim of this chapter is to present a schema or diagram that shows the ways in which its various topics link together and why. The chapter argues for a plan of conceptualization of a number of rather complex topics in relation to each other rather than for the topics themselves. Its emphasis will be on the

A Paradigm for a Free Society

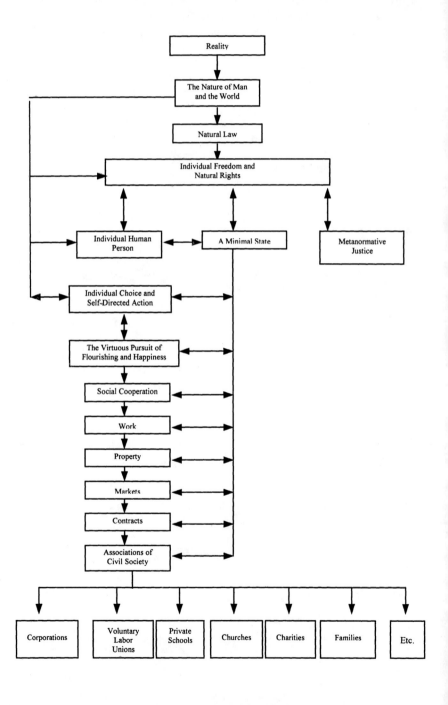

interconnections between the elements of the flow chart presented in this paper. Rather than providing proof or validation of the concepts and principles themselves, the goal of this chapter is to provide a schema that demonstrates the interrelationships among the concepts and principles.

The approach of this chapter is expository and does not engage in formal academic debate or argumentation. My approach is simply to search for correct ideas and to promote what is true and right. Because I am not a professional economist or philosopher, my inquiry does not extend beyond a systematic level that relies heavily on logic and common sense. I will defer to scholars in these and other disciplines to evaluate, critique, and extend my systematic understanding. They are better equipped to deal with subtle and deep concerns and the construction of a more detailed, exact, and consistent formulation of principles. Given that a paradigm combining insights from various thinkers is possible and desirable, it follows that it may require extensions, refinements, and revisions for reasons of coordination and consistency. This can occur in an atmosphere of open rational inquiry, as additional value can be found in the work of many contemporary scholars who engage and extend the notion of combining the doctrines of an assorted range of philosophers and economists. Of course, it will be inevitable that there will be opportunities for different interpretations and developments as more work is done on this edifice. The resulting synergy may provide a superior basis for communicating to the general public why a capitalist society is the best society for human beings.

To construct a conceptual framework, we must be concerned with observed or experienced phenomena. Induction, generalization from perceptual experiences of reality, is used to form axioms, concepts, and constructs. The observational order and the conceptual order must correspond with one another if we are to conceive of things properly. It is through the analysis of inductively derived ideas that the appropriate principles of society can be deduced. A correctly constructed, internally consistent conceptual framework represents the real world in constructs and language. A conceptual framework should be logically consistent and based on reality so that inferences derived from it can be said to be deductively valid.

From a deductive perspective, philosophy precedes and determines politics, which, in turn, precedes and determines economics. On the other hand, the philosopher must begin by inductively studying the fundamental nature of existence, of man, and of man's relationship to existence. This is the point at which we will begin our review of the conceptual foundations of a free society.

The Nature of Man and the World

In developing a conceptual framework for capitalism, it is necessary to focus our attention on the enduring characteristics of reality. Men live in a universe with a definite nature and exist within nature as part of the natural order. Using their minds, men have the ability to discover the permanent features of the world. A unified theoretical perspective and potent intellectual framework for analyzing the social order must be based on the constraining realities of the human condition. Reality is not optional.

To ascertain man's nature, we must, through a process of abstraction, remove all that is accidental to any specific man. What is left must be man's distinctive features and potentialities. It is man's ability to reason that separates him from other vital organisms. Man's rational faculty distinguishes him from all other living species. Conceptualization based on reason is man's unique and only proper way of dealing with the rest of the natural world. It is in man's nature to use his rational powers, to form concepts, to integrate them, to evaluate alternatives, to make choices, and so on. In order to survive and flourish, men must come to terms with the requirements of reality.

The ability to control one's actions (i.e., natural liberty) is an inborn condition of man. In the nature of things, no person can use the mind, senses, or appendages of another. Man is free to use his faculties provided that he does not harm others in his use of them. All thinking and acting is done by individual persons in their own spatiotemporal localities—a society cannot think nor act, although men can choose to act in a coordinated manner with one another. Men have the ability to cooperate and achieve through voluntary action.

To properly construct a paradigm for a free society it is necessary to go back to absolute fundamentals in human nature. We need to have a precise understanding of the nature of the human person. Human beings are a distinct species in a natural world whose lives are governed by means of each person's free will and individual conceptual consciousness. Unlike other beings, a person's survival and flourishing depends on cognition at a conceptual level. People are all of one species with a definite nature, uniquely configured because of their individuating features.

There is a biological case for human diversity with the individual as the primary reality. We must respect the condition of human diversity and the fact that people are not interchangeable. Individuality is vital to one's nature. A person is responsible for achieving and sustaining the human life that is his own. Each person has potentialities, is the steward of his own time, talents, and energies, and is responsible for becoming the person he has the potential to become by means of his own choices and actions.

Human beings possess a stable nature with certain definite, definable, and delimitable characteristics. Consciousness and free will are essential attributes of man's nature. Reason is man's guiding force. Human activities are self-conscious, purposeful, and deliberately chosen. One's actions are caused by his own volition, which is a capacity of human nature. A human being can initiate and make choices about what he will do. Human action involves purposeful, intentional, and normative behavior. Mental action or thinking is the ultimate free action, is primary, and includes the direct focus and willing of the person. Behavior thus takes place after a judgment or conceptualization has been made. It follows that there is a moral element or feature of action because human beings possess free will, which can cause most (or at least some) of what they do.

The distinguishing features of human nature (i.e., rationality and free will) provide objective standards for a man's choice of both means and ends. Man is a volitional being whose reason should guide his selection of both ends and means to those ends. Volition is a type of causation—it is not an exception to the law of causality. Men can think, choose, act, and cause. Human beings act, choose means to achieve ends, and choose both means and ends. In human action, a person's free will choice is the cause and this cause generates certain effects. Such causality is a prerequisite of action and is primarily concerned with a person's manipulation of objects external to himself.

Free will is not the negation of causality, but rather is a type of causality that relates to man. Causality is an association between an entity and its mode of action. It is not the relationship between actions and earlier actions. For a human being, a cause can be the change in his assessment of the relative importance of his values. A person uses his knowledge to correlate his values with his various plans. The concept of purpose underlies the idea of causality as motivated action. Action in behavior is directed at attaining a purpose. Human action has a teleological character because it is rational conduct aimed at a goal. A person can consciously act to initiate a sequence of causation by changing or moving an attribute of his body. This act implies that he has a contemplated objective that he wants to attain. This initial change in a person's body is intended to cause other events to take place and to eventually lead to the accomplishment of the desired goal. The success or failure of a person in attaining his objective depends on his ability to isolate correctly the relevant causal features of a situation and to predict the future accurately both in the presence and in the absence of one's own contemplated actions.

The idea of human action depends upon the introspectively valid fact that there is a type of conduct that is peculiarly human. This kind of conduct coincides with the consciousness of volition. Actions are free only if they are controlled by a faculty that functions volitionally. A person knows via introspection that he experiences physical variables and properties, creates concepts, chooses values, and changes physical variables and properties because he constantly does those activities. Introspection supplies the knowledge that we can make metaphysically free decisions to attempt to attain our values.

What is known (i.e., the object) is distinct from, and independent of, the knower (i.e., the subject). Men are born with no innate conceptual knowledge. Such knowledge is gained via various processes of integration and differentiation from perceptual data. For example, a person apprehends that he has a conscious mind by distinguishing between external objects and events and the workings of his mind. Self-awareness is thus attained when a person reflects upon what he has observed.

Reality is what there is to be perceived. Reality exists independently of a man's consciousness. It exists apart from the knower. It follows that empirical knowledge is acquired through observational experience of external reality. People can observe goal-directed actions from the outside. An individual attains an understanding of causality and other categories of action by observing the actions of others to reach goals. He also learns about causality by means of his own acting and his observation of the outcomes. Action is thus a man's conscious adjustment to the state of the world.

It is necessary to provide a realistic foundation for a true paradigm for a free society. Therefore, a comprehensive moral defense of individualism and its political implications is founded appropriately on a naturalistic philosophy. An Aristotelian metaphysics such as those supplied by Carl Menger or Ayn Rand would be an excellent starting point for a political and economic framework based on the requirements of reality and of man's nature.

Logic is pivotal to correct human thought because reality corresponds to the principles of logic. Men are capable of comprehending the workings of the world through the application of logic. Logic is the method by which a volitional consciousness conforms to reality. It is reason's method. The method of logic reflects the nature and needs of man's consciousness and the facts of external reality.

Principles such as the laws of identity and noncontradiction underpin the observable fact that there are innumerable distinct types of being in reality. Human beings are a unique class, characterized by the real attributes of reason and free will that introduce a dimension of value into nature. Human existence represents a distinct ontological realm different from all others. A human being can choose and is thus a moral agent. This moral nature is grounded in the facts of nature. What a thing must be or do depends on the kind of object or entity that it is. The values (and virtues) of life are discovered by means of an understanding of human nature and the nature of the world.

Natural Law

The idea of natural law has played an important role in political and economic philosophy and in ethics for more than 2,500 years. Elements of natural law can be found in the writings of many ancient and medieval thinkers, including Lao Tzu, Aristotle, the Stoics, Cicero and the Romans, Epicurus, and Thomas Aquinas. The development of natural law thought was continued by Spinoza, Hugo Grotius, John Locke, A. R. J. Turgot, Adam Smith, J. B. Say, Herbert Spencer, and Carl Menger as well as by others. Contemporary natural law thinkers include Ayn Rand, Murray Rothbard, and Michael Novak, among many others. Throughout history, both the secular natural law tradition and the Christian natural law tradition have stressed individual personal responsibility and have advanced the defense of a free society and classical liberal thought.

There are ontological necessities, constraints, possibilities, and impossibilities regarding the way the world works that exist regardless of what we believe of the world or how we represent it—the world works through a variety of laws, causal processes, and interactions. There is one universe in which everything is interconnected through the inescapable laws of cause and effect. There is a natural order with various types of beings whose fulfillment comes from developing and perfecting their potentialities. Differences abound in nature and reality is nuanced in its varieties. There is a stable human nature that establishes limits regarding how human beings should act. To survive and flourish, a man must recognize that nature has its own imperatives. There is a natural law that derives from the nature of man and the world and that is discernible through the use of reason. It is necessary for men to discover the natural order and to adhere to it. It follows that one needs to examine human nature—a sound, feasible, and viable conception of human nature is required.

Human nature is what it is. It follows that the law of human nature is the only law that man, possessing free will, is free to try to disobey. Of course, a man must be prepared to experience the consequences of his "disobedience". If a person desires to prosper, he should not ignore natural law. We could say that the efficacy of human nature is, in a sense, dependent upon human willfulness. The law of nature is revealed by reason and man can choose to violate it. Moral concerns are matters of fact and standards of morality are grounded in the facts of nature. It is only if moral standards can be freely adhered to or avoided that a framework for moral standards can arise. In order to have such freedom, each person must be protected from intrusion by others. What is required is a social structure that accords each person a moral space over which he has freedom to act—natural rights define this moral space.

Natural laws exist and we can discern what they are. Natural law is universal and unchanging and is discovered rather than made. The principles produced through natural law analysis are important and nonarbitrary human constructs or concepts and are firmly rooted in the real world. To derive objective concepts from reality requires a rational epistemology involving both induction and deduction. Natural law reveals an objective moral order knowable through reason and favorable to the survival and flourishing of human beings in the world. Natural law's moral order provides individuals with motivations to fulfill their potential as human beings. Of course, putting natural law principles into practice requires judgment and practical reason. Aristotle taught the benefits of a virtuous life in accordance with the law of human nature. He explained that man's particular nature, different from all other entities and objects, gives him the ability to make moral judgments.

Natural law provides the groundwork for the Aristotelian idea of human flourishing and links moral commitments to facts about the natural world. Because human nature is what it is, ethical naturalism is rooted in a biological understanding of human nature. Natural law addresses the problem of how individual human persons should live their lives. Human beings are not fungible— each individual is responsible for his conduct in the context of his personal attributes and circumstances. Of course, the laws of nature do not guarantee that every person will flourish—they only offer the opportunity to flourish. Human beings can flourish and attain happiness by living their lives according to laws inscribed in their beings.

Natural law doctrines have generally been said to include, but are not limited to, the state of nature, natural rights, the social contract, and the rule of law.

Because natural law can be inferred from what is innate in the nature of man and the world, it would be compelling even if God did not exist. Natural law can be deduced with or without a religious framework. Natural law doctrines are discovered through the use of reason.

The state of nature includes the suppositional circumstances that are assumed to have existed before the institution of a civil government. Because all persons are free and equal in the state of nature, it follows that no one person has the natural right to reign over any of the others.

Society is natural to man as an associative being. It is within society that man can make voluntary exchanges that please and fulfill him. Furthermore, government (or a system of private competing legal and protection agencies) is essential to enable each man to keep what is his and to live peacefully while having mutually beneficial voluntary relations with others. The state is not society. It is simply the entity charged with the function of protecting society that overflows the boundaries of the state. If a society was synonymous with the state, it would not be free because all human activity would be prescribed and governed by law.

According to some thinkers such as Turgot, Spencer, and arguably Hayek, the ideas of social cooperation, spontaneous order, and progressive evolution of the social order are included within natural law. That which is appropriate for society is appropriate for human nature, and thus, according to natural law. If the law emerges and evolves spontaneously, then it has its roots in human nature and human intelligence.

The natural law insists that everything stands under the test of reason grounded in reality. The particular nature of entities requires particular actions if the desired ends are to be attained. Natural laws of human action, discoverable through the use of reason, necessitate specific means and arrangements to affect the desired ends. The laws of nature determine the consequences. The free society works because it is in accord with nature. Natural law provides for reasoning and verification about what is good and what is not good.

Natural law underpins the inalienable rights of life, liberty, and the pursuit of happiness. Negative liberty, the absence of constraints and restraints coercively imposed upon a person by other persons, can be arrived at by studying the distinctive faculties and abilities of human beings and abstracting away the particular levels or amounts that specific individuals possess with respect to their faculties and abilities. What remains is the ability of each man to think his own thoughts and control his own energies in his attempts to act according to those thoughts. Negative freedom is thus a natural requirement of human existence.

Freedom from coercive, man-made constraints and obstacles is a necessary condition to fulfill the potentialities of one's nature. This does not mean freedom from obstacles in general. Not having the abilities or resources is not coercion and therefore does not constitute a lack of freedom.

According to the precepts of natural law, a person should not be forced into acting or using his resources in a way in which he has not given his voluntary consent. It follows that man has certain natural rights to life, to the use of one's faculties as one wills for one's own ends, and to the fruits of one's labor. These rights inhere in man's nature and predate government, constitutions, and courts. Natural rights are derived from the facts of human nature and are respected because they protect individual self-directedness.

The social contract is the tacit agreement of all which is essential, in the nature of things, to the existence of society. It is the implicit and concurrent covenant not to use violence, to fulfill agreements, not to trespass, not to deny others the use of their property, etc. The social contract is the understood, timeless, and universal contract that necessarily must exist if people are to live peacefully within society.

Social interactions and associations offer great benefits to individuals, including friendships, more information, specialization and the division of labor, greater productivity, a larger variety of goods and services, etc. Throughout history, economic activities have been the main type of social interaction and cooperation among people. Government thus became increasingly necessary as the range and complexity of market transactions grew.

Government (of a natural order of competing security and conflict resolution agencies) is needed in order to enable people to live well in society. It is needed to prohibit and punish the private violation of the natural rights of those who peacefully use their energies and resources, to punish fraud and deception, and to settle disputes that may arise.

Of course, the existence of a natural order prior to government means that government's role should be limited and restrained. Natural law theory limits government to its proper sphere, sets bounds to its actions, and subjects the government itself to the law. It follows that to circumscribe government to its proper role, power must be separated into its different functions and power must be counterbalanced to keep those who govern from exceeding their legitimate bounds. This is important because when those who govern act outside the law, they do so with the full coercive power of the government.

Under the rule of law, everyone, including the government, is bound by rules. The idea that the government is under the law is a condition of the liberty of the people. The rule of law requires law to be general and abstract, known and certain, and equally applicable to all persons in any unknown number of future instances.

A constitution is a law for governments. Constitutional governments are characterized by specific restraints and enumerations of their powers. The force behind constitutional governments is the idea of a higher natural law restricting the operations of the government.

The notion of metanormative justice, an idea in harmony with natural law, is concerned only with the peaceful and orderly coordination of activities of any possible human being with any other in a social setting. This type of justice refers to equal treatment under social and legal conditions that include a collection of known rules regarding allowable and nonallowable actions that will lead to unequal positions, with no one knowing in advance the particular result this arrangement will have for any specific person.

Similarly, the state can properly be said to be ensuring the common good when it protects man's natural right to seek his own happiness. Only protected liberty (or self-directedness) can be said to be good for, and able to be possessed by, all persons simultaneously. No other definition of the common good can be in harmony with an ordered universe and the natural law. The common good properly understood is protected freedom that permits persons to pursue happiness or the good that each defines for himself. The government achieves the common good when its functions are limited to protecting the natural right to liberty and preserving peace and order.

There is a critical distinction between the legitimacy of a right and the morality of exercising that right. The government should only be concerned with questions such as the domain of rights, the proper role of violence, and the definitions of aggression and criminality. The government should not be concerned with all personal moral principles. There is a huge difference between establishing the permissibility of an action and the goodness or morality of it. The state should be concerned with the rights of men and not with the oughts of men.

It follows that because religion is a private matter, the government has no right to enter the field of religious beliefs on the side of theism or on the side of atheism. People are free to hold any religious or nonreligious view they choose. Religion is a matter of personal conviction.

A healthy, differentiated social order relies on a separation of political, economic, and moral-cultural-religious systems. The power of the state should not be enhanced by the identification with religion. Churches need to be free from state power and vice versa. The U.S. Constitution and Bill of Rights correctly state that neither a state nor a federal government can set up a religion nor can they pass laws that aid one religion, aid all religions, or prefer one religion over another. Neither can they force or influence a person to go to or remain away from church against his will or force him to profess a belief or disbelief in any religion. The state is properly required to be neutral in its relations with groups of religious believers and nonbelievers.

Human Flourishing and Natural Rights

Natural law is an older concept than the idea of natural rights. John Locke and his predecessor, Hugo Grotius, are frequently credited with ushering in the modern concept of natural rights. Historically, the doctrine of natural rights appears to have developed either within, or at least consonant with, the framework of the natural law tradition. There is some debate among philosophers as to whether the idea of natural rights is based on the idea of natural law, whether the concept of natural law is derived from the concept of natural rights, or whether they are separately developed, but related, concepts. Either way, natural law and natural rights are compatible ideas each of which is rooted in human nature itself—both require an ontological foundation. Both natural law and natural rights are based on epistemological realism.

People are all of one species with a definite nature who are also each uniquely configured because of their individuating attributes—individuality is essential to one's nature. Having reason and free will, each person has the capacity and responsibility to choose to attempt to actualize his potential for being a flourishing individual human being—it is a person's moral responsibility to be as good as possible at living his own life. Morality is the good of man in his individual instantiation—it does not aim at the common good. There is only flourishing of individual human beings. The human telos is the standard for morality and the individual human person is the center of the moral world. This classical teleological eudaimonistic approach to ethics states that the proper moral task of each person is to seek his personal flourishing and happiness in his life—one's needs and purposes in life are determined by his humanity and individuality. It follows that the morally good is subject to the determination by each individual person who is responsible for his own life—the human moral good is connected with individual initiative. There is a connection between respecting each person's right to liberty and one's attempt to flourish by answering questions of morality and by acting accordingly.

Each unique individual human person is morally autonomous and should be held responsible for his actions. It is essential to respect human autonomy and uniqueness so that individuals can attain self-actualization. There is an inviolable moral space around each person that protects him from intrusion by others. Rights involve a delineation of jurisdiction within which an individual may decide what to do. A person's own discerned potentialities tell him what to do and the standard of flourishing provides a criterion for one's wants and desires. Each person is responsible for living the type of life that realizes his distinctiveness. The notion of responsibility is a key concept for understanding rights, morality, and human flourishing. Agential direction involves autonomous acting on decisions made via a process of examination, reflection, deliberation, and choice.

Individual uniqueness is the source from which value pluralism flows— from value differences emanate the need to engage in peaceful exchanges and for voluntary associations. Individuality entails varieties of value and diversity with respect to human flourishing—in a society of varied individuals, the outcomes of human flourishing will reflect that variety. It follows that what is required is freedom of action to allow for a plurality of ends and for a diversity of approaches to the attainment of human flourishing. Responsible agents require a moral space for living their lives in accordance with their nature as individual human persons. A protected moral space is needed for the possibility of self-direction. The doctrine of natural rights attributes to human beings moral rights which others are obligated to respect. Natural rights justify the context in which human actions take place and determine the moral principles that establish what is permissible within that context. Mutual noninterference provides the context and proper setting for social interactions.

Natural rights are derived by reason from human nature and supply a comprehensive principle that applies universally to all persons and to all acts. Natural rights are based on the common aspects of human beings, whereas each life to be lived is the life of some individual person—the human telos is individualized and agent relative. The cognition of the universal idea of natural rights involves abstraction without precision and is based on the consideration of human nature. Natural rights provide a context of self-directedness that is common to every act of human flourishing. Common features give rise to universal standards—some principles are irrefutable and indispensable. Natural rights provide a sphere of rightful defensible authority for individuals to live their own lives according to their nature as individual human beings. The designation "natural" refers to the justification of these rights.

The ultimate justification of an ethic of human flourishing is consequentialist and agent-based, endorsing each person's pursuit of his individual well-being. On the other hand, the doctrine of natural rights can be viewed as having a deontic dimension, informing people what restrictions they must accept. There is a distinction between ethical principles that are teleological and those that are deontic. According to teleological principles, the moral value of an action depends upon the consequences of the action—human flourishing is a consequence-based theory of right action. According to deontic principles, the propriety of an action stems from something other than the consequences—deontic restrictions are moral prohibitions against imposing specific forms of treatment upon other people. There are deontic restrictions that are correlative to the rights of others. We could say that rights and responsibilities are relational in the nature of human persons. It would be inconsistent or contradictory to maintain the right to direct one's own life and not to advocate others' rights to direct their own lives. It follows that an individual is not limited personally regarding his own pursuits but he is limited interpersonally with respect to others' actions.

In his various writings, Eric Mack explained that there is a distinctive correspondence or correlation between the doctrines of human flourishing and natural rights. Endorsing human flourishing makes it rationally necessary to also endorse natural rights. Although human flourishing is not the mainspring or source of rights, the two doctrines are complementary systematizing principles within an ethical framework that is rational because it contains both of these coordinating and integrating components. The rationality of advocating the doctrine of human flourishing depends upon the support of the doctrine of natural rights.

The doctrine of natural rights provides a conception of freedom that establishes the context for other senses of freedom. Natural rights portray the appropriate setting for social interactions and specify the conditions for meaningful senses of moral virtue and human flourishing. Natural rights delineate conceptually the moral space within which individuals need to be free (and self-directed) to make their own choices regarding their possible pursuit of their self-actualization without interfering with the like pursuit of others with whom they interact socially.

Natural rights do not enforce themselves. Securing natural rights should be the primary and central concern of the political and legal order. The notion of natural rights should inform the formation of law and government. Political liberty should involve a state of organized social life in which persons are not deprived of their sovereignty. Human flourishing can best occur when there exists a minimal state that takes no actions except to uphold the negative natural rights of all of its citizens. Politics and law should not have a direct role in how people ought to live their lives. Politics should be concerned only with the limited ends of peace and security—politics and law should be separated from personal morality.

The book *Norms of Liberty* embodies the most complete expression, and best statement to date, of Douglas B. Rasmussen and Douglas J. Den Uyl's thesis that liberalism is a political philosophy of metanorms that does not guide individual conduct in moral activity. Arguing that politics is not suited to make men moral, they proclaim the need to divest substantive morality from politics. The purpose of liberalism, as a political doctrine, is to secure a peaceful and orderly society. Political philosophy should only be concerned with providing a framework within which people can make moral choices for themselves. This framework creates a moral space for value-laden activity. Politics should be concerned solely with securing and maintaining the conditions for the possibility of human flourishing that is real, individualized, agent-relative, inclusive, self-directed, and social. Liberalism requires conduct so that conditions may be obtained where moral actions can take place—liberalism is not an equinormative system. Metanormative and normative levels of ethical principles are split because of their different relationships to self-perfection. Rights are metanormative principles—they are ethical principles, but they are not normative principles.

What is required is the existence of an ethical principle that aspires not to guide human conduct in moral activity, but instead to regulate conduct so that conditions can be achieved where moral actions can occur. Rasmussen and Den Uyl explain that rights are an ethical concept that is not directly concerned with human flourishing, but rather is concerned with context-setting—establishing a political/legal order that will not require one form of human flourishing to be preferred over any other form. A two-level ethical structure consists of metanorms (also referred to as political norms) and personal ethical norms.

Ethics are not all of one category. Whereas some regulate the conditions under which moral conduct may exist, others are more directly prescriptive of moral conduct. Of course, the conditions for making any type of human flourishing possible are less potent than conditions that serve to advance forms of human flourishing directly. Natural rights do not aim at directly promoting human flourishing—the context of natural rights is as universal as possible. Self-direction is the common crucial element in all concrete distinct forms of human flourishing and the negative natural right to freedom is a metanormative principle because it protects the possibility of self-direction in a social context. According to Rasmussen and Den Uyl, the purpose of rights is to protect the possibility of self-directedness. Although they acknowledge that human flourishing is man's telos, their argument for rights does not justify rights for their being conducive to achieving human flourishing. The natural right to liberty permits each individual a sphere of freedom in which self-directed activities can be undertaken without the interference of other people.

A neo-Aristotelian ethical perfectionism is consistent with, and supportive of, a nonperfectionist view of politics. A person's human nature calls for his personal flourishing, which, in turn, requires practical wisdom and self-directedness. The purpose of rights is to protect self-directedness. It follows that self-directedness can be viewed as an intermediate factor between metanormative natural rights and normative human flourishing. Self-perfection requires self-direction and pluralism—diverse forms of flourishing are ethically compossible under the rubric of universal metanorms.

Rasmussen and Den Uyl have extended and refined ideas from political philosophy that began in ancient times. These are the ideas that the state should not use or permit coercion against peaceful people and that the state should have nothing to do with fostering individual personal morality and virtue—people participate in political life so that they are not harmed rather than to be made to flourish. Elements of these notions can be found in the writings of a number of philosophers such as Lao Tzu, Epicurus, and especially Spinoza, who strongly warned people about the dangers of the moralization of politics.

Rasmussen and Den Uyl state that, based on the nature of man and the world, certain natural rights can be identified and an appropriate political order can be instituted. Rasmussen and Den Uyl base their view of natural rights as metanormative principles on the universal characteristics of human nature that call for the protection and preservation of the possibility of self-directedness in society regardless of the situation. Because they do not base natural rights on human flourishing, they believe they have formulated a strong argument for a nonperfectionist and non-moralistic minimal-state politics. Rasmussen and Den Uyl see a problem in putting a moral principle (i.e., natural rights) as the subject of political action or control. Their goal is to abandon legal moralism—the idea that politics is institutionalized ethics. They say that statecraft is not soulcraft and that politics is not appropriate to make men moral.

Morality and Human Flourishing

Moral values enter the world with human life. There is a close connection between an objective normative structure for understanding human life and economics. Human flourishing or happiness is the standard underpinning the assessment that a goal is rational and should be pursued. This common human benchmark implies a framework for evaluating a person's decisions and actions. It follows that the fundamental ethical task for each man is the fullest development of himself as a human being and as the individual that he is. Human life thus provides the foundation and context of the realm of ethics. The idea of value is at the root of ethics. A man's immediate needs for survival are economic and are values for his life. Economic production is necessary to satisfy these needs or material values. A productive man is a rational, self-interested, and virtuous man. He is doing what he ought to do to sustain his life.

To survive and flourish a man must grasp reality. To do this requires a rational epistemology and an objective theory of concepts. These have been supplied by Ayn Rand. A person needs to observe reality, abstract essentials, and form objective concepts and laws. The objective nature of the world circumscribes the operations that must be accomplished if goals and values are to be attained. Reality is what is there to be perceived and studied. Everyone is constrained by what is metaphysically real. Fortunately, people have the capacity to objectively apprehend reality. A man's mind can identify, but cannot create, reality. Knowability of the world is a natural condition common both to the external world and the human mind.

Ayn Rand's conception of universals (or essences) as epistemological (she really means contextual and relational) is arguably superior to the traditional interpretation given to Aristotle's ideas or universals as being metaphysical. Rand explains that knowledge is acquired by an active, conscious agent through the processes of induction and deduction. In order to deduce from axioms and general statements, we must first have inductive inferences. We can know via the senses, inferences from data supplied by the senses, and introspective understanding. Once it is acknowledged that Mises's action axiom could be derived through an inductive process, it will then be legitimate to follow and adopt his logical arguments that all the core principles and relationships of economics can be deduced from that axiom.

Capitalism is the consequence of the natural order of liberty, which is based on the ethic of individual happiness. Freedom is connected with morality, ethics, and individual flourishing. Men are moral agents whose task it is to excel at being the human being that one is. In order to be moral agents people need to be free and self-directed. It follows that capitalism is the political expression of the human condition. As a political order relegated to a distinct sphere of human life, it conforms with human nature by permitting each person to pursue happiness, excellence, and the perfection of his own human life through the realization of his rational and other capacities. A free society, one that respects an individual's natural rights, acknowledges that it is an individual's moral responsibility to be as good as possible at living his own life. Of course, such a society cannot guarantee moral and rational behavior on the part of its members. It can only make such conduct possible.

Free will is critical to human existence and human flourishing. A person has the ability to choose to actualize his potential for being a fully developed individual human being. A man depends on his rationality for his survival and flourishing. He must choose to initiate the mental processes of thinking and focusing on becoming the best person he can be in the context of his own existence. He is responsible for applying reason, wisdom, and experience to his own specifically situated circumstances. Rationality is the virtue through which a man exercises reason.

Rand explains that men know they have volition through the act of introspection. The fact that people are regularly deciding to think or not to think is directly accessible to each person. Each person can introspectively observe that he can choose to focus his consciousness or not. A person can pay attention or not. The implication of free will is that men can be held morally responsible for their actions.

The idea of free will does not imply that a person has unlimited power with respect to the operation of his own mind. Man's consciousness has a particular nature, structure, set of powers, and characteristics. Action can be said to be influenced by physiological, psychological, sociological, and other factors, but there is at least some residual amount of free will behind the action that operates independently of the influencing factors. An action is not totally determined by a man's inheritance.

Although a man's choices are ultimately free, there is, in all probability, some connection to a person's physical endowments, facticity, urges, past choices, articulated preferences for the future, scarcity of a good, acquisition of new knowledge, and so on. None of these deterministically causes value. Something is only of value when some human being has decided to act to gain or sustain it. An object can only become a value by means of a person's free choice. Certainly each person is subject to his unconscious mind, biological constraints, genetic inheritances, feelings, urges, environment, etc. However, none of these denies the existence of free will, but only shows that it may be challenging for a person to use his free will to triumph over them.

Each person shares some attributes with other human beings, such as free will and the capacity to reason. It follows that at a basic or metanormative level what is objectively moral or ethical is universally the same. In addition, a person's moral decisions depend, to a certain degree, on his particular circumstances, talents, and characteristics. The particular evaluations a person should make are made through a process of rational cognition. A rational ethical action is what a person believes he should do based on the most fitting and highest quality information acquired about human nature and the individual person that one is. When people approach life rationally, they are more likely to conclude that virtues and ethical principles are necessary for human flourishing. They discover that human beings have a profound need for morality.

Human purposefulness makes the world understandable in terms of human action. Human action is governed by choice and choice is free. Choice is a product of free will. A voluntaristic theory of action recognizes the active role of reason in decisions caused by a human person who wills and acts. Choosing both ends and means is a matter of reason. Because human action is free it is potentially moral. It therefore follows that human actions necessarily include moral or ethical considerations. Values cannot be avoided. Free will means being a moral agent.

Mises views social cooperation and coordination as a proxy for happiness, which is similar to the Aristotelian notion of human flourishing. He deduces that the coordination of free prudent different actions leads to social coordination. It follows that virtuous and moral human actions based on freedom and singularity foster the coordination process.

Reconciling Subjective and Objective Value Theories

The preeminent theory within Austrian value theory is the Misesian subjectivist school. Mises maintained that it is by means of its subjectivism that praxeological economics develops into objective science. The praxeologist takes individual values as given and assumes that individuals have different motivations and prefer different things. The same economic phenomena means different things to different people. In fact, buying and selling takes place because people value things differently. The importance of goods is derived from the importance of the values they are intended to achieve. When a person values an object, this simply means that he imputes enough importance to it to be willing to start a chain of causation to change or maintain it, thus making it a thing of value. Misesian economics does not study what is in an object, as does the natural scientist, but rather, studies what is in the subject.

On the other hand, Menger and Rand agree that the ultimate standard of value is the life of the valuer. Human beings have needs and wants embedded in their nature. Both Menger and Rand begin with the ultimate value of human life and determine the values that a man needs. Their respective objective approaches to value hold that value is only meaningful in relationship to some valuing consciousness. A value must be a value to an existing human being. The differences between the ideas of Menger and Rand on value is that Menger was exclusively concerned with economic values whereas Rand was interested in values of all types. For Rand, all human values are moral values that are essential to the ethical standard of human nature in general and the particular human life of who the agent is.

Although Menger speaks of economic value while Rand is concerned with moral value, their ideas are essentially the same. Both view human life as the ultimate value. Their shared biocentric concept of value contends that every value serves biological needs. Value thus has its roots in the conditional nature of life. Life can perish. Objective values support man's life and originate in a relationship between a man and his survival requirements.

Menger was concerned with the many values whose pursuit is mainly an economic matter. Because anything that satisfies a human need is a value, that which satisfies a man's material needs for food, shelter, health care, wealth, production, and so forth, is deemed to be an economic value. People require a certain degree of prosperity with respect to their needs, desires, and wants.

Rand explains that the idea of value enters the world with the phenomenon of life and that the nature of values depends on the type of life in question. Good and bad are objective relational features of living beings. It follows that the human good is connected to human nature, which involves life, the source of value, and free will, the element of responsibility. Of course, a human being can choose to pursue or reject life. Moral judgment is concerned with what is volitional. Moral principles are useful only to beings with conceptual consciences who can choose their actions.

From Ayn Rand's perspective, every human value is a moral value (including economic value) that is important to the ethical standard of man's life qua man. Rand viewed virtually every human choice as a moral choice involving moral values.

Both Rand and Menger espouse a kind of contextually relational objectivism in their theories of value. Value is seen as a relational quality dependent on the subject, the object, and the context or situation involved. The subject, object, and the situation that combine them are the antecedents of value.

Values come into existence with the emergence of life. Only living things have values. Values are linked to life, and moral values are linked to human life. The ultimate value is life itself. Whereas all living things pursue values, it is only human beings that hold this ultimate value by choice. The idea of human value presupposes a valuer with a conceptual consciousness. In addition to a valuer for whom a thing is a value, other prerequisites of human value are an end to which the value is a means and man's life as an end in itself (i.e., a final end that is not a means to a further end). Life's conditionality (i.e., the alternative of life or death) makes action necessary to achieve values.

In order for a person to survive and flourish, he must obtain the means or fulfill the requirements and needs of his life. A need is a condition whose presence improves a person's ability to survive or flourish or whose absence hinders that ability. Needs arise from a man's nature and thus have a rational foundation. It is natural to satisfy one's needs. In fact, a person's needs can be viewed as the bridge between the natural sciences (especially biology) and the human sciences. Whatever satisfies a need can be deemed to be a value. Value depends on man's needs.

The act of valuing is one of discovering what maintains, advances, and enhances the life of the individual. Objective values support a man's life and objective disvalues jeopardize it. We can say that values are objective when particular objects and actions are good to a specific person and for the purpose of reaching a particular goal. It is possible for a person to value objects that are not actually valuable according to the standard of life. This is because a man is fallible or may choose not to use his capacity to be rational and self-interested. Menger has correctly stated that values correspond to an objective state of affairs when men value what they objectively require to sustain themselves. Value is an objective relationship between a man and an aspect of reality. This relationship is not arbitrary.

Objective value involves a proper connection between conceptual human consciousness (i.e., reason) and the facts of reality. A specific thing's value is a function of the relationship which it has to a given person's life. Whether or not the relevant relationship exists is a matter of fact. Metaphysically, an objective value must exist in a life-affirming relationship to a man. Epistemologically, an objective value must obtain in a proper relationship to his consciousness.

A person properly starts with the specific needs of human life, examines his own capacities, and then determines what values are proper for him. Next, in order to achieve values, a person needs to gain and use conceptual knowledge.

Action is required to reach one's values. However, before one acts in his efforts to gain a value, he should use his reason to identify pertinent causal factors and means-ends relationships. A human being freely chooses to initiate his own actions. He is the fundamental cause of his own behavior.

Some objective values are universal and stem from common human potentialities and characteristics. There are also values that are objective but not universal. Objective values depend on both an individual's humanity and his individuality. A person's individuality is consistent with realism and with an all-embracing consistent explanation of existence. Since individualism is a fundamental feature of the human species, each person is able to employ his unique attributes, talents, and situations in his efforts to do well at living his own individual life. Each person needs to consider his needs, his capacities, the nature of the world, and the opportunities it offers for human action.

Values are metaphysically objective when they are based on the facts that are relevant to him as an individual. A person's moral responsibility, from the perspective of ethical naturalism, is to make the fullest possible development of himself as an individual rational being in the context of the world in which he lives. What a person is, together with what the world is, reveals how he should live his life. A person should use reason to satisfy his needs, choose what goals to pursue, and determine what actions will achieve them.

As we have seen, there is an important dissemblance within Austrian value theory between Menger and Mises. However, it is possible for Menger's more objective-value-oriented theory to coexist and complement Mises's pure subjectivism, which is based on the inscrutability of individual values and preferences. Although Menger agreed with Mises that an individual's chosen values are personal and therefore subjective and unknowable to the economist, he also contended that a person ought to be rationally pursuing his objective life-affirming values. Menger thus can be viewed as a key linchpin thinker between Misesian praxeology and Objectivist ethics.

Production and Economic Laws

Production is the means to the fulfillment of men's material needs. The production of goods, services, and wealth metaphysically precedes their distribution and exchange. When a man acts rationally and in his own self-interest, he makes wealth creation, economic activity, and the scientific study of economics possible. To survive and flourish, men have to produce what is necessary for their existence. The requirements of life must be objectively identified and produced. The facts regarding what enhances or restrains life are objective, established by the facts of reality, and based on proper cognition. There are requirements and rules built into the nature of things which must be met if we are to survive and prosper.

Both Austrian economists and Objectivists agree with the French classical economist Jean-Baptiste Say that production is the source of demand. Products are ultimately paid for with other products. Consumption (i.e., demand) follows from the production of wealth. Supply metaphysically comes before consumption. The primacy of production means that we must produce before we can consume. Demand does not create supply, and consumption does not create production.

The idea that supply comprises demand is true in a money economy as well as in a barter economy. Money is an intermediate good that allows people to buy the things they desire. What ultimately permits men to buy is not the possession of money but rather the possession of productive assets through which they can earn money in the market economy. It follows that when individuals spend money they are demanding from the wealth what their production created.

Productiveness is a virtue. People tend to be productive and successful when they are rational and self-interested. Production requires people who practice the virtues of rationality and self-interest. Rationality, a common standard in human nature, is a discerning approach to the selection of both ends and means. Self-interest is also a virtue because living for human beings is ultimately an individual task. Because the maintenance of each person's life is conditional, it is necessary for each individual to choose to think, plan, and produce if he wants to survive and flourish.

As volitional beings, men have the capacity to be rational and self-interested. In fact, it is only to the degree that men are rational and self-interested that they can produce and it is only to the extent that they produce that an objective science of economics can emerge. Economic laws are based on rational, self-interested actions and are concerned with the universal abstract aspects of phenomena. Because a man's life is conditional, he needs to acquire economic and other values in order to live. Material wealth (i.e., value) is necessary to maintain one's life. A man has the capacity to choose to produce and exchange values. Most people do choose to live and thus are productive. To be productive, a person must be rational and self-interested. People produce in order to consume (i.e., to live). Economic behavior occurs and is regular when men act rationally and in their own self-interest. Because most people want to survive, they attempt to rationally comprehend the facts of the world and choose to create and trade values. Normative, descriptive, and explanatory economic laws are possible because of the regularity that is evidenced in economic activity due to most people acting in their own rational self-interest. Causal connections are manifested in the phenomena of economic life. Rational self-interest is the driving force of both production and consumption. It is easy to see why both Menger and Mises viewed the field of economics as one of exact laws and exact inquiry. According to Menger, exact laws assume that men are rational, self-interested, informed, and free. Similarly, Rand saw economic laws as objective laws.[1]

Human Action

Praxeology is the general theoretical science of human action. Mises grounds economics upon the action axiom that states that men exist and act by making purposive choices. Misesian praxeology refers to the set of sciences that derive by logical inference exclusively from the axiom of human action. Economics is thus a division of praxeology and is made up of apodictically true statements that are not empirically testable. Praxeological laws are universal doctrines whose applicability is independent of any particular empirical circumstances. Praxeology is a unifying framework that unites all types of human decisions, actions, and interactions.

Mises emphasized the central role that "acting man" plays in economics and the necessity to work within a framework conducive for real acting persons. Because axioms expound bedrock metaphysical facts that are self-evident, it is obvious why Mises is in error when he identified action as a primary axiom. Action depends upon a thing's nature. Action is not an irreducible primary. What is primary in studying human action is the nature of man. This leads to a consideration of man's modes of action and their related causal factors. The action axiom is thus more appropriately seen as a secondary axiom to the primary axiom of identity, which states that a thing is what it is. The significance of any given action is relational and changes depending upon what or who is performing the specific action.

Rand explains that entities act in accordance with their natures, and the causality is the axiom of identity applied to action. It follows that action cannot be a primary independent of something's nature. In other words, action depends on the underlying characteristics of the thing. This presupposes the axiom of existence, which means that "existence exists" and that there is a definite something that exists.

Mises explains that a man's introspective knowledge that he is conscious and acts is a fact of reality and is independent of external experience. Mises deduced the principles of economics and the complete structure of economic theory entirely through the analysis of the introspectively derived, a priori idea of human action. While it is certainly important to understand and acknowledge the useful role of introspection in one's life, it is also necessary to realize that its role is limited, secondary, and adjunct to the empirical observation and logical analysis of empirical reality. It would have been better if Mises had said that external observation and introspection combine to reveal that people act and employ means to achieve ends. Introspection aids or supplements external observation and induction in disclosing to a man the fundamental purposefulness of human action.

Murray Rothbard defends Mises's methodology but goes on to construct his own edifice of Austrian economic theory. Although he embraced nearly all of Mises's economics, Rothbard could not accept Mises's Kantian extreme aprioristic position in epistemology. Mises held that the axiom of human action was true a priori to human experience and was, in fact, a synthetic a priori category. Mises considered the action axiom to be a law of thought and thus a categorical truth prior to all human experience.

Rothbard, working within an Aristotelian, Thomistic, or Mengerian tradition, justified the praxeological action axiom as a law of reality that is empirical rather than a priori. Of course, this is not the empiricism embraced by positivists. This kind of empirical knowledge rests on universal inner or reflective experience in addition to external physical experience. This type of empirical knowledge consist of a general knowledge of human action that would be considered to be antecedent to the complex historical events that mainstream economists try to explain. The action axiom is empirical in the sense that it is self-evidently true once stated. It is not empirically falsifiable in the positivist sense. It is empirical, but it is not based on empiricism as practiced by today's economics profession. Praxeological statements cannot be subjected to any empirical assessment whether it is falsificationist or verificationist.

Both induction and deduction are required. Initially, the concept of action is formally and inductively derived from perceptual data. Next, the whole systematic structure of economic theory would be deduced from the notion of human action. The categories, theorems, and laws implied in the idea of action include, but are not limited to, value, causality, ends, means, preference, cost, profit and loss, opportunities, scarcity, choice, marginal utility, marginal costs, opportunity cost, time preference, originary interest, association, etc.

There is a dimension of interiority for human beings who have the ability to imagine new futures for themselves and to invent projects and paths for their personal development. Each person is responsible for, and provident over, his own actions and identity. The human person, the acting person, can reflect, deliberate, choose, initiate action, and assume responsibility for his own actions. In addition to the Austrian economists noted economic personalists such as Pope John Paul II and Michael Novak herald the acting person's interior life of insight, reflection, and decision.

Introspection is a reasonably reliable but ancillary source of evidence and knowledge with respect to what it means to be a rational, purposeful, volitional, and acting human being. Each person knows universally from introspection that he chooses. In other words, observation is introspective in the case of free will. Universal inner or reflective experience is an important adjunct to external, empirical, physical experience.

Free will means that a person is able to perform actions that are not determined by forces outside of his control. This means that at least some choices and actions are not caused by antecedent factors or governed by physical laws or physical events. A human being has the power to reflect, weigh, arrange, and select from among various courses of behavior. In order for an action to be free, it must be because no antecedent factors were enough to make the person carry out exactly that action. A human action is thus not merely a reaction to some prior force or action. We can say that free will exists if a change in a physical variable or property is not due to a prior change in some other physical variable or property. Because a man has reason and free will, he can create concepts, form values, and develop plans aimed at actualizing those values. A person recognizes opportunities to improve his well-being and pursues actions to attain the preferable state of affairs. Actions are intended mainly because of what is desired and thought to be possible. Means-end rationality presumes that people can imagine futures that are different from the present. In devising a plan, a man imagines the future conditions he believes he would experience if he decides to act.

Physical events cannot cause praxeological events. There is a qualitative difference between human actions and deterministic reactions of totally corporeal objects. Action embodies a forward-looking character. Human beings can cause goal-directed, self-generated behavior. Reaction in a determined entity can theoretically and potentially be followed back in time until the beginning of the universe. It follows that, in the natural sciences, the researcher deals with things and the regular relationships that can be discovered to be functioning between them. While we find determinism in physical nature, we discover that a human being possesses specific, delimited control over his consciousness. Every existent is constrained to be what it is and to not be anything else. Men's thoughts and actions are therefore irrelevant to the natural scientist but crucial to philosophers and economists.

A person discovers relationships between his values and his plans. He also strives to learn the relationships between various pertinent causal variables and strives to create those relationships. He must act to acquire the factors or goods he believes are required to accomplish the plans that will achieve his values. Of course, as he gains knowledge, his values may change, which, in turn, may result in a change of his plans. A person is always free to change the significance of his values and plans and may decide to act in a different manner than before. People learn from their experiences, past choices, and discoveries, and revise their plans accordingly.

According to Mises, economics is a value-free science of means, rather than of ends, that describes but does not prescribe. However, although the world of praxeological economics, as a science, may be value-free, the human world is not value-free. Economics is the science of human action, and human actions are inextricably connected with values and ethics. It follows that praxeological economics needs to be situated within the context of a normative framework. Praxeological economics does not conflict with a normative perspective on human life. Economics needs to be connected with a discipline that is concerned with ends such as human flourishing. Praxeological economics can stay value-free if it is recognized that it is morally proper for people to take part in market and other voluntary transactions. Such a value-free science must be combined with an appropriate end.

Economics, for Mises, is a value-free tool for objective and critical appraisal. Economic science differentiates between the objective, interpersonally valid conclusions of economic praxeology and the personal value judgments of the economist. Critical appraisal can be objective, value-free, and untainted by bias. It is important for economic science to be value-free and not to be distorted by the value judgments or personal preferences of the economist. The credibility of economic science depends upon an impartial and dispassionate concern for truth. Value-freedom is a methodological device designed to separate and isolate scientific work from the personal preferences of the given economic researcher. His goal is to maintain neutrality and objectivity with respect to the subjective values of others.

Misesian economics focuses on the descriptive aspects of human action by offering reasoning about means and ends. The province of praxeological economics is the logical analysis of the success or failure of selected means to attain ends. Means only have value because, and to the degree that, their ends are valued.

The reasons why an individual values what he values and the determination of whether or not his choices and actions are morally good or bad are certainly significant concerns, but they are not the realm of the praxeological economist. The content of moral or ultimate ends is not the domain of the economist qua economist. There is another level of values that defines value in terms of right preferences. This more objectivist sphere of value defines value in terms of what an individual ought to prefer.

Simply because Mises expounds a value-free science of economics, it does not mean that he believes that a man's behavior lacks moral content. Because a human being is not compartmentalized, economic values and moral values coexist in a man's consciousness, frequently affect one another, and oftentimes overlap. Sooner or later, some moral values must be referred to before the propositions of praxeological economics can be used in men's concrete situations and in service of their ultimate ends. It follows that theories of the moral good are compatible with Austrian economics because they exist on a different plane.

Knowledge gained from praxeological economics is both value-free (i.e., value-neutral) and value-relevant. Value-free knowledge supplied by economic science is value-relevant when it supplies information for rational discussions, deliberations, and determinations of the morally good. Economics is reconnected with philosophy, especially the branches of metaphysics and ethics, when the discussion is shifted to another sphere. It is fair to say that economic science exists because men have concluded that the objective knowledge provided by praxeological economics is valuable for the pursuit of both a person's subjective and ultimate ends.

Advocating or endorsing the idea of "man's survival qua man" or of a good or flourishing life involves value judgments. To make value judgments, one must accept the existence of a comprehensive natural order and the existence of fundamental absolute principles in the universe. This acceptance in no way conflicts with the Misesian concept of subjective economic value. Natural laws are neither discovered nor are not arbitrary relationships, but instead are relationships that are already true. A man's human nature, including his attributes of individuality, reason, and free will, is the ultimate source of moral reasoning. Value is meaningless outside the context of man.

Knowledge of the consequences of alternative social arrangements is necessary and useful in deciding from among different social structures. The choice of the best model of political economy is a value-laden endeavor that is underpinned by the value-free logic of praxeological economics. Given the nature of a human being, it is only he who can decide, and has the right to decide, upon the relative importance of different values and whether or not to act upon them. Since a person has free will, he can choose to cause physical changes to occur without any prior physical causes. Values are metaphysically freely chosen and acted upon when there is an absence of coercion. Man's distinctiveness from other living species is his ability to originate an act of his consciousness. This process of thought is originated volitionally. Freedom is the degree of independence of an individual's plans from the plans of others. Freedom can be assessed by examining the autonomy a man would have under various social arrangements. Praxeological analysis reveals that a free market society results in the optimum amount of freedom, social cooperation, and social coordination.

Praxeological economics and the philosophy of human flourishing are complementary and compatible disciplines. Economics teaches us that social cooperation through the private property system and division of labor enables most individuals to prosper and to pursue their flourishing and happiness. In turn, the worldview of human flourishing informs men how to act. In making their life-affirming ethical and value-based judgments, men can refer to and employ the data of economic science.

Bounded Man in a Circumscribed World

Human nature is essentially unchanging and unchangeable. Men have always been imperfect in their knowledge, in their integrity, and in their ability to love and respect their fellow men. Men possess all of the frailties of a finite nature. Accept them as they are and don't expect human behavior to improve much over the long run. Men are essentially self-centered, but conditions can be improved within that constraint by relying primarily on incentives (i.e., rewards and punishments) rather than on dispositions. Because of human limitations and imperfections, man's ability to improve society is restricted.

Social outcomes are mainly a function of incentives presented to individuals and of the conditions under which they interact in response to them. Given man's moral and intellectual limitations and egocentricity, the fundamental challenge is to make the best of the possibilities within the constraints of man's nature.

In addition, resources are always inadequate to fulfill all the desires of all of the people. There are no solutions, only trade-offs that leave man's desires unfulfilled. We must accept the reality of economic constraints and the trade-offs they imply. We need to realize that human limitations are moral as well as intellectual and that resources are taken from other uses. Men choose between alternatives, regulate their behavior deliberately, and act purposively to attain their chosen ends.

As emphasized by F. A. Hayek and Thomas Sowell, it is imperative to have the right processes for making trade-offs and correcting inevitable errors. We need to maximize individuals' ability to use scattered fragments of knowledge and to correct mistakes as quickly as possible. Societal progress is most effectively and equally attained through systemic social processes (e.g., moral tradition, the market, the law, and families) rather than through solutions proposed by government officials. Society is a spontaneous order not under anyone's design or control. It cannot be a field of problems awaiting solutions because no one knows enough to successfully engage in comprehensive social and political experiments.

Human beings cannot flourish unless they direct their own actions. Each man is ultimately responsible for what happens to him and has the potential to rise above influences of environment, heredity, and chance to alter and determine his own future. The task of human persons is to do well in their own lives. Men, by virtue of being human, possess the capacity to exercise free will and have the inalienable right to do so. The natural order can be altered by men using their reason and free will, but who can also choose to treat others rightly or wrongly. Natural law grounds the propriety of human actions and values in the facts of reality and human nature. There is a natural order, which would result in the consonance of everyone's interests, if all people would participate in life fairly and justly.

Whereas potential natural resources are the given, the variable is human action. Human beings are unique individuals as well as members of a distinct species. It follows that each singular person's self-enhancement is a matter of what suits him best. Human variability in abilities and tastes is a source of comparative advantage that results in specialization, division of labor, and exchange. Similarly, the uneven distribution of natural resources, climate variability, and the diversity of human abilities lead to the ideas of the comparative advantage of nations and free trade. Variation leads to differential attainment in all areas of human endeavor and the dissimilar acquisition of income and wealth. Because the natural order of human society is variety, diversity, and inequality, virtue, charity, and compassion can only exist in a world of free and unequal individuals. In a free society, in accord with the natural order, natural differences among people would result in some being better off than others, but there would be no political inequality—everyone would be equal before the law and possess equal rights, freedom to choose, and equality of opportunity.

Although environmental factors can mitigate or intensify mental and physical differences, nonequality will continue to be the natural order. The differences in individual talents, motivations, and resources that each of us has are not inherently unjust—there will always be inequalities among people. The idea of justice does not apply to the metaphysically given. It is not unjust for some people to be born with less ability or resources than others.

Economic and social equality can only be attained at the cost of political equality, if it is possible to attain it all. Because people differ in intelligence, physical abilities, and drive, it follows that, given freedom, people will also vary in achievement, income, wealth, and status. People are unequal in reality. In fact, to say that persons are equal simply means that they are equal in one or more respects—not in all respects.

Once freedom has been achieved, a man is free to do and act according to his plans and decisions. Of course, having the capacity to choose does not exempt him from the law of cause and effect. A man can choose to act in agreement or disagreement with natural law. However, once a choice has been made, the inviolate and inexorable workings of natural law and cause and effect come into play by supplying a reward or a penalty as a result of the choice made. A person cannot manifest real freedom unless he is willing to accept the natural consequences of his freely made choices.

The Pursuit of Flourishing and Happiness

Personal flourishing requires the rational use of one's talents, abilities, and virtues in the pursuit of one's freely chosen goals and values. Happiness is the positive experience that accompanies or flows from the use of one's individual human potentialities in the pursuit of one's goals and values. In other words, personal flourishing leads to happiness.

Virtues are the means to values and goods, and together the virtues, values, and goods enable individuals to attain human flourishing and happiness. Living by, and acting on, rational moral principles cultivates corresponding virtues, which in turn, lead to value attainment, flourishing, and happiness. An appropriate set of general evaluative principles provides basic guidance in living well. Virtues such as rationality, honesty, independence, justice, integrity, productiveness, courage, trustworthiness, benevolence, and pride (moral ambitiousness) must be applied, although differentially, by each person in his task of human flourishing. Human flourishing is the reward of virtues and values and happiness is the goal and reward of human flourishing.

The right of private property is a precondition for making the pursuit of one's flourishing and happiness possible. No more fundamental human right exists than the right to use and control one's things, thoughts, and actions so as to manage one's life as one sees fit. If one has the right to sustain his life, then he has the right to whatever he is able to produce with his own time and means. Each person has the right to do whatever he wants with his justly held property as long as in so doing he does not violate the rights of another. Without private ownership, voluntary free trade and competition would be impossible.

As men found specialization desirable, an exchange mechanism evolved through which one person, who could produce an item more efficiently than others, could exchange it for an article that he could not make as efficiently as another person could make it. As trade and commerce developed, this giving-

and-getting arrangement became more and more protected by formal contract. The idea of sanctity of contract is essential to a market economy and one of the most important elements that holds a civilized society together.

A market economy is a voluntary association of property owners for the purpose of trading to their mutual advantage. The market accommodates people who seek to improve their circumstances by trading goods and services in a non-coercive setting. Markets are efficient and effective mechanisms for ensuring that society is arranged to maximize individuals' ability to act on their best vision of their well-being. The market process reflects both social cooperation and voluntarism in human affairs. A market economy is a necessary condition for a free society.

Private markets encourage people to interact, cooperate, learn, and prosper from their diversity. The market economy inspires people to seek out others who are different from them, treat their differences as opportunities, and garner mutual gains through their cooperative interaction. When two people make a deal, each one expects to gain from it. Each person has a different scale of values and a different frame of reference. The market mechanism permits people to maximize their results while economizing their efforts.

The price of any good or service is whatever others willingly give in voluntary exchange in particular circumstances. The judgments of all parties are continually and everlastingly changing. There is no one optimal product or service specification. Not only do consumer tastes vary among prospective purchasers at any one point in time, they also change over time and situationally so that experimentation and research in product and service specifications is a continuous process.

The market is an effective communicator of data. With its continuing flow of positive and negative feedback, the market allows decision makers to review a constantly changing mix of options and resulting trade-offs and to respond with precision by continually making incremental adjustments. The role of prices as transmitters of knowledge economizes the amount of information required to produce a given economic result. No one person need have complete information in order for the economy to convey relevant information through prices and achieve the same adjustments that would obtain if everyone had that knowledge. Prices are a mechanism for carrying out the rationing function and are a fast, efficient conveyor of information through a society in which fragmented knowledge must be coordinated. Accurate prices, resulting from voluntary exchanges, allow the economy to achieve optimal performance in terms of satisfying each person as much as possible by his own standards without sacrificing others' rights to act according to their own standards.

Work is built into the human condition. Men have to work in order to sustain themselves. The things by which people live do not exist until someone creates them. Man survives by using his reason and other faculties to adjust his environment to himself. Productive work is also a means through which people attain purpose in their lives. Work is at the heart of a meaningful life and is essential for personal survival and flourishing. Work is necessary not only to obtain wealth but also to pursue one's purpose and self-esteem. There are integrated links between reality, reason, self-interest, productive work, goal attainment, personal flourishing, and happiness.

There is an inextricable association between purposeful work and individual freedom. Both employees and employers are parties to a voluntary agreement, the terms of which both parties are legally and morally obliged to honor. Both seek to gain from the arrangement. As independent moral agents, the employee and employer agree to terms in a matter that affects their lives, their values, and their futures. A freely chosen job can be a source of one's happiness and self-respect.

Because a large portion of an individual's potentialities can only be realized through association with other human beings, personal flourishing requires a life with others—family, friends, acquaintances, business associates, etc. These associations are instrumentally valuable in the satisfaction of nonsocial wants and desirable for a person's moral maturation, including the sense of meaning and value obtained from the realization of the consanguinity of living beings that accompanies such affiliations.

Men are necessarily related to others and they can determine to a great extent the persons they will be associated with and the ways in which they will be associated. Each person is responsible for choosing, creating, and entering relationships that enable him to flourish. Voluntary, mutually beneficial relations among autonomous individuals using their practical reason is necessary for attaining authentic human communities. Human sociality is also open to relationships with strangers, foreigners, and others with whom no common bonds are shared—except for the common bond of humanity.

Unlike the state, which is based on coercion, civil society is based on voluntary participation. Civil society consists of natural and voluntary associations such as families, private businesses, unions, churches, clubs, charities, etc. Civil society, a spontaneous order, consists of a network of associations built on the freedom of the individual to associate or not to associate. The voluntary communities and associations of civil society are valuable because human beings need to associate with others in order to flourish and achieve happiness. For example, freely given charity may be considered as an embodiment of one's struggle for self-perfection. In this context, charitable activities may be viewed as fulfillment of one's potential for cooperation and as a specific demonstration of that capacity—not as an obligation owed to others.

A person's moral maturation requires a life with others. Charitable conduct can therefore be viewed as an expression of one's self-perfection. From this viewpoint, the obligation for charity is that the benefactor owes it to himself, not to the recipients. If a benefit is owed to another, rendering it is not a charitable act—charity must be freely given and directed toward those to whom we have no obligation. Charitable actions may be viewed as perfective of a person's capacity for cooperation and as a particular manifestation (i.e., giving to those in need) of that capacity. Kindness and benevolence, as a basic way of functioning, are not impulses or obligations to others but rational goals. Compassion is not charity and sentiment is not virtue. This nonaltruistic, noncommunitarian view of charity (and the other virtues) is grounded in a self-perfective framework under which persons can vary the type, amount, and object of their charity based on their contingent circumstances. Other contemporary concepts of charity rely on adherence to duty expressed as deontic rules or as the maximization of social welfare.

Business is the way a free society arranges its economic activities. Business deals with the natural phenomena of scarcity, insatiability, and cost in a valuable and efficient manner. The business system creates equality of opportunity and rewards businessmen who take advantage of opportunities by anticipating consumer preferences and efficiently using resources to satisfy those preferences. Through his thought and action, the businessman enables other people to obtain what they want.

Progress is difference and change. If individuals were not free to try new things, then we would never have any improvements. In order to have progress, there must be freedom to attempt new advances. Progress is impossible unless people are free to be different. Regulation and controls stifle innovation and experimentation. Bureaucracy gets in the way of change. Capitalism has made advances possible, not solely in providing life's necessities, but in science, technology, and knowledge of all types upon which human society depends. Freedom attracts innovators and explorers and gives life to their ideas. Freedom for people to act in their own self-interest is the mainspring for a diversity of ideas, innovations, and experiments that lead to the discovery of new products, services, and other means of production.

Progress requires the use of information that exists only as widely dispersed knowledge that each person has with respect to his own circumstances, conditions, and preferences. Such tacit, locationally specific knowledge is only useful if people are free to act upon it. A free market permits prices to emerge from the use of people's localized knowledge. These prices contain more and better information and result in better decisions than what can be achieved under a regime of central planners. Limited government and decentralized markets permit more freedom and foster more prosperity than do state-dominated and centralized bureaucracies.

Wealth, in the form of goods and services, is created when individuals recombine and rearrange the resources that comprise the world. Wealth increases when someone conceives and produces a more valuable configuration of the earth's substances than the combination that existed previously. It is the existence of unremitting change that summons entrepreneurs in their search for profits. The entrepreneur predicts, responds to, and creates change regarding the discovery of new resource sources, new consumers' desires, and new technological opportunities. He seeks profit by creating new products and services, new businesses, new production methods, and so on. An entrepreneur attains wealth and his other objectives by providing people with goods and services that further flourishing on earth. Entrepreneurs are specialists in prudence—the virtue of applying one's talents to the goal of living well.

Technology is an attempt to develop means for the ever more effective realization of individuals' ideas and values. The purpose of technological advancement is to make life easier through the creation of new products, services, and production methods. These advances improve people's standard of living, increase their leisure time, help to eliminate poverty, and lead to a great variety of products and services. New technologies enhance people's lives as both producers and consumers. By making life easier, safer, and more prosperous, technological progress permits a person more time to spend on higher-level concerns such as religion, character development, love, and the perfection of one's soul.

The corporation occupies an important position within civil society. The corporation is a social invention with the purpose of providing goods and services in order to make profits for its owners, with fiduciary care for shareholders' invested capital. Corporate managers thus have the duty to use the stockholders' money for expressly authorized purposes that can run from the pursuit of profit to the use of resources for social purposes. Managers have a contractual and moral responsibility to fulfill the wishes of the shareholders and, therefore, do not have the right to spend the owners' money in ways that have not been approved by the stockholders, no matter what social benefits may accrue by doing so.

Unionism currently consists of both voluntary and coercive elements. Voluntary unions restrict themselves to activities such as mass walkouts and boycotts. They do nothing to violate the rights of others by using violence against them. Coercive unions use physical force (e.g., picketing when its purpose is to coerce and physically prevent others from crossing the picket line and from dealing with the struck employer) aimed at nonaggressing individuals. Mass picketing that obstructs entrance or exit is invasive of the employer's property rights, as are sit-down strikes and sit-ins that coercively occupy the property of the employer. People who are willing to work for a struck employer have a legitimate right (but currently not a legal right in many states) to do so. In addition, the struck employer has a legitimate right to engage in voluntary exchanges with customers, suppliers, and other workers.

Coercive unions achieve their goals through the coercive power of the state. Most states' legislation excludes nonunion workers when a majority of the workers choose a particular union to be their exclusive bargaining agent. The state should not be concerned with a private citizen's agreement to work with a particular firm. In a free society, one based on natural law principles, each person would be free to take the best offer that he gets. In a free society, unions could merely be voluntary groups trying to advance their members' interests without the benefit of special privileges. In such a society, some workers would join one union, some would join other unions, and some would choose to deal with the employer directly and individually.

There are a great many coercive challenges, encroachments, and constraints that have inhibited the establishment of a society based on the natural liberty of the individual and the realities of the human condition. By nature, these barriers tend to be philosophical, economic, and political. Some of the strongest attacks on, and impediments to, a free society include: collectivist philosophies, cultural relativism, communitarianism, environmentalism, public education, taxation, protectionism, antitrust laws, government regulation, and monetary inflation. These bureaucratic and socialistic ideologies and schemes tend to stem from various sources such as true human compassion, envy, the insecurity of people who want protection from life's uncertainties, categorical "solutions" proposed to solve problems, idealism, and the tendency to think only of intended, primary, and immediate results while ignoring unintended, ancillary, and long-term ones.

Toward an Integrated Conceptual Framework

Philosophy provides the conceptual framework necessary to understand man's behavior. To survive a person must perceive the world, comprehend it, and act upon it. To survive and flourish a man must recognize that nature has its own imperatives. He needs to have viable, sound, and proper conceptions of man's nature, knowledge, values, and action. He must recognize that there is a natural law that derives from the nature of man and the world and that is discoverable through the use of reason.

Ultimately, the truth is one. There is an essential interconnection between objective ideas. It follows that academicians should pay more attention to systems building rather than to the extreme specialization within a discipline. They should endeavor to take positive steps toward an overarching theoretical perspective and truth-based paradigm.

A sound paradigm requires internal consistency among its components. By properly integrating insights from past and current thinkers, we can avoid the errors of rationalism and empiricism and develop a general theory that can be separated from historical circumstances. Such a framework would reframe the argument for a free society and would elucidate a theory of the best political regime on the basis of proper conceptions of the nature of man, human action, and society. This natural-law-based paradigm would uphold each man's sovereignty, moral space, and natural rights. It would hold that men require a social and political structure that recognizes natural rights and accords each person a moral space over which he has freedom to act and pursue his personal flourishing.

It is acceptable to mix and match components from different paradigms in our efforts to achieve a deeper understanding of the nature of man and the world. By extracting information from existing paradigms it is possible to create a paradigm that is more reflective of reality. Specifically, it may be desirable to refine and fuse together the following components: (1) an objective, realistic, natural-law-oriented metaphysics; (2) a natural rights theory based on the nature of man and the world; (3) an objective epistemology which describes essences or concepts as relational and contextual rather than as metaphysical; (4) a bio-centric theory of value; (5) praxeology as a tool for understanding how people cooperate and compete and for deducing universal principles of economics; and (6) an ethic of human flourishing based on reason, free will, and individuality.

Our goal is to have a paradigm or system in which the views of reality, knowledge, human nature, value, and society make up an integrated whole. The suggested synthesis can provide a foundation for such a paradigm. Of course, the paradigm will grow and evolve as scholars engage, question, critique, interpret, and extend its ideas. Such a systematic approach and/or its components must be viewed as a vibrant, living framework that aims at the truth.

Note

1. See Richard M. Salsman, *Economic and Rational Self Interest*, four audio lectures (New Milford, CT: Second Renaissance Books, 1995).

Recommended Reading

Annas, Julia. *The Morality of Happiness*. New York: Oxford University Press, 1993.

Backhouse, R. E. *Economists and the Economy: The Evolution of Economic Ideas*. 2nd ed. New Brunswick, NJ: Transaction Press, 1994.

Blaug, Mark. *Economic Theory in Retrospect*. Cambridge: Cambridge University Press, [1985] 1992.

Boaz, David. *Libertarianism: A Primer*. New York: Free Press, 1997.

Bonar, James. *Philosophy and Political Economy*. New Brunswick, NJ: Transaction Publishers, 1992.

Brue, Stanley L. *The Evolution of Economic Thought*. Mason, OH: Thomson Learning, 2000.

Buckle, Stephen. *Natural Law and the Theory of Property*. Oxford: Oxford University Press, 1991.

Caldwell, Bruce C., ed. *Carl Menger and His Legacy in Economics*. Durham, NC: Duke University Press, 1990.

Conway, David. *Classical Liberalism: The Unvanquished Ideal*. London: MacMillan, 1997.

Copleston, Frederick. *A History of Philosophy*. New York: Doubleday, 1985.

Den Uyl, Douglas J. *The Virtue of Prudence*. New York: Peter Lang, 1991.

Den Uyl, Douglas J., and Douglas B. Rasmussen. "Rights as Metanormative Principles." In *Liberty for the Twenty-First Century*, edited by Tibor R. Machan and Douglas B. Rasmussen. Lanham, MD: Rowman & Littlefield., 1995.

Ebeling Richard M., ed. *Austrian Economics: Perspectives on the Past and Prospects for the Future*. Hillsdale, MI: Hillsdale College Press, 1991.

———. *Human Action: A 50-Year Tribute*. Hillsdale, MI: Hillsdale College Press, 2000.

Finnis, John. *Natural Law and Natural Rights*. Oxford: Oxford University Press, 1980.

Fuller, Lon. *The Morality of Law*. New Haven, CT: Yale University Press, 1964.

Gierke, Otto von. *Natural Law and the Theory of Society*. Translated by Ernest Barker. Boston: Beacon Press, 1957.

Hart, H. L. A. "Are There Any Natural Rights?" *Philosophical Review* (October 1955).

———. *The Concept of Law*. Oxford: Oxford University Press, 1961.

Hazlitt, Henry. *The Foundations of Morality*. Los Angeles: Nash Publishing, 1972.

Hospers, John. *Libertarianism: A Political Philosophy for Tomorrow*. Los Angeles: Nash Publishing, 1971.

Hunt, Lester H. "Flourishing Egoism." *Social Philosophy and Policy* (Winter 1999).

Hurka, Thomas. *Perfectionism*. New York: Oxford University Press, 1993.

Hursthouse, Rosalind. *On Virtue Ethics*. New York: Oxford University Press, 2002.

Jones, W. T. *A History of Western Philosophy*. New York: Harcourt, Brace & World, 1962.

Kenny, Anthony. *A Brief History of Western Philosophy*. Oxford: Blackwell, 1998.

LeFevre, Robert. *The Fundamentals of Liberty*. Santa Ana, CA: Rampart Institute, 1988.

Lepage, Henri. *Tomorrow Capitalism*. LaSalle, IL: Open Court, 1978.

Locke, John. *Essays on the Law of Nature*. Edited by W. von Leyden. Oxford: Clarendon Press, 1952.

Lomasky, Loren E. *Persons, Rights, and the Moral Community*. Oxford: Oxford University Press, 1987.

Machan, Tibor R. *Human Rights and Human Liberties*. Chicago: Nelson-Hall, 1974.

———. *Individuals and Their Rights*. LaSalle, IL: Open Court, 1989.

———. *Capitalism and Individualism*. New York: St. Martin's Press, 1990.

———. *Classical Individualism*. London: Routledge, 1998.

Mack, Eric. "Moral Individualism: Agent Relativity and Deontic Restraints." *Social Philosophy and Policy* (Autumn 1989).

———. "Deontic Restrictions are not Agent-Relative Restrictions." *Social Philosophy and Policy* (1998).

———. "On the Fit Between Egoism and Rights." *Reason Papers* (Fall 1998).

Menger, Carl. *Principles of Economics*. New York: New York University Press, [1871] 1981.

———. *Investigations into the Method of the Social Sciences with Special Refer-ence to Economics*. New York: New York University Press, [1883] 1985.

Mises, Ludwig von. *Human Action: A Treatise on Economics*. New Haven, CT: Yale University Press, 1949.

———. *Epistemological Problems of Economics*. Princeton, NJ: Van Nostrand, 1960.

———. *Liberalism in the Classical Tradition*. Irvington, NY: Foundation for Economic Education, [1927] 1985.

Narveson, Jan. *The Libertarian Idea*. Philadelphia: Temple University Press, 1988.

Norton, David. *Personal Destinies*. Princeton, NJ: Princeton University Press, 1976.

Peikoff, Leonard. *Objectivism: The Philosophy of Ayn Rand*. New York: Dutton, 1991.

Rand, Ayn. *Atlas Shrugged*. New York: Random House, 1957.

———. *Capitalism: The Unknown Ideal*. New York: Signet, 1967.

———. *Introduction to Objectivist Epistemology*. New York: The Objectivist, 1967.

Rasmussen, Douglas B. "Individual Rights and Human Flourishing." *Public Affairs Quarterly* 3 (1989).

———. "Community versus Liberty." In *Liberty for the Twenty-First Century*, edited by Tibor R. Machan and Douglas B. Rasmussen. Lanham, MD: Rowman & Littlefield, 1995.

———. "Human Flourishing and the Appeal to Human Nature." *Social Philosophy and Policy* (Winter 1999).

Rasmussen, Douglas B., and Douglas J. Den Uyl. *Liberty and Nature*. La Salle, IL: Open Court, 1991.

———. *Norms of Liberty*. University Park: The Pennsylvania State University Press, 2005.

Reisman, George. *Capitalism*. Ottawa, IL: Jameson Books, 1996.

Roncaglia, Allesandro. *The Wealth of Ideas: A History of Economic Thought*. Cambridge: Cambridge University Press, 2005.

Rothbard, Murray N. *Man, Economy, and State*. Mission, KS: Sheed, Andrews & McMeel, 1962.

———. *The Ethics of Liberty*. Atlantic Highlands, NJ: Humanities Press, 1982.

Rowley, Charles Kershaw, ed. *Classical Liberalism and Civil Society*. Cheltenham, UK: Edward Elgar, 1998.

Sabine, George H. *A History of Political Theory*. New York: Holt, Rinehart, & Winston, 1961.

Sciabarra, Chris Matthew. *Total Freedom: Toward a Dialectical Libertarianism*. University Park: Pennsylvania State University Press, 2000.

Shue, Henry. *Basic Rights*. Princeton, NJ: Princeton University Press, 1980.

Skoble, Aeon, ed. *Reading Rasmussen and Den Uyl: Critical Essays on Norms of Liberty*. Lanham, MD: Lexington Books, 2008.

Slote, Michael. *From Morality to Virtue*. New York: Oxford University Press, 1992.

Smith, Barry. *Austrian Philosophy: The Legacy of Franz Brentano*. LaSalle, IL: Open Court, 1994.

Smith, Tara. *Viable Values*. Lanham, MD: Rowman & Littlefield, 2000.

Sowell, Thomas. *Knowledge and Decisions*. New York: Basic Books, 1980.

Spiegel, Henry William. *The Growth of Economic Thought*. 3rd ed. Durham, NC: Duke University Press, 1971.

Strauss, Leo. *Natural Rights and History*. Chicago: University of Chicago Press, 1953.

Strauss, Leo, and Joseph Cropsey, eds. *History of Political Philosophy*. Chicago: University of Chicago Press, 1987.

Sumner, L. W. *The Moral Foundations of Rights*. Oxford: Oxford University Press.

———. *Welfare, Happiness, and Ethics*. Oxford: Clarendon Press, 1996.

Tuck, Richard. *Natural Rights Theories: Their Origin and Development*. Cambridge: Cambridge University Press, 1979.

Veatch, Henry B. *For an Ontology of Morals*. Evanston, IL: Northwestern University Press, 1971.

———. *Human Rights: Fact or Fancy*. Baton Rouge: Louisiana State University Press, 1985.

Wild, John Daniel. *Plato's Modern Enemies and the Theory of Natural Law*. Chicago: University of Chicago Press, 1953.

Windleband, Wilhelm. *History of Philosophy*. New York: Harper and Row, 1958.

Younkins, Edward W. *Capitalism and Commerce: Conceptual Foundations of Free Enterprise*. Lanham, MD: Lexington Books, 2002.

———, ed. *Philosophers of Capitalism: Menger, Mises, Rand, and Beyond*. Lanham, MD: Lexington Books, 2005.

Index

About the Author

Edward W. Younkins is professor of accountancy and director of graduate programs in the Department of Business at Wheeling Jesuit University. He is the founder of the university's undergraduate degree program in political and economic philosophy. He is also the founding director of the university's Master of Business Administration (M.B.A.) and Master of Science in Accountancy (M.S.A.) programs. In addition to earning state and national honors for his performances on the Certified Public Accountant (CPA) and Certified Management Accountant (CMA) exams, respectively, Dr. Younkins also received the Outstanding Educator Award for 1997 from the West Virginia Society of Certified Public Accountants. The author of numerous articles in accounting and business journals, his free-market-oriented articles and reviews have appeared in numerous publications. He is the author of *Capitalism and Commerce: Conceptual Foundations of Free Enterprise* (2002), and has edited *Philosophers of Capitalism: Menger, Mises, Rand, and Beyond* (2005) and *Ayn Rand's* Atlas Shrugged: *A Philosophical and Literary Companion* (2007).